HONDA 1969-1978

WORKSHOP MANUAL

750cc SINGLE O.H.C. FOUR CYLINDER

A Floyd Clymer Publication
This edition published in 2022 by
www.VelocePress.com

All rights reserved. this work may not be reproduced or transmitted in any form without the express written consent of the publisher.

INTRODUCTION

Welcome to the world of digital publishing ~ the book you now hold in your hand was printed using the latest state of the art digital technology. The advent of print-on-demand has forever changed the publishing process, never has information been so accessible and it is our hope that this book serves your informational needs for years to come. If this is your first exposure to digital publishing, we hope that you are pleased with the results. Many more titles of interest to the classic automobile and motorcycle enthusiast, collector and restorer are available via our website at www.VelocePress.com. We hope that you find this title as interesting as we do.

NOTE FROM THE PUBLISHER

The information presented is true and complete to the best of our knowledge. All recommendations are made without any guarantees on the part of the author or the publisher, who also disclaim all liability incurred with the use of this information.

TRADEMARKS

We recognize that some words, model names and designations, for example, mentioned herein are the property of the trademark holder. We use them for identification purposes only. This is not an official publication.

INFORMATION ON THE USE OF THIS PUBLICATION

This manual is an invaluable resource for those interested in performing their own maintenance. However, in today's information age we are constantly subject to changes in common practice, new technology, availability of improved materials and increased awareness of chemical toxicity. As such, it is advised that the user consult with an experienced professional prior to undertaking any procedure described herein. While every care has been taken to ensure correctness of information, it is obviously not possible to guarantee complete freedom from errors or omissions or to accept liability arising from such errors or omissions. Therefore, any individual that uses the information contained within, or elects to perform or participate in do-it-yourself repairs or modifications acknowledges that there is a risk factor involved and that the publisher or its associates cannot be held responsible for personal injury or property damage resulting from the use of the information or the outcome of such procedures.

WARNING!

One final word of advice, this publication is intended to be used as a reference guide, and when in doubt the reader should consult with a qualified technician.

CONTENTS

CHAPTER ONE

TUNE-UP 2

- General information
- Oil and filter
- Spark plugs
- Breaker points
- Timing
- Valves
- Cam chain
- Air cleaner
- Fuel delivery
- Carburetor
- Clutch
- Battery

CHAPTER TWO

ENGINE 26

- Removal
- Installation
- Lubrication
- Oil filter
- Oil pump
- Camshaft
- Cylinder head
- Piston and cylinder
- Crankshaft
- Connecting rods
- Primary drive
- Kickstarter

CHAPTER THREE

CLUTCH AND TRANSMISSION 54

- Operation
- Disassembly
- Inspection
- Reassembly

CHAPTER FOUR

CARBURETORS AND FUEL TANK 64

- CB 750 carburetor
- CB 750 K1 carburetor
- Fuel tank
- Fuel valve

CHAPTER FIVE

IGNITION AND CHARGING SYSTEMS 73

- Coil
- Breaker points
- Spark advance
- Alternator
- Regulator
- Rectifier
- Battery

CHAPTER SIX

STARTER 86
    Starting motor   Magnetic switch
    Starting clutch

CHAPTER SEVEN

FRONT SUSPENSION AND STEERING 91
    Front fork   Steering

CHAPTER EIGHT

REAR SUSPENSION 96
    Rear shocks   Rear fork

CHAPTER NINE

WHEELS AND FINAL DRIVE 100
    Front wheel   Rear wheel
    Wheel balancing   Final drive

CHAPTER TEN

BRAKES 107
    Front brakes   Inspection
    Rear brakes   Bleeding
    Disassembly   Adjustment

CHAPTER ELEVEN

FRAME 114
    Frame disassembly   Exhaust system
    Oil tank

CHAPTER TWELVE

LIGHTING, WIRING, AND INSTRUMENTS 118

Instrument group
Headlight
Tail and stop lights
Turn signal
Flasher relay
Ignition switch
Starter and lighting switch

Turn signal and horn switch
Front stop switch
Rear stop switch
Oil pressure switch
Neutral switch
Wiring harness

CHAPTER THIRTEEN

SUPPLEMENTS 126

CB 750 K1 - K4 126
CB 750 K5 158
CB 750 F 162
CB 750 K6 ('76) 186
CB 750 K7 ('77) 190
CB 750 F2 ('77) 202
CB 750 K8 ('78) 212
CB 750 F3 ('78) 218
Wiring diagrams 221

CHAPTER FOURTEEN

TROUBLESHOOTING 231

Operating requirements
Starting difficulties
Poor idling
Misfiring
Flat spots
Power loss
Overheating
Backfiring
Engine noises

Piston seizure
Excessive vibration
High oil consumption
Clutch slip or drag
Transmission problems
Poor handling
Brake problems
Lighting problems

INDEX 235

CHAPTER ONE

TUNE-UP

Introduction

Regular maintenance is the best guarantee of a trouble-free, long lasting motorcycle. An afternoon spent now, cleaning and adjusting, can prevent costly mechanical problems in the future and unexpected breakdowns on the road.

The tune-up procedures outlined in this chapter should hold no terrors for an owner of average ability. The operations are outlined step by step and it is difficult to go wrong.

How Often

The factory recommends a complete tune-up every 3,000 miles or six months, whichever comes first. The one exception is changing oil, which should be done every 1,000 miles.

Tools and Parts

In addition to basic tools, a tune-up requires a static timing light, a strobe light or dwell tachometer, vacuum gauges to synchronize carburetors, a float gauge, and a set of flat feeler blades and round wire gauges calibrated in millimeters. The only expensive special tool is the gauge set—about $75—but a less expensive alternative is discussed in the carburetor section of this chapter.

Parts required for a tune-up are four spark plugs matched to the anticipated running conditions (discussed in text), two sets of points and condensers, three quarters of oil, and a filter.

Tune-up Procedures

The following pages cover servicing or replacement of the oil and filter, spark plugs, breaker points and condensers, static and advanced timing, valve clearances, cam chain, air cleaner, fuel valve, carburetors, clutch, and battery. The tune-up should be performed in the order the operations are listed in this chapter.

Other routine servicing procedures, such as bleeding the brakes, adjusting headlights, and lubricating the chain, are covered in other chapters.

OIL AND FILTER

Frequency

The engine oil should be changed every 1,000 miles (1,500 km) or 60 days, whichever occurs first. In areas of extreme cold, change the oil every 30 days. The time interval is important because acids formed by gasoline and water vapor will contaminate the oil even if the cycle is not run for several months. If the cycle is operated under dusty conditions, the oil will get dirty more quickly, so change it more often.

Quality and Viscosity

Use only a detergent oil with an API rating

TUNE-UP

of MS, DG or DM. These quality ratings usually are stamped on the top of the can. Try to always use the same brand of oil. The factory recommends against using additives.

SAE 10W 40 oil is recommended for normal operation in moderate climates. Contrary to some editions of the Honda 750 owners manual, heavier weight oils should be used if the motorcycle is to be run hard in high temperatures. SAE 20W 50 is recommended.

The factory recommends the following alternate weight oils according to prevailing temperature:

59°F and above	SAE 30 or 30W
32°F to 59°F	SAE 20 or 20W
32°F and below	SAE 10W

Draining Oil

1. Warm up the engine, unless the valves are to be adjusted later. Warm oil drains faster and carries more sludge with it than cold oil.
2. Place a drip pan of at least one gallon capacity under the oil tank. Remove the oil tank filler cap with its attached dipstick.
3. Remove the 19mm oil tank drain plug, **Figure 1**, and allow to drain.

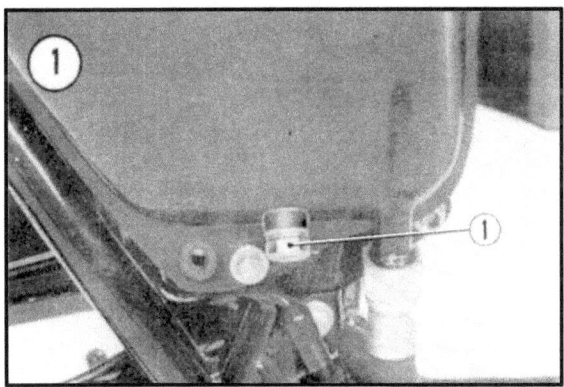

① Oil tank drain plug

4. Shift the catch pan under the crankcase and remove the 19mm drain plug, **Figure 2**. Allow the oil to drain.
5. Crank the engine several times with the kickstarter to force out any oil trapped in the engine's internal recesses.

> TIP: *Pour the used oil into plastic bottles, such as those used for laundry bleach. Cap them and dischard in trash can.*

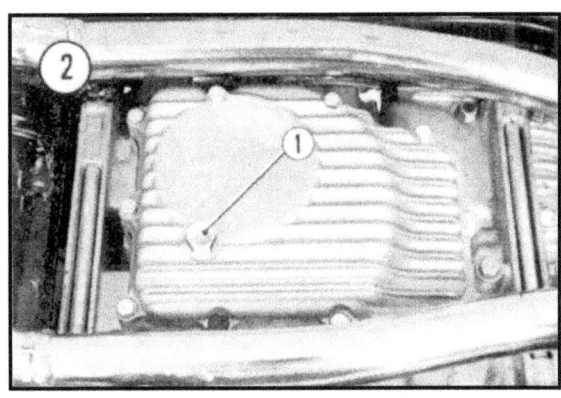

① Crankcase oil drain plug

Changing Oil Filter

The Honda 750 has two different types of oil filter housings, depending on when the machine was manufactured. Starting with engine No. CB750E-1000001 the smooth case was reinforced with radial ribs, for extra cooling, and the center bolt was reduced in size from 14mm to 12mm. The switch was made in 1970.

Figure 3 is a photo of the old cover and **Figure 4** is an exploded view of the later version.

① Oil filter retaining bolt   ② Oil filter cover

1. Remove the 14mm or 12mm retaining bolt from the cover, and pull the assembly from the engine. Throw away the dirty filter element, and examine the O-ring seal for damage.
2. Clean the cover and its internal parts of dirty oil and sludge, using solvent—and dry.
3. Install a new element and a new O-ring, if required, and reinstall the assembly on the engine.

Filling with Oil

1. Replace the two drain plugs and their gaskets in the crankcase and oil tank.

TUNE-UP

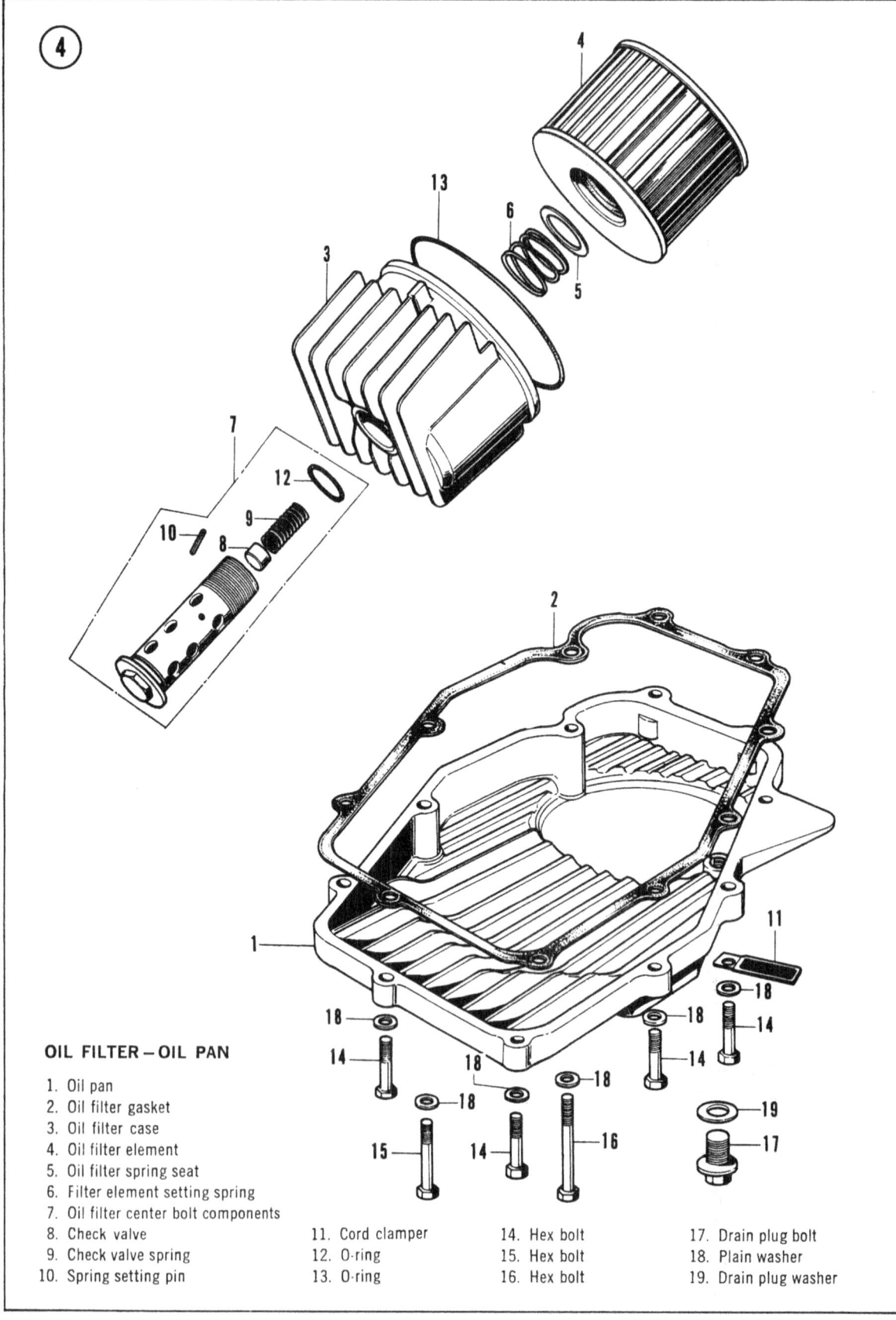

OIL FILTER – OIL PAN

1. Oil pan
2. Oil filter gasket
3. Oil filter case
4. Oil filter element
5. Oil filter spring seat
6. Filter element setting spring
7. Oil filter center bolt components
8. Check valve
9. Check valve spring
10. Spring setting pin
11. Cord clamper
12. O-ring
13. O-ring
14. Hex bolt
15. Hex bolt
16. Hex bolt
17. Drain plug bolt
18. Plain washer
19. Drain plug washer

TUNE-UP

2. Fill tank with three quarts of recommended oil. Check the level with the dipstick cap.

3. Run the engine at 1,000 to 1,500 rpm for two minutes. Then stop the engine and check for seepage from the plugs and filter. Top up the oil tank if required.

SPARK PLUGS

Removal

1. Blow out any debris from the recesses around the spark plugs.

2. Gently remove the insulated plug leads, pulling up and out. Do not jerk. The wires could pull out of the insulator caps.

3. Back out the plugs with a socket that has a rubber insert to grip the insulator.

CAUTION
The plugs in No. 2 and No. 3 cylinders are hard to reach. If dropped, they can lodge in the recesses in the cylinder head.

Inspection

The normal color of the spark plug tip ranges from a light tan to a chocolate brown, depending on the concentration of lead in the gas.

Figure 5 shows some of the abnormal tip conditions and probable causes. Plug heat ranges are discussed later.

The Two-Plug System

Spark plugs for the Honda 750 are available in various heat ranges above and below the normal plug originally installed in the machine. Use plugs designed for the load under which the bike will be run, and the temperatures in which it will be used.

In general, use a lower numbered plug for low speeds, a low load, and low temperatures. Use a higher numbered plug for higher speeds, a high engine load, and high temperatures.

More important than any one of these factors is the combination. A motorcycle ridden at high speeds with a high load in freezing weather would require a plug on the high side of the normal heat range.

The factory recommends what it calls a "two-plug" system—a high plug number for hard riding in summer, and a low number for winter and slower riding.

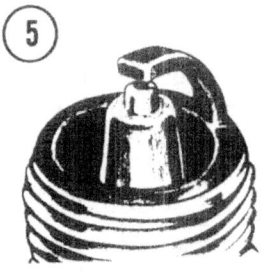

Black carbon deposit

Fuel mixture too rich
Dirty air cleaner
Prolonged idling
Low heat range

Oil fouling (wet tip)

Worn pistons or rings
Timing off
Plug loose
Worn valve guides

White crust

Fuel mixture too rich
Timing off
Loose plug
Hot heat range

Use of incorrect heat ranges can result in seizing of pistons, scoring of cylinder walls, and holes in the piston crowns.

The rule of thumb in choosing plug heat range is to install the highest number plug that will not foul. Most fouling occurs because of prolonged low speeds, shifting at too low an rpm, poor quality gas, or other causes listed in the chart. Examine driving habits if persistent fouling occurs.

The factory recommends NKG plugs, claiming the copper core makes NKG's more flexible in adjusting to different operating conditions.

The plug selection guide below begins with the hot heat ranges (lower numbers for low speeds) up to cold plugs with higher numbers for high speeds.

Type	Uses
NKG D-7ES	Short distances, low speeds
NKG D-8E	Low rpms, city riding, use if D-7ES fouls.
NKG D-8ES	Normal touring, city or highway
NKG D-10E	Competition, extreme engine speeds or temperatures

TUNE-UP

Old Plugs

If the old plugs are to be used again, inspect them for cracked insulators, damaged threads, or worn electrodes. Discard the entire set if any of these conditions are present.

Cleaning

Clean the tips with a sandblasting machine—some gas stations have them—or with a wire brush and solvent, followed by compressed air.

Adjusting Gap and Installing

1. Referring to **Figure 6**, adjust the gap to .6mm to .7mm (.024 in. to .028 in.) using a feeler gauge.

> NOTE: *Vary the gap by bending only the outside electrode. The distance is correct when the gauge slips through with a slight amount of drag.*

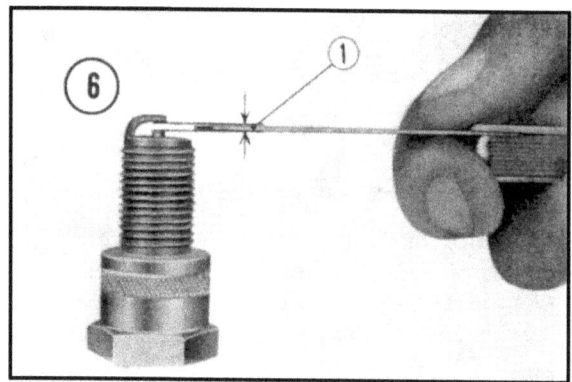

① Spark plug gap

2. Screw the plugs back into the cylinder head, finger turning the socket until the plug is seated. Then tighten one half to three quarters of a turn more.

CAUTION
Overtightening can change the gap, damage threads, and make the plug hard to remove the next time.

BREAKER POINTS

Inspection

1. Remove breaker point cover by removing the two Phillips head screws. If the cover does not come off easily, tap it loose with a rubber or rawhide mallet.

2. Pry open the points gently with a finger, and inspect the two sets for alignment and wear. **Figure 7** shows what to look for. Replace the points if they are severely pitted or worn.

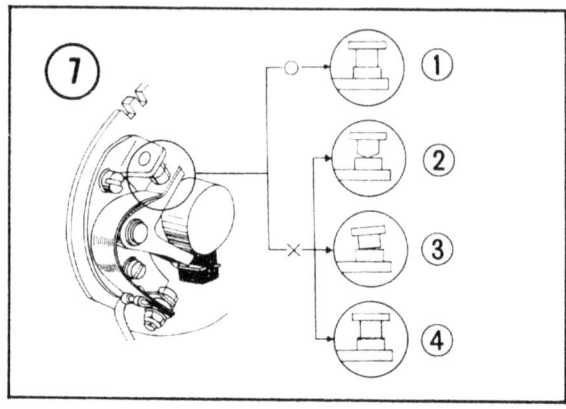

① Correct
② Contact is worn
③ One side contact
④ Contamination of the contact

Cleaning

1. Gray discoloration is normal. Dress the contact surfaces with a point file. Never use sandpaper or emery cloth.

2. Blow away the residue, and then clean the contacts with a chemical point cleaner or a piece of unwaxed stiff paper, such as a clean business card. Make certain the contact surfaces are absolutely clean. Even oil from a fingerprint can affect performance.

3. If the same points are to be used, skip the next section outlining replacement procedure.

Replacement

> NOTE: *It is recommended that the two condensers routinely be replaced along with the points. Parts are usually sold in sets. Refer to* <u>FIGURE 8</u>.

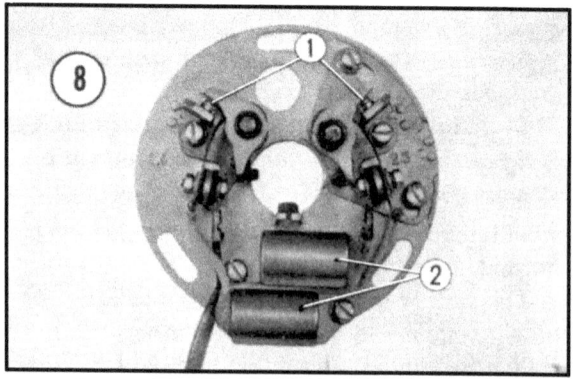

① Contact breaker   ② Condenser

TUNE-UP

1. Note **Figure 9**, and disconnect the yellow and blue leads located on the lower right side of the center of the frame.

① Contact breaker lead

2. Remove the 6mm hex nut and its washer as shown in **Figure 10**, and remove the three breaker plate holding screws.

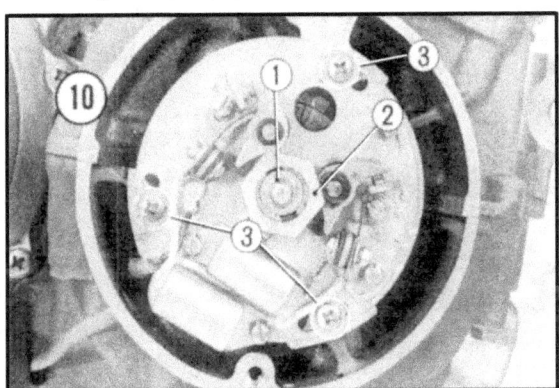

① 6mm hex nut
② Special washer
③ Contact breaker setting screws

3. Pull out the unit.

4. Remove the points and condensers, referring to the exploded view in **Figure 11**. When installing the new parts, take care to install the insulating washers in the same positions.

> NOTE: *If the layout seems confusing, remove one wire at a time; install the new lead before going to the next one.*

Adjusting the Gap

There are two methods for determining the gap—the static operation with a feeler gauge, and the dwell meter procedure with the engine running. The points must still be adjusted manually, no matter which method is used.

Static Procedure:

1. Rotate the crankshaft clockwise, in the direction of the arrow in **Figure 12**, until the cam lobe fully opens one of the point sets.

① Contact breaker points
② Contact breaker plate locking screw

2. The gap should be .3mm to .4mm (.012 in to .016 in). Check with a feeler gauge.

3. To adjust, loosen the set screw shown in Figure 12, in a counterclockwise direction.

4. To vary the distance of the gap, set the tip of a flat blade screwdriver in the notch in the point arm, and move it by gently prying against the two leverage buttons set into the base plate next to the point.

5. When the gap is correct (.3mm to .4mm), tighten the lock screw. Check again with the feeler gauge.

> NOTE: *The act of tightening the lock screw can throw off the adjustment. The gap may have to be reset several times to get it right.*

6. To adjust the other set of points, rotate the crankshaft until the points are open to a maximum, and repeat steps three and four.

Dwell Method:

Definition: "Dwell" is the number of degrees that the breaker point cam rotates while the points are closed. The longer the dwell, the smaller the point gap. The shorter the dwell, the wider the gap.

The dwell in a Honda 750 should be between 92 degrees and 98 degrees if the points are adjusted correctly. The meter is an extremely accurate method of measuring the point gap, but if the distance is off, the points still have to be adjusted manually as in the preceding section.

TUNE-UP

NOTE: *Be sure the dwell meter is designed for motorcycle or small gasoline engines of two cylinders (one point set controls 2 cylinders in the Honda 750).*

1. Hook up the meter according to its instructions—usually with one lead attached to the points, and the other grounded to the engine.

2. Start the engine and read the dwell angle. It should be 92 to 98 degrees. This is equivalent to .3mm to .4mm gap.

NOTE: *If the points are worn, the correct reading will result in too small a gap. Replace the points.*

3. If the points need adjusting, proceed according to steps three and four in the Static Adjustment section.

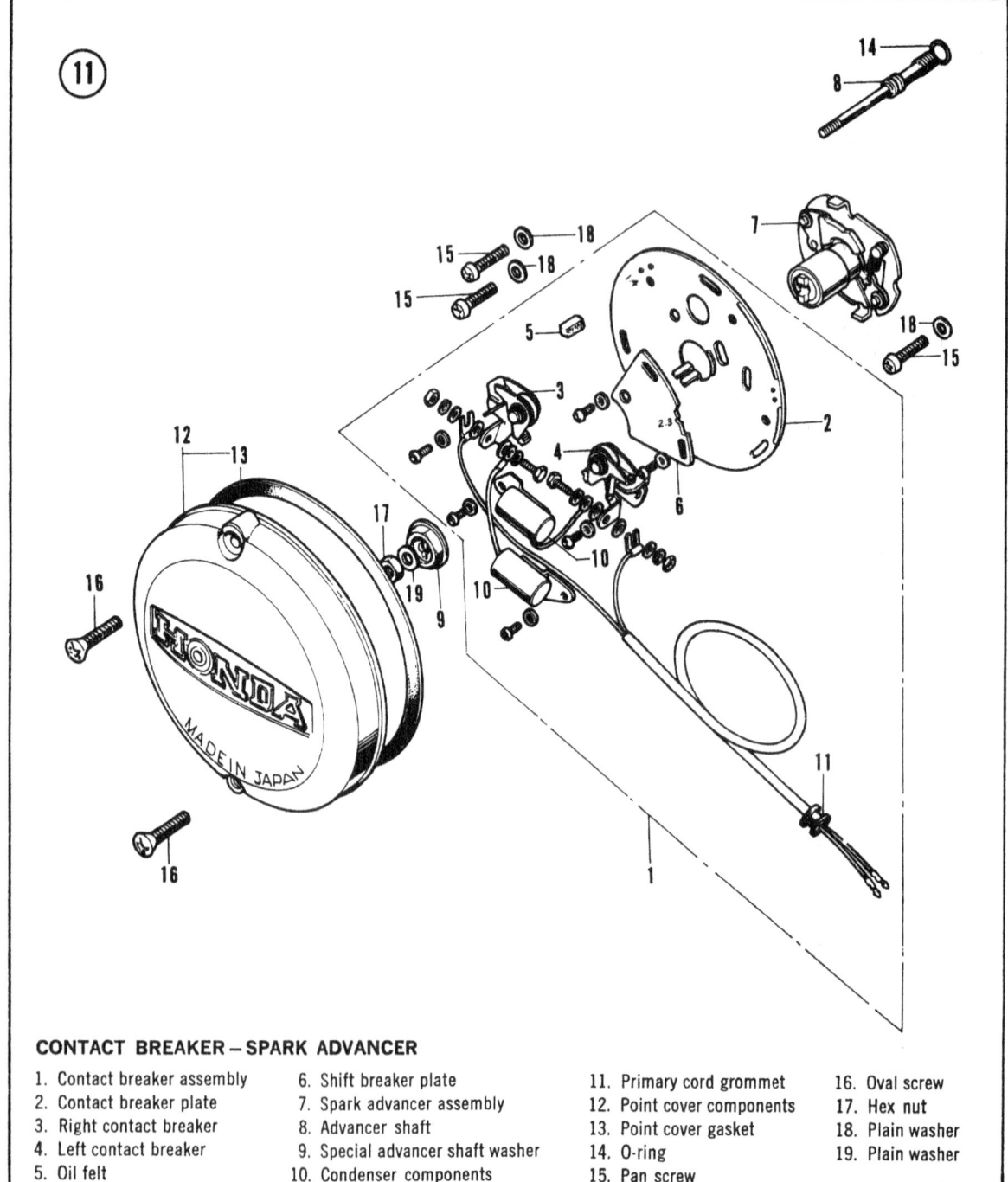

CONTACT BREAKER – SPARK ADVANCER

1. Contact breaker assembly
2. Contact breaker plate
3. Right contact breaker
4. Left contact breaker
5. Oil felt
6. Shift breaker plate
7. Spark advancer assembly
8. Advancer shaft
9. Special advancer shaft washer
10. Condenser components
11. Primary cord grommet
12. Point cover components
13. Point cover gasket
14. O-ring
15. Pan screw
16. Oval screw
17. Hex nut
18. Plain washer
19. Plain washer

TUNE-UP

Lubrication

The final step in adjusting the points is to lubricate the cam with a thin coating of cam grease. Do not use an excessive amount, or it will contaminate the contact surfaces.

> NOTE: *If the engine is to be timed, do not replace the breaker point cover.*

TIMING

Just as there are two ways to set the breaker points, one more accurate than the other, so are there two methods to adjust the timing of the engine—the static procedure and the more precise method using a stroboscopic light.

The static operation requires something that can signal when an electric circuit is opened and closed. This can be a buzz box, an ohmmeter, or a continuity light. The latter, more commonly called a timing light, is the easiest to use.

Such lights are available for under $2 at parts stores. A homemade light consists of a light bulb, a socket to hold it, and two wires attached to the socket with alligator clips at the ends.

Static Timing

1. As shown in **Figure 13**, the cylinders controlled by each set of points are stamped next to the breaker set on the base plate. Begin the static timing with the set for Cylinders No. 1 and No. 4.

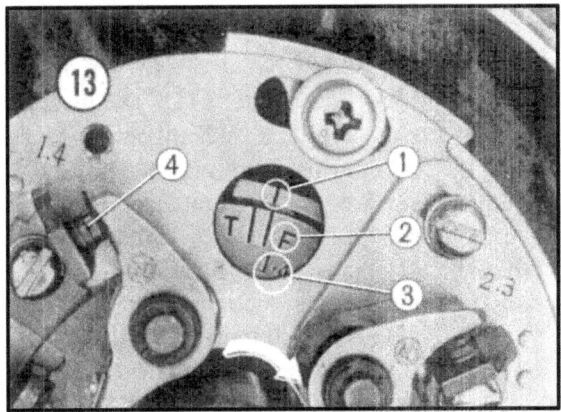

① Index mark
② "F" mark
③ Cylinder number
④ 1.4 cylinder breaker points

2. Clip one wire from the timing light to the 1-4 points, and ground the other wire to the engine. Turn on ignition.

3. Examine Figure 13 again. The timing marks are visible through the peephole in the base plate. Slowly rotate the crankshaft in a clockwise direction (arrow) until the "1-4 F" mark is even with the index mark on the outer ring.

4. At that instant the timing light should go on as the points begin to open. If not, the timing is off.

5. To adjust, loosen the three base plate screws shown in **Figure 14**, and rotate the plate to retard or advance the timing until the light flickers. Tighten the three base plate screws.

⑤ Contact breaker base plate
⑥ Base plate locking screw
⑦ Contact breaker right base plate
⑧ Right base plate locking screws
⑨ 2-3 cylinder breaker points

6. Check the point gap or dwell again before proceeding.

7. Connect the light to the other set of breaker points, those controlling the No. 2 and No. 3 cylinders.

8. Rotate the crankshaft one half revolution until the "2-3 F" mark is aligned with the outer index mark.

9. If the light does not flicker at that point, adjust by loosening the two right base plate locking screws, referring again to Figure 14. These two screws are different from the ones used to adjust the No. 1 and No. 4 cylinder timing.

10. Remove the light and turn off ignition. Replace the breaker point cover unless using the method below.

Stroboscopic Timing

Strobe timing lights are also commonly available. Beware of cheap ones, because they usually are not durable.

1. Connect the light according to its instruc-

tions. Improper hookup can result in incorrect timing.

2. Connect the timing light spark plug lead to plug No. 1 or No. 4.

3. Start the engine and set it to idle—between 850 and 950 rpm.

4. Aim the light at the peephole in the breaker plate base. If the "1-4 F" mark lines up with the index mark, the timing is correct.

5. If the timing is off, adjust according to steps five and six in the section on Static Timing.

6. Turn off the engine and connect the plug lead to the No. 2 or No. 3 spark plug.

7. Check the timing at the "2-3 F" mark and adjust according to step nine under Static Timing.

Advance Check

The strobe light is also used to check the timing advance mechanism. A bent or out-of-center advance shaft will cause inaccurate timing. The remedy is discussed in Chapter Five.

1. Connect the strobe light to either set of cylinders.

2. Start the engine and run it at about 2,500 rpm.

3. Advance is correct if the index mark appears between the two timing marks located 23.5 to 26.5 degrees ahead, or advanced, of the "F" mark.

VALVES

Incorrect clearances between the tappets and valve stems can damage the valves and mar performance. To forestall premature wear and a costly regrind, adjust clearances regularly.

NOTE: *This procedure is performed with the engine cold.*

1. Turn off the fuel valve. Release the seat catch and raise the cushion. Pull off the rubber buffer from the rear mount for the gas tank. Slide the tank to the rear, taking care not to stretch the fuel lines, until the top of the engine is accessible.

2. If the breaker point cover is not already removed, do so now, by backing out the two Phillips head screws.

3. Referring to **Figure 15**, use a 17mm wrench to remove the eight caps over the tappet access holes. There are four holes in back and four in front.

NOTE: *In the following steps the cylinders are designated by number. They are numbered one through four starting from the left as seen when sitting astride the bike and facing the front. The intake valves are at the back of the engine, and the exhaust valves are at the front.*

4. Slowly rotate the crankshaft clockwise, in the direction of the arrow in **Figure 16**, until the "T 1-4" mark, seen through the peephole in the breaker point base plate, is even with the index mark on the outer ring as shown in the illustration.

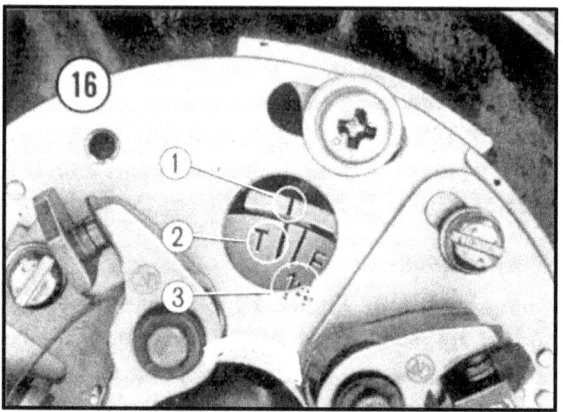

① Index mark   ③ 1·4 Cylinder mark
② "T" mark

5. At this point either No. 1 or No. 4 cylinder will be at the top dead center (TDC) of its compression stroke. Find out which one it is by feeling the rocker arms of both cylinders through the adjustment holes. The cylinder at TDC will have both rocker arms loose, signifying that both inlet and exhaust valves are closed.

The standard clearances are:
Inlet valve (rear) .05mm (.002 in)
Exhaust valve (front) .08mm (.003 in)

6. Check the valve clearances in the TDC cylinder with a feeler blade, as shown in **Figure 17**. If the gaps are off, adjust as follows.

7. Refer to Figure 17, and loosen the tappet screw lock nut with a 10mm wrench.

8. Turn the tappet adjusting screw clockwise to tighten it and reduce the clearance; counterclockwise to loosen it and increase clearance.

TUNE-UP

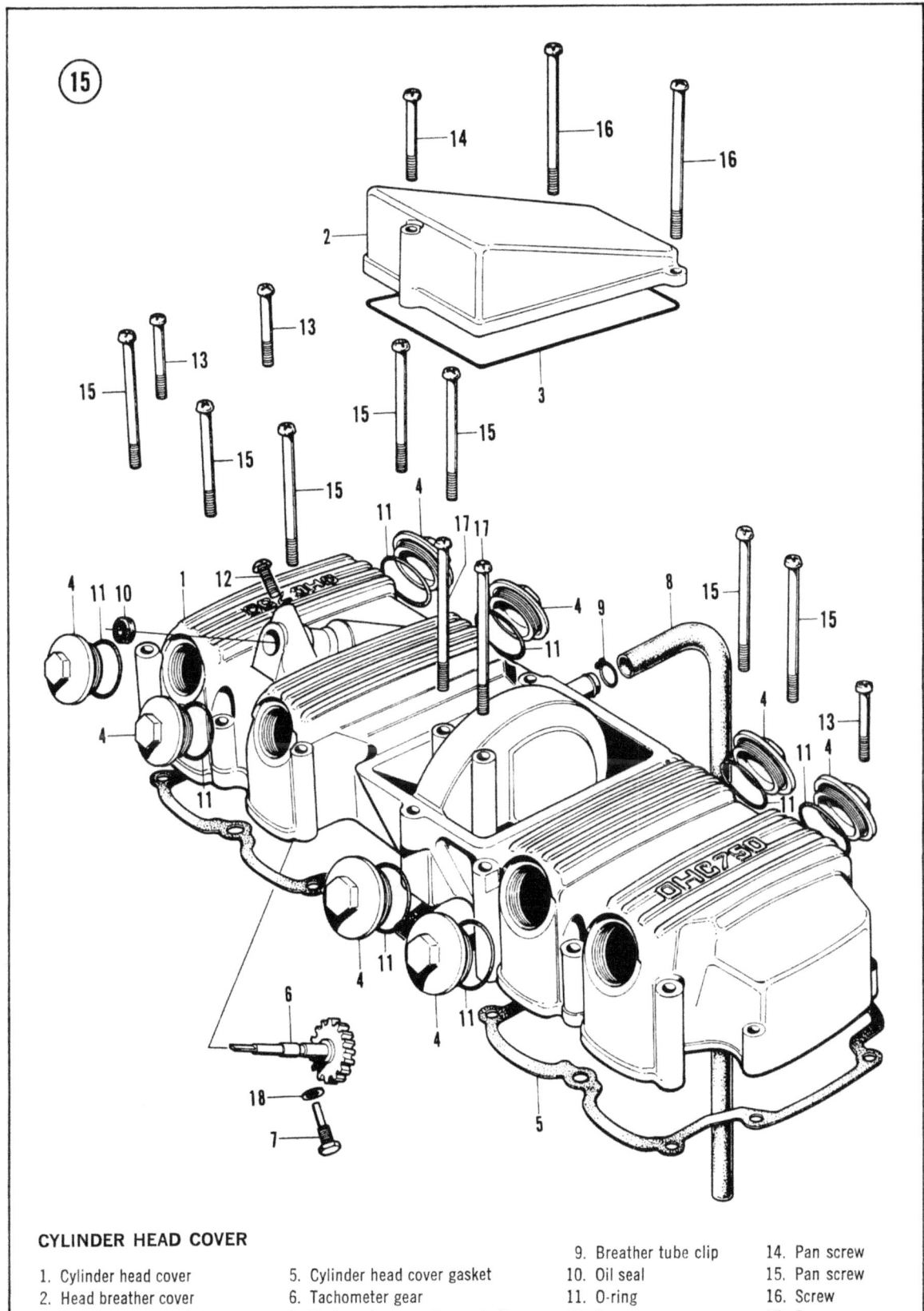

CYLINDER HEAD COVER

1. Cylinder head cover
2. Head breather cover
3. Breather cover gasket
4. Tappet adjusting hole cap
5. Cylinder head cover gasket
6. Tachometer gear
7. Tachometer gear stopper bolt
8. Breather tube
9. Breather tube clip
10. Oil seal
11. O-ring
12. Pan screw
13. Pan screw
14. Pan screw
15. Pan screw
16. Screw
17. Pan screw
18. Plain washer

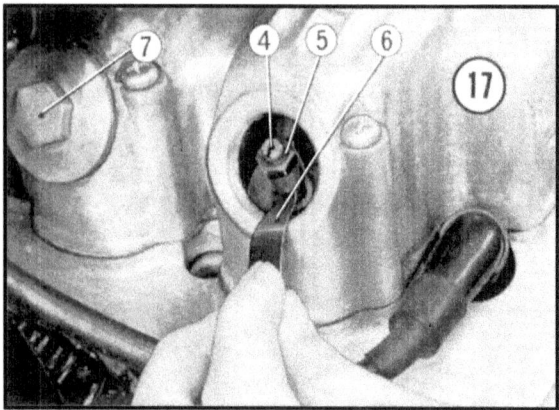

④ Tappet adjusting screw ⑥ Thickness gauge
⑤ Lock nut ⑦ Hole cap

Gap is correct when there is a slight drag on the feeler blade.

9. When clearance is correct, tighten the lock nut and recheck to make sure the tightening did not upset the setting.

10. These adjustment steps should be performed on both valves for the cylinder at TDC.

11. Rotate the crankshaft clockwise 360 degrees until the "T 1-4" timing mark is lined up again with the index line.

12. The other cylinder now is at TDC, and it may be checked and adjusted by repeating steps six through ten above.

13. To set up the valves in cylinders No. 2 and No. 3 for adjustment, rotate the crankshaft clockwise again until the "T 2-3" mark is even with the index line.

14. Determine which cylinder is at TDC by the method in step five, then check and adjust the clearance.

15. Rotate the crankshaft 360 degrees until the "T 2-3" mark is again lined up with the index mark, and adjust the last cylinder.

16. Replace the tappet hole caps and their gaskets.

> NOTE: *If the cam chain tensioner is to be adjusted (next procedure) do not replace the caps for the No. 1 cylinder.*

CAM CHAIN

A loose cam chain is noisy and will affect both valve timing and performance. It is simple to adjust. **Figure 18A** shows how a spring loaded push bar keeps tension on an idler wheel against the chain.

1. Rotate the crankshaft clockwise until it is 15 degrees after top dead center (ATDC) for the No. 1 cylinder. See **Figure 18B**. This position puts the chain slack at the rear of the engine and duplicates running conditions.

> NOTE: *When the No. 1 piston is at TDC, both valves will be closed and the rocker arms will be loose. The drawing shows the timing setting for 15 degrees ATDC.*

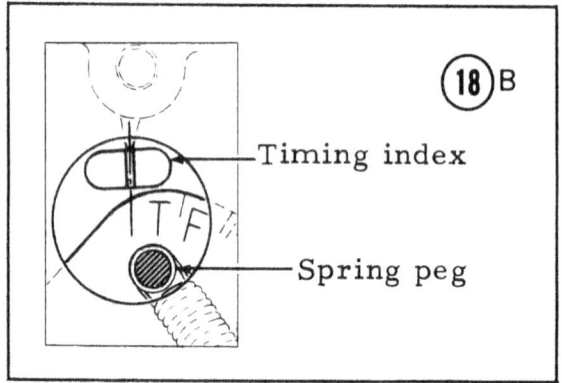

2. Referring to **Figure 19**, loosen the lock nut with a 10mm wrench. Then back off the adjusting bolt with a 10mm wrench. This releases the bar. The spring automatically adjusts the force to the correct amount of tension on the chain.

① Lock nut ② Tensioner lock bolt

3. Tighten the adjusting bolt until it seats lightly. Do not overtighten. Then tighten the lock nut.

4. Replace the cap over the tappet adjusting hole of the No. 1 cylinder, using a new O-ring if the old one is worn or damaged.

TUNE-UP

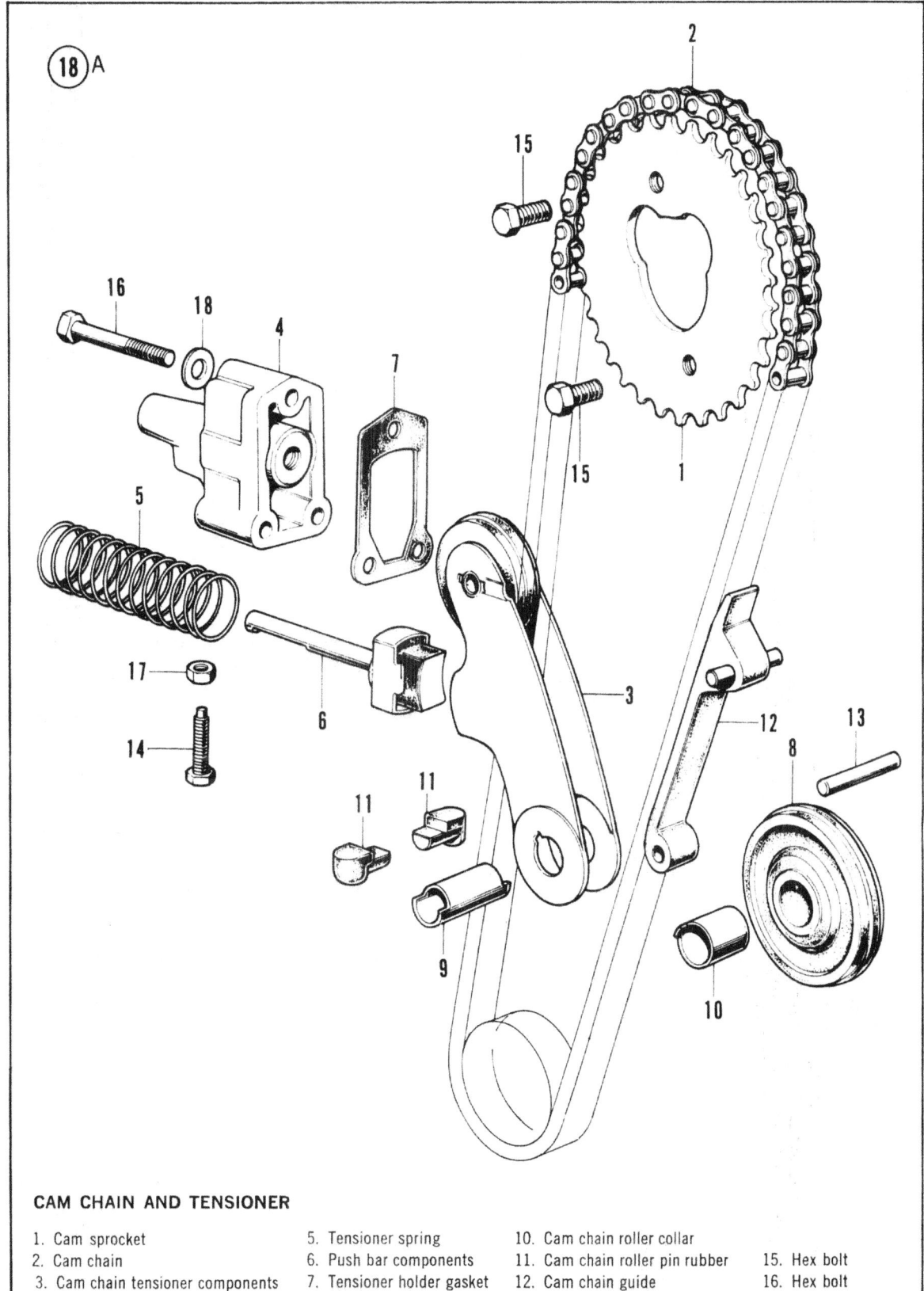

CAM CHAIN AND TENSIONER

1. Cam sprocket
2. Cam chain
3. Cam chain tensioner components
4. Cam chain tensioner holder components
5. Tensioner spring
6. Push bar components
7. Tensioner holder gasket
8. Cam chain guide roller
9. Cam chain roller pin
10. Cam chain roller collar
11. Cam chain roller pin rubber
12. Cam chain guide
13. Cam chain guide pin
14. Tensioner adjusting bolt
15. Hex bolt
16. Hex bolt
17. Hex nut
18. Plain washer

AIR CLEANER

A properly functioning air cleaner is important to engine efficiency and life. It should be checked at each oil change, or at least every 2,000 miles. If the motorcycle is operated under dusty conditions, inspect the air cleaner more often. **Figure 20** is a cutaway view of the system.

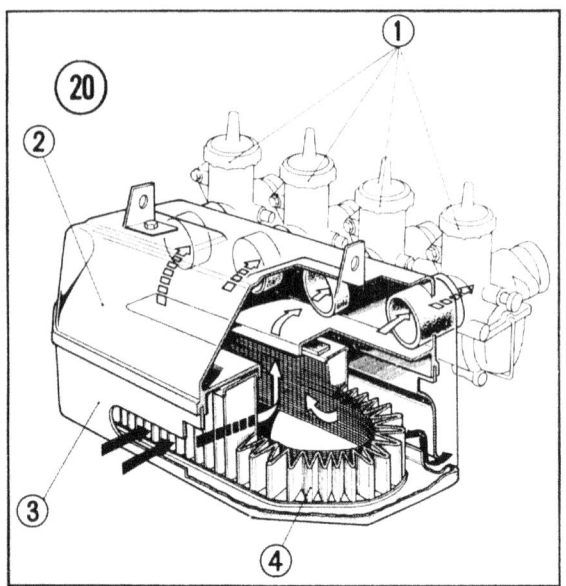

① Carburetors   ③ Air cleaner cover
② Air cleaner case   ④ Air cleaner element

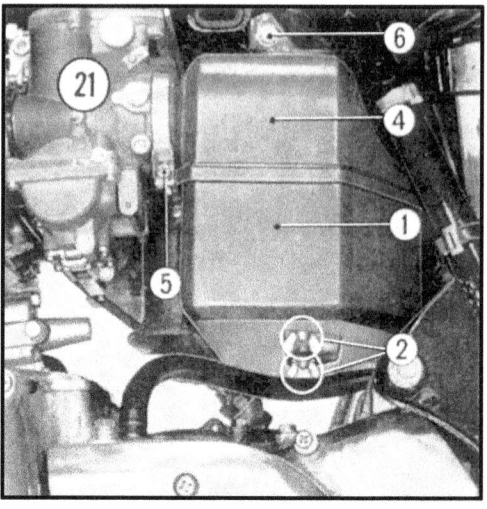

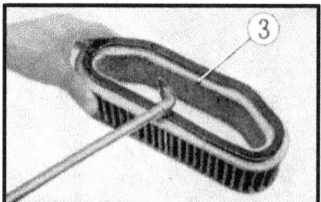

① Air cleaner lower case
② Wing nut
③ Air cleaner element
④ Air cleaner upper case
⑤ Air cleaner hose clamp screw
⑥ Air cleaner mounting bolt

1. Referring to **Figure 21**, loosen the two wing nuts on the underside of the cover, and remove the lower half.

2. Remove the filter element. Replace it with a new one if the filter is clogged with dirt, oil soaked, or if the bonding material is cracked.

3. Light dust can be shaken off the element by tapping it while using a soft brush on the outside. A better method, if compressed air is available, is to force air through the element from the inside.

4. Replace the lower housing and the filter element. If the carburetors are to be adjusted, remove the upper case by loosening the four clamps on the air hoses, and removing the mounting bolts. See Figure 21.

FUEL DELIVERY

Figure 22 is an exploded view of the fuel tank and the petcock that controls gas flow to the carburetors. The float bowls should also be inspected during this procedure.

1. Make sure there is gas in the tank, and then turn the valve to the off position.

2. Disconnect the fuel line at the carburetors. Put the end in a can to catch the fuel.

3. Turn petcock on. Fuel should flow into the catch can.

4. Move the valve to the reserve position. Fuel should flow.

5. Move valve to stop position. Fuel should cease flowing.

> NOTE: *If fuel does not flow at "on" or "reserve" positions, check supply lines for kinks. If fuel flows in "off" position, the valve packing is defective.*

6. Replace hose at carburetor. Make sure petcock is off.

7. The fuel valve strainer is located in a cup on the underside of the valve. See **Figure 23**. Remove the cup by using the nut at the bottom to unscrew it.

8. **Figure 24** shows the mesh filter and the O-ring. Clean the strainer with solvent and replace the O-ring if it is damaged.

TUNE-UP

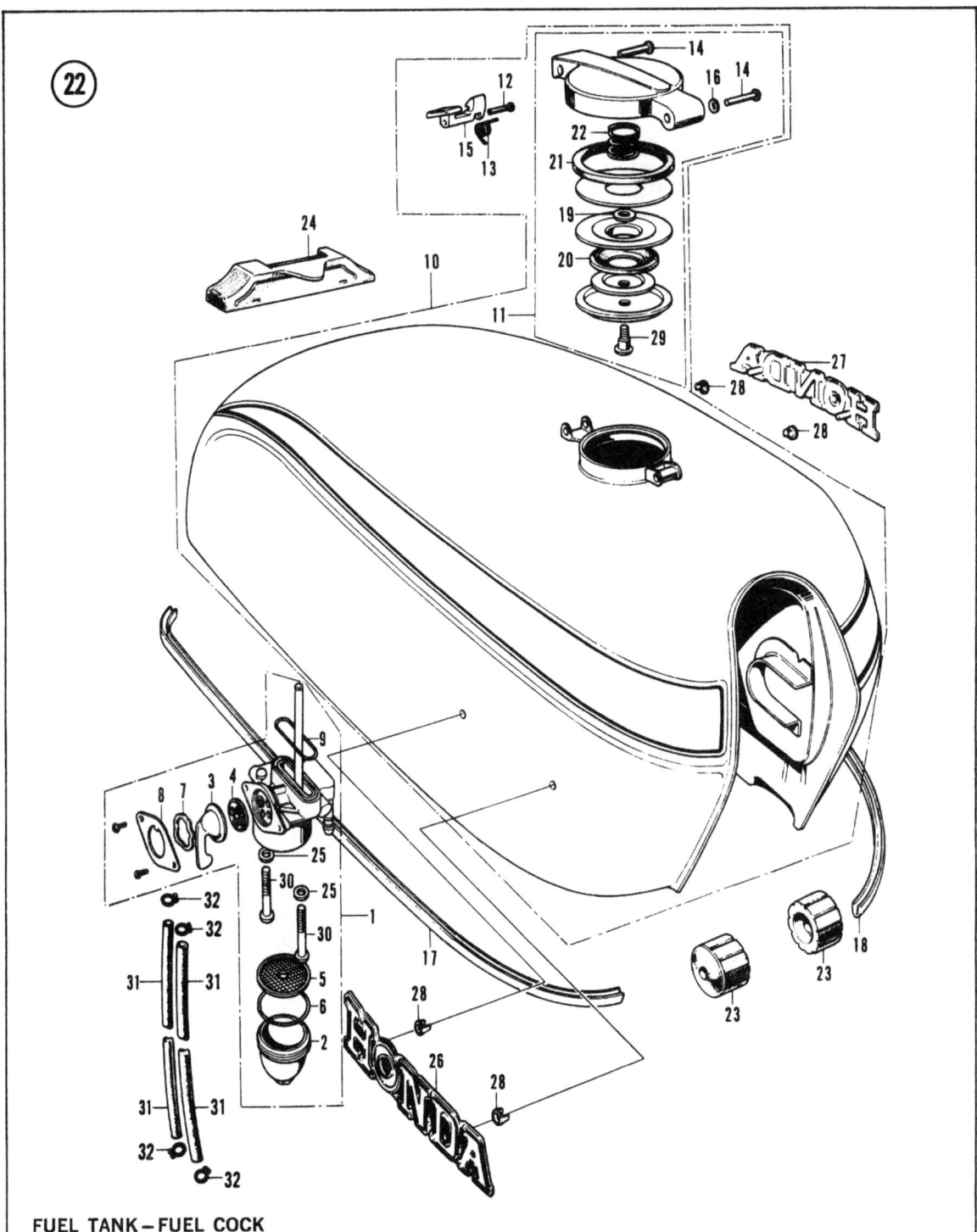

FUEL TANK – FUEL COCK

1. Fuel cock assembly
2. Fuel strainer cup
3. Fuel cock lever
4. Fuel cock valve packing
5. Fuel strainer screen
6. Fuel strainer gasket
7. Cock lever spring
8. Fuel cock lever setting plate
9. O-ring
10. Fuel tank
11. Fuel filler cap components
12. Fuel filler cap check pin
13. Cap check spring
14. Fuel filler cap pin
15. Fuel filler cap check
16. Fuel filler cap friction washer
17. Right fuel tank molding
18. Left fuel tank molding
19. Plain washer
20. Fuel separator
21. Fuel filler cap gasket
22. Seat spring
23. Fuel tank front cushion
24. Fuel tank rear cushion
25. Fuel cock fixing gasket
26. Right fuel tank emblem
27. Left fuel tank emblem
28. Rear fuel tank emblem
29. Fuel cap screw
30. Pan screw
31. Fuel tube
32. Fuel tube clip

TUNE-UP

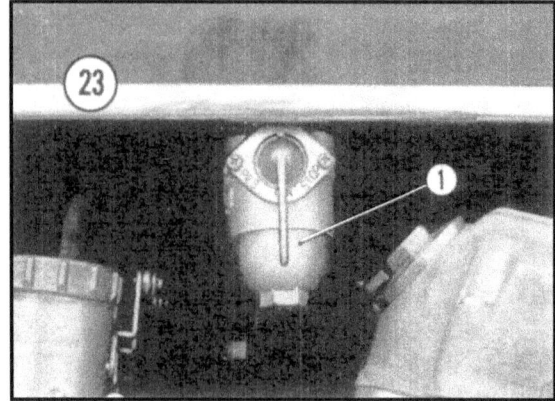

① Fuel valve body

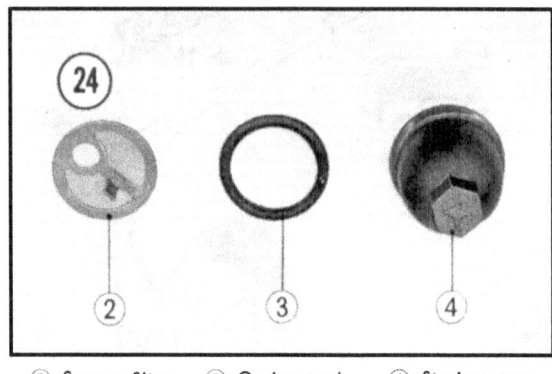

② Screen filter ③ O ring seal ④ Strainer cap

9. Reinstall the strainer, O-ring, and cup, taking care not to overtighten the cup casting.

Float Level

The operations below for cleaning carburetor float bowls and adjusting the levels, apply both to the early CB 750 and the later CB 750 K1.

The float valve is a mechanism for maintaining a constant level of fuel in the bowl on the bottom of the carburetor to supply the demands of varying engine speeds and throttle openings. As the chamber fills with fuel, a float rises and shuts off the incoming fuel by closing a valve. As the fuel level drops, the float does the same, opening the valve to replenish the supply of gas.

Honda sells a special gauge to set the float level (Tool No. 07144-99962). Use this tool to measure the float level rather than estimating it with a ruler. See **Figure 25**.

1. Remove float bowls by slipping the snap ring toward the front of the engine.

> NOTE: *Remove carefully. The bowls will contain gasoline. Be sure not to damage the floats or the float valves.* <u>FIGURE 26</u> *shows the layout.*

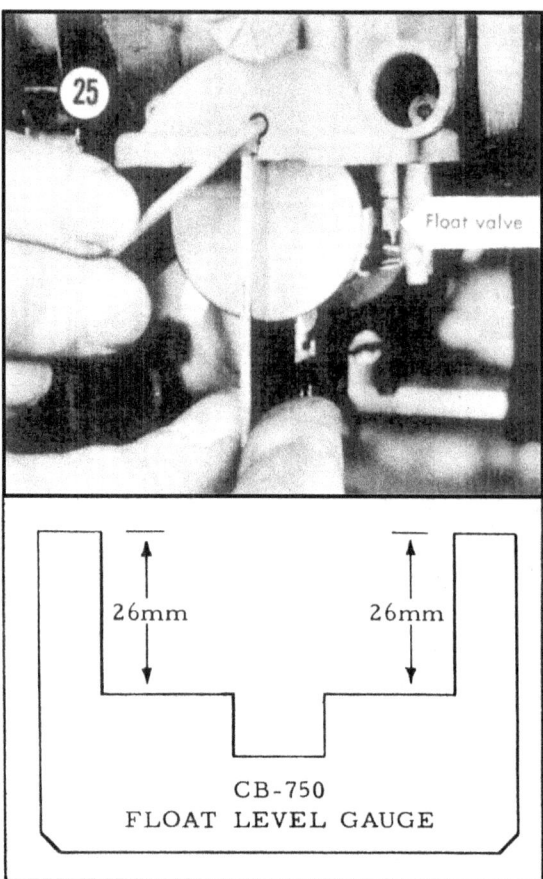

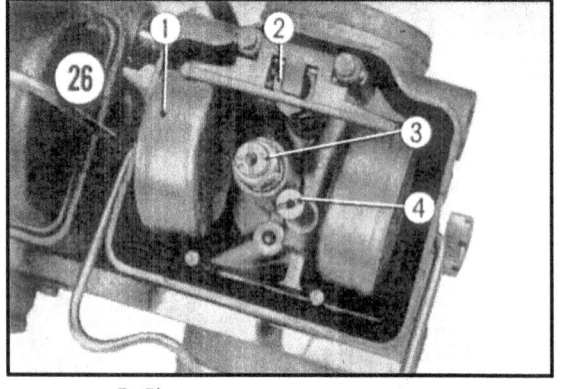

① Float   ③ Main jet
② Float valve set ④ Slow jet

2. Check float bowls for sediment, and flush with solvent.

3. Use the gauge as shown in **Figure 27** to check the float setting. It should be 26mm (1.023 in) measured from the base of the carburetor to the bottom edge of float.

> NOTE: *The measurement should be taken when the float arm is just barely touching the valve, but not compressing the valve spring.*

TUNE-UP

17

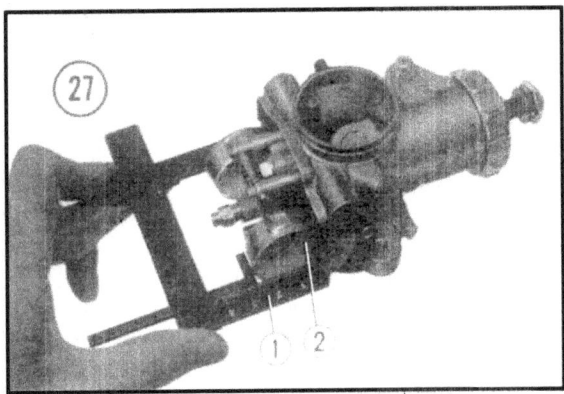

① Float
② Float level gauge

4. Adjust the setting if necessary by carefully bending the float arm tab that contacts the valve. Use a narrow, flat-blade screwdriver. At the correct setting, the float should just barely touch the gauge.

5. Repeat the inspection and adjustment operations on all four carburetors.

6. Replace the bowls and gaskets, making sure the bowl lips are seated properly and that the clips are secure.

CARBURETOR

Two different carburetor throttle linkages are used on the Honda 750. Early versions use a single throttle cable from the twist grip to the carburetor linkage, with a spring employed to close the throttle. Starting in late 1970, this was modified to a two-cable arrangement designed to give a more positive "push-pull" action to opening and closing the throttle. The CB 750 has the single cable, and the CB 750 K1 has two cables. The adjustment and synchronization operations for each models are outlined separately in this section. The change was made with engine No. CB750E-1044813.

A special set of gauges is required for this procedure. Honda sells a set of four vacuum gauges with tubes and adapters to connect them to the carburetors. The unit costs about $75, but it enables synchronization to be performed quickly and easily.

Less costly gauges which measure air flow are available, and results are just as accurate if they are used carefully. But a gauge such as the inexpensive "Uni-Syn" is inconvenient because the settings on the four carbs cannot be measured simultaneously.

In the sequence of operations that follows, the factory gauges are used.

CB 750

Figure 28 shows the major parts of the carburetor involved in the adjustment process.

1. Remove the fuel tank, making sure to disconnect the fuel lines at the valve assembly underneath. Remove the air cleaner.

2. Check each of the four throttle stop screws, **Figure 29**, to make sure the "T" mark is aligned with the index mark on the carburetor body. If not, adjust to the setting shown in **Figure 30**. Check all four carburetors.

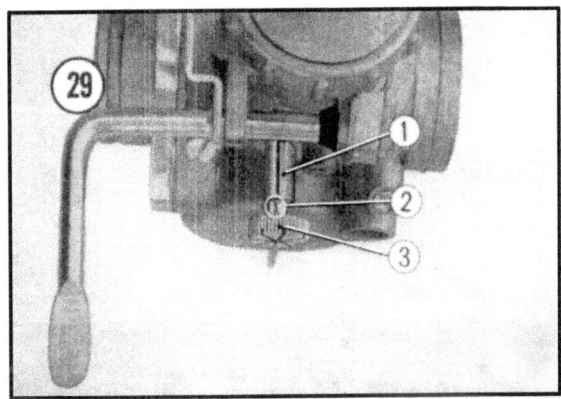

① Index mark ③ Throttle stop screw
② "T" mark

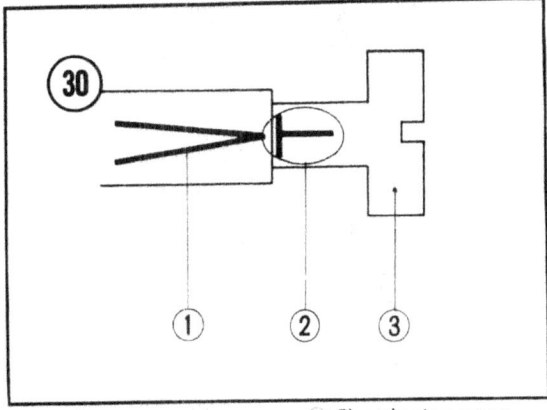

① Index mark ③ Throttle stop screw
② "T" mark

3. Referring to **Figure 31**, loosen the lock nut and turn the throttle cable adjusting nut so that free play in the cable is between 1mm and 2mm (.04 in and .05 in). Tighten the lock nut. The play should be even on all four carburetors, as shown in **Figure 32**.

TUNE-UP

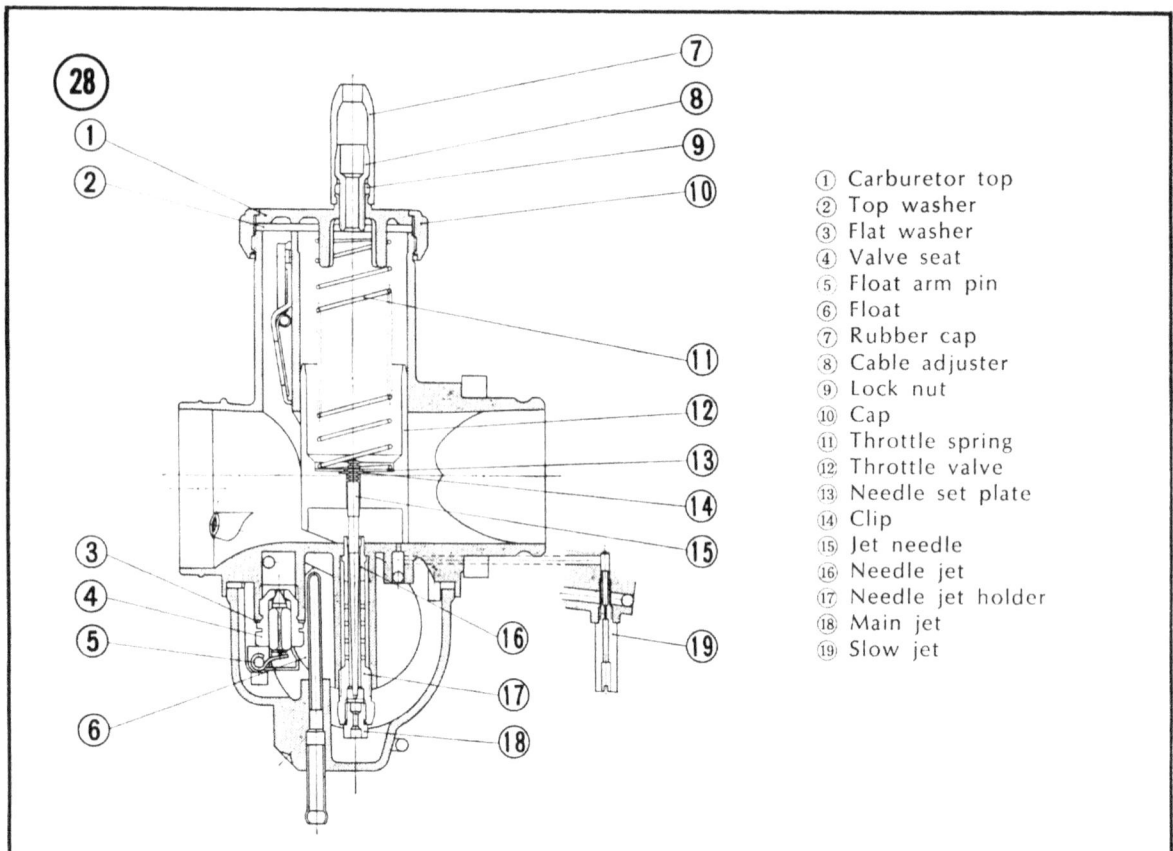

- ① Carburetor top
- ② Top washer
- ③ Flat washer
- ④ Valve seat
- ⑤ Float arm pin
- ⑥ Float
- ⑦ Rubber cap
- ⑧ Cable adjuster
- ⑨ Lock nut
- ⑩ Cap
- ⑪ Throttle spring
- ⑫ Throttle valve
- ⑬ Needle set plate
- ⑭ Clip
- ⑮ Jet needle
- ⑯ Needle jet
- ⑰ Needle jet holder
- ⑱ Main jet
- ⑲ Slow jet

- ④ Carburetor cap
- ⑤ Throttle cable adjuster
- ⑥ Adjuster lock nut

- ① Air screw
- ② Throttle stop screw

4. Perform a preliminary fuel mixture adjustment by turning in each of the idle air screws, **Figure 33**, until they seat gently. Back each out counterclockwise one full turn.

5. Install air cleaner and the fuel tank.

6. Start the engine and warm it up to operating temperature.

7. Stop engine and remove the plugs from the vacuum gauge attachment holes, **Figure 34**, taking care not to drop the flat-head screws.

0.04~0.08 in (1~2mm)

① Cable adjuster ② Cable adjuster lock nut

TUNE-UP   19

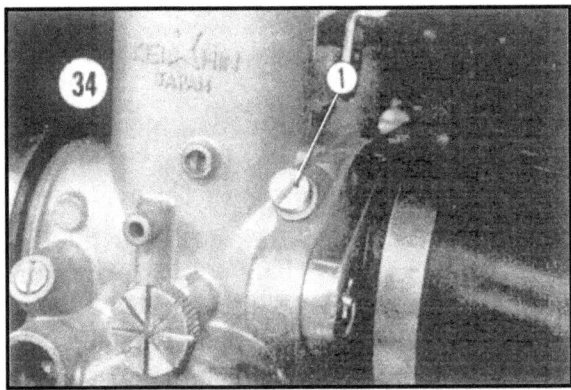

① plug

8. Connect the vacuum gauges as shown in **Figure 35**. The long adapters are for the inside carburetors and the short ones for the outboard carbs. **Figure 36** shows one way to rig the gauges over the handlebars.

① Vacuum gauge adapter

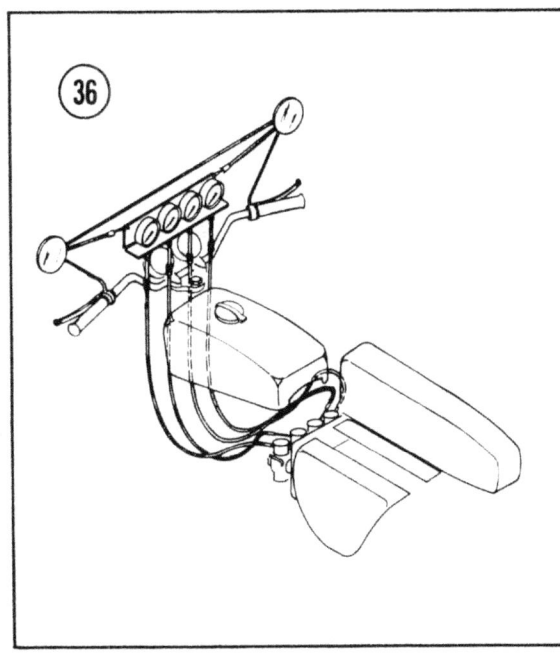

9. Start the engine and let it idle. Adjust the speed to between 1,000 rpm and 1,100 rpm by turning the adjuster screw at the throttle grip, **Figure 37**. The lock nut must be loosened to make the adjustment.

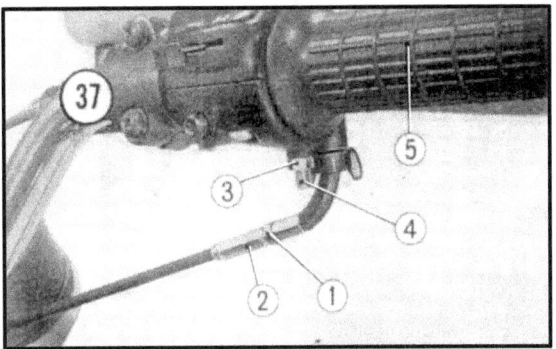

① Throttle cable adjuster lock nut
② Throttle cable adjuster
③ Damper adjusting screw lock nut
④ Damper adjusting screw
⑤ Throttle grip

10. Steady the gauge needles by adjusting the damping valves in the hoses, **Figure 38**. The needles will flutter slightly but should not move beyond one graduation.

11. The carburetor vacuum readings are not as important as the equal balance between carburetors. Generally, eight inches of vacuum is the average for machines with under 30,000 miles.

12. If the vacuum readings vary between carburetors, adjust them as outlined below using the one with the lowest vacuum as a reference.

13. Raise the dust boot from the top of the carburetor, being careful not to tear the soft rubber.

14. Loosen the lock nut at the base, Figure 38.

15. Rotate the adjuster clockwise to increase the vacuum, and counterclockwise to decrease the vacuum.

> NOTE: *Check the balance with the throttle grip opened about one quarter turn. Note if the vacuum drop of one carburetor is not equal to the others when the throttle is opened. If the drop is too fast, turn the adjuster clockwise. Turn it in the other direction if the drop is too slow.*

16. After the carbs are synchronized, tighten the lock nuts and replace the dust covers.

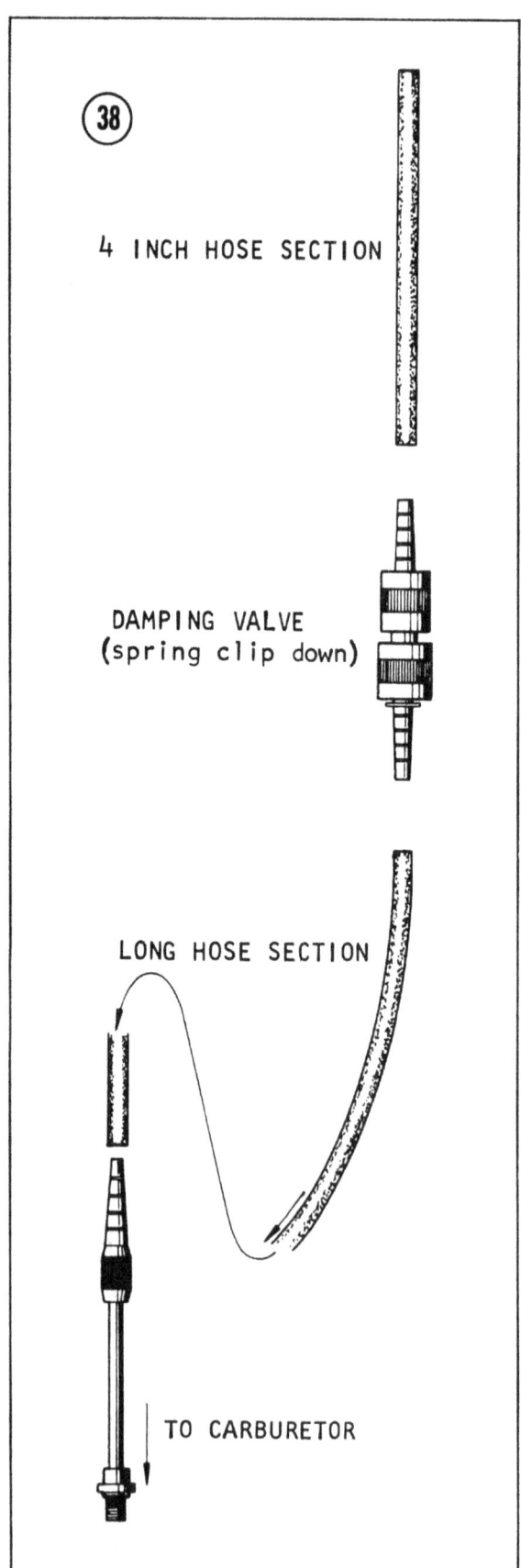

17. Slack off the main throttle cable by backing off the adjustment screw near the grip. See Figure 37.

18. Turn the idle speed screws slowly clockwise until the idle speed is between 1,000 rpm and 1,100 rpm with the vacuum balanced.

19. Referring to Figure 37, adjust the throttle cable at the grip. For the most positive engine response, the free play in the grip should be between 10 and 15 degrees of the total rotation.

20. To adjust, loosen the lock nut to free the adjuster screw. Turn the screw until the desired free play is achieved.

> NOTE: *A similar lock nut and adjusting screw setup is used to adjust the damping action of the grip. See Figure 37.*

21. Stop engine and remove the gauge set from the carburetors.

CB 750 K1

Figure 39 (next page) shows the major carburetor parts involved in the adjustment process.

1. Warm up the engine to operating temperature. Make sure the chokes are open.

2. Turn in the four idle air screws, **Figure 40**, until they gently seat; then back each out, one full turn.

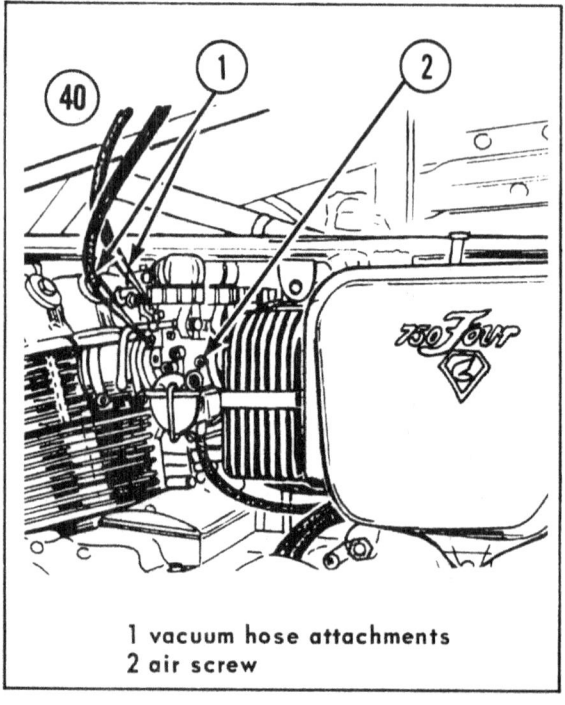

1 vacuum hose attachments
2 air screw

TUNE-UP

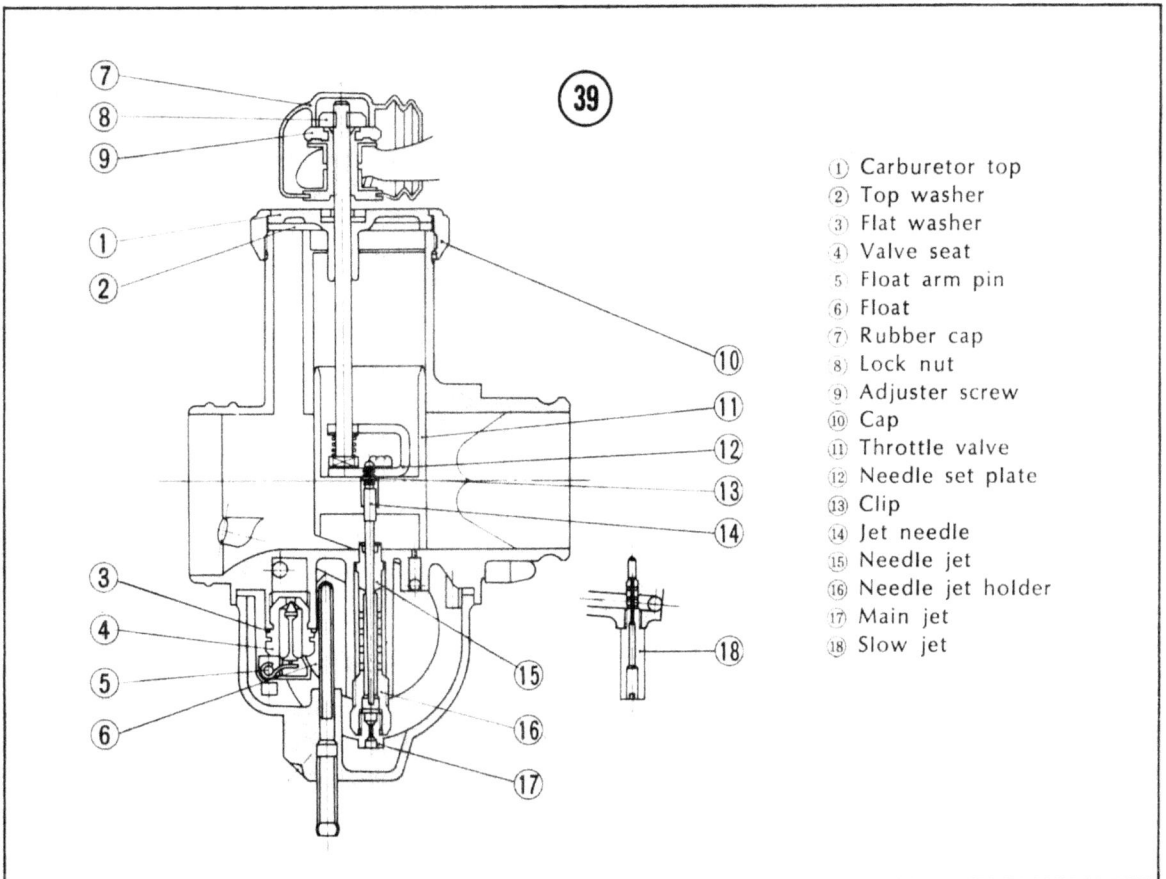

- (1) Carburetor top
- (2) Top washer
- (3) Flat washer
- (4) Valve seat
- (5) Float arm pin
- (6) Float
- (7) Rubber cap
- (8) Lock nut
- (9) Adjuster screw
- (10) Cap
- (11) Throttle valve
- (12) Needle set plate
- (13) Clip
- (14) Jet needle
- (15) Needle jet
- (16) Needle jet holder
- (17) Main jet
- (18) Slow jet

3. Referring to **Figure 41**, set the engine idle speed to 1,000 rpm by adjusting the throttle stop screw. Turn it clockwise to increase idle speed, and counterclockwise to reduce it.

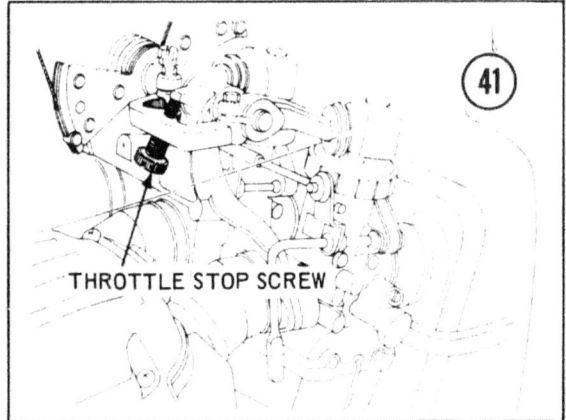

4. Stop the engine. Open the seat and prop up the fuel tank to provide access to the carburetors. Be careful not to stretch the fuel lines.

5. Remove the rubber dust covers from the throttle rod adjusters on top of the four carburetors.

6. Remove the plugs from the vacuum gauge attachment holes in the carburetors, Figure 39, and hook up the gauge hoses—the long hoses to the inside carburetors, and the short ones to the outside carbs. Start the engine.

7. Stabilize the gauges by adjusting the damping valves on the hoses until the needles flutter only slightly and do not move more than one graduation.

8. Equalize the vacuum readings between the four gauges to either around eight inches or until all are equal to the lowest initial reading.

9. To raise or lower the vacuum of an individual carburetor, refer to **Figure 42**, and adjust the throttle rod by loosening the lock nut and turning the adjusting nut. Note: Turn nut clockwise to reduce vacuum. Turn nut counterclockwise to increase vacuum.

CAUTION
When performing the synchronization, make sure to leave the throttle rods extended at least one thread above the lock nut, as in <u>FIGURE 43</u>.

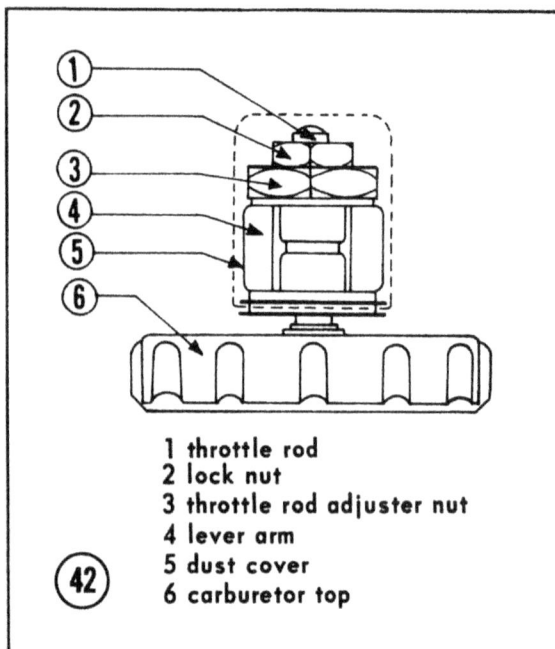

1 throttle rod
2 lock nut
3 throttle rod adjuster nut
4 lever arm
5 dust cover
6 carburetor top

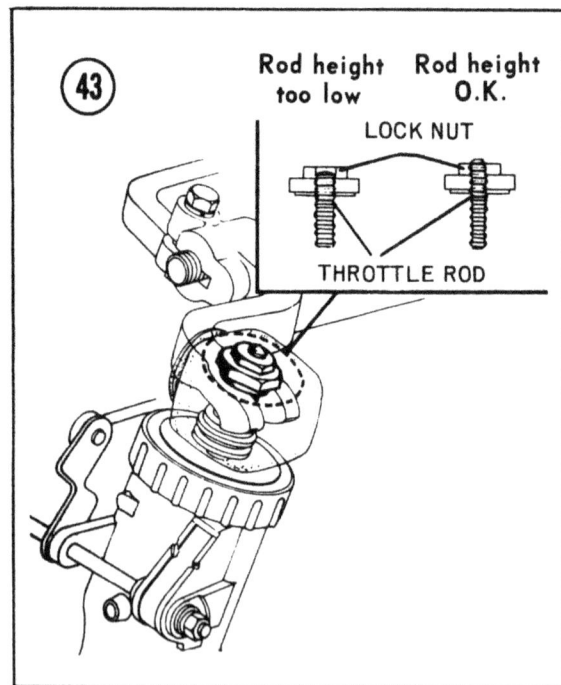

10. When the carbs are balanced, tighten the lock nut.

CAUTION
Hold adjusting bolt with a 17mm wrench when tightening lock nut. If the adjusting nut is left loose, the torque can transfer through to the throttle rod and twist or break it. Lock nut torque should be 12kg-cm to 20kg-cm (.8 ft. lb. to 1.4 ft. lb.).

11. Rev the engine several times and check the vacuum readings again. Readjust if the carbs are not balanced.

12. Refer to the drawing (**Figure 44**) to oil and grease the throttle linkage. Apply the grease to the throttle rods with the throttle grip opened all the way.

13. Reinstall dust covers, making sure the bottom rims are seated in the groove at the base of the throttle rod adjuster. Incorrect seating can interfere with operation of the linkage.

14. Stop the engine. Remove the vacuum gauges and replace the plug screws in the carburetor orifices.

15. If the idle speed has changed, adjust it to 1,000 to 1,100 rpm with the stop screw. Rev the engine several times to make sure the idle is stable.

Throttle Cable Adjustments

The last procedure in adjusting the carburetors is to set the throttle cable. There are three points in the linkage that must be adjusted.

1. Look at **Figures 45 and 46**, which show the linkage for preventing overtravel when the throttle grip is snapped to the closed position.

2. Adjust by loosening the lock nut and turning the eccentric link pin until the clearance between the throttle lever and the pin is between 2mm and 3mm (.081 in and .12 in).

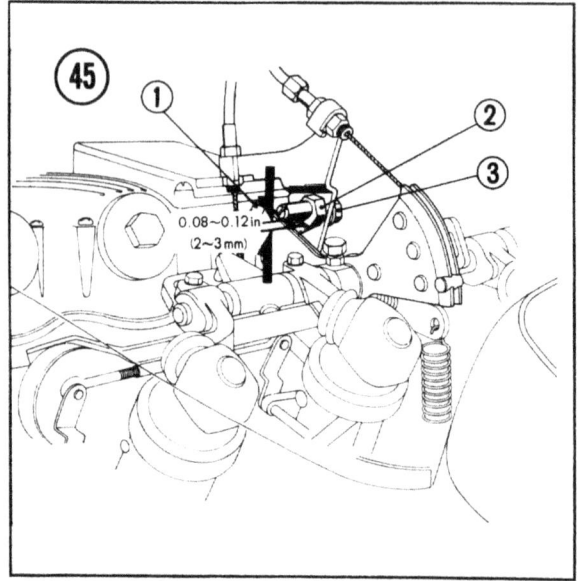

① Throttle lever   ③ Lock nut
② Eccentric link pin

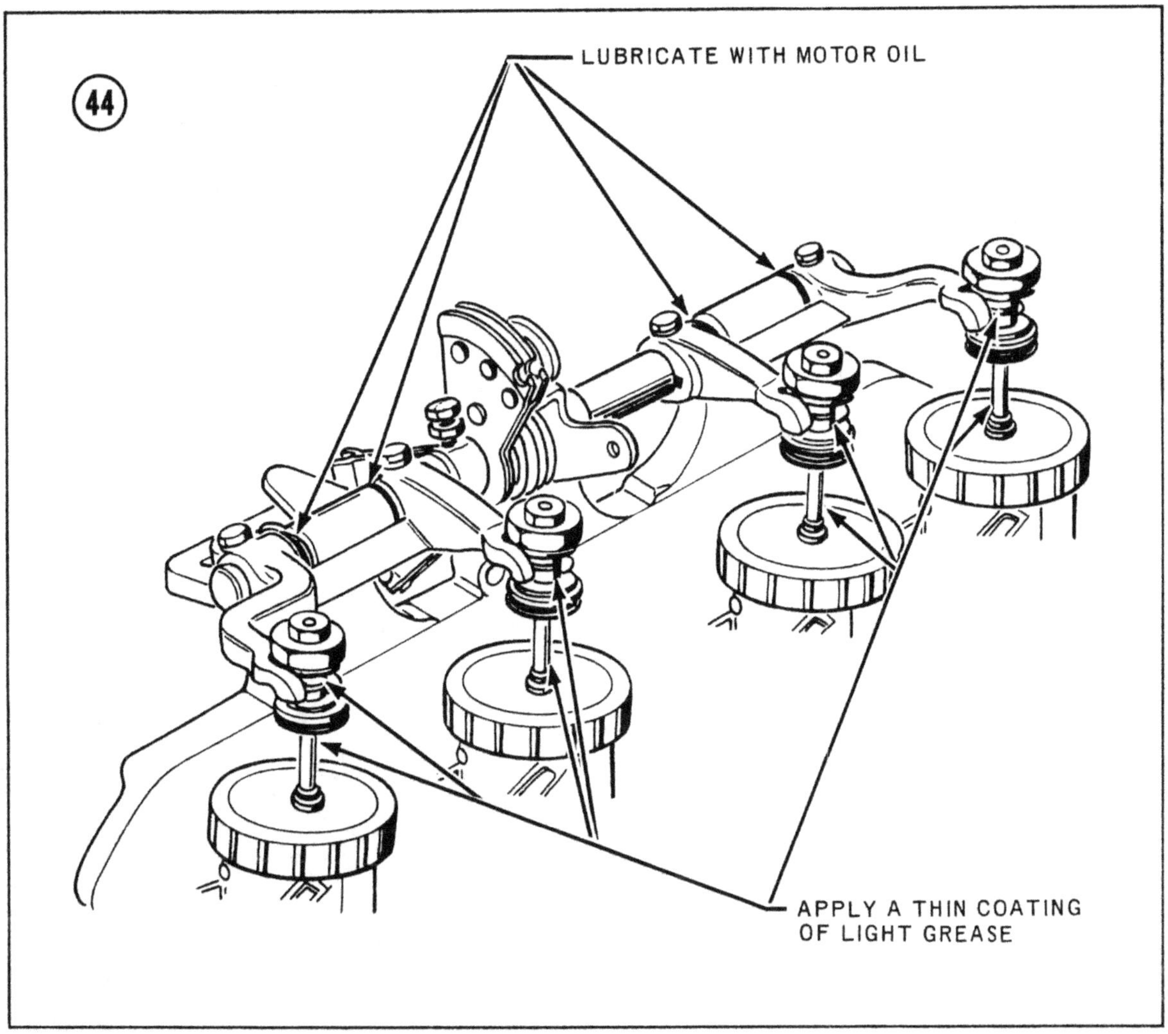

TUNE-UP

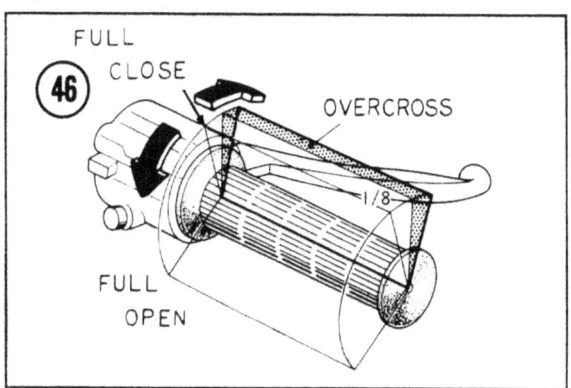

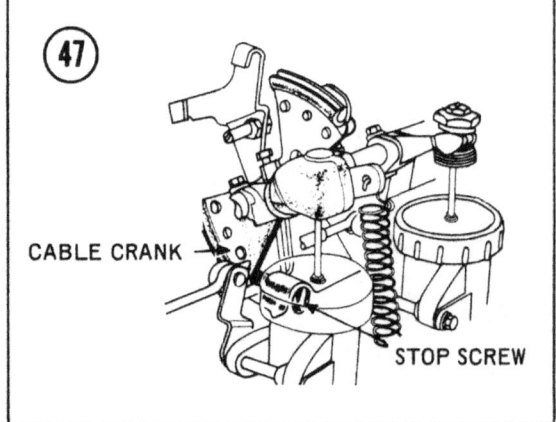

3. Next, refer to **Figure 47** for the detail of the stop screw that limits opening travel and excessive pressure on the throttle valve. The air cleaner must be removed to gain access.

4. There are two methods of adjustment; both are with the throttle grip held open all the way.

   A. Turn the stop screw so that the gap between the top and the screw is 32.5mm to 33mm (1.28 in to 1.29 in).

   B. Back out the stop screw, and turn it in so it just touches the throttle lever. Then turn it in an additional three quarters to one turn.

5. The final adjustment is shown in **Figure 48**. The throttle cable should have about 3mm (.12 in) of free play when measured as rotation of the throttle grip.

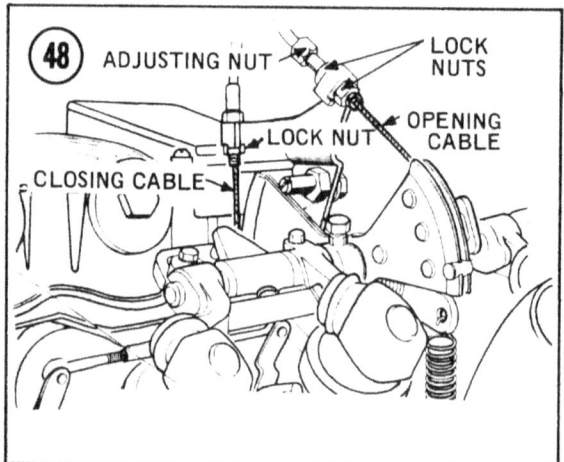

6. Loosen the lock nut at the carburetor end of the cable, and turn the adjusting nut to provide 3mm to 4mm (.12 in to .16 in) play at the grip flange.

CLUTCH

If the clutch slips when engaged, or if the motorcycle creeps forward when in gear even with the clutch disengaged, the free play is out of adjustment.

1. Screw in the clutch cable adjusting bolt at the grip lever, **Figure 49**, in the direction of the arrow until it stops against the bracket.

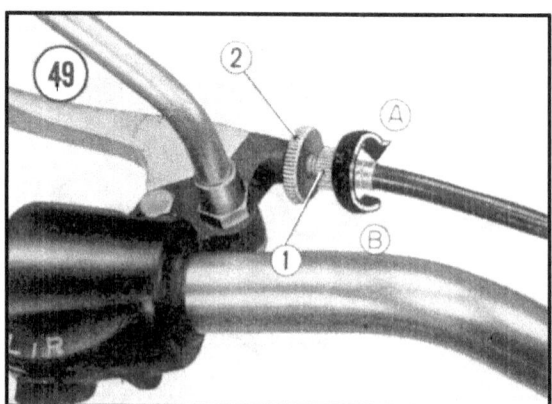

① Clutch cable adjusting bolt
② Lock nut

2. Referring to **Figure 50**, turn the adjusting bolt at the clutch housing in the direction of the arrow to slack off the cable.

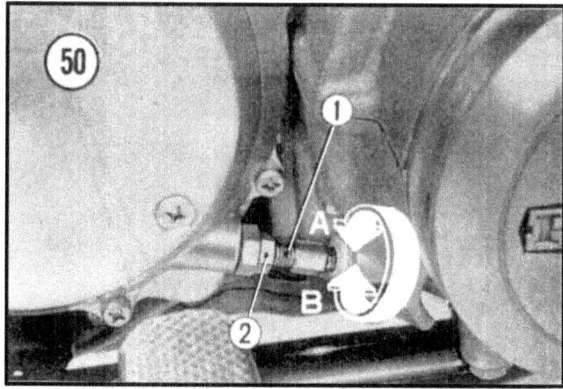

① Clutch cable adjusting bolt
② Lock nut

3. Remove the clutch cover, and referring to **Figure 51**, loosen the lock nut and turn the lifter adjusting screw counterclockwise until a slight resistance is felt. Now turn the screw one quarter turn back, clockwise.

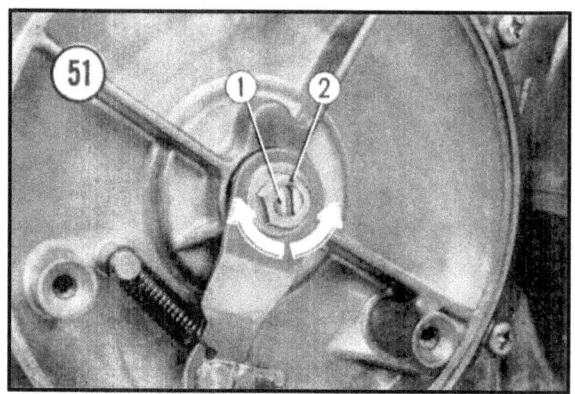

① Clutch adjusting screw
② Lock nut

4. Tighten the lock nut and replace the cover.

5. The final adjustment is made with the adjusting bolt at the clutch grip lever. In step one, this was screwed up to the bracket.

6. Back off the adjusting bolt until the standard free play of 10mm to 25mm (.4 in to 1 in) is achieved.

BATTERY

The battery is the heart of the electrical system, and its condition should be checked regularly.

CAUTION
Do not spill battery electrolyte on painted surfaces. The liquid is corrosive and can damage the finish.

TUNE-UP

1. Remove the left side cover from the battery. See **Figure 52**.

2. Check the level of the electrolyte. **Figure 53** shows the maximum and minimum level marks.

3. If necessary, top up with distilled water only. Be careful not to overfill.

4. Inspect the terminals. Flush off any oxidation using a solution of baking soda and water to neutralize acids. Lightly coat the terminals with Vaseline or a silicon grease to retard corrosion.

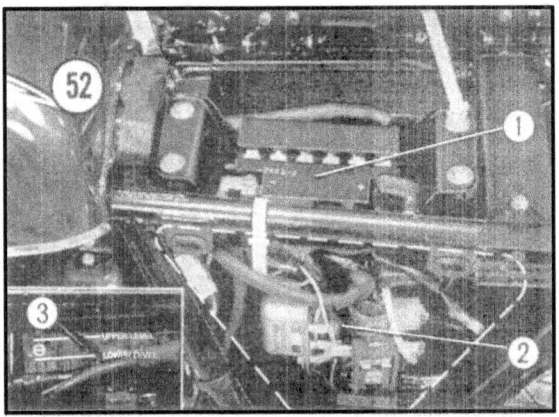

① Battery   ② Left cover   ③ Battery case

① Upper level mark   ② Lower level mark

CHAPTER TWO

ENGINE

REMOVING THE ENGINE

The engine, clutch, and transmission are a single unit attached to the frame by four mounting bolts. **Figures 1 and 2** are different views of this unit when removed from the cycle.

1. Turn off the fuel tank valve and disconnect the tubes running from it to the tank. Raise the seat and remove the fuel tank.
2. Drain oil from the crankcase and the oil tank, and remove the filter.
3. Remove the mufflers.
4. Refer to **Figure 3** and disconnect the tachometer cable.

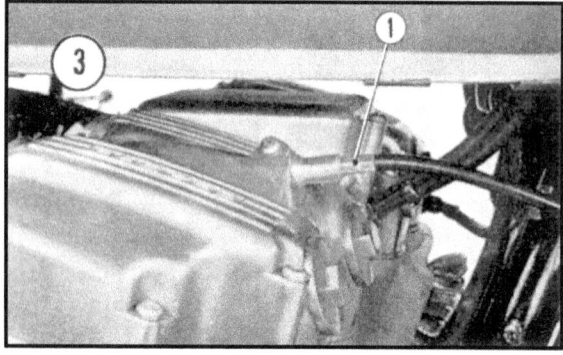

① Tachometer cable

5. Remove the throttle valves from the four carburetors, disconnect the carbs from the inlet pipes, and remove them.
6. Remove the air cleaner case, kickstarter pedal, and the clutch cover.
7. Disconnect the clutch cable from the clutch lever. See **Figure 4**.
8. Disconnect the spring for the stop switch and remove the brake pedal and its step bar.

ENGINE

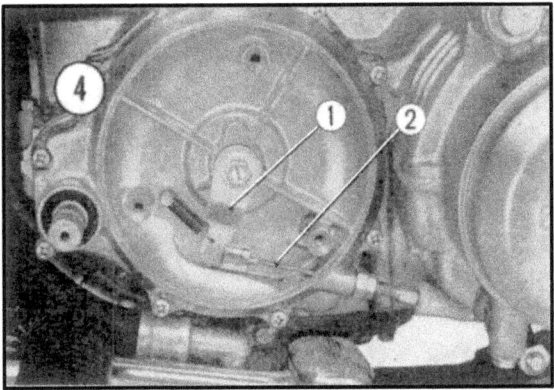

① Clutch lever ② Clutch cable

9. See **Figure 5** and remove the two oil hoses at the engine. Then remove the oil tank and disconnect the breather cap from the crankcase.

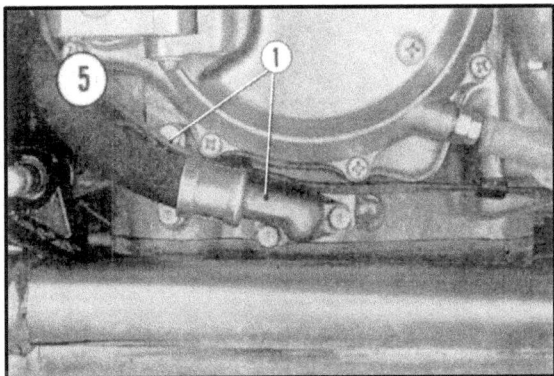

① Engine oil hoses

10. Remove the gearshift pedal and the drive chain cover. Disconnect the drive chain, and wire the ends together to keep it from coiling.

11. Disconnect the negative lead from the battery to prevent a short circuit, then disconnect the starter motor cable, **Figure 6**, at the magnetic switch. Also disconnect the dynamo leads and the lead to the stop switch as shown.

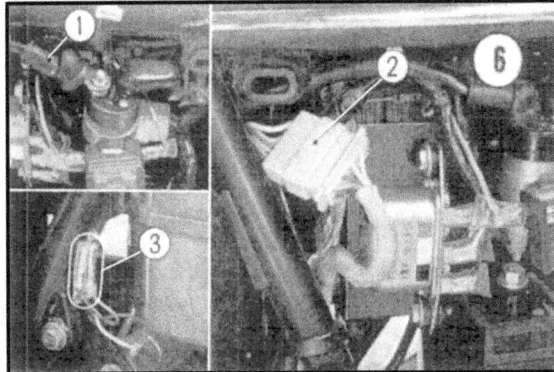

① Starter motor cable ③ Stop switch lead
② Dynamo leads connector

12. **Figure 7** shows the location of the mounting bolts. Unscrew them, lift the rear of the engine, and remove it from the right side of the bike.

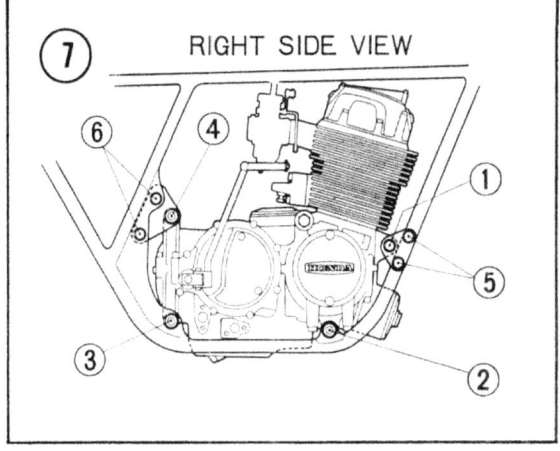

① 10 mm bolt
② Engine hanger bolt A
③ Rear engine hanger lower bolt
④ Engine hanger bolt C
⑤ 8 mm × 56 bolt
⑥ 8 mm × 45 bolt

INSTALLING THE ENGINE

1. Place the engine in the frame from the right side.

2. Install the mounting bolts. Note that the ground strap from the battery is connected to the frame at the upper rear bolt, shown in **Figure 8**. The mounting bolts also do double duty to connect the hanger plate and the stop switch stay.

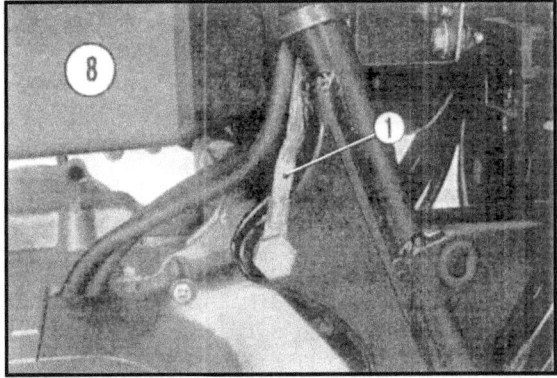

① Ground cable

3. Connect the electrical wiring and the tach cable.

4. Connect the drive chain and install its cover. Install the gearshift pedal.

5. Refer to **Figure 9** and install the brake pedal and the spring for the stop switch.

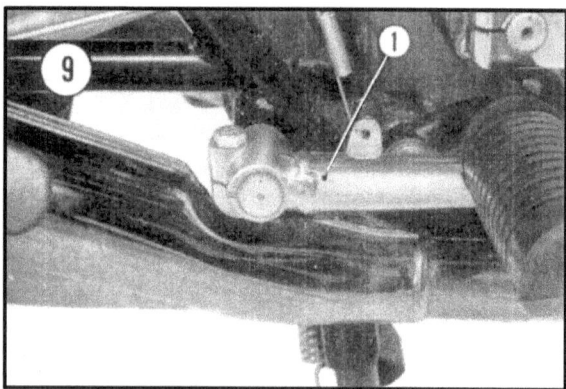

① Rear brake pedal

6. Connect the clutch cable to the lever, install the clutch pedal, and then the clutch cover.

7. Mount the carburetors and the air cleaner case. Connect the throttle valves and the spark plug leads.

8. Mount the oil tank, install the hoses, and connect them to the engine. Be careful not to mistake the supply hose for the scavenge hose.

9. Install the mufflers, referring to **Figure 10** for the positioning of the bands.

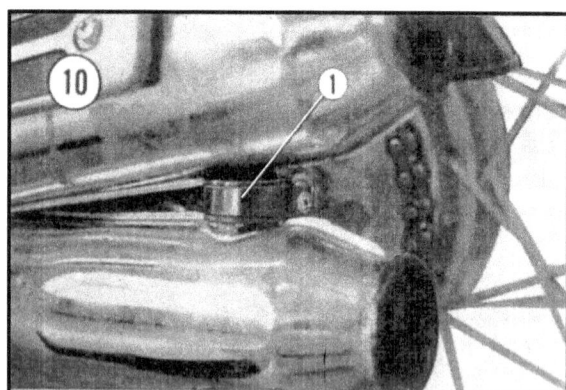

① Exhaust muffler band

10. Replace the fuel tank and connect the tubes to the fuel valve.
11. Refill with oil.

LUBRICATION

Figure 11 shows the dry sump lubrication system of the Honda 750. Oil from a reservoir tank is pressurized by a pump and forced through a filter to the engine components. A scavenge pump returns oil accumulated in the crankcase sump to the tank.

OIL FILTER

The full-flow, replaceable element filter cleanses the oil of impurities before it is routed to the engine. **Figure 12** shows the normal path of oil through the filter.

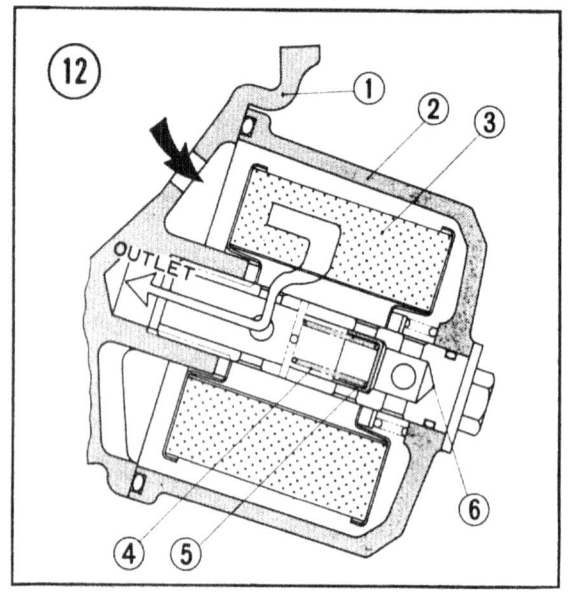

① Crankcase   ④ By-pass valve spring
② Oil filter case   ⑤ By-pass valve
③ Oil filter element ⑥ Center bolt

If the element becomes clogged, a by-pass valve opens to allow a continued supply of oil to the engine. **Figure 13** shows oil routed directly to the main gallery when the by-pass valve is open.

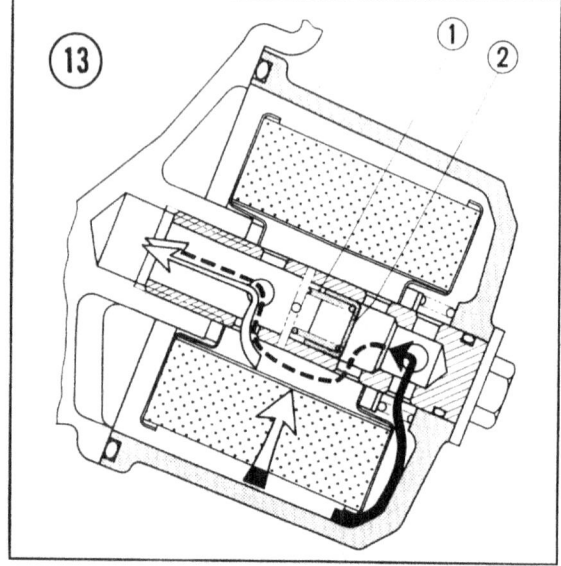

① By-pass valve spring
② By-pass valve

ENGINE

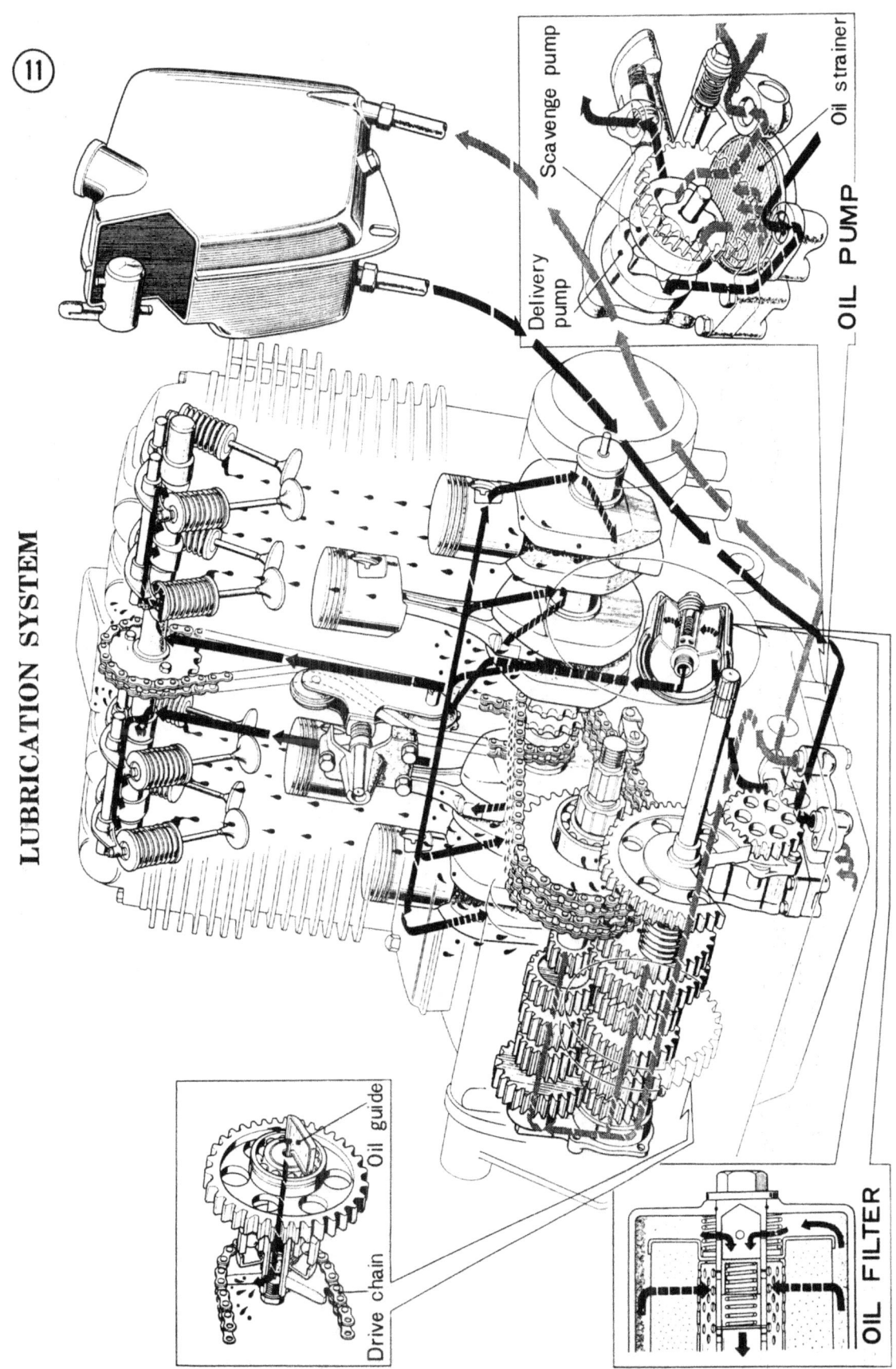

ENGINE

OIL PUMP

Refer to **Figure 14** for construction of the oil pump. It is not necessary to remove the engine from the frame in order to remove and inspect the pump.

Disassembly

1. Remove the oil filter case by unscrewing the center bolt at the base of the cover.

2. Remove the oil pan from the base of the crankcase.

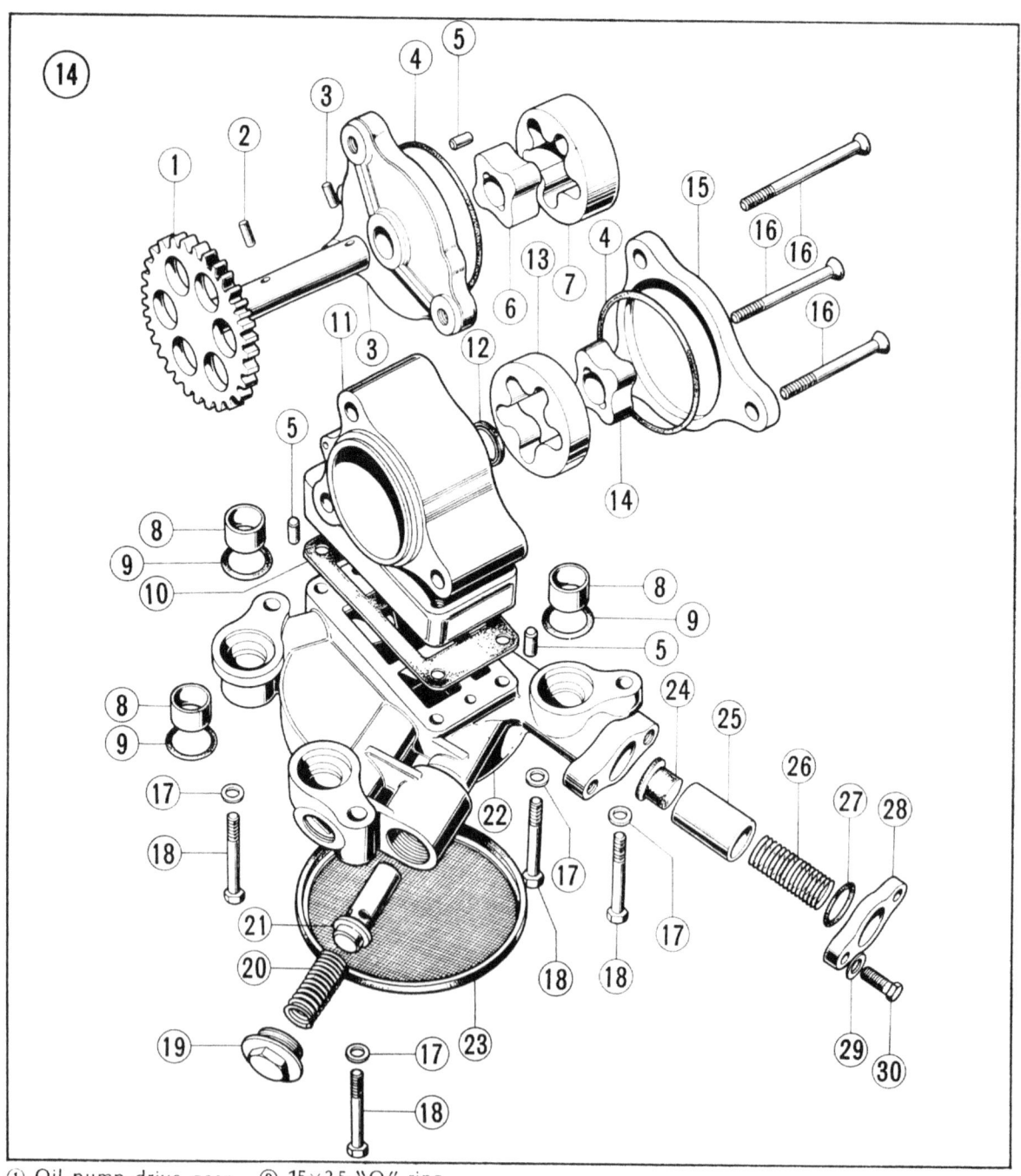

① Oil pump drive gear
② 4×14.8 mm pin
③ Oil pump right cover
④ 46×2 "O" ring
⑤ 4×8 dowel pin
⑥ Inner rotor B
⑦ Outer rotor B
⑧ "O" ring collar
⑨ 15×2.5 "O" ring
⑩ Oil pump gasket
⑪ Oil pump body
⑫ 11×15×3 Oil seal
⑬ Outer rotor A
⑭ Inner rotor A
⑮ Oil pump left cover
⑯ 6×59 flat screw
⑰ 6 mm flat washer
⑱ 6×32 hex bolt
⑲ Relief spring cap
⑳ Relief valve spring
㉑ Relief valve
㉒ Oil pump base
㉓ Oil strainer screen
㉔ Oil leak stopper seal
㉕ Oil leak stopper valve
㉖ Oil leak stopper spring
㉗ 15×2.5 "O" ring
㉘ Oil leak stopper cap
㉙ 6 mm flat washer
㉚ 6 mm hex bolt

ENGINE

3. Unscrew the three mounting bolts, **Figure 15**, and remove the oil pump.

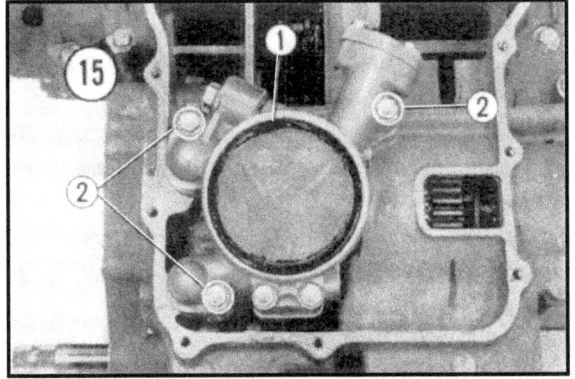

① Oil pump
② Oil pump mounting bolts

4. Take off the side cover, and referring again to the exploded view in Figure 14, remove the "A" rotor from the delivery side.

5. Remove the dowel pin shown in Figure 15, and pull the shaft from the body. This will free the "B" rotor so it can be removed from the scavenge side.

6. Remove the round mesh filter, **Figure 16**, and then the pump body by unscrewing the four 6mm bolts.

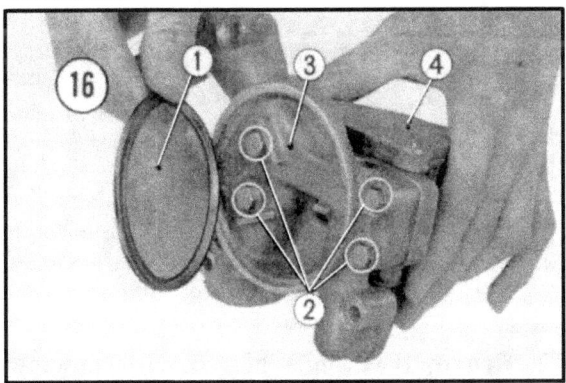

① Metal oil screen   ③ Oil pump base
② 6 mm hex bolts   ④ Oil pump body

7. **Figure 17** shows the function of the stopper valve to cut off oil flow from the tank when the engine is stopped. To disassemble, refer to **Figure 18** and remove the cap bolts. Then remove the stopper cap, spring, and valve from the pump.

8. **Figure 19** shows the relief spring which opens when the oil pressure exceeds the normal level and by-passes oil to the sump. This maintains the same oil pressure in the engine. To remove

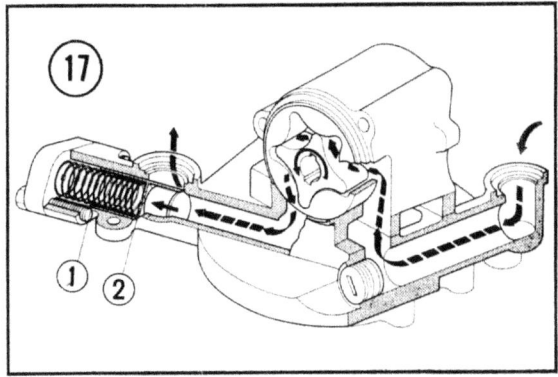

① Oil leak stopper spring
② Oil leak stopper valve

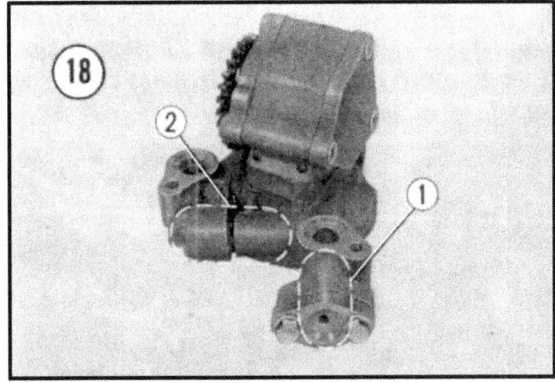

① Leak stopper valve
② Relief valve

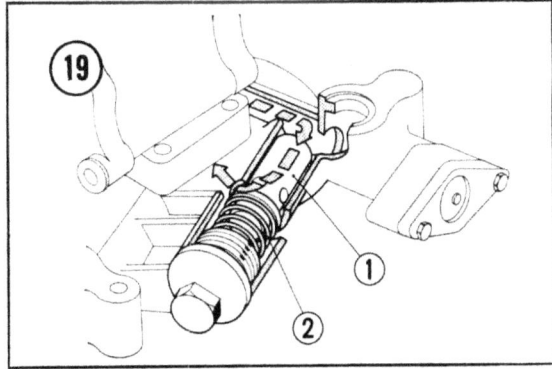

① Relief valve
② Relief valve spring

the valve, unscrew the spring cap, Figure 18, and remove the assembly.

Inspection

1. Check the side cover for cracks.

2. Measure the clearance between the outer rotor and the body as shown in **Figure 20**. If the clearance is more than .35mm (.014 in) the worn part must be replaced.

ENGINE

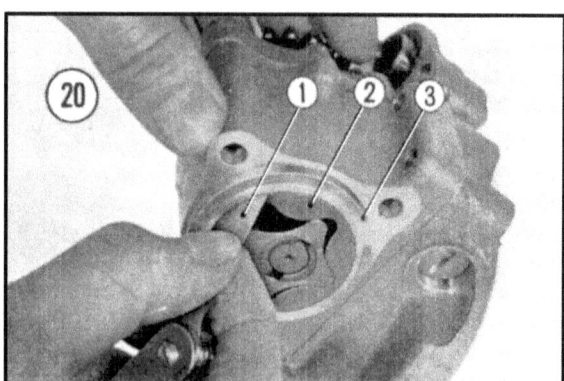

① Thickness gauge ③ Pump body
② Outer rotor

3. Measure the clearance between the inner and outer rotor at the tip, **Figures 21**. If the clearance is more than .35mm (.014 in) the rotors should be replaced in a set.

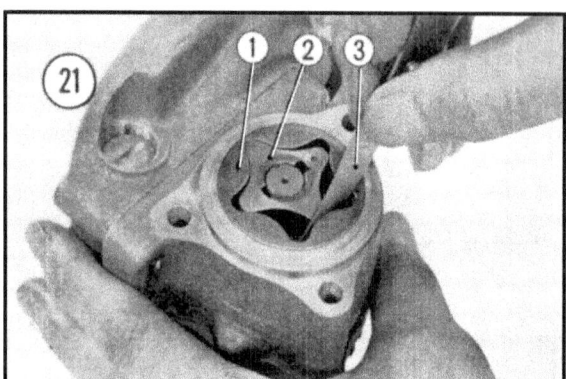

① Outer rotor ③ Thickness gauge
② Inner rotor

4. Use a dial gauge or micrometer to measure the inside diameter of the pump body, and the outside diameter of the oil leak stopper valve (refer to Figure 14). If the difference between the two measurements is more than .17mm (.007 in), the worn part must be replaced.

5. Use a dial gauge or micrometer to measure the inside diameter of the body, and the outside diameter of the relief valve. If the difference is greater than .1mm (.004 in), the worn part should be replaced.

6. Measure the thickness of the rotor with a micrometer, and its depth using a depth micrometer. If the clearance with the body is more than .12mm (.005 in), the parts should be replaced.

7. Before reassembling the pump, clean the round strainer with solvent. If the seal is damaged, replace the part.

Reassembly

1. Reassemble the oil pump in reverse order of disassembly.

2. Assemble the relief valve and its spring, taking care to screw on the cap securely.

3. Assemble the stopper valve, its spring, the O-ring, and the cap. Tighten the two bolts securely.

4. Mount the "B" inner and outer rotors into the pump body, and insert the drive gear, making sure the dowel pin also is installed.

5. Mount the "A" inner and outer rotors.

CAMSHAFT

The single overhead camshaft is driven by a chain off the timing sprocket at the crankshaft. **Figure 22** shows the drive system with the tensioner, guide roller, and chain guide.

Disassembly

1. Remove the breather cover by unscrewing the three 6mm Phillips screws **Figure 23**.

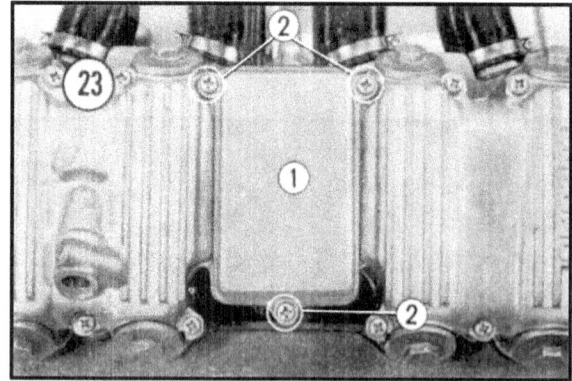

① Breather cover ② Cross screws

2. Remove the cylinder head cover by unscrewing the 6mm Phillips screws circled in **Figure 24**.

① Cylinder head cover

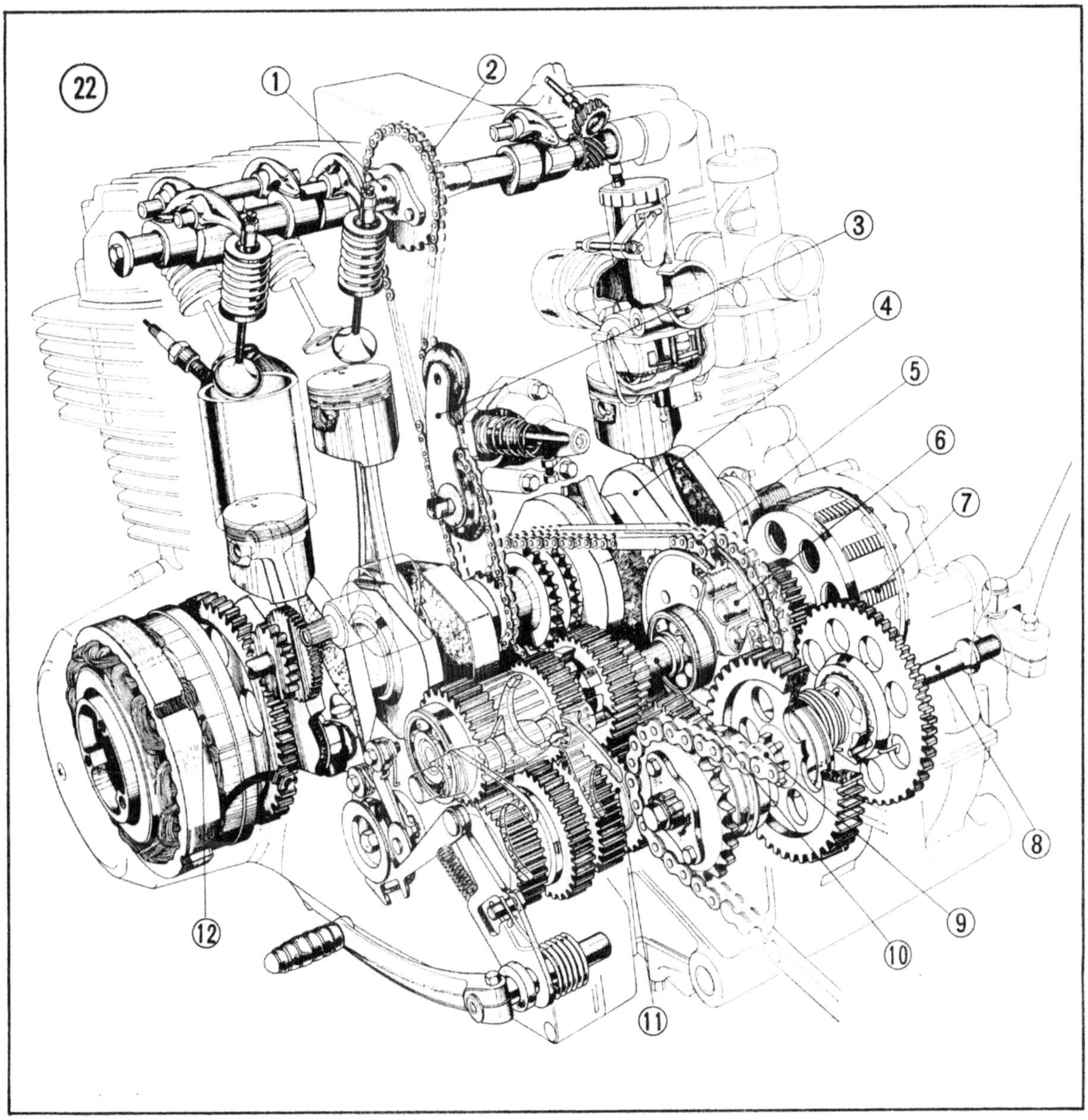

ENGINE

![Engine cutaway diagram labeled 22]

① Camshaft   ④ Crankshaft   ⑦ Clutch   ⑩ Mainshaft
② Camchain   ⑤ Primary chain   ⑧ Kick starter spindle   ⑪ Countershaft
③ Camchain tensioner   ⑥ Primary driven sprocket   ⑨ Final driven shaft   ⑫ A.C. generator

3. Refer to **Figure 25** and rotate the crankshaft to align the timing marks on the cam end with the joint between the holder cap and head. The key groove should be at 12 o'clock.

4. Remove the cam holder cap by loosening the two bolts.

5. Refer to **Figure 26** and remove the cam chain tensioner from the engine.

6. Remove the two mounting bolts from the cam sprocket, and loosen the lock nuts and the adjusting screws on the valve tappets.

① Camshaft ② Timing index marked lines

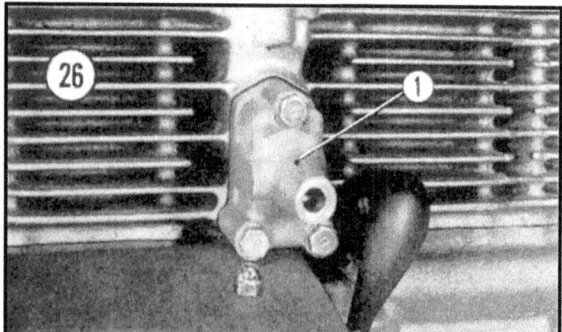

① Cam chain tensioner holder

7. Refer to **Figure 27** for construction of the rocker arm assembly. Unscrew the four mounting bolts on the rocker arm shaft and remove the shaft. Honda makes a special tool (No. 07050-30001) for this operation, shown in **Figure 28**.

NOTE: *Rocker arms No. 1 and No. 3, and No. 2 and No. 4 are identical. Tag them for identification when they are removed.*

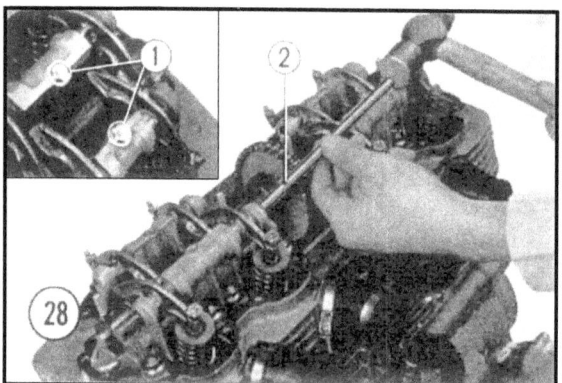

① Rocker arm shaft mounting bolts
② Rocker arm shaft remover

8. Remove the cam chain from the sprocket, **Figure 29**, and pull out the cam from the holder on the left side.

9. Remove the holder from the head.

① Camshaft   ② Cam sprocket

10. To remove the cylinder head, the 16 mounting nuts and the five mounting bolts, circled in **Figure 30**, must be unscrewed. Refer to the tightening sequence in Figure 42, later in this section, and remove the head in the reverse order. Honda tool No. 07078-30001 is used to loosen the six bolts.

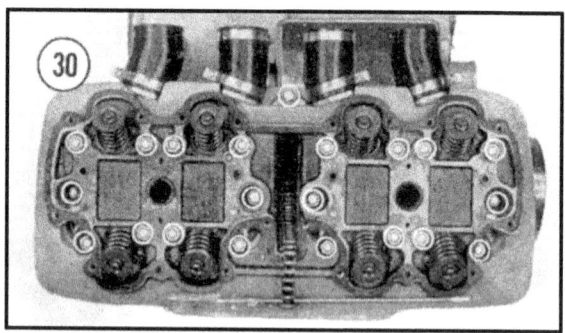

11. Refer to **Figure 31** and remove the two mounting rubbers, and then remove the chain tensioner assembly.

① Tensioner roller mounting rubbers
② Cam chain tensioner

12. The guide roller can then be removed from the chain tensioner by pushing the roller pin. Refer to **Figure 32** for locations of these parts.

13. Remove the guide pin from the bottom of the block, **Figure 33**, and remove the guide.

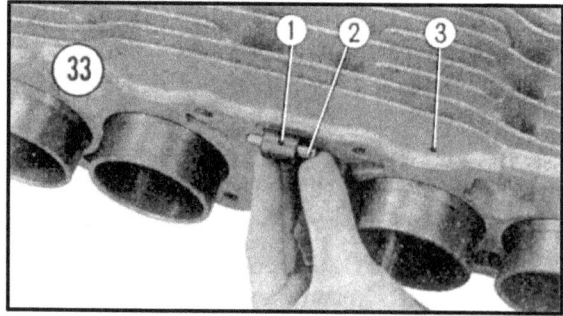

① Cam chain guide   ③ Cylinder
② Cam chain guide pin

ENGINE

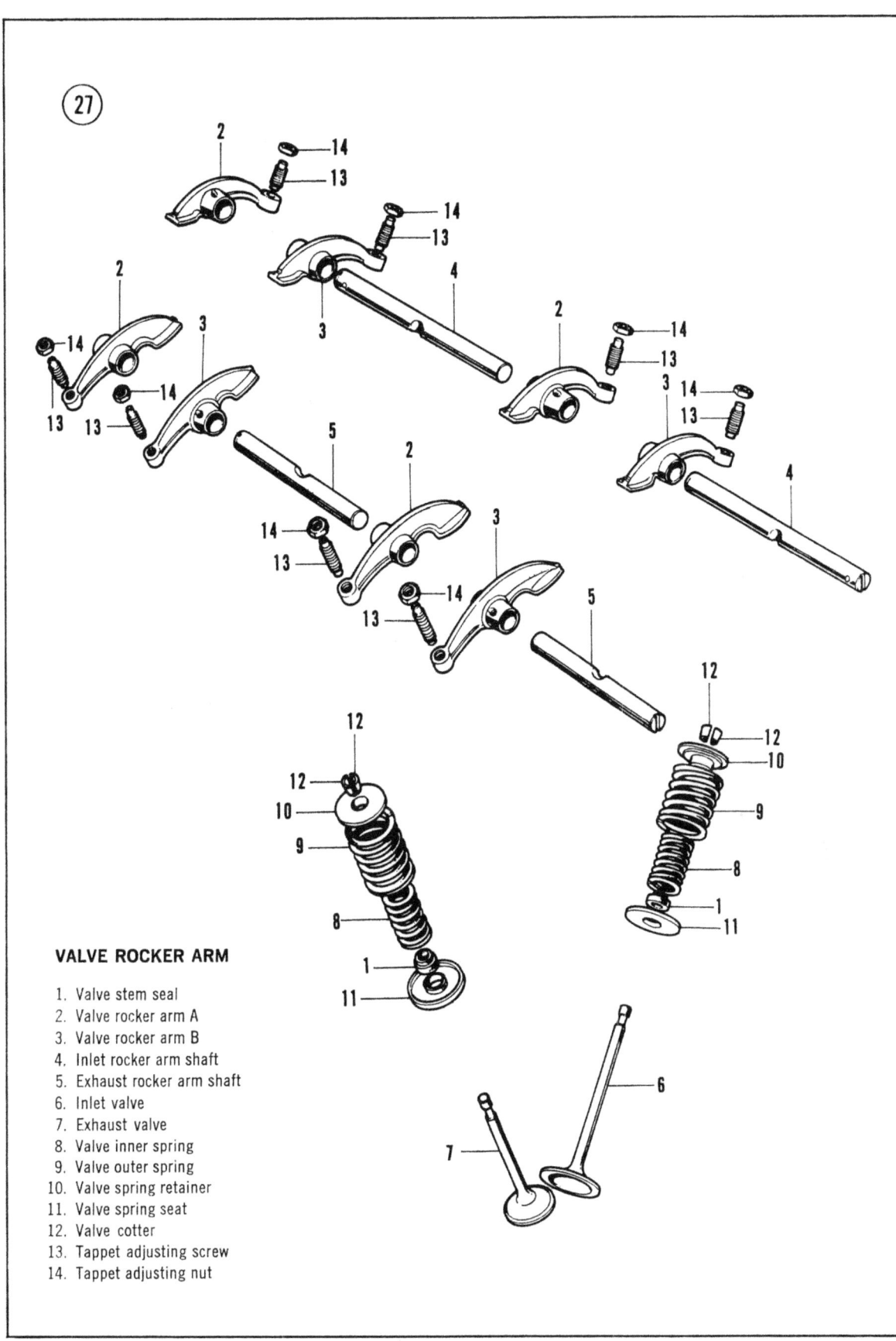

VALVE ROCKER ARM

1. Valve stem seal
2. Valve rocker arm A
3. Valve rocker arm B
4. Inlet rocker arm shaft
5. Exhaust rocker arm shaft
6. Inlet valve
7. Exhaust valve
8. Valve inner spring
9. Valve outer spring
10. Valve spring retainer
11. Valve spring seat
12. Valve cotter
13. Tappet adjusting screw
14. Tappet adjusting nut

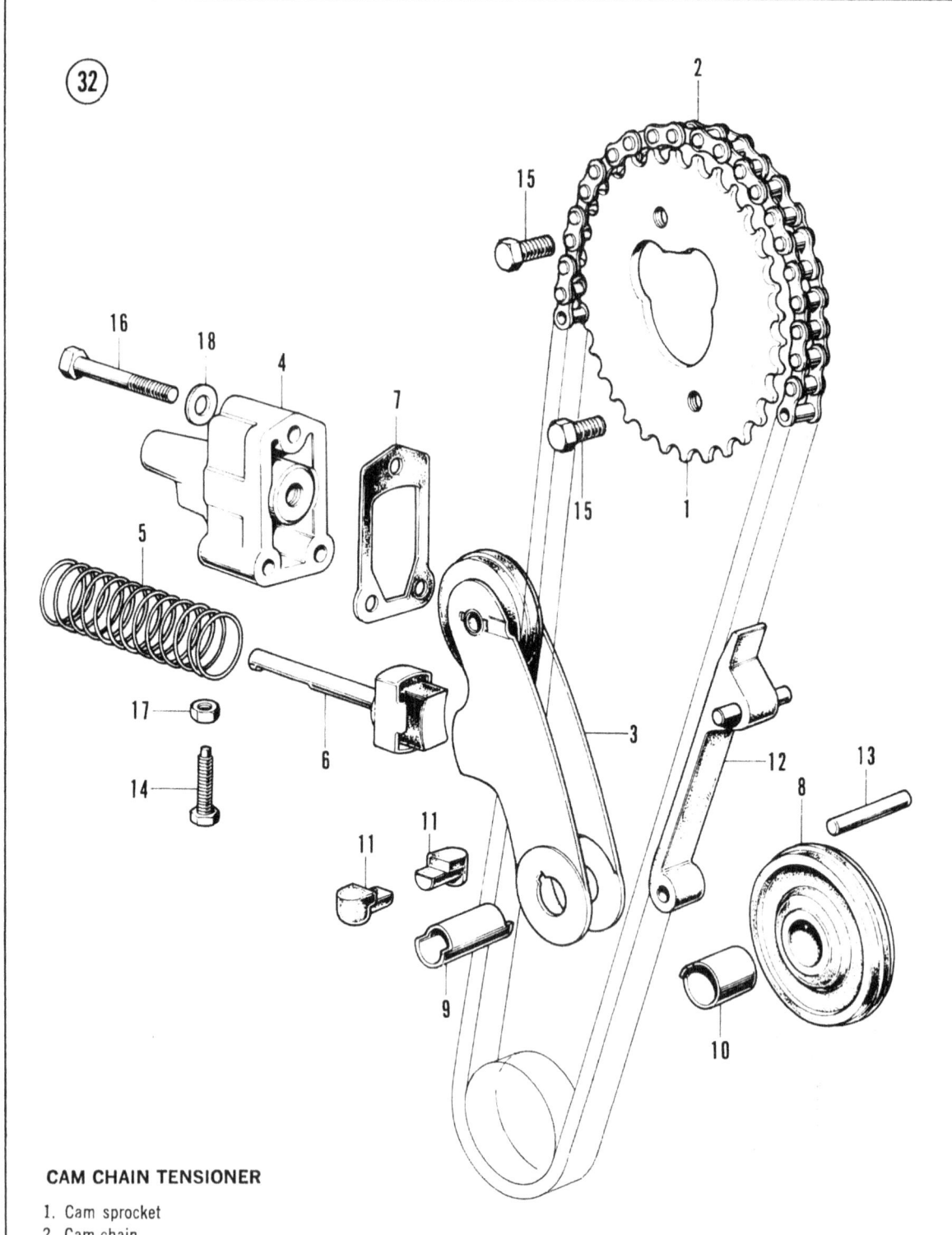

CAM CHAIN TENSIONER

1. Cam sprocket
2. Cam chain
3. Cam chain tensioner components
4. Cam chain tensioner holder components
5. Tensioner spring
6. Push bar components
7. Tensioner holder gasket
8. Cam chain guide roller
9. Cam chain roller pin
10. Cam chain roller collar
11. Cam chain roller pin rubber
12. Cam chain guide
13. Cam chain guide pin
14. Tensioner adjusting bolt
15. Hex bolt
16. Hex bolt
17. Hex nut
18. Plain washer

ENGINE

Inspection and Measurement

1. Assemble the cam holder on the head, and torque down the cap to 80 kg-cm to 110 kg-cm (6 ft-lbs to 8 ft-lbs).

2. Use an inside dial gauge to measure the average inside diameter of the bearing, **Figure 34**, both vertically and horizontally. Then measure the camshaft bearing surface with a micrometer, **Figure 35**, and calculate the shaft clearance by subtracting the two values. If the clearance is more than .21mm (.008 in) the holder and cap should be replaced as a set.

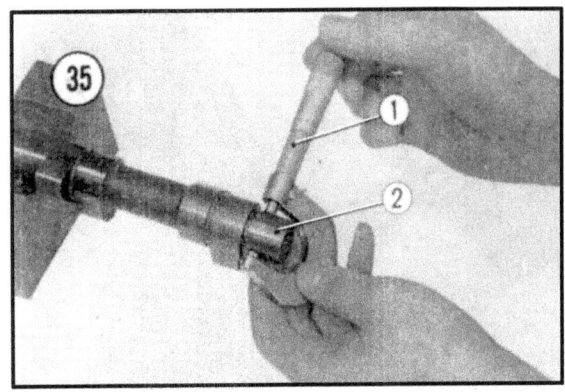

① Micrometer
② Camshaft bearing

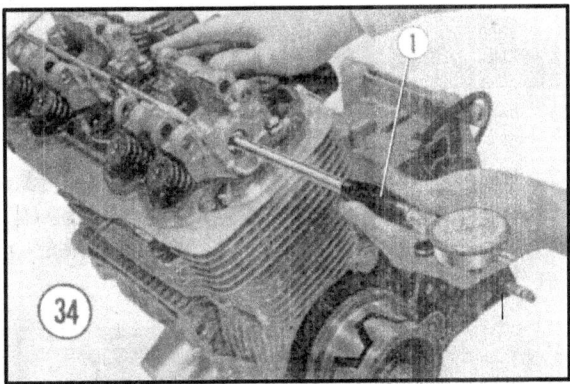

① Inside dial gauge

NOTE: *The sets available from Honda have identical codes, usually a letter and a number, stamped on both pieces, as shown in* <u>FIGURE 36</u>. *There are two types available, with the newer version for engine No. CB750E-1010338 and later numbers.*

3. Check cam lift by measuring the lobe with a micrometer, as shown in **Figure 37**. The camshaft should be replaced if the inlet cam height is less than 35.86mm (1.411 in), or the exhaust

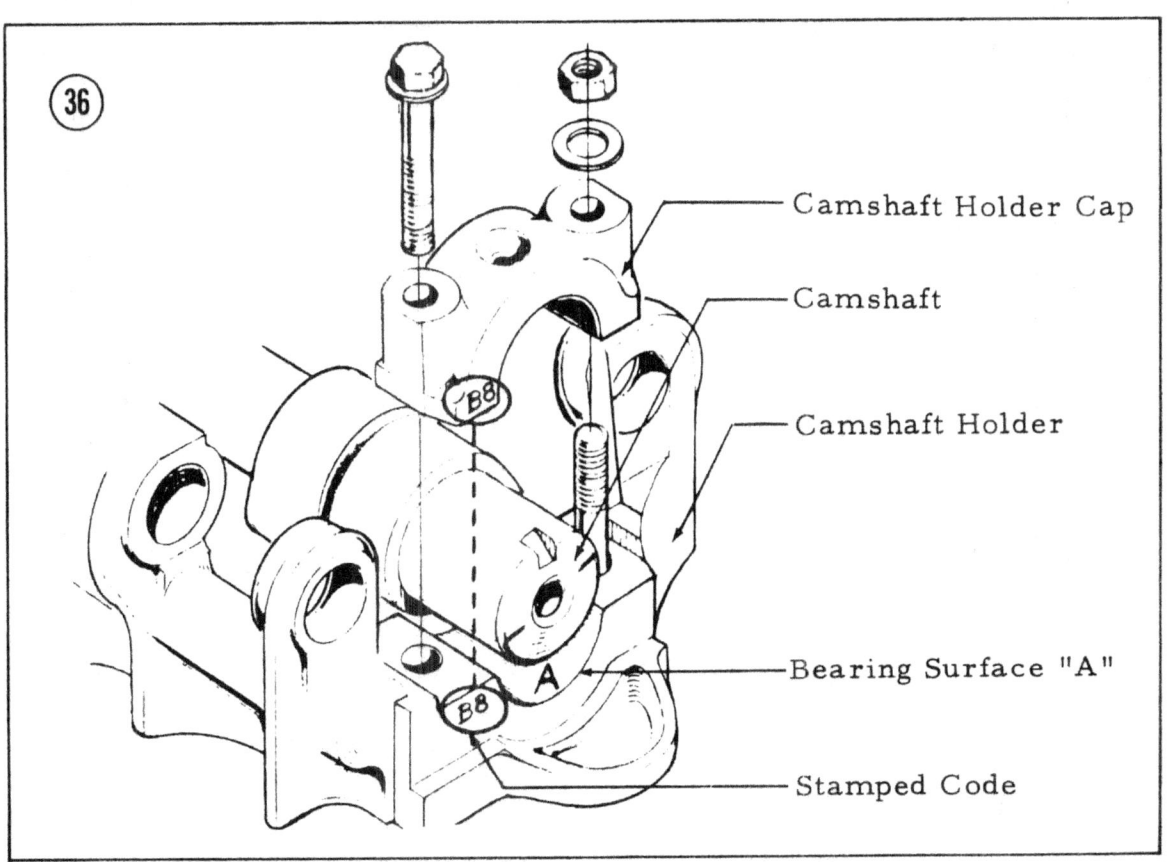

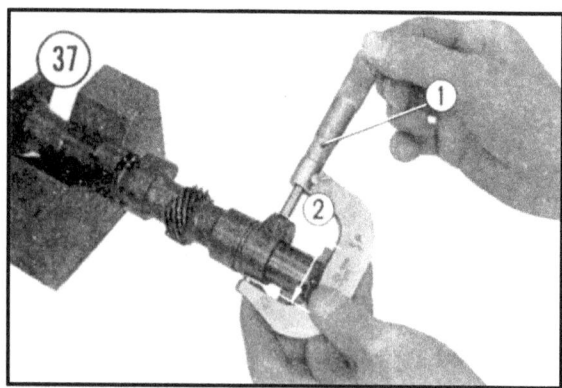

① Micrometer ② Cam height

cam height is less than 35.36mm (1.392 in), or the base circle is less than 27.93mm (1.099 in).

4. Check for bend in the camshaft with a dial gauge as shown in **Figure 38**. If the runout is more than .1mm (.005 in), the camshaft should be replaced.

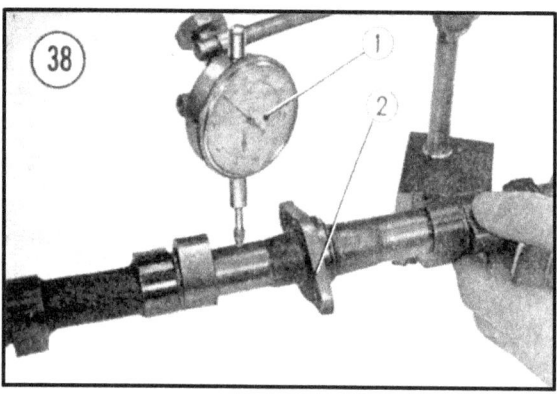

① Dial gauge ② Camshaft

5. Check the camshaft and holder for cracks and scratches.

6. Check the chain guide roller, **Figure 39**, for wear. Replace if necessary.

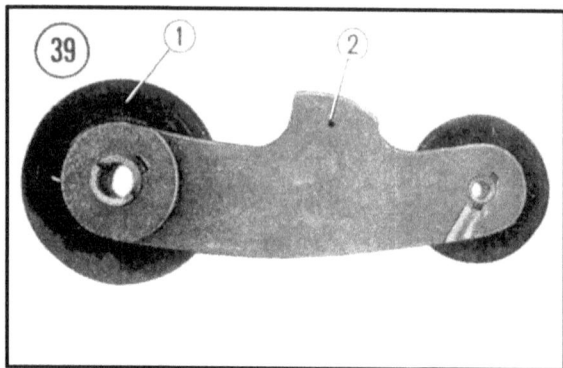

① Cam chain guide roller
② Cam chain tensioner

Reassembly

1. Refer to **Figure 40** and run the chain through the tensioner roller, mount it on the crankcase, and install the rubbers.

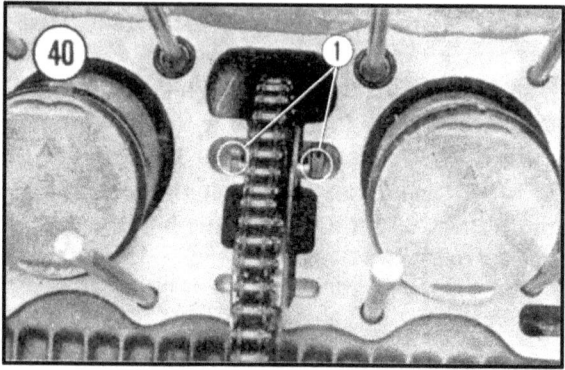

① Tensioner roller mounting rubbers

2. Install the head gasket, two dowel pins, two O-rings, and the cylinder head on the block, **Figure 41**. Be careful not to damage the pistons or the rings.

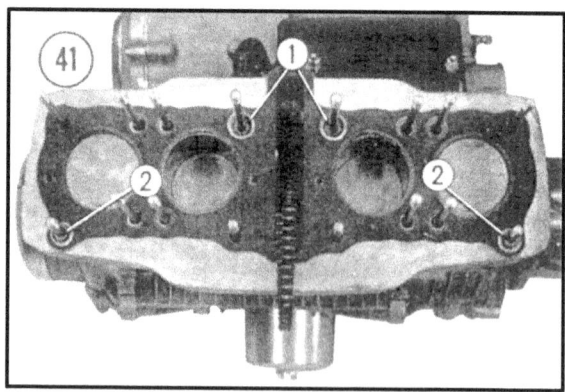

① "O" rings ② Dowel pins

3. Torque down the head mounting nuts and bolts in the sequence shown in **Figure 42** to 1.9 kg-m to 2.1 kg-m (13.7 ft-lbs to 15.2 ft-lbs).

4. Time the valves by setting the No. 1 and No. 2 cylinders to top dead center (TDC) by aligning the "T 1-4" mark on the spark advance under the breaker points with the index mark, as shown in **Figure 43**.

5. Put the sprocket on the camshaft, and run the chain through the right side.

6. Put the camshaft in the holder and align the timing line on the shaft end, as shown in **Figure 44**, so it is parallel with the horizontal surface of the holder. The key groove should be at 12 o'clock.

ENGINE

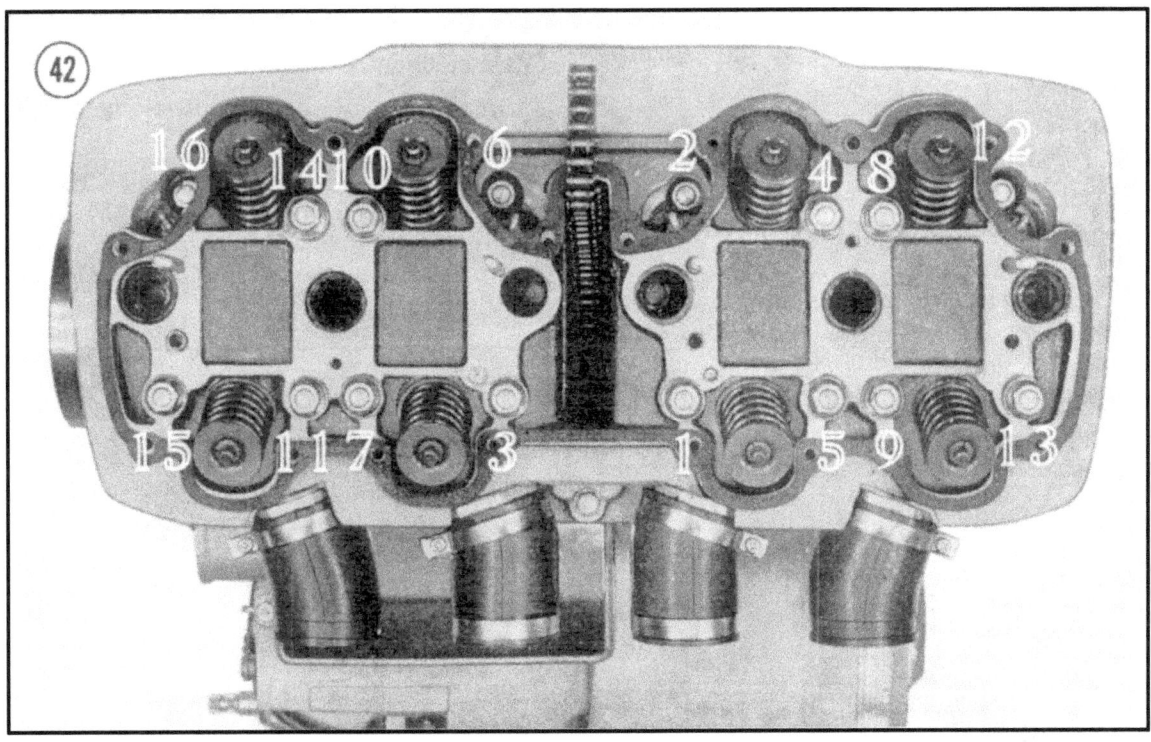

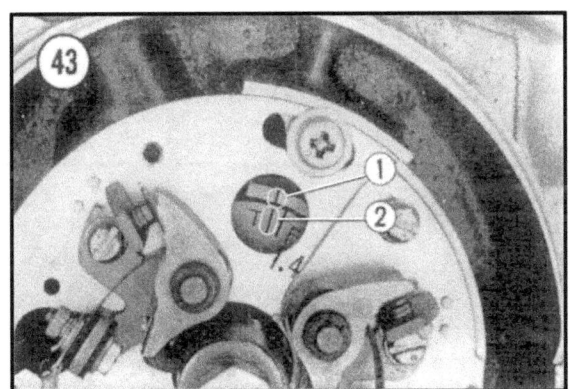

① Index mark   ② "T" mark

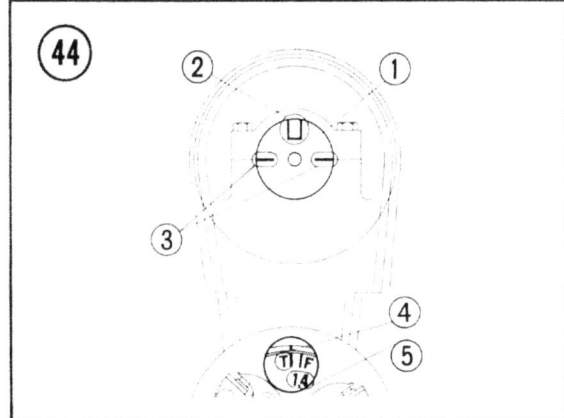

① Camshaft   ④ "T" mark
② Groove   ⑤ 1.4 mark
③ Index lines

7. Mount the sprocket and cam chain on the shaft with the two bolts as in **Figure 45**.

① Cam sprocket mounting bolts

8. Mount the rocker arms on the shaft, and install the mounting bolts, **Figure 46**, making sure

① Rocker arm shaft mounting bolts

that No. 1 and No. 3, and No. 2 and No. 4 rocker arms are put back in the original positions.

9. Install the camshaft holder and cap by torquing the bolts to 90 kg-cm—130 kg-cm (6.5 ft-lbs — 9.4 ft-lbs). Note that the sets are matched by identical codes stamped on the parts.

10. Install the push bar cam chain tensioner, and install the housing on the engine, **Figure 47**. Loosen the adjusting bolt to allow the push bar to automatically tension the chain, and then tighten the bolt and the lock nut.

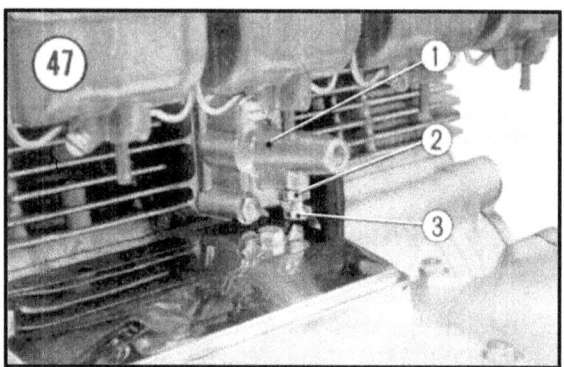

① Cam chain tensioner holder
② Lock nut
③ Tensioner adjusting bolt

11. Adjust the valve tappet clearances, **Figure 48**, as outlined in Chapter One. Briefly, set the gap with the valve closed by turning the adjusting screw. The clearances should be .05mm (.002 in) for the inlet valves, and .08mm (.003 in) for the exhaust valves.

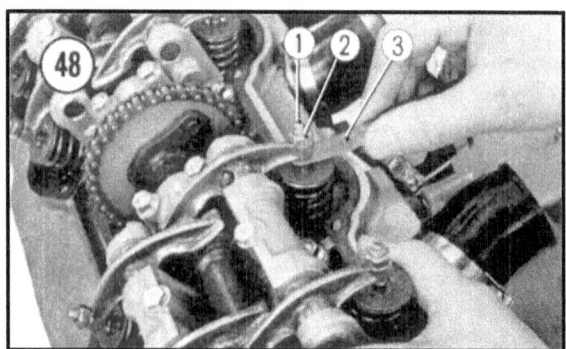

① Valve tappet adjusting screw
② Valve tappet lock nut
③ Thickness gauge

12. Install the cylinder head cover using the Phillips head screws, and mount the breather cover with its three screws.

CYLINDER HEAD

Disassembly

1. Remove the cylinder head from the block as outlined in the camshaft section.

2. Refer to **Figure 49** and disassemble the head using a valve remover, Honda tool No. 07031-30001, shown in **Figure 50**. Remove parts in this order: cotter, retainer, valve spring, stem seal, and spring seat.

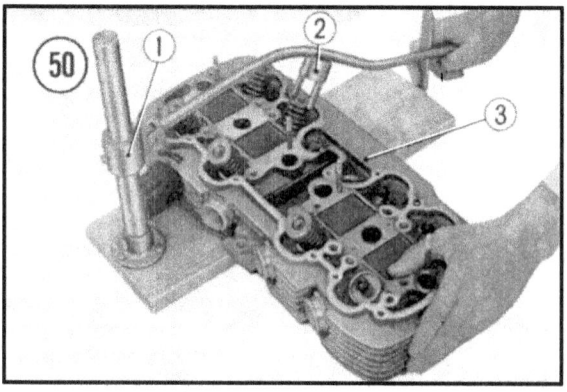

① Valve remover
② Valve remover attachment
③ Cylinder head

3. Use Honda tool No. 07046-30001 to remove the valve guides, **Figure 51**.

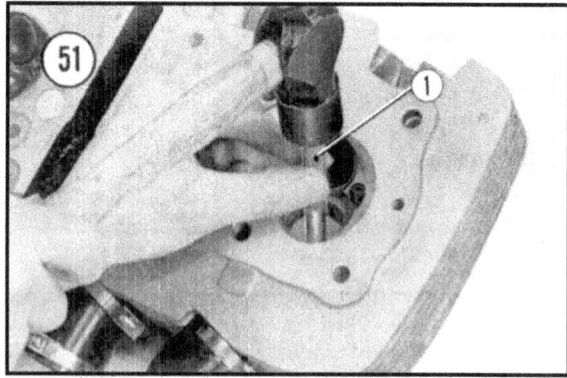

① Valve guide removing tool

Inspection

1. Refer to **Figure 52** for measurement of the clearance between the valve stem and its guide. Insert the valve into the guide and use a dial gauge to measure clearance for both the X and Y dimensions. If the clearance is more than .08mm (.003 in) for an inlet valve or .1mm (.004 in) for an exhaust valve, the valve and its guide should be replaced as a set.

2. The new valve guide should be oversize.

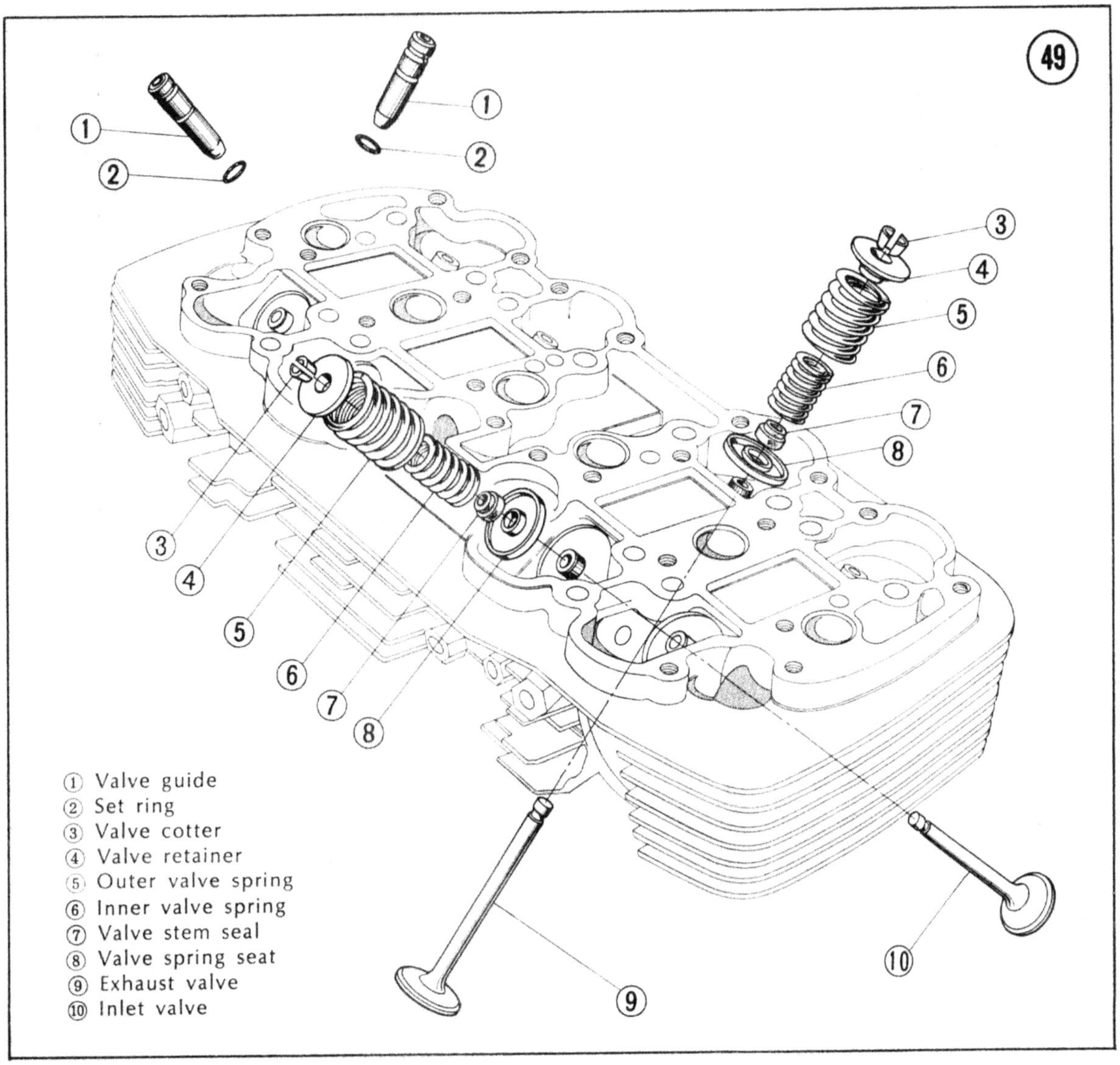

49
1
2
3
4
5
6
7
8
9
10
① Valve guide
② Set ring
③ Valve cotter
④ Valve retainer
⑤ Outer valve spring
⑥ Inner valve spring
⑦ Valve stem seal
⑧ Valve spring seat
⑨ Exhaust valve
⑩ Inlet valve

52
1
2
Y
X

① Valve ② Dial gauge

53
1
2

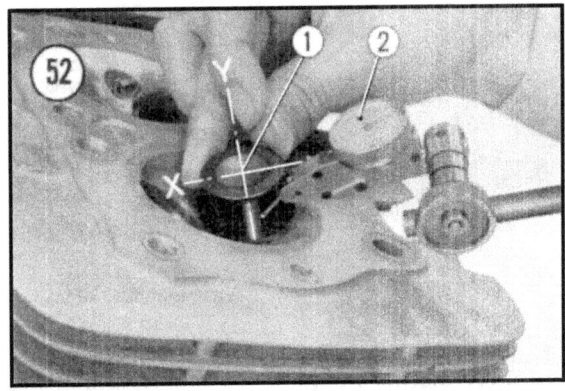

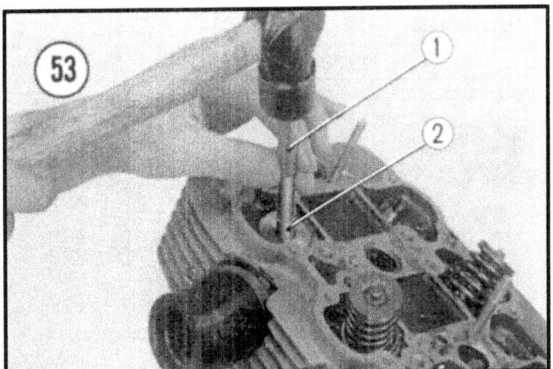

① Valve guide driving tool ② Valve guide

Drive the new guide into the head with Honda tool No. 07046-30001, shown in **Figure 53**. Then ream out the oversize guide to the standard dimension with a reamer, tool No. 07008-30001. The guide diameter should be 6.6mm to 6.61mm (.260 in to .2603 in).

3. Measure the vertical runout of the valve face with a dial gauge as shown in **Figure 54**. If the

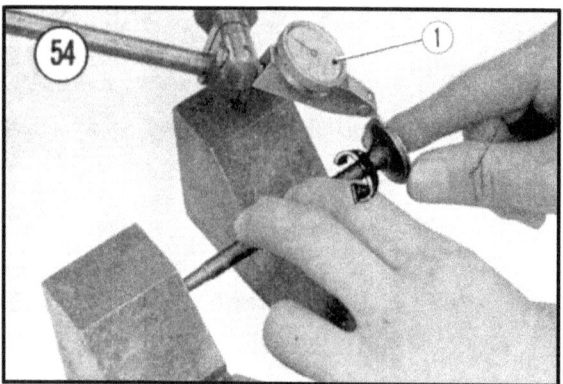

① Dial gauge

runout is more than .05mm (.002 in), replace the valve.

4. Measure the width of the contact area on the valve face. If it is more than 2mm (.079 in), replace the valve.

5. Check the edge of the valve for burned spots, and replace if necessary.

6. Check if the valve is seating in the head properly. If it is not seating completely, the seats must be reground. This is a job for a machine shop.

7. Measure the free height of the valve springs with a vernier caliper, **Figure 55**, and measure the force it takes to compress the spring. Replace any which do not conform to the values below.

	Standard	Useable	Spring force
Inner spring	38.1mm (1.5 in)	37mm (1.457 in)	22.8kg-26mm to 25.8kg-26mm
Outer spring	41.2mm (1.622 in)	40mm (1.475 in)	45.6kg-28mm to 51.6kg-28mm

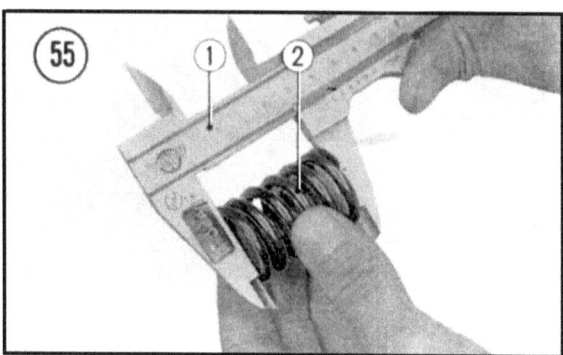

① Vernier caliper   ② Spring

8. Measure the support area of the rocker arm shaft with a micrometer, and the bearing diameter with an inside micrometer as shown in **Figure 56**. The clearance should not be greater than .11mm (.005 in). If it is, one or both of the parts must be replaced.

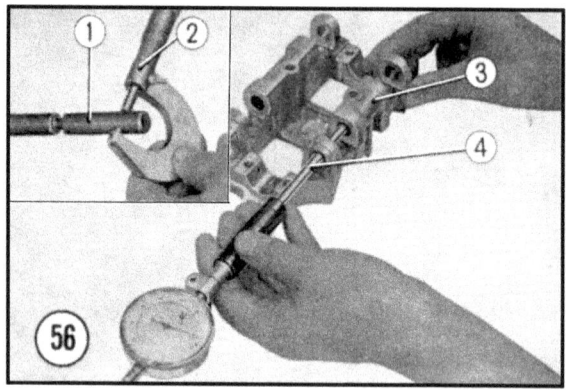

① Rocker arm shaft   ③ Camshaft holder
② Micrometer   ④ Inner dial gauge

9. Insert the valves into the combustion chamber, and scrape or brush off the carbon, taking care not to scratch the metal.

10. Check the trueness of the head by placing a straight-edge across the surface, **Figure 57**, and checking the clearance with a feeler blade. If the clearance is greater than .25mm (.009 in) the head must be replaced or re-machined. The standard allowable warp is a maximum of .05mm (.002 in).

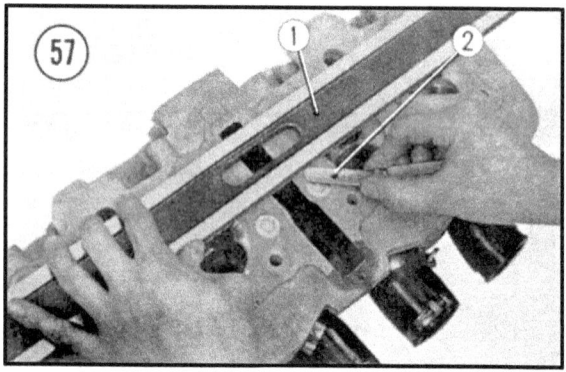

① Stretch   ② Thickness gauge

Reassembly

1. Reassemble the head in reverse order, referring to the exploded view for the sequence of parts.

2. Set valve tappet clearance according to the section in Chapter One. Briefly, the clearances between the tappets and the valve stem ends, with the valve closed, should be .05mm (.002 in)

ENGINE

for inlet valves, and .08mm (.003 in) for the exhaust valves.

3. Install the cylinder head and breather covers.

PISTON AND CYLINDER

The pistons are made of light alloy aluminum. The low weight increases high speed performance, while this metal dissipates heat rapidly. **Figure 58** (next page) shows block and pistons.

Disassembly

1. Remove the cylinder head as described in the camshaft section.

2. Refer to **Figure 59** and remove the clip, wrist pin, and connecting rod from the piston. Be careful not to drop the clip into the crankcase.

3. Remove the rings from the pistons.

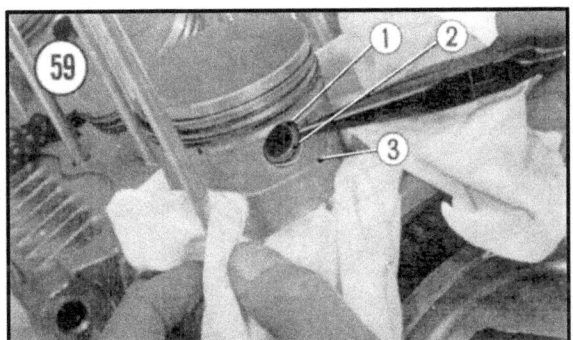

① Piston pin clip ③ Piston
② Piston pin

Inspection

1. Use a cylinder gauge as shown in **Figure 60** to measure the bore at the top, center, and bottom. The cylinder must be bored if diameter is more than 61.1mm (2.406 in), or if the taper and out-of-round are more than .05mm (.002 in).

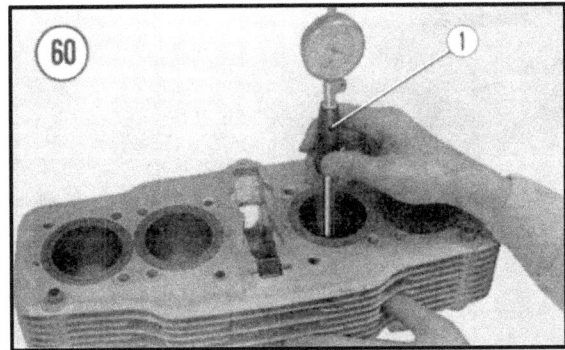

① Cylinder gauge

2. Have the cylinder bored out at a machine shop to a diameter greater than the point of maximum wear. Beforehand, select the proper oversize pistons. They are available from .25mm to 1mm oversize in .25mm increments. All cylinders must be bored to the same size.

3. Measure the diameter of the pistons at the skirt and 90 degrees from the wrist pin hole, as in **Figure 61**. Pistons should be replaced if the diameter is less than 60.85mm (2.394 in).

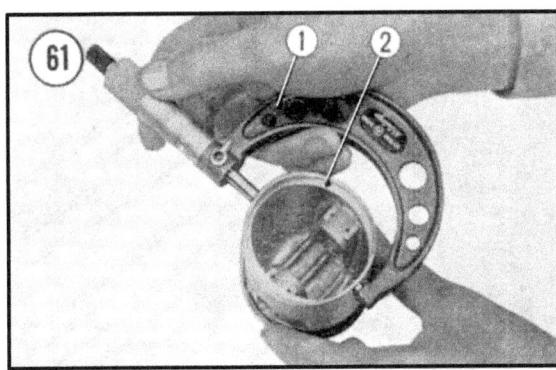

① Micrometer ② Piston

4. Scrape the carbon from the top of the piston and the ring groove. If the groove is damaged or worn, the piston should be replaced.

5. Measure the end gap of the ring by fitting it into the cylinder and checking with a feeler blade, as in **Figure 62**. The rings are serviceable if the gap is .7mm (.028 in).

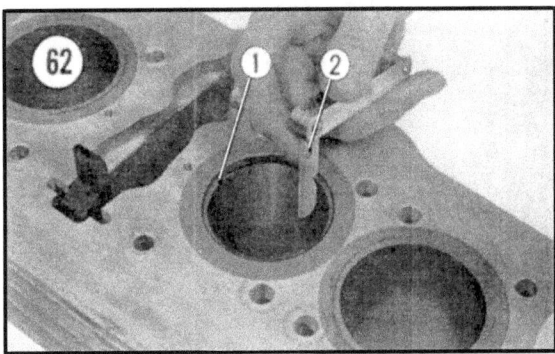

① Piston ring ② Thickness gauge

6. Use a feeler blade as in **Figure 63** to measure the clearance between the rings and the lands. Replace rings if clearances are greater than the standard values.

Top ring	.18mm (.0071 in)
Second ring	.165mm (.0065 in)
Oil ring	.114mm (.0045 in)

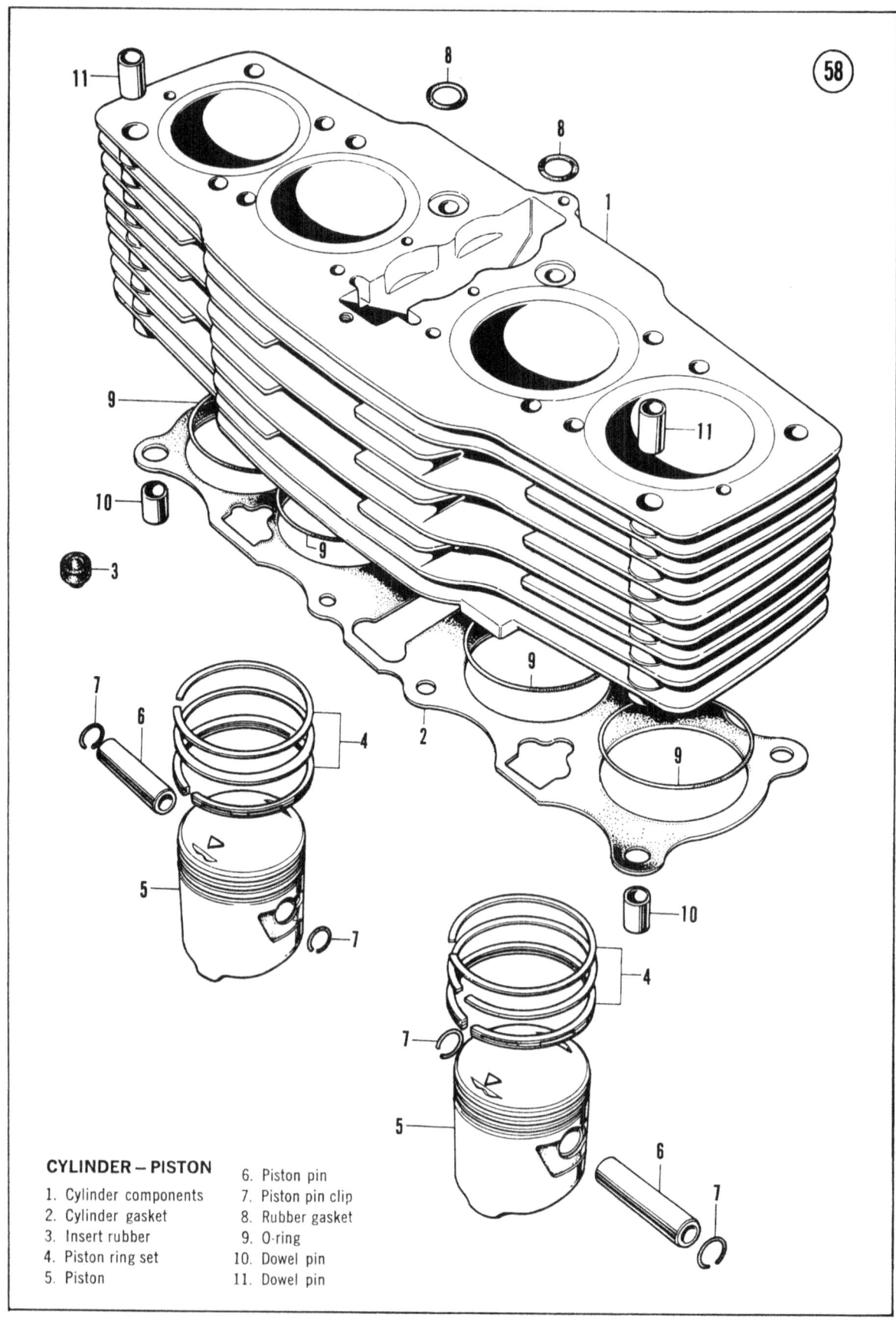

CYLINDER – PISTON

1. Cylinder components
2. Cylinder gasket
3. Insert rubber
4. Piston ring set
5. Piston
6. Piston pin
7. Piston pin clip
8. Rubber gasket
9. O-ring
10. Dowel pin
11. Dowel pin

ENGINE

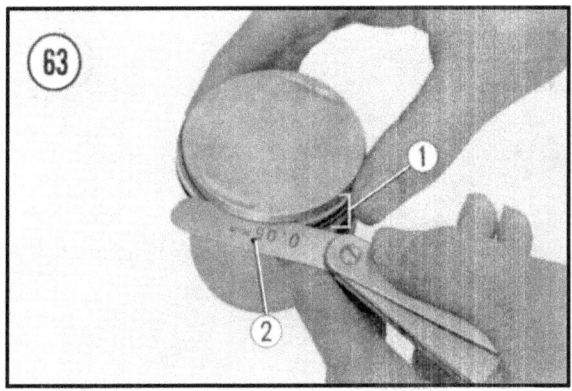

① Piston ring ② Thickness gauge

7. Use a dial gauge or an inside micrometer to measure the bore of the pin hole. Replace the piston if the reading is more than 15.08mm (.594 in).

Reassembly

1. Before putting new rings on a piston, roll the rings in the grooves as shown in **Figure 64** to make sure the clearances are correct.

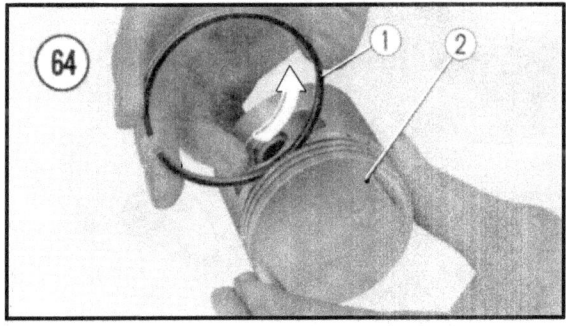

① Piston ring ② Piston

2. Install the rings, making sure the manufacturer's mark is toward the top, and the gaps are spaced 120 degrees apart.

3. Attach the piston to the connecting rod so the arrow marks on the tops, **Figure 65**, are pointed forward toward the exhaust ports.

4. Use new pin clips when reassembling.

CRANKSHAFT AND CONNECTING RODS

The forged crankshaft is supported by five main bearings of tin alloy. **Figure 66** shows crank and rod components.

Disassembly

1. Remove the cylinder head pistons, and cam chain tensioner according to the steps in the camshaft section.

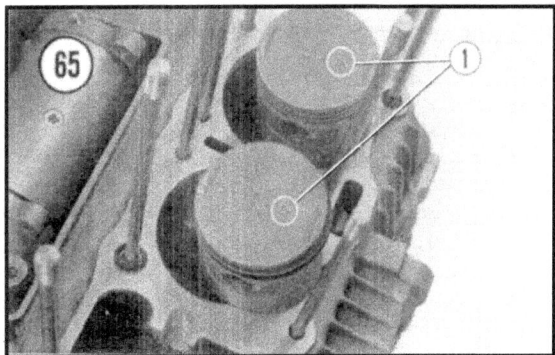

① Arrow marks

2. Remove the dynamo cover, unscrew the generator mounting bolt, and remove the rotor with the special puller, Honda tool No. 07011-30001, shown in **Figure 67**.

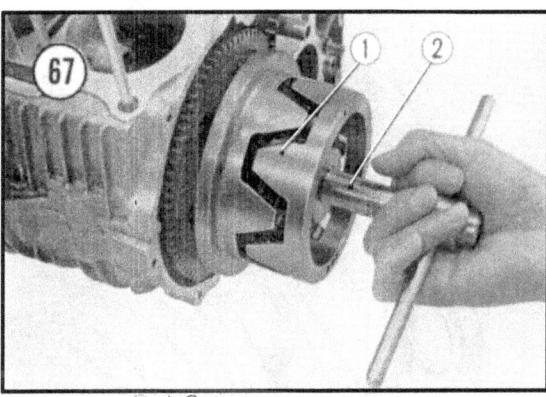

① A.C. generator rotor
② Rotor puller

3. Refer to **Figure 68** and remove the reduction and clutch gears.

① Starting clutch gear
② Starting motor reduction gear

4. Refer to **Figure 69** and remove the gearshift arm, drum stopper, and the positive stopper.

5. Remove the point cover and unscrew the hex nut, **Figure 70**, and remove it with the advance

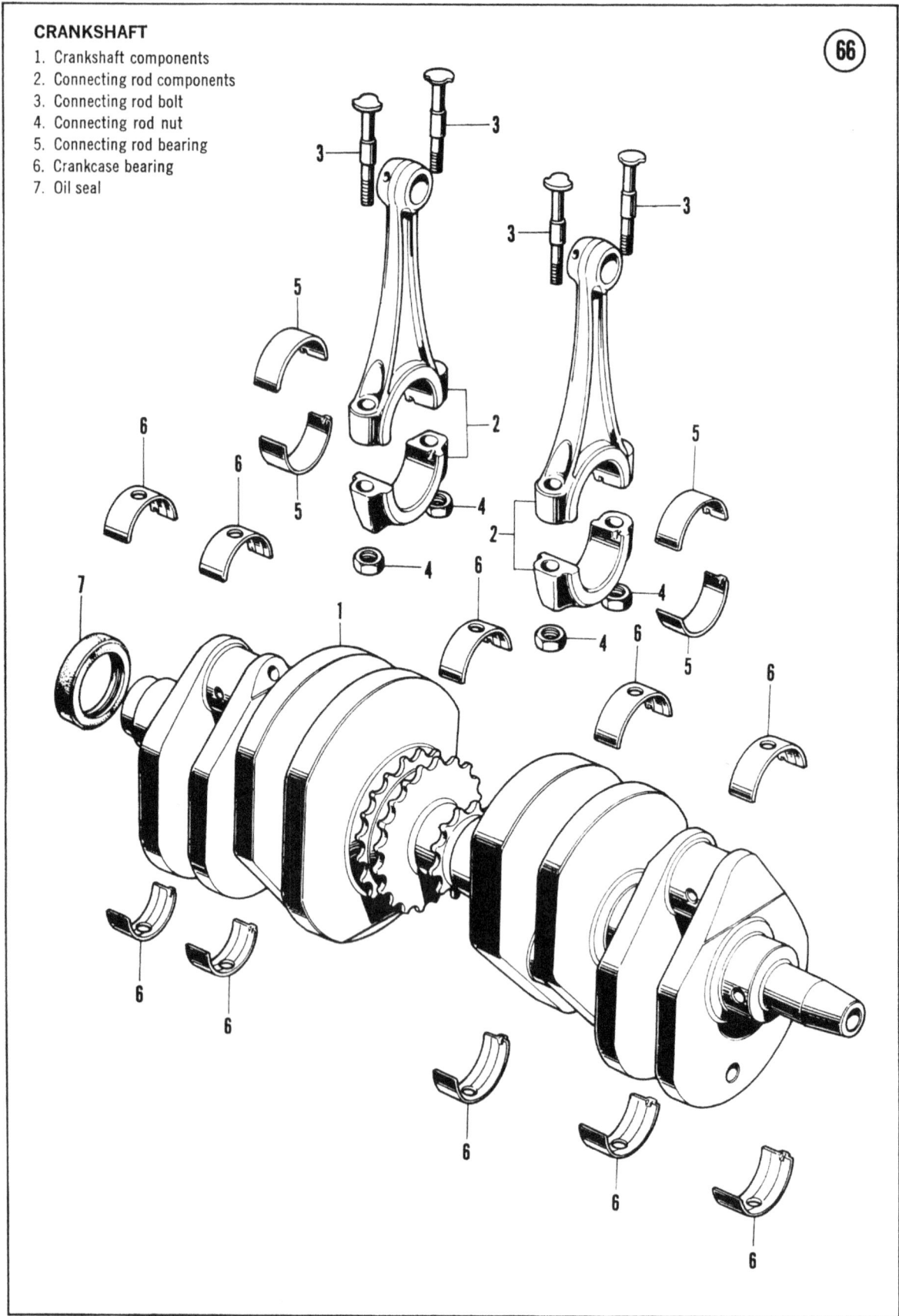

ENGINE

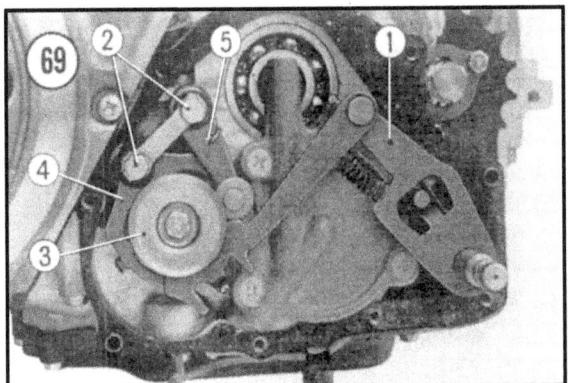

① Gear shift arm
② 6 mm bolts
③ Gear shift side plate
④ Gear shift positive stopper
⑤ Shift drum stopper

① 6 mm hex. nut
② Advancer shaft special washer
③ Breaker assembly mounting screws

shaft washer. Unscrew the mounting screws and remove the breaker point unit.

6. Remove the spark advancer and the advance shaft.

7. Remove the clutch as outlined in Chapter Three.

8. Remove the countershaft bearing holder shown in **Figure 71**.

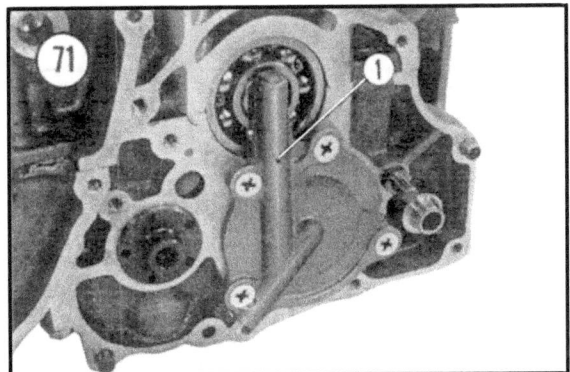

① Counter shaft bearing holder

9. Remove the lower crankcase by loosening the upper mounting bolts, shown in **Figure 72**, and then removing the lower mounting bolts circled in **Figure 73**.

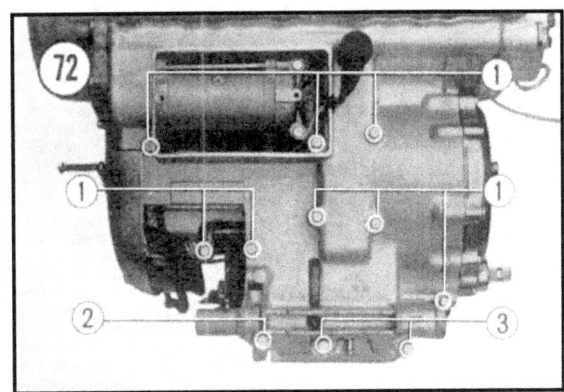

① 6 mm bolts   ③ 8 mm bolts
② 10 mm bolt

① 8 mm bolts   ③ 10 mm nut
② 6 mm bolts   ④ 8 mm nut

10. Lift up the transmission mainshaft, **Figure 74**, remove the primary sprocket, and the chain.

① Primary sprocket
② Transmission mainshaft

11. Lift the crankshaft from the upper crankcase, **Figure 75**.

12. Remove the connecting rods, **Figure 76**, by unscrewing the cap bolts and removing the caps.

① Crankshaft

① Connecting rod bolts ③ Connecting rod
② Connecting rod nuts

Inspection

1. Measure for bends in the crank with a dial gauge as shown in **Figure 77**. Runout should be .05mm (.002 in) or less. If it is greater than that value, the crank must be straightened in a press. This is a precision job for an expert.

2. To measure wear in the crankshaft journals, cut a piece of Plasti-gauge to the length of the bearing parallel to the crank. Keep it clear of the oil hole. Assemble the crankshaft into the lower case with the Plasti-gauge in place, and torque down the mounting bolts. Do not turn the crankshaft. Now disassemble and read the gauge according to the instructions that came with it. Replace the bearings as a set if clearance is more than .08mm (.0032 in). Standard clearance is .02mm to .046mm (.0008 in to .0018 in).

3. Check each journal for damage or wear. The limit of taper or out-of-roundness is .05mm (.002 in).

4. The size of the bearings originally fitted to the crankshaft are identified by matching the code letters stamped on the side of the crankshaft weight adjacent to the drive sprocket, as in **Figure 78**. This system, effective with engine No. CB750E-1015587, supersedes the earlier code which used Japanese characters. The letters refer to the journals starting from the left end of the crank. See **Figure 79**. Refer to the table below for the corresponding sizes and color codes. The numbers refer to the crank pins, discussed later.

① Dial gauge ② Crankshaft

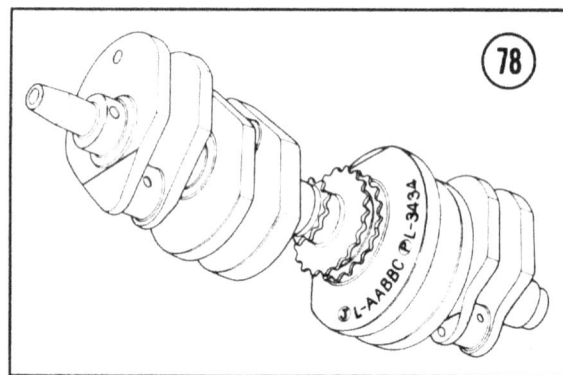

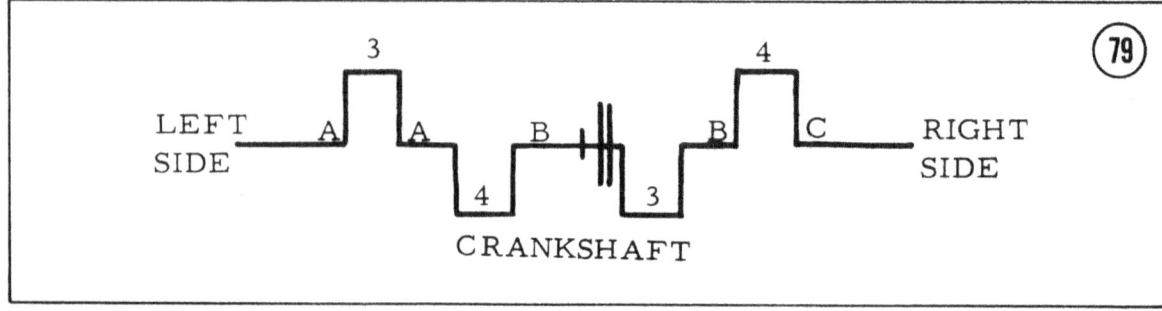

ENGINE

CRANK PIN BEARING INSERTS

Code	Connecting Rod			Crank Pin			Bearing Insert			
	1	2	3	3	4	5	Black	Brown	Green	Yellow
Dimension (mm)	39.000-39.008	39.008-39.016	39.016-39.024	36.000-35.995	35.995-35.990	35.990-35.985	1.502-1.498	1.498-1.494	1.494-1.490	1.490-1.486
Clearance (μ)*										
20 - 41	1				3		Yellow (13218-300-013)			
22 - 43	1					5	Green (13217-300-013)			
25 - 46	1				4		Yellow			
20 - 41		2			3		Green			
22 - 43		2				5	Brown (13316-300-013)			
25 - 46		2			4		Green			
20 - 41			3		3		Brown			
22 - 43			3			5	Black (13315-300-013)			
25 - 46			3		4		Brown			

* μ is the Greek letter representing the micron, commonly noted as 0.001mm.

5. When inserting a new bearing, be careful not to damage the thin shell. When it is mounted into the crankcase, the top should extend above the flange .068mm to .098mm (.0027 in to .0039 in).

6. The connecting rod bearings are measured by first taking a micrometer reading of the crank pin diameter. Next put the bearing into the connecting rod and torque the cap to 2 kg-m (14.5 ft-lbs). Measure the inside diameter of the bearing. An alternate method is using the press gauge following the same steps as in the crankshaft journal measurement section. The average clearance should be .02mm to .046mm (.0008 in to .0018 in). If the clearance is greater than .08mm (.0032 in), replace the bearings as a set.

7. Refer to the table below, and the preceding diagram of the number code, to determine the original size of the bearings.

Reassembly

1. Put the cam and primary chains on the crankshaft, and assemble it in the upper crankcase.

2. Put the primary chain on the sprocket, **Figure 80**, and install the sprocket on the mainshaft.

3. Refer to **Figure 81** and install the two dowel pins, the oil pass collar, and the O-ring on the upper crankcase. Coat the mating surface with

CRANKSHAFT JOURNAL BEARING INSERTS

Code	Crankcase			Crankshaft Journal			Bearing Insert			
	A	B	C	A	B	C	Black	Brown	Green	Yellow
Dimension (mm)	39.000-39.008	39.008-39.016	39.016-39.024	36.000-35.995	35.995-35.990	35.990-35.985	1.502-1.498	1.498-1.494	1.494-1.490	1.490-1.486
Clearance (μ)*										
20 - 41	A			A			Yellow (13318-300-013)			
22 - 43	A					C	Green (13317-300-013)			
25 - 46	A				B		Yellow			
20 - 41		B		A			Green			
22 - 43		B				C	Brown (13316-300-013)			
25 - 46		B			B		Green			
20 - 41			C	A			Brown			
22 - 43			C			C	Black (13315-300-013)			
25 - 46			C		B		Brown			

* μ is the Greek letter representing the micron, commonly noted as 0.001mm.

① Transmission mainshaft
② Bearing set rings

① Oil pass collar & "O" ring
② Dowel pins

Permatex. Set the lower crankcase on top and install the mounting bolts.

4. Torque in the sequence shown in **Figure 82** to 2.3 kg-m to 2.5 kg-m (16.6 ft-lbs to 18.1 ft-lbs).

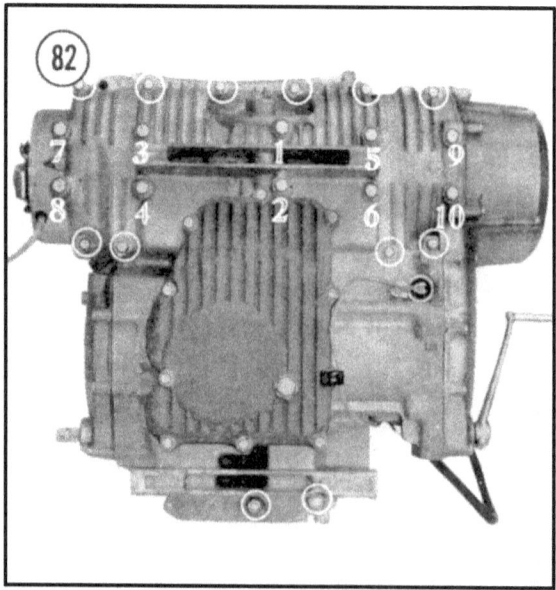

Tightening sequence

5. Tighten the bolts in the upper crankcase.

6. Refer again to Figure 69 and install the countershaft bearing, gearshift positive stopper, drum stopper, and shift arm.

7. Install the clutch, referring to Chapter Three.

8. Refer to **Figure 83** and mount the spark advance shaft and advancer, making sure that the pin on the back side fits into the crankshaft pin hole.

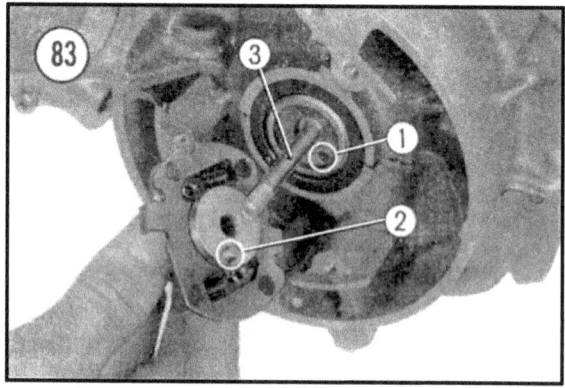

① Pin hole ③ Spark advancer shaft
② Spark advancer pin

9. Install the breaker point assembly with the washer and nut.

10. Install the starting motor reduction and clutch gears.

11. Install the generator, then torque the mounting bolt to 10 kg-m (72.3 ft-lbs).

12. Install the pistons and cylinder head according to the previous sections on the camshaft, pistons, and rods.

PRIMARY DRIVE

Power is transmitted from the crankshaft through two chains to the primary sprocket, and then through the clutch to the transmission. The speed of the crankshaft is reduced by a 1.708 ratio.

> NOTE: *The stretch of the primary drive chain can be checked without disassembling the engine.*

Inspection

1. Drain the oil from the crankcase, and drop the pan by removing the 10 mounting bolts.

2. Refer to **Figure 84** and use a vernier caliper to measure the distance between the primary tensioner bracket and the pan mounting flange.

ENGINE

51

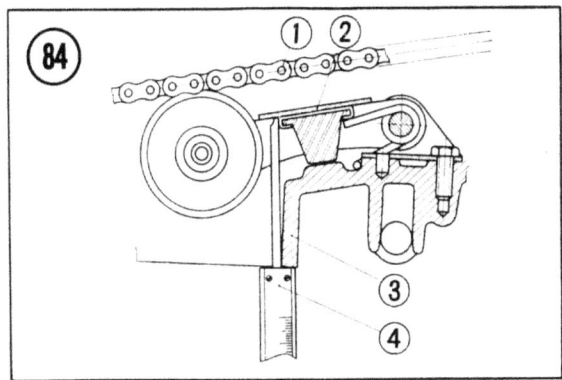

① Primary chain   ③ Lower crankcase
② Primary chain tensioner   ④ Vernier caliper

① Primary chain   ③ Transmission mainshaft
② Primary sprocket

Replace the chain if the distance is more than 70mm (2.756 in).

3. Inspect the rubber roller for wear or deterioration, and replace if necessary.

Disassembly

1. Remove the cylinder head, pistons, and crankcase, referring to the appropriate sections of this chapter.

2. Remove the primary sprocket, **Figure 85**, by lifting the transmission mainshaft. Then remove the chain from the sprocket.

3. Raise the crankshaft and remove the chain.

4. Refer to **Figure 86** for details, and remove the primary chain tensioner from the lower crankcase. See **Figure 87**.

Reassembly

1. Reverse the above procedure and reassemble the crankcase, pistons, and cylinder head.

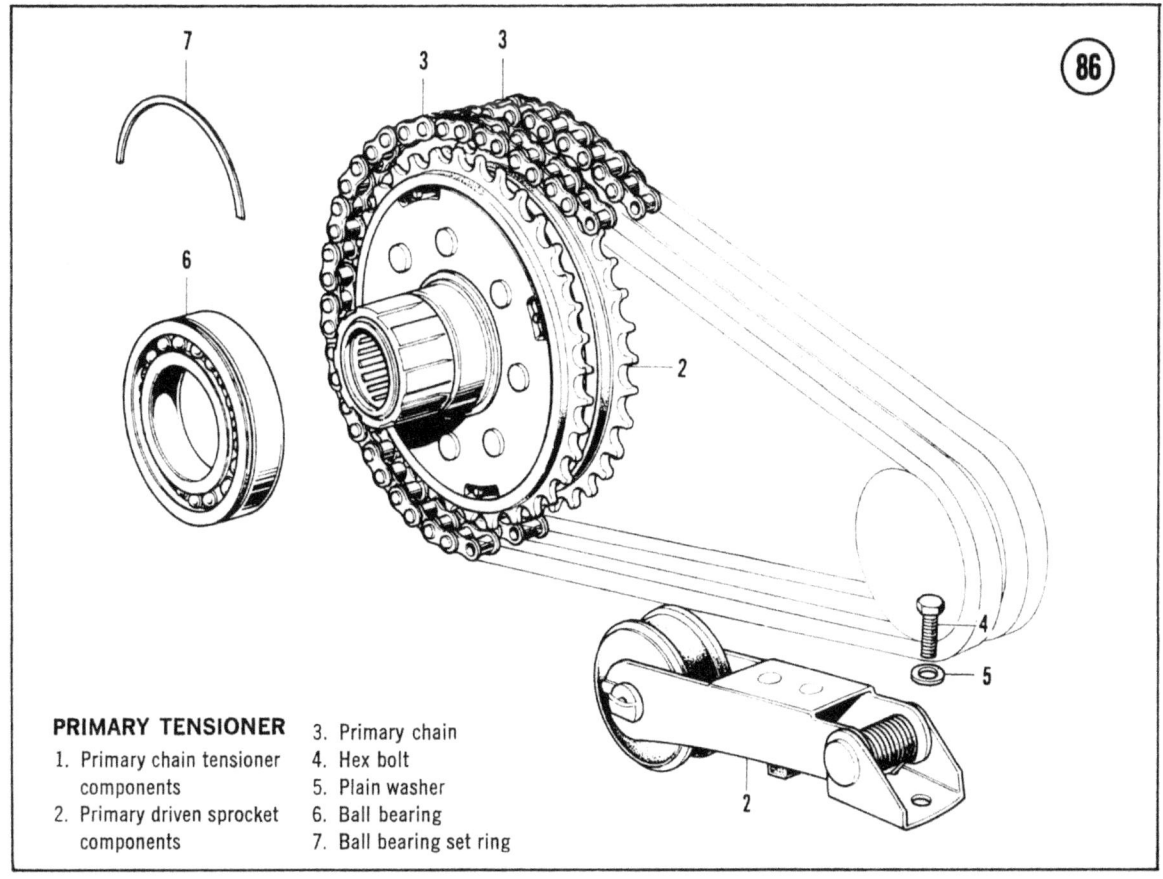

PRIMARY TENSIONER
1. Primary chain tensioner components
2. Primary driven sprocket components
3. Primary chain
4. Hex bolt
5. Plain washer
6. Ball bearing
7. Ball bearing set ring

① Primary chain tensioner

KICKSTARTER

See **Figure 88** for the operation of the kickstarter. When the pedal is kicked, the spindle turns in the direction of the arrow. The pawl engages the groove on the starter gear, and the rotary force is transmitted from the spindle through the gear and clutch to the crankshaft. When the engine catches, crankshaft force is transmitted back to the clutch and gear where the pawl disengages.

Disassembly

1. Remove the cylinder head, cam chain tensioner, and crankcase in accordance with the earlier sections of this chapter.

2. Refer to **Figure 89** and remove the stopper pin and the shaft.

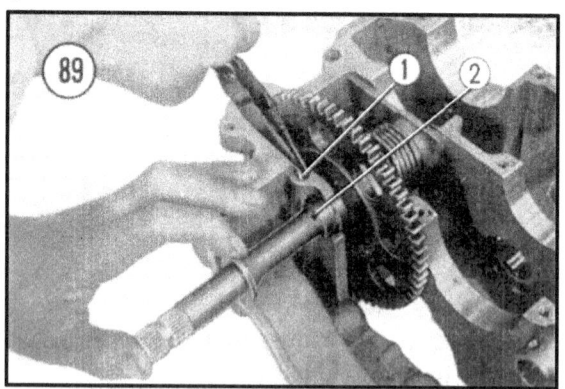

① Kick starter shaft stopper pin
② Kick starter shaft

3. Remove the gear assembly, shown in **Figure 90**, and the return spring.

4. Remove the ratchet spring from the kickstarter flange, and then the starter pawl.

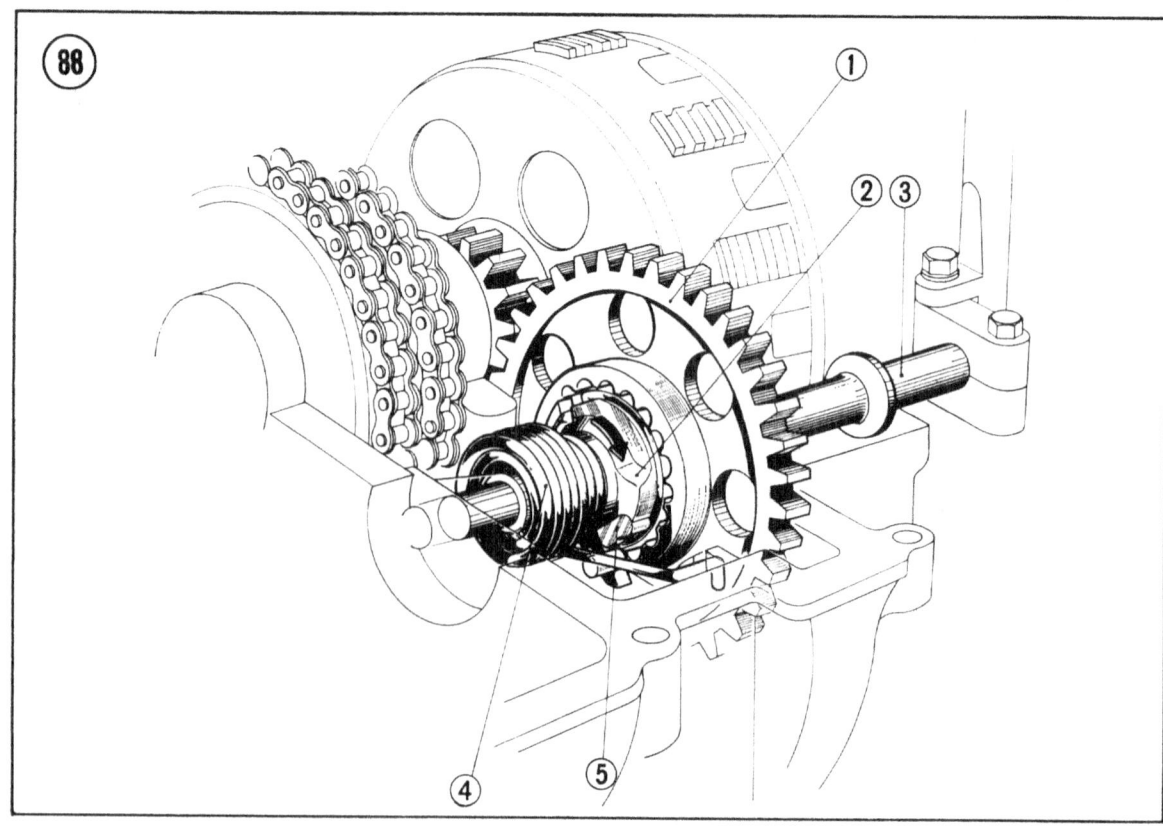

① Kick starter gear
② Kick starter flange
③ Kick starter spindle
④ Kick starter return spring
⑤ Kick starter pawl

ENGINE

① Kick starter gear ③ Kick starter return spring
② Kick starter flange

Inspection

1. Operate the kick gear to make sure it turns smoothly in one direction and locks in the reverse direction.

2. Use an inside dial gauge to check the bore of the kick gear, **Figure 91**, and a micrometer to check the starter shaft. Replace the parts if the gear bore is more than 20.075mm (.7904 in), or the shaft diameter is less than 19.930mm (.7847 in).

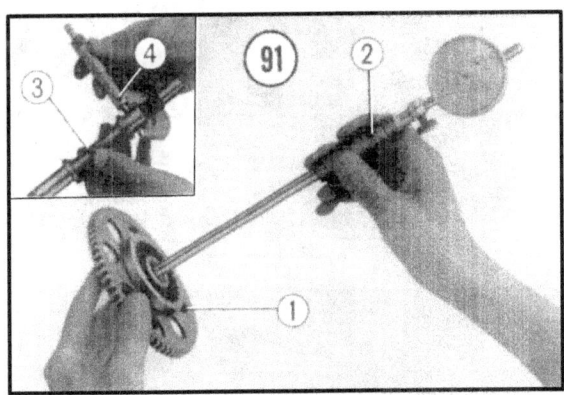

① Kick gear   ③ Kick starter shaft
② Inside dial gauge ④ Micrometer

Reassembly

1. Assemble the kick gear, starter flange, and return spring in the lower crankcase, **Figure 92**. Make sure the return spring is hooked to the case. Use a screwdriver to force down the flange, and hook it on to the pin.

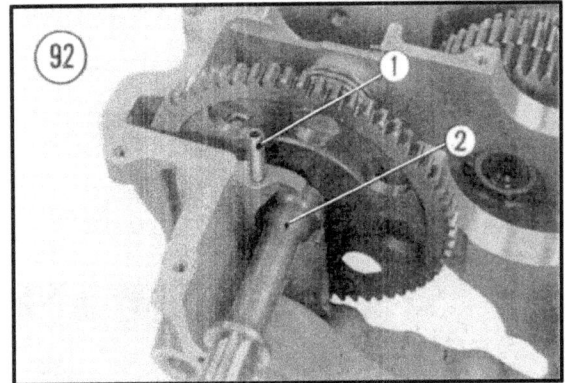

① Kick spindle stopper pin
② Kick starter spindle

2. Install the spindle, **Figure 93**, and the stopper pin.

3. Assemble the crankcase, pistons, and cylinder head.

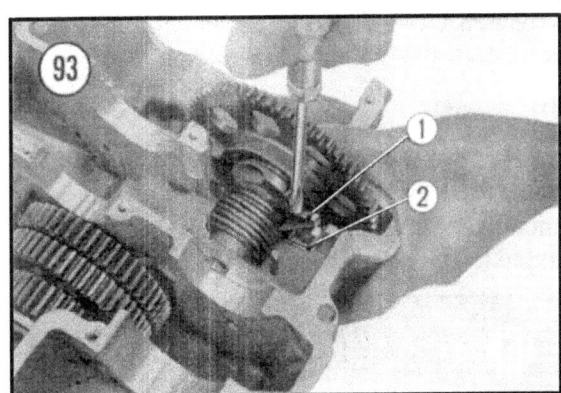

① Kick starter flange
② Return spring

CHAPTER THREE

CLUTCH AND TRANSMISSION

CLUTCH

The Honda 750 has a multiple disc, wet type clutch with seven cork mold discs, six clutch plates, and four clutch springs. **Figure 1** is an exploded view of the clutch assembly. **Figure 2** is a cutaway diagram of the clutch mechanism.

Disassembly

1. Remove the clutch cover and disconnect the cable from the lever, as in **Figure 3**. Remove the mounting screw and the clutch case. See the exploded view in **Figure 4** (page 57).

① Clutch lifter plate

① Clutch lever ② Clutch cable ③ Clutch case

2. Refer to **Figure 5** and unscrew the four mounting bolts, then remove the lifter plate and the spring.
3. Remove the lock nut, **Figure 6**, using tool

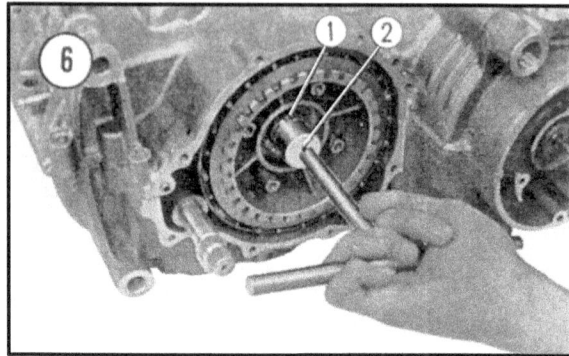

① Clutch lock nut ② Box wrench

No. 07086-30001. Then remove the tabbed washer, the spring washer, and the clutch center.
4. Refer to **Figure 7** and remove the "B" friction disc and the outer ring. Then remove friction disc "A" and the clutch plates.

CLUTCH AND TRANSMISSION

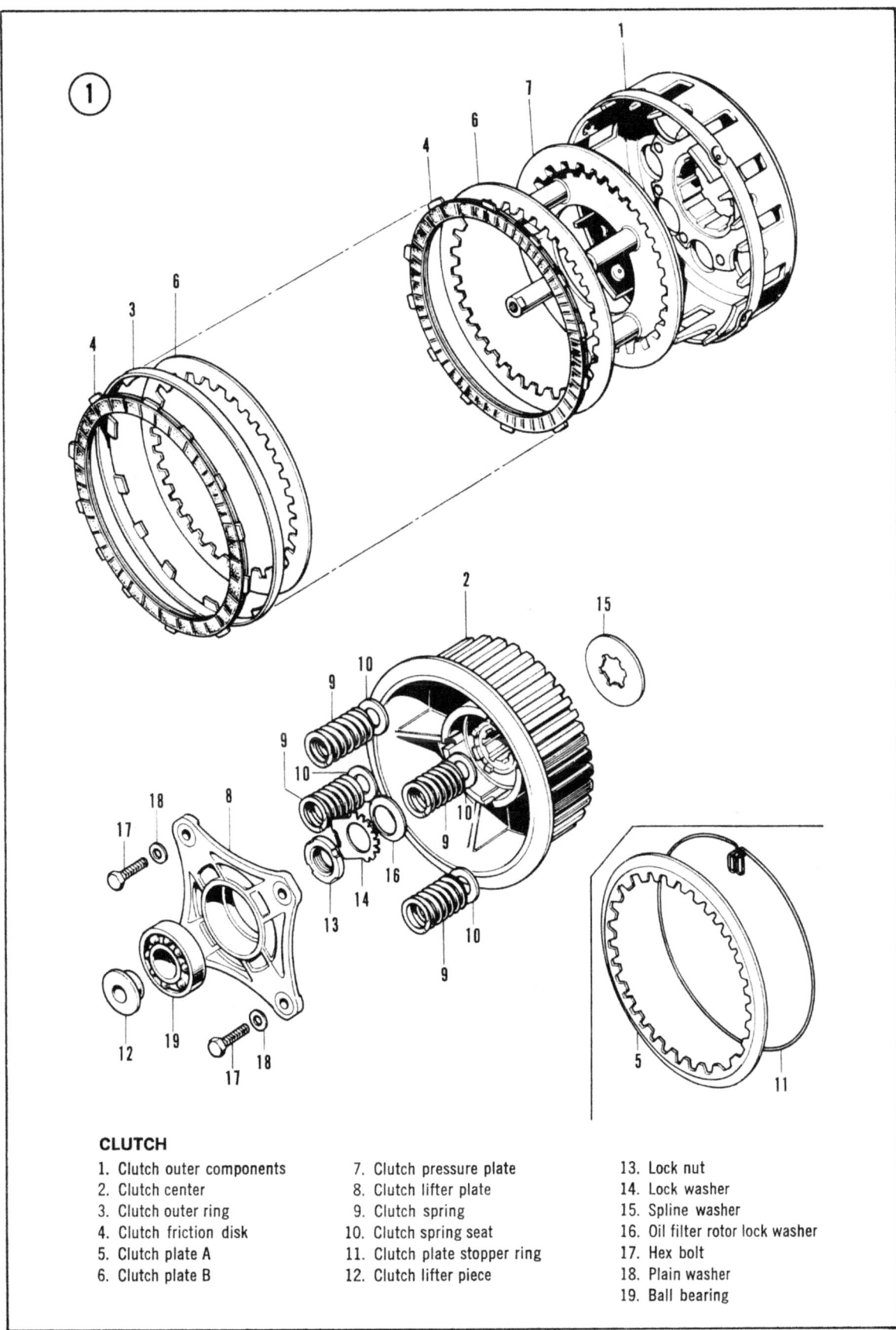

CLUTCH

1. Clutch outer components
2. Clutch center
3. Clutch outer ring
4. Clutch friction disk
5. Clutch plate A
6. Clutch plate B
7. Clutch pressure plate
8. Clutch lifter plate
9. Clutch spring
10. Clutch spring seat
11. Clutch plate stopper ring
12. Clutch lifter piece
13. Lock nut
14. Lock washer
15. Spline washer
16. Oil filter rotor lock washer
17. Hex bolt
18. Plain washer
19. Ball bearing

CLUTCH AND TRANSMISSION

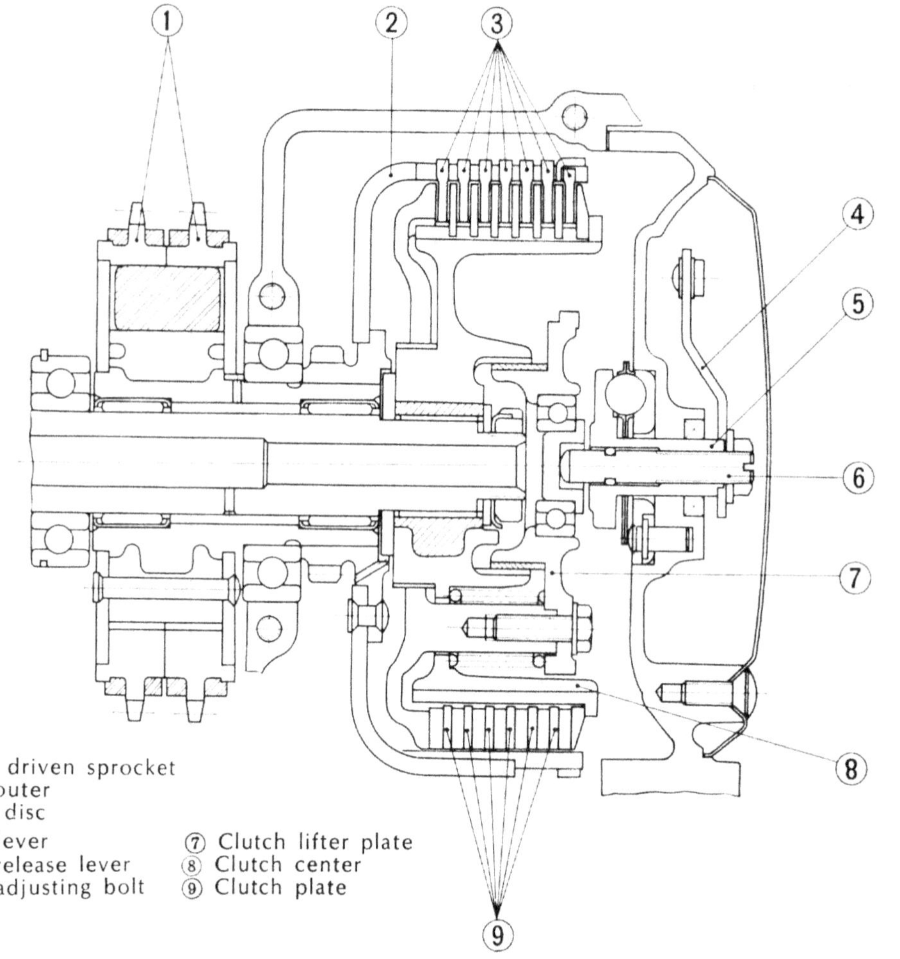

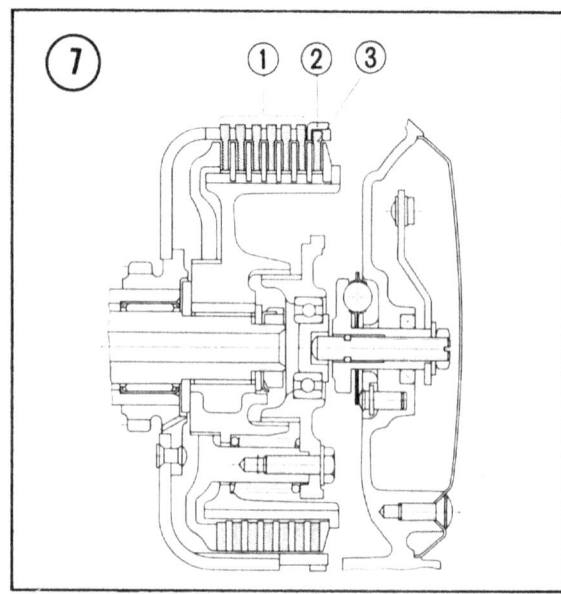

① Primary driven sprocket
② Clutch outer
③ Friction disc
④ Clutch lever
⑤ Clutch release lever
⑥ Clutch adjusting bolt
⑦ Clutch lifter plate
⑧ Clutch center
⑨ Clutch plate

① Clutch friction disc A
② Clutch outer ring
③ Clutch friction disc B

5. Remove the clutch washer, pressure plate, and the outer clutch from the mainshaft.

Inspection

1. Use a vernier caliper as shown in **Figure 8** to check the thickness of the friction disc. If the thickness is less than 3.10mm (.122 in) the disc should be replaced. Check the trueness of the clutch plate, and replace the disc if the plate is warped more than .3mm (.012 in).

2. Measure the uncompressed length of the clutch spring with a vernier caliper as shown in **Figure 9**. If the length is less than 30.5mm (1.2 in), replace it. All four springs should be the same length.

Reassembly

1. Put the outer clutch and the 25mm spline washer on the mainshaft, referring to **Figure 10**. Then assemble the pressure plate.

CLUTCH AND TRANSMISSION

CLUTCH COVER
1. Clutch cover
2. Clutch adjusting cover
3. Clutch cover gasket
4. Clutch lever components
5. Clutch lever spring
6. Clutch release shaft
7. Clutch lifter cam components
8. Clutch adjusting bolt
9. Clutch ball retainer components
10. Head washer
11. Oil seal
12. Oil seal
13. O-ring
14. Pan screw
15. Pan screw
16. Oval screw
17. Hex nut
18. Dowel pin

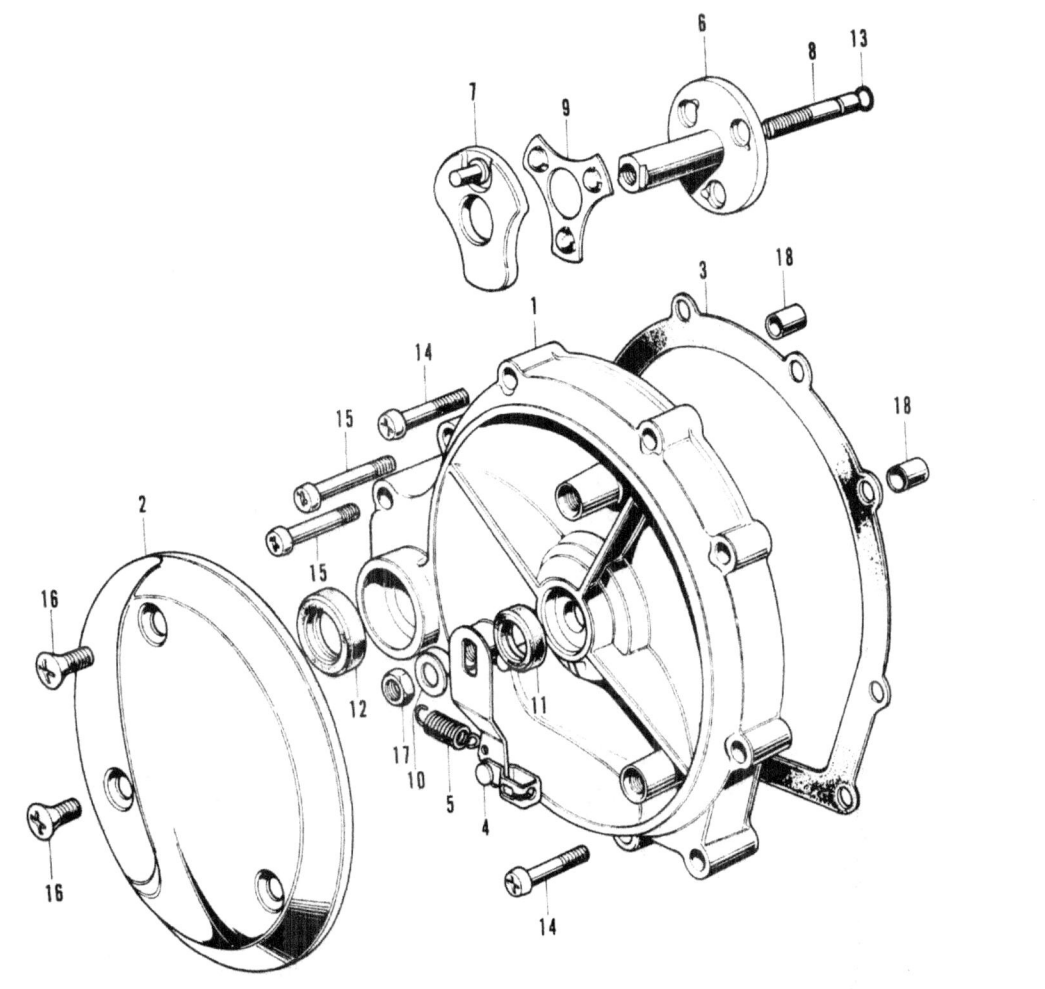

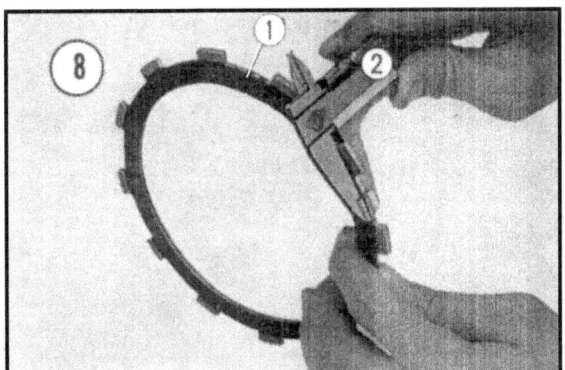

① Friction disc   ② Vernier caliper

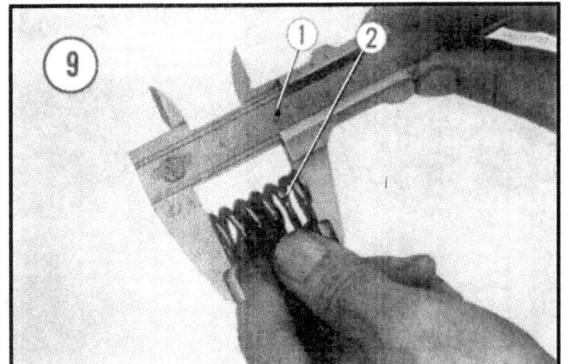

① Vernier caliper   ② Clutch spring

CLUTCH AND TRANSMISSION

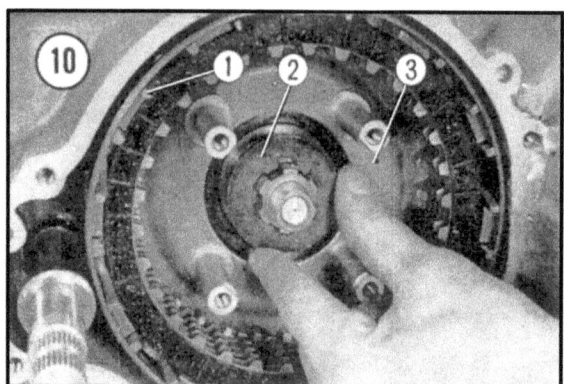

① Clutch outer
② 25 mm spline washer
③ Clutch pressure plate

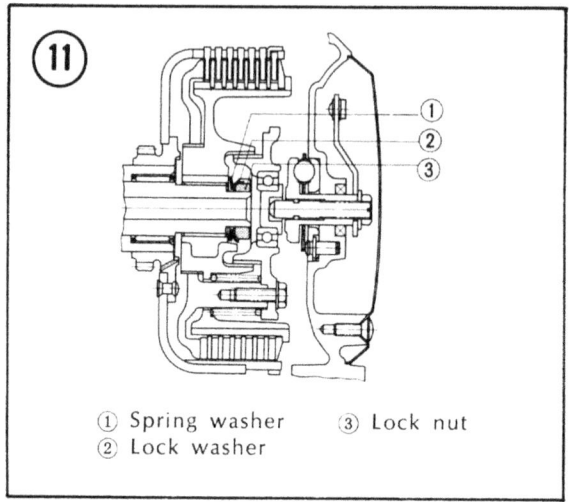

① Spring washer   ③ Lock nut
② Lock washer

2. Refer again to Figure 7 and assemble the six friction discs "A," the clutch plates, and the clutch center into the outer clutch. Next install the outer ring, making sure the tabs are lodged in the friction disc grooves.

3. Assemble friction disc "B," referring to Figure 7.

4. Assemble the clutch center in the following order, referring to **Figure 11**: spring washer with its tab facing front, lock washer, and lock nut. Torque with the special tool to 4.5 kg-m to 5 kg-m (32.5 ft-lbs to 36.2 ft-lbs).

5. Assemble the four clutch springs, and mount with the four lifter bolts.

6. Refer to the clutch section in Chapter One for adjustment.

TRANSMISSION

The Honda 750 has a constant mesh, five-speed transmission. **Figure 12** shows the power train of the transmission in various gears.

The shift mechanism, **Figure 13**, incorporates three forks. When the shift pedal is depressed, the shift spindle rotates, causing the shift arm to turn the drum. The shift forks are moved sideways by the action of the groove cut in the body of the drum.

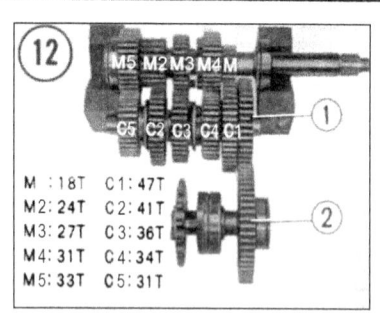

① Final drive gear (47 T)
② Final driven gear (56 T)

M : 18T C1: 47T
M2: 24T C2: 41T
M3: 27T C3: 36T
M4: 31T C4: 34T
M5: 33T C5: 31T

1st gear (C_4 gear shifted)

2nd gear (C_5 gear shifted)

3rd gear (C_4 gear shifted)

4th gear (M_2-M_3 gear shifted)

5th gear (M_2-M_3 gear shifted)

CLUTCH AND TRANSMISSION

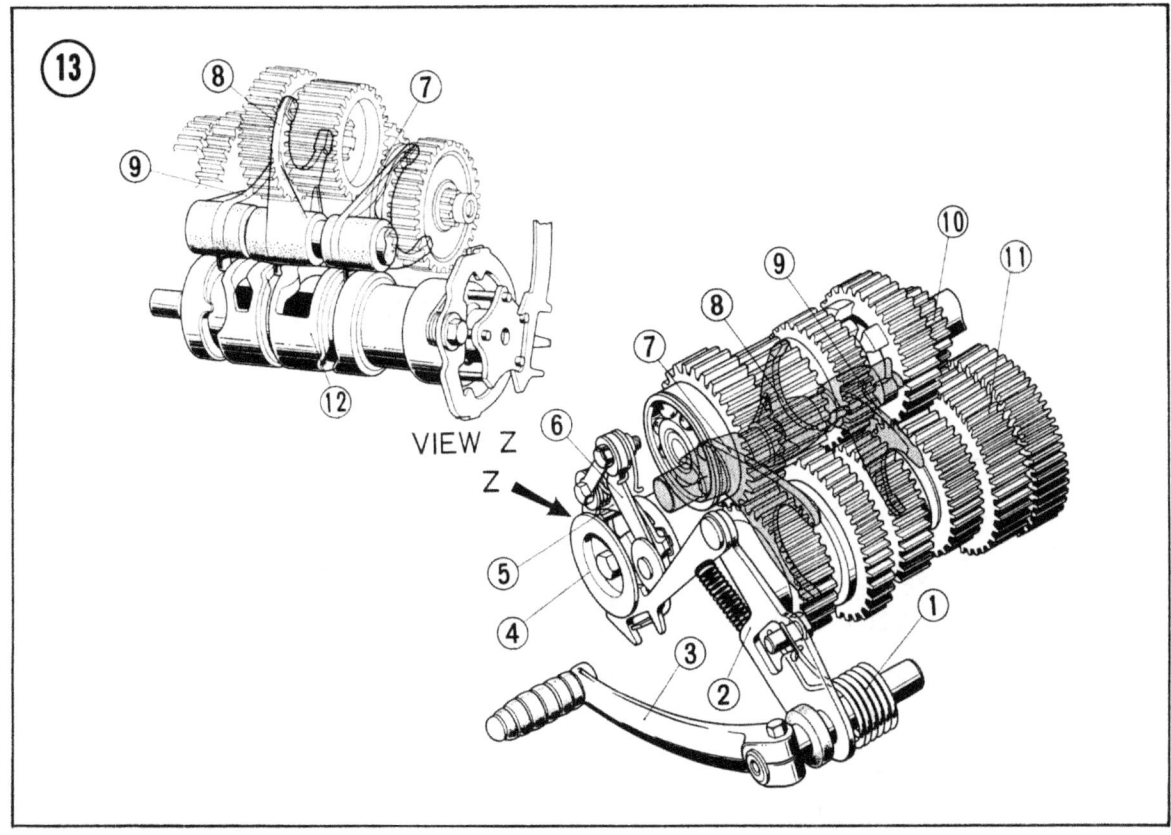

1. Gear shift return spring
2. Gear shift spindle
3. Gear change pedal
4. Gear shift side plate
5. Gear shift positive stopper
6. Shift drum stopper
7. Left gear shift fork
8. Center gear shift fork
9. Right gear shift fork
10. Transmission mainshaft
11. Transmission countershaft
12. Gear shift drum

Disassembly

1. Remove the cylinder head, pistons, cam chain tensioner, and the crankcase according to the operations in the Engine Chapter.

2. Raise the transmission mainshaft, **Figure 14**, and remove the primary sprocket and the mainshaft gear assembly from the upper crankcase.

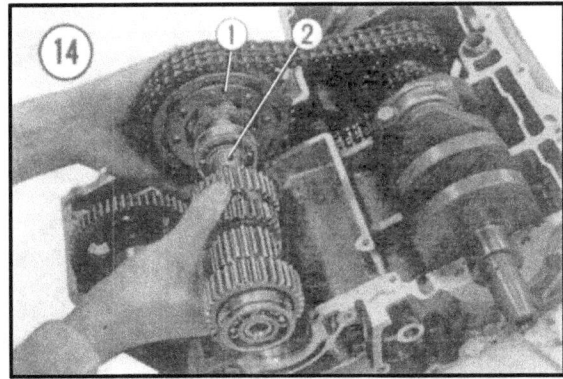

1. Primary sprocket
2. Transmission mainshaft

3. Remove the oil guide shaft and the final shaft from the upper crankcase, shown in **Figure 15**.

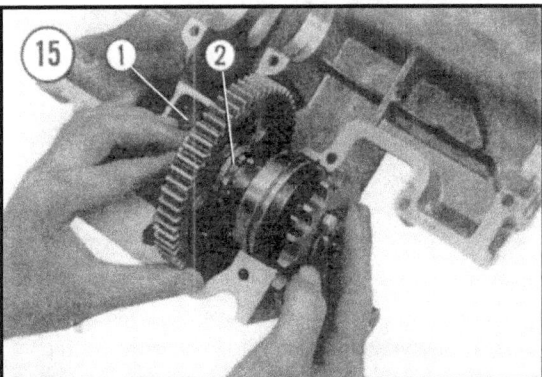

1. Final shaft oil guide
2. Final shaft assembly

4. Pull out the shaft for the shift forks, **Figure 16**, and then remove the forks.

5. Remove the neutral stopper bolt and the stopper. Remove the shift drum.

6. Remove top gear, **Figure 17**, from the countershaft and then remove the gear assembly.

① Gear shift forks
② Gear shift fork shaft

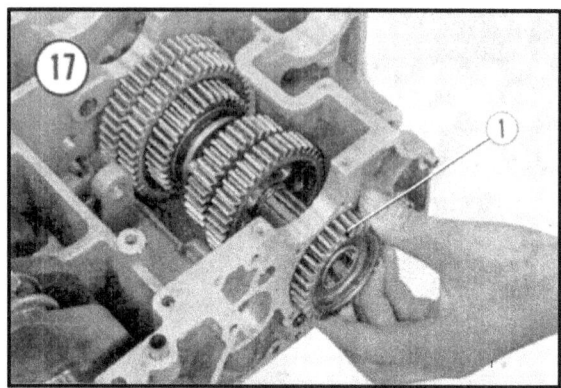

① Countershaft top gear

7. Use a bearing puller, Honda tool No. 07048-30025, to remove the right countershaft bearing from the lower crankcase, shown in **Figure 18**.

① Countershaft bearing ② Bearing puller

8. Refer to the exploded view of the gears, **Figure 19**, and disassemble them from the shafts.

Inspection

1. Measure gear backlash with a small dial gauge. Place the pointer against the teeth, **Figure 20**, lock the mating gear, and obtain a reading.

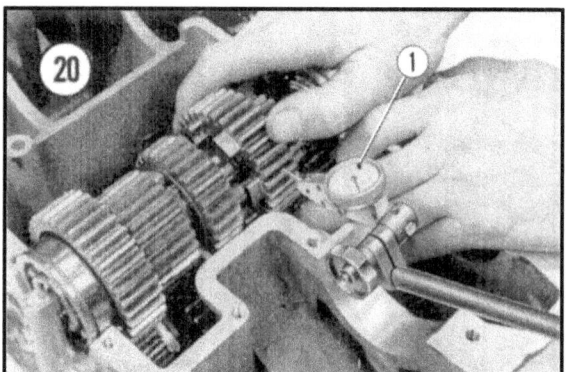

① Small dial gauge

Replace the shafts or the gears as a set if the backlash exceeds the standards below:

	Standard	Useable limit
First gear	.044mm to .140mm	.2mm
	(.0017 in to .0052 in)	(.008 in)
Second through fifth gears	.046mm to .140mm	.2mm
	(.0018 in to .0052 in)	(.008 in)

2. Inspect the dogs on the gears. If they are excessively worn or damaged, replace the respective gears.

3. Measure clearance between the gears and their shafts by measuring the gear bore with an inside micrometer, and the diameter of the shaft with a micrometer. Subtract to find the clearance. Standard clearances are .04mm to .082mm (.0016 in to .0032 in). Replace the gear and shaft if the clearance is more than .182mm (.0072 in).

4. Check the tines on the shift forks with a micrometer, **Figure 21**, and replace if worn beyond 6.1mm (.240 in). If the dog is worn more than the same standard, replace the gear.

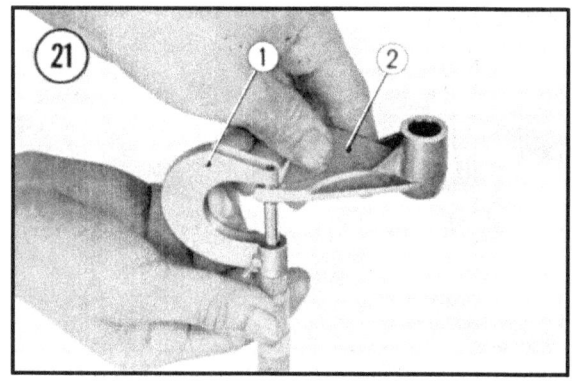

① Micrometer   ② Gear shift fork

CLUTCH AND TRANSMISSION

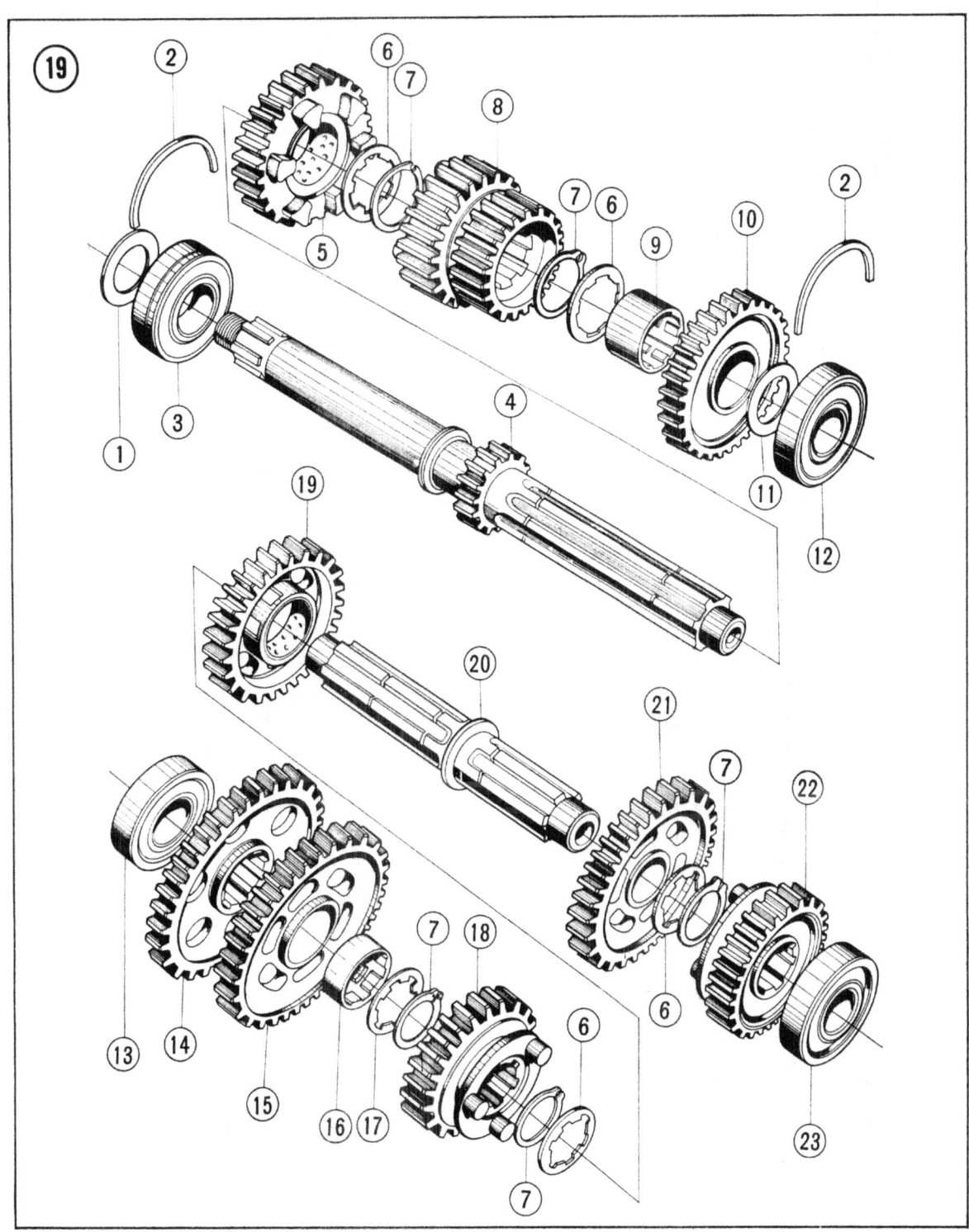

1. 25 mm thrust washer
2. Ball bearing set ring A
3. 6205 special ball bearing
4. Transmission mainshaft
5. Mainshaft fourth gear (37 T)
6. 25 mm thrust washer
7. 25 mm circlip
8. Mainshaft second & third gear (24 T & 27 T)
9. 28 × 20.5 bush
10. Mainshaft top gear (33 T)
11. 20 mm thrust washer
12. 6304 HS radial ball bearing
13. N-6304 radial ball bearing
14. Final drive gear (48 T)
15. Counter shaft low gear (47 T)
16. 28 × 14 bush
17. 25 × 33 thrust washer
18. Countershaft fourth gear (34 T)
19. Countershaft third gear (36 T)
20. Transmission countershaft
21. Countershaft second gear (41 T)
22. Countershaft top gear (31 T)
23. 6204 ball bearing

5. Measure the inside diameter of the shift forks with a micrometer, **Figure 22**. If the distance is more than 13.04mm (.5134 in), replace the fork.

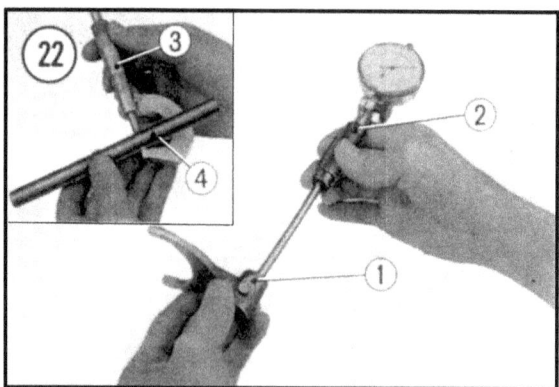

① Gear shift fork ③ Micrometer
② Inside dial gauge ④ Gear shift fork shaft

6. Measure the fork shaft with a micrometer, Figure 22. If worn to less than 12.9mm (.5079 in), replace it.

7. Measure the outside diameter of the shift drum, **Figure 23**, with a micrometer. Standard measurements are 11.95mm (.5154 in) for the right side and 35.92mm (1.4142 in) for the left side. If worn below these standards, replace the drum.

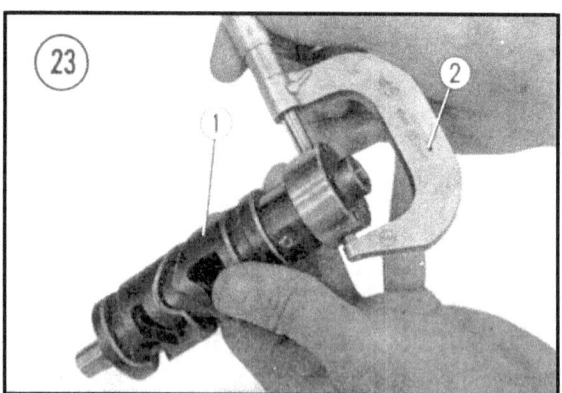

① Gear shift drum
② Micrometer

Reassembly

1. Mount the tensioner for the primary chain on the crankcase.

2. Refer to **Figure** 19 and mount the gears on their shafts, using new clips and making sure they are seated in the proper grooves.

3. Refer to **Figure 24** and use the driver tool, No. 07048-30020 to push the countershaft bearing into the lower crankcase.

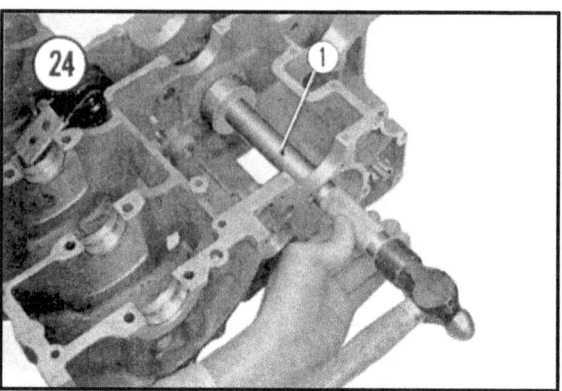

① Bearing driver tool

4. Mount the countershaft with all its gears except for 5th (top) which is inserted later. Refer to **Figure 25**.

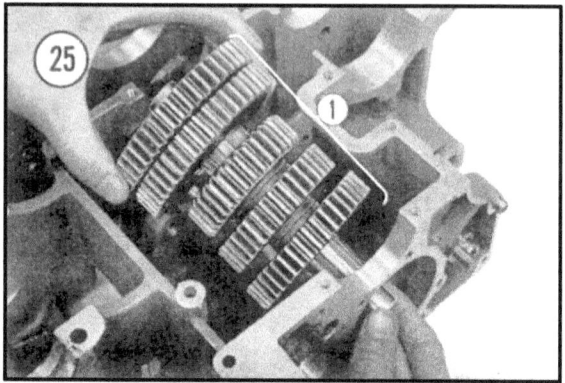

① Countershaft gear assembly

5. Mount the shift drum and install the neutral stopper with its bolt. The depression on the drum is the neutral position.

6. Assemble the shift forks as shown in **Figure 26**. The letters **R**, **C** and **L** are stamped on the sides. Forks **R** and **L** are fitted into the fourth and fifth gears on the countershaft, while the **C** fork is used with the mainshaft's second and third gears. The dog on the back of this fork fits into the groove on the shift drum.

① Gear shift forks

CLUTCH AND TRANSMISSION

7. Refer to **Figure 27** and install the final shaft assembly into the upper crankcase. Make sure to install the set ring. Then, install the final shaft oil guide.

① Final shaft oil guide ② Final driven shaft

8. Mount the primary sprocket on the mainshaft assembly, and install the unit in the upper crankcase.

9. Install the two dowel pins, the oil collar, and the O-ring in the upper crankcase. Smear Permatex on the flange, and assemble the lower crankcase.

> NOTE: *Make sure that the transmission is in neutral, with the center fork between second and third gears on the mainshaft.*

10. Install the crankcase, cam chain tensioner, pistons, and cylinder head.

CHAPTER FOUR

CARBURETORS AND FUEL TANK

CARBURETORS

The differences between the early model CB 750 carburetors and those on the later CB 750 K1 lie chiefly in the throttle linkages.

The original one-cable design was modified to a more positive, two-cable arrangement designed to open and close the throttles with a "push-pull" action. A machine with one throttle cable is a 750 and one with two cables is a 750 K1.

Routine adjustment procedures for both versions are outlined in the tune-up chapter. This chapter covers disassembly and inspection. There are separate sections for removal of the 750 carburetors and those on the K1. Elsewhere, instructions apply to both.

CB 750 Disassembly

Figure 1 (page 66) shows the major parts of the CB 750 carburetor. Refer to it while performing the following operations.

1. Remove the fuel tank.
2. Remove the throttle valve, **Figure 2**, from each of the carburetors.
3. Remove the insulating and connecting bands, **Figure 3**, and then remove the four carburetors as an assembly.
4. Refer to **Figure 4** and dismount the carburetors from the stay plate by unscrewing the

① Throttle valve

① Air cleaner connecting band
② Carburetor insulator band

6mm screws, two for each carb, and separate by disconnecting the individual choke rods.

5. Remove the needle jet, **Figure 5**, by disconnecting the throttle cable from the throttle valve,

CARBURETORS AND FUEL TANK

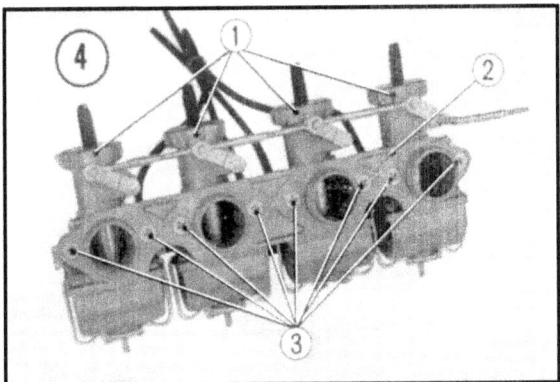

① Carburetor ③ Setting screws
② Carburetor stay plate

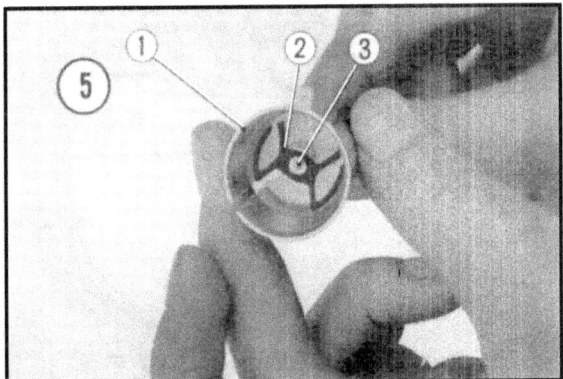

① Throttle valve ③ Jet needle
② Needle set plate

and then removing the needle set plate from the valve.

6. Slip the retaining clip from the float chamber, and referring to **Figure 6**, carefully remove the slow jet, main jet, needle jet holder, float, and float valve set.

> NOTE: *Do not mix up the jets. Store them in individually labeled envelopes to avoid confusion.*

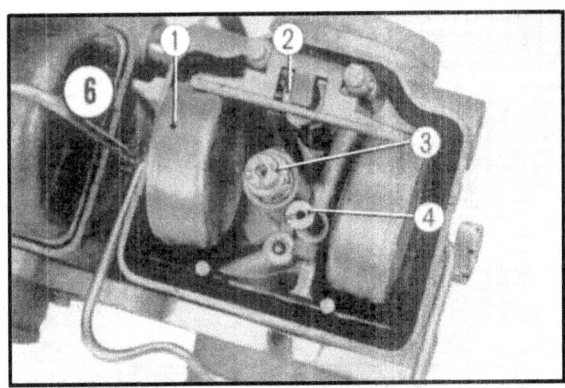

① Float ③ Main jet
② Float valve set ④ Slow jet

CB 750 K1 Disassembly

Figure 7 (page 68) shows the parts of the K1 carburetor. Refer to it while performing the following operations.

1. Remove the fuel tank.

2. Disconnect the throttle cables at the link lever, **Figure 8**, loosen the air cleaner connecting and insulator bands, **Figure 9**, and then remove the carburetors as an assembly.

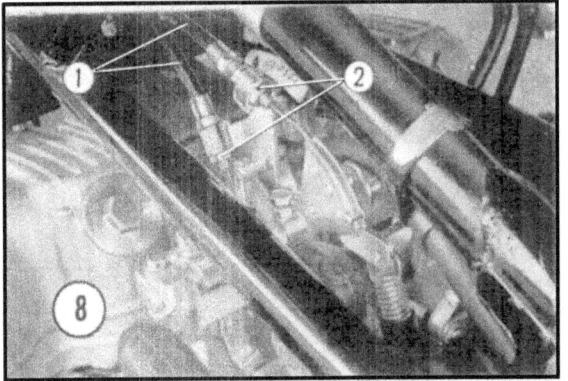

① Throttle cable ② Lock nuts

① Air cleaner connecting band
② Carburetor insulator band

3. Refer to **Figure 10** and dismount each carburetor from the stay plate by removing the 6mm screws, two for each carb. Separate the carburetors by disconnecting the individual choke rods.

4. Remove the needle set plate, **Figure 11**, and then remove the needle jet from the throttle valve.

5. Remove the clip from the float chamber and remove the bowl. With a small screwdriver, and referring to **Figure 12**, remove the slow jet, main jet, needle jet holder, float, and float valve set.

> NOTE: *To avoid mixing up the jets, store them in individually labeled envelopes.*

CARBURETORS AND FUEL TANK

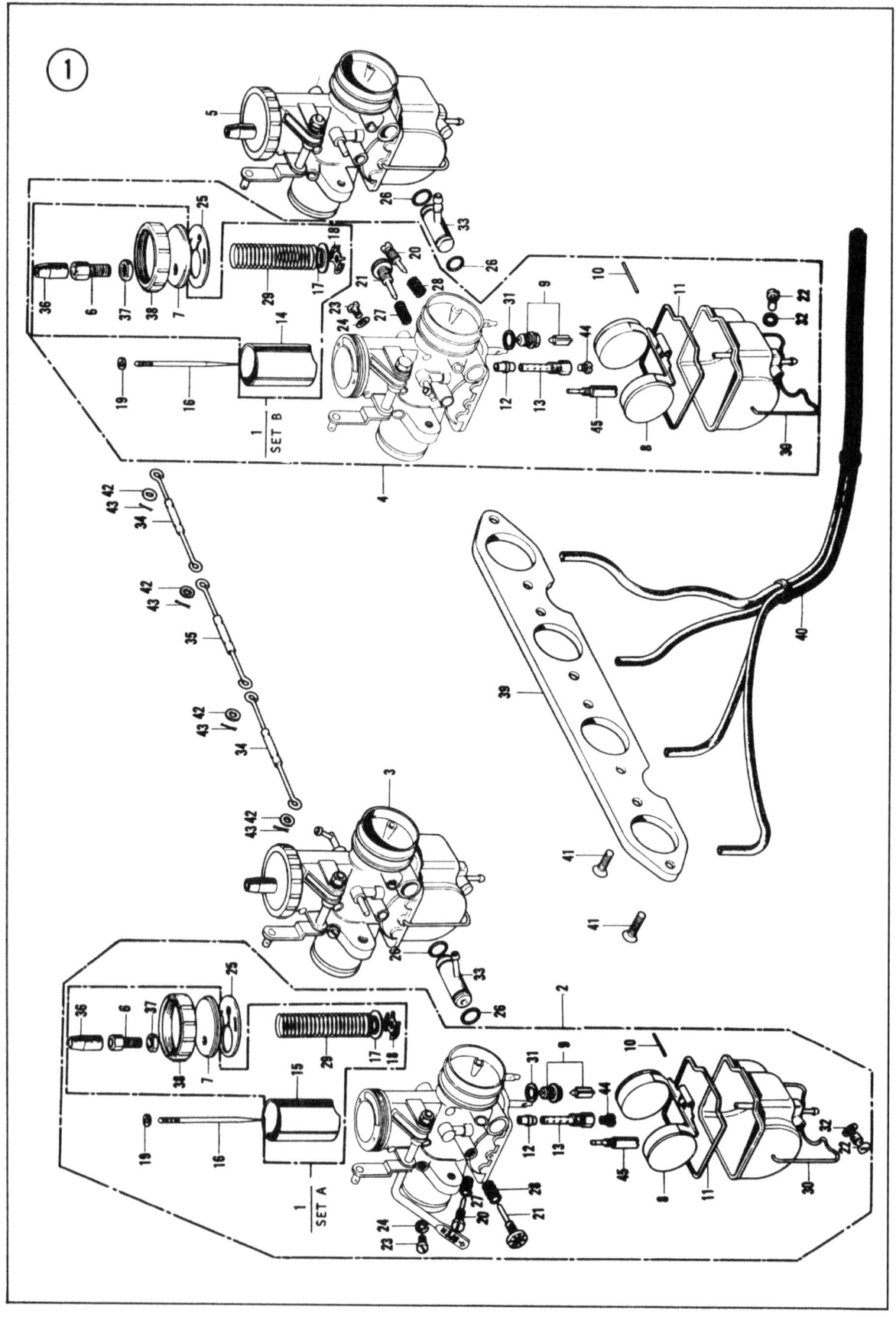

CARBURETORS AND FUEL TANK

CARBURETOR (CB750)

1. Carburetor top assembly
2. Carburetor assembly I
3. Carburetor assembly II
4. Carburetor assembly III
5. Carburetor assembly IV
6. Cable adjuster
7. Top
8. Float
9. Float valve-set
10. Float arm pin
11. Float chamber washer
12. Needle jet
13. Needle jet holder
14. Right throttle valve
15. Left throttle valve
16. Jet needle
17. Washer guide
18. Needle setting plate
19. Bar clip
20. Air screw
21. Throttle stop screw
22. Drain screw
23. Plug screw
24. Plain washer
25. Top washer
26. O-ring
27. Air screw spring
28. Throttle stop screw spring
29. Throttle spring
30. Float chamber setting clip
31. Plain washer
32. Plain washer
33. Fuel tube T-type joint
34. Choke rod A assembly
35. Choke rod B assembly
36. Rubber cap
37. Hex nut
38. Cap
39. Stay plate
40. Carburetor overflow tube assembly
41. Oval screw
42. Plain washer
43. Split pin
44. Main jet
45. Slow jet

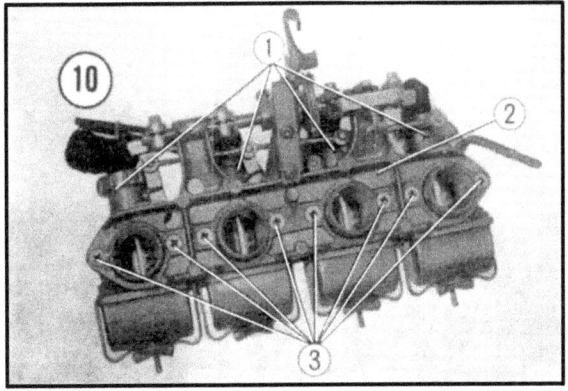

① Carburetor   ③ Setting screws
② Carburetor stay plate

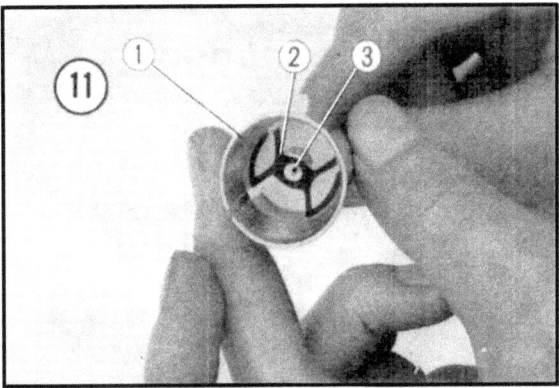

① Throttle valve   ③ Jet needle
② Needle set plate

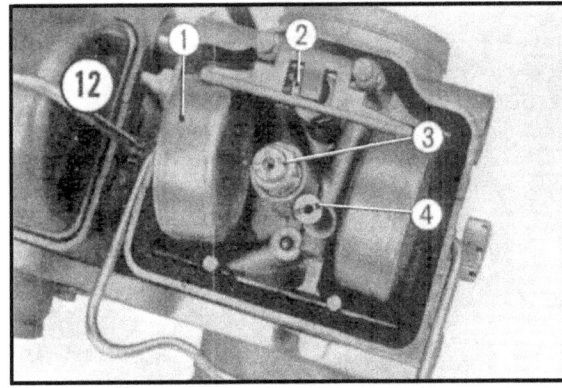

① Float   ③ Main jet
② Float valve set   ④ Slow jet

Inspection and Adjustment, CB 750 and CB 750 K1

1. Check the float level. This procedure was shown in Chapter One. Briefly, measure the level vertically as shown in **Figure 13** with a special gauge. The height of the float above the carburetor body should be 26mm (1.023 in). Adjust by bending the float arm with a narrow screwdriver.

2. Check the needle jet and its valve for wear.

CARBURETORS AND FUEL TANK

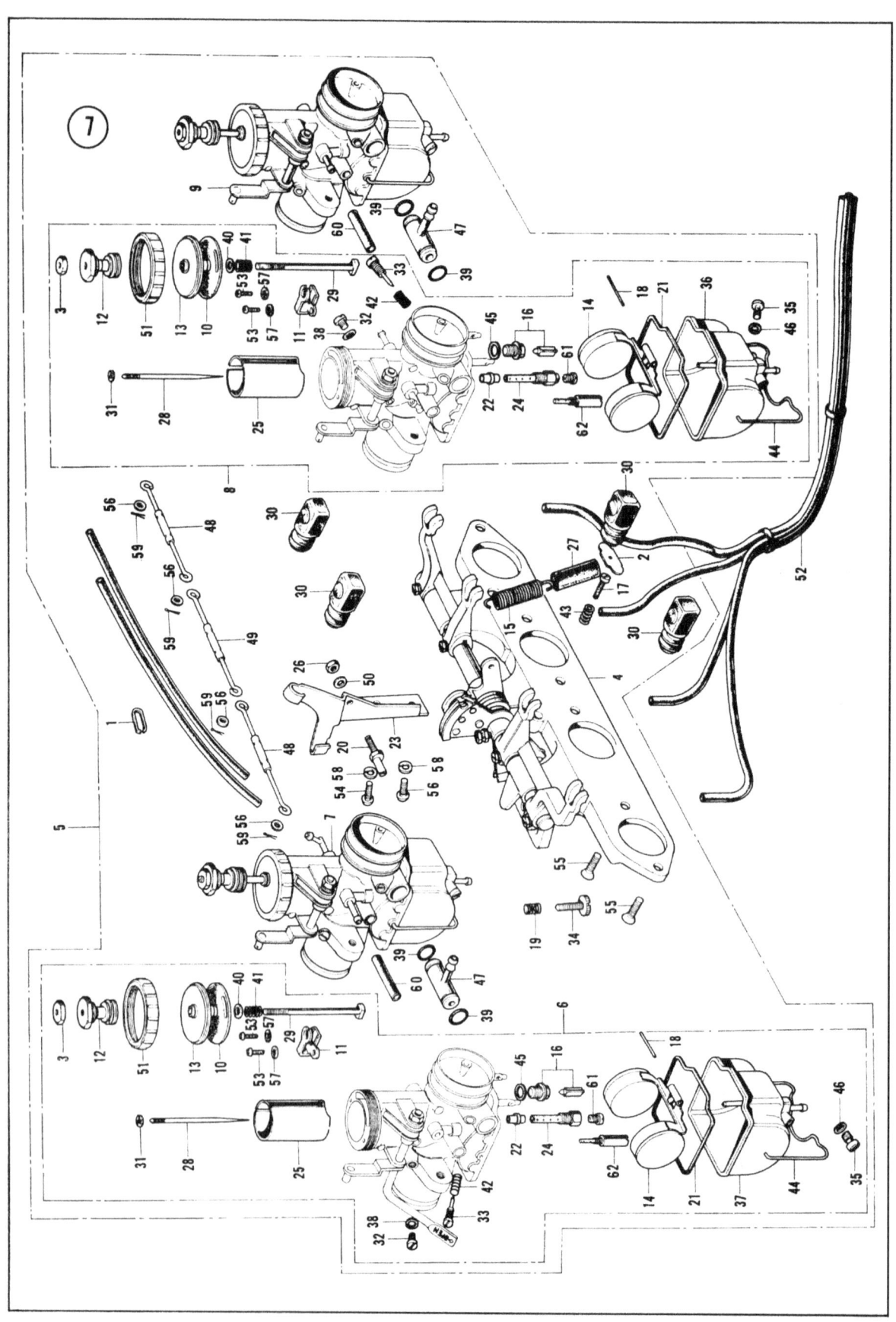

CARBURETORS AND FUEL TANK

CARBURETOR (CB750K1)

1. Carburetor breather pipe setting band
2. Spring setting plate
3. Special nut
4. Carburetor setting plate
5. Carburetor assembly
6. Carburetor assembly A
7. Carburetor assembly B
8. Carburetor assembly C
9. Carburetor assembly D
10. Top washer
11. Needle clip plate
12. Cable adjuster
13. Top
14. Float
15. Throttle return spring
16. Float valve-set
17. Throttle stop screw
18. Float arm pin
19. Throttle stop spring
20. Screw stopper pin
21. Float chamber washer
22. Needle jet
23. Throttle cable stay
24. Needle jet holder
25. Throttle valve
26. Hex nut
27. Protector tube
28. Jet needle
29. Throttle rod
30. Dust cap
31. Bar clip
32. Plug screw
33. Air screw
34. Throttle stop screw
35. Drain screw
36. Float chamber A
37. Float chamber B
38. Plain washer
39. O-ring
40. Washer
41. Air screw spring
42. Air screw spring
43. Stop screw spring
44. Float chamber setting clip
45. Plain washer
46. Plain washer
47. T-type fuel tube joint
48. Choke rod A assembly
49. Choke rod B assembly
50. Interior tooth washer
51. Cap
52. Carburetor overflow tube assembly
53. Pan screw
54. Pan screw
55. Oval screw
56. Plain washer
57. Spring washer
58. Spring washer
59. Split pin
60. Fuel tube
61. Main jet
62. Slow jet

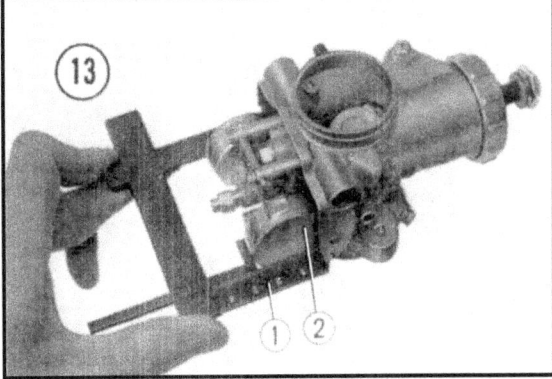

① Float ② Float level gauge

The needle moves constantly during operation, and if excessively worn it should be replaced.

3. Clean each jet by blowing out with compressed air. Never use a wire to poke dirt from the jets. A straw from a broom is permissible.

4. Clean all parts with carburetor cleaner, and blow dry with compressed air.

Reassembly

Refer to **Figure 14** and the earlier exploded views, and reassemble in reverse order of disassembly. Be careful not to overtighten the jets. **Figure 15** shows where the main and slow jets are installed.

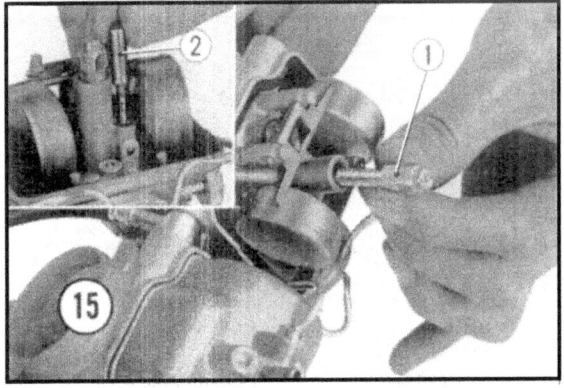

① Main jet ② Slow jet

Adjustment and Balancing

Final adjustment and synchronizing of the carburetors is covered in the tune-up chapter.

FUEL TANK AND FUEL VALVE

Figure 16 (page 71) is an exploded view of the fuel tank and the valve that controls the flow of fuel to the carburetors. **Figure 17** (next page) shows how the tank is mounted on the frame.

CARBURETORS AND FUEL TANK

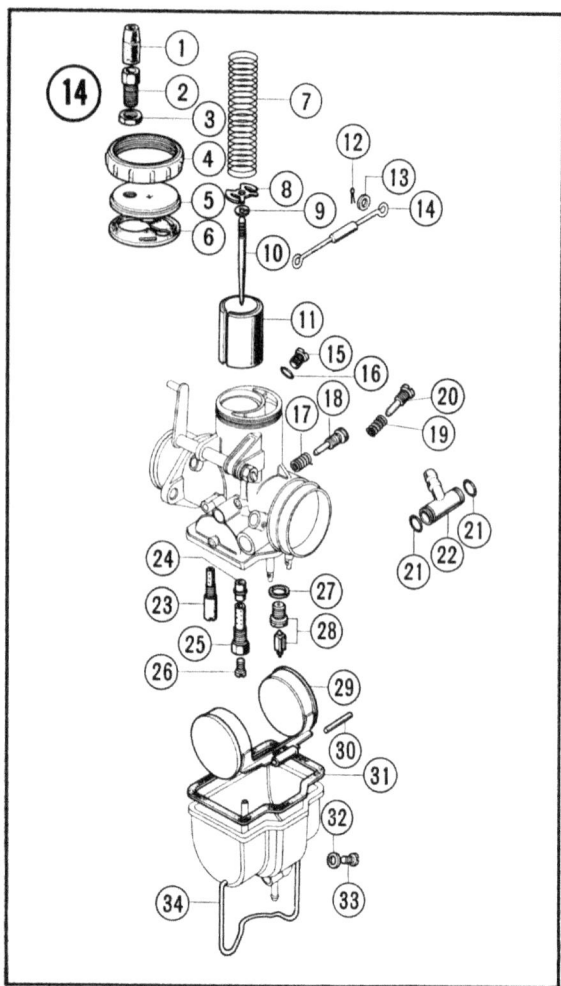

① Rubber cap
② Cable adjuster
③ Lock nut
④ Cap
⑤ Top
⑥ Top washer
⑦ Throttle spring
⑧ Needle set plate
⑨ Clip
⑩ Jet needle
⑪ Throttle valve
⑫ 1.0×10 split pin
⑬ 5 mm flat washer
⑭ Choke rod
⑮ Plug screw
⑯ Flat washer
⑰ Air screw spring
⑱ Air screw
⑲ Stop screw spring
⑳ Throttle stop screw
㉑ 7.9×1.9 O-ring
㉒ T-type fuel tube joint
㉓ Slow jet
㉔ Needle jet
㉕ Needle jet holder
㉖ Main jet
㉗ Flat washer
㉘ Float valve set
㉙ Float
㉚ Float arm pin
㉛ Float chamber washer
㉜ 6 mm flat washer
㉝ Drain plug
㉞ Float chamber set clip

Disassembly

1. Shut the fuel valve and remove the fuel tube from the tank at the valve, **Figure 18**.

2. Lift the seat, raise the rear cushion, pull the tank to the rear, and raise it up and away with the valve attached.

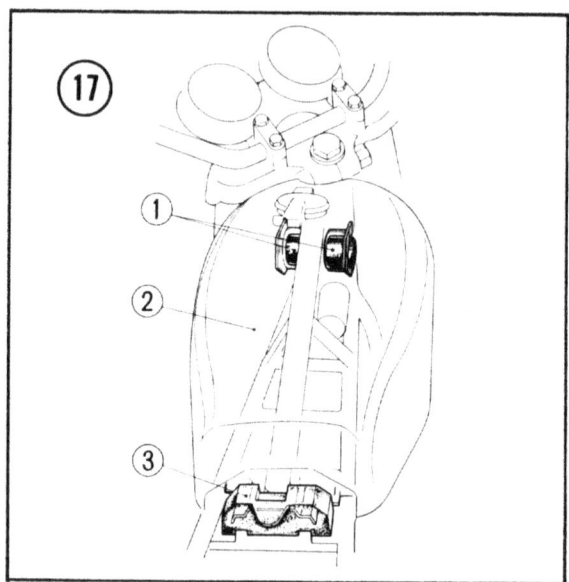

① Fuel tank front cushions
② Fuel tank
③ Fuel tank rear cushion

① Fuel tube   ② Fuel valve

3. Remove the cup from the base of the valve using the bolt on the bottom as a purchase. Then remove the O-ring gasket and the fuel strainer.

4. Refer to **Figure 19** and remove the two mounting screws. Then remove the valve from the tank.

① Fuel valve
② Fuel valve mounting screws

CARBURETORS AND FUEL TANK

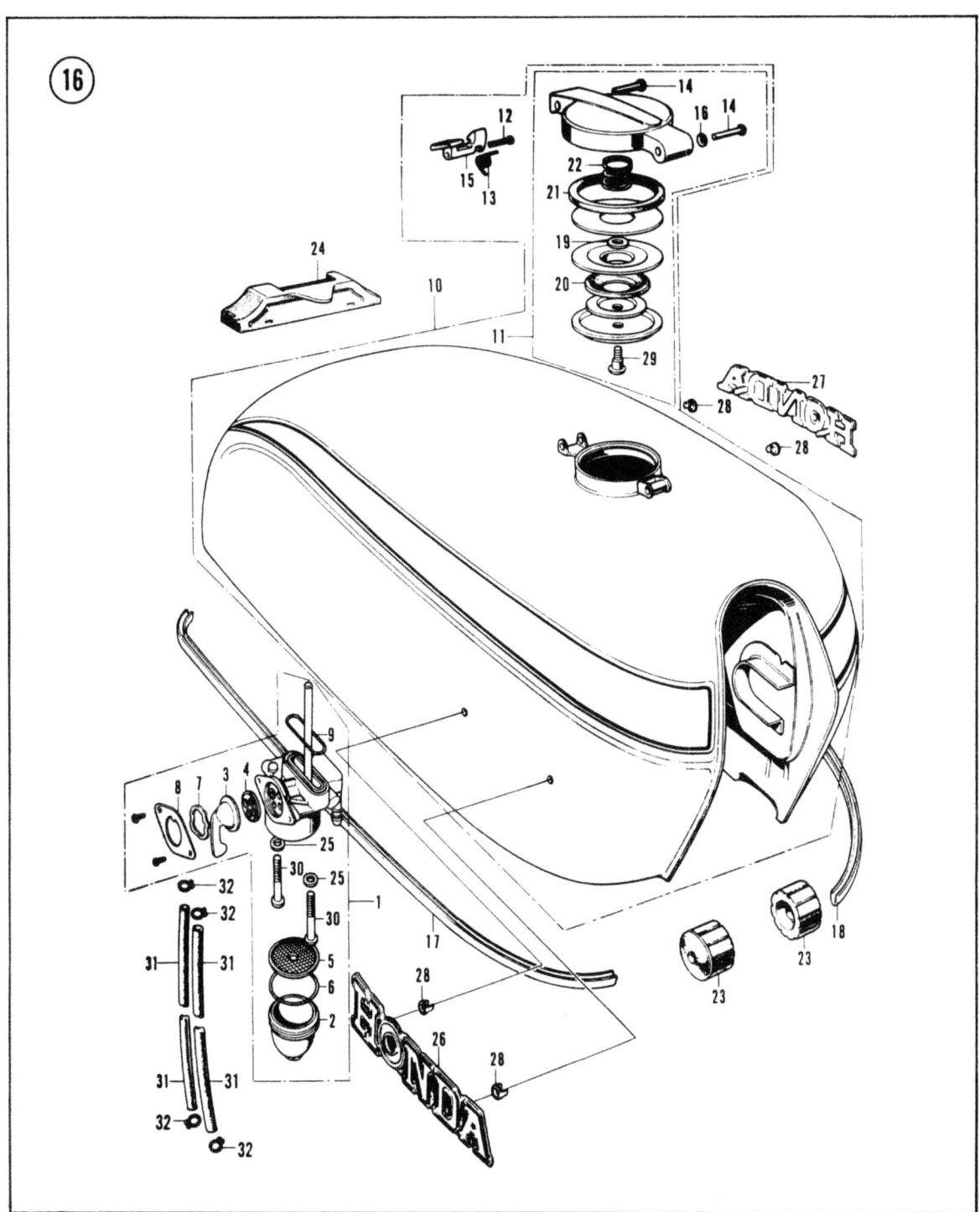

FUEL TANK — FUEL COCK

1. Fuel cock assembly
2. Fuel strainer cup
3. Fuel cock lever
4. Fuel cock valve packing
5. Fuel strainer screen
6. Fuel strainer gasket
7. Cock lever spring
8. Fuel cock lever setting plate
9. O-ring
10. Fuel tank
11. Fuel filler cap components
12. Fuel filler cap check pin
13. Cap check spring
14. Fuel filler cap pin
15. Fuel filler cap check
16. Fuel filler cap friction washer
17. Right fuel tank molding
18. Left fuel tank molding
19. Plain washer
20. Fuel separator A
21. Fuel filler cap gasket
22. Seat spring
23. Fuel tank front cushion
24. Fuel tank rear cushion
25. Fuel cock fixing gasket
26. Right fuel tank emblem
27. Left fuel tank emblem
28. Rear ornament clamp nut
29. Fuel cap screw
30. Pan screw
31. Fuel tube
32. Fuel tube clip

Inspection

1. Inspect the tank for leaks, and make sure the vent hole is not clogged.

2. Check the rubber mounts for deterioration, and replace if necessary.

3. Refer to **Figure 20** and check for damage to the petcock and the filter screen. Clean the mesh of dirt, and the bowl of sediment.

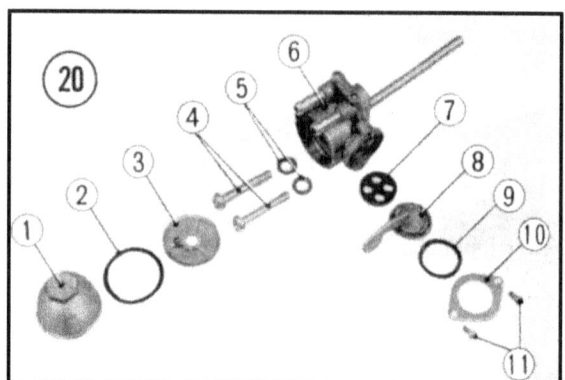

① Fuel strainer cup ② O ring ③ Fuel strainer screen ④ 6mm cross screws ⑤ Fuel cock fixing packing ⑥ Fuel valve body ⑦ Fuel cock valve packing ⑧ Fuel cock lever ⑨ Cock lever spring ⑩ Setting plate ⑪ Cross screws

4. Inspect the fuel tube for leaks or cracks, and replace if required.

Reassembly

1. Assemble the fuel valve, and install it on the tank with the two mounting screws.

2. Install the front and rear rubber mounts on the frame. Fit the front mount by pushing the tank from the rear, **Figure 21**. Fit the tank, being careful to route the wiring correctly.

3. Install the fuel line.

4. Turn the valve to open, and check for leaks.

① Fuel tank

CHAPTER FIVE

IGNITION AND CHARGING SYSTEMS

This chapter covers the ignition system, charging system, and the battery. Routine adjustment instructions for the ignition system were covered in the tune-up chapter.

IGNITION

The Honda 750 ignition system consists of the battery, two coils, two sets of contact breaker points, and the four spark plugs. There is no distributor.

The schematic, **Figure 1**, traces the flow of current from the battery through the primary ignition windings to the breakers and then the plugs. One set of points supplies current to the No. 1 and No. 4 cylinders, and the other to cylinders No. 2 and No. 3.

This section gives instructions for removal

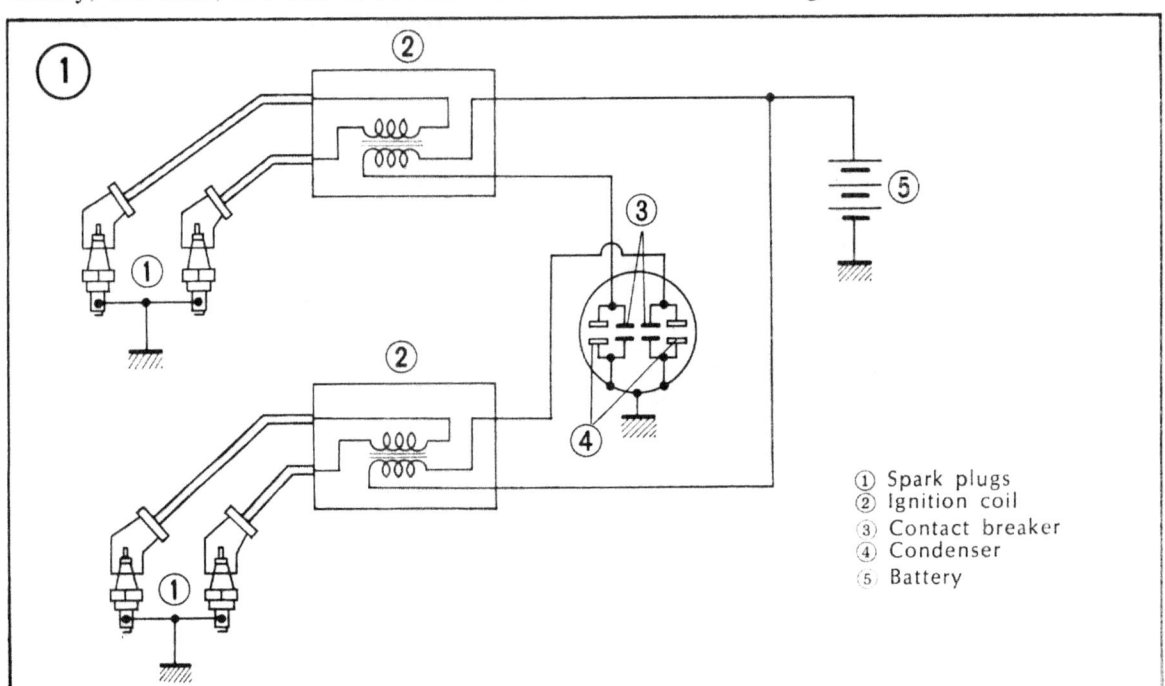

1. Spark plugs
2. Ignition coil
3. Contact breaker
4. Condenser
5. Battery

and testing of the coils, servicing the points assemblies, and disassembly of the spark advance mechanism.

COIL

The primary windings consist of 380 turns, and the secondaries number 15,000 turns. The core is made of laminated steel sheets, **Figure 2**.

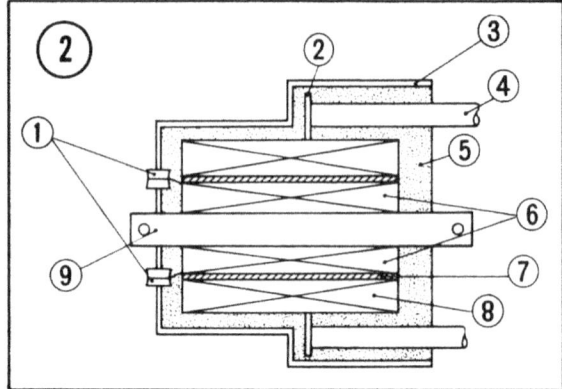

① Primary terminal
② High tension terminal
③ Case
④ High tension cord
⑤ Synthetic resin
⑥ Primary coil
⑦ Bobbin
⑧ Secondary coil
⑨ Core

Disassembly

1. Remove the fuel tank.

2. Disconnect the three electrical leads, as shown in **Figure 3**. They are color-coded yellow, blue, and black-white.

3. Unscrew the two mounting bolts, **Figure 3**, and remove the coils from the frame.

① Ignition coil   ③ Leads connectors
② Mounting bolts

Coil Testing

The coils must be checked on a bench testing device like the one shown in **Figure 4**. Most

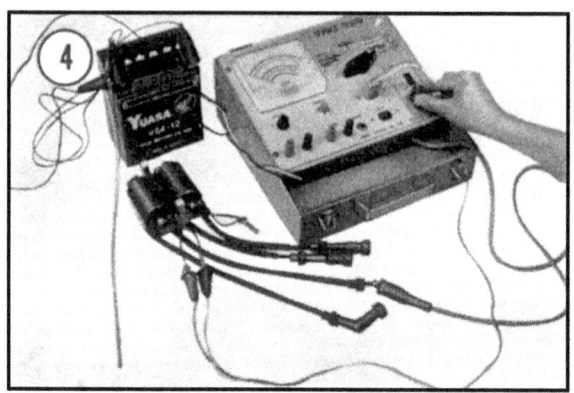

testers are similar to this one, on which the following instructions are based.

1. Connect the power cord to the 12-volt battery, and ground the black lead to complete the circuit.

2. Plug the primary cord into the tester, and connect the other end to the primary terminal of the coil to be checked.

3. Connect the red test lead to the black terminal.

4. Connect the white lead to the yellow or blue terminal, depending on which coil is being tested.

5. Connect the red high tension cable to the secondary terminal.

6. Set the selector knob to "coil test" or the equivalent.

7. Refer to **Figure 5A** and adjust the three-point spark tester to the greatest distance that will maintain a spark. If the gap is more than 7mm (.28 in), the coil is serviceable.

NOTE: <u>FIGURE 5B</u> *shows the appearance of the spark when the test leads are attached to the coil in reverse.*

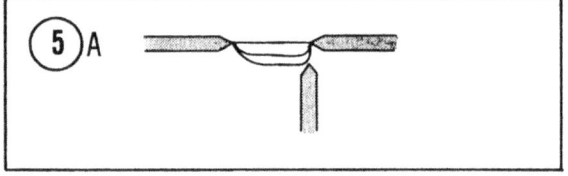

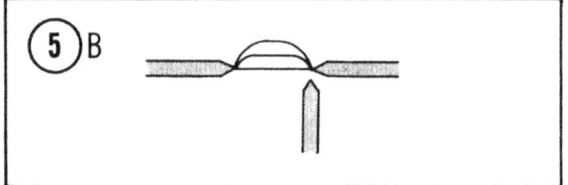

IGNITION AND CHARGING SYSTEMS

Testing Coil on the Engine

1. Do not use the external battery. Connect the tester ground lead to the frame.

2. Remove the cap from either No. 1 or No. 4 cylinder, and install the special attachment to the terminal. Then connect the high voltage test lead to the attachment, and reinstall the plug cap.

3. Turn on the ignition switch and turn the engine over with the kickstarter or starting motor. Note the maximum sparking distance of the coil. It should be more than 7mm (.28 in).

4. Repeat the operation using the plug from cylinders No. 2 or No. 3.

Reassembly

1. Mount the coils with the two bolts.

2. Connect the yellow, blue, and black-white leads to the wiring harness.

3. Install the fuel tank. Be careful not to crimp the electrical leads.

BREAKER POINTS

Servicing of the points and condensers was covered in Chapter One. Only the removal of the assembly is outlined here.

Disassembly

1. Remove point cover.

2. Disconnect the yellow and blue leads at the junction point in the center of the frame, **Figure 6**.

① Contact breaker lead

3. Referring to **Figure 7**, unscrew the 6mm hex nut and remove the assembly.

> NOTE: *Do not replace the breaker point assembly if the spark advance mechanism is to be serviced.*

① 6mm hex nut
② Special washer
③ Contact breaker setting screws

SPARK ADVANCE

The spark advance mechanism is mounted on the crankshaft inboard of the breaker point assembly. This device advances the point cam as the engine speed increases to cause earlier ignition. Operation is by weights that move outward against spring tension as the rpm increase, **Figure 8**.

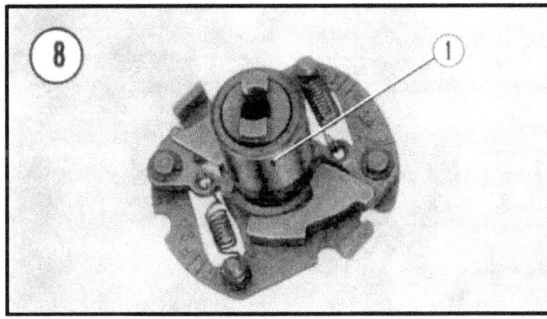

① Spark advancer

Disassembly

1. Remove the breaker point assembly as outlined in the preceding section.

2. Pull the advance mechanism from the advancer shaft, **Figure 9**.

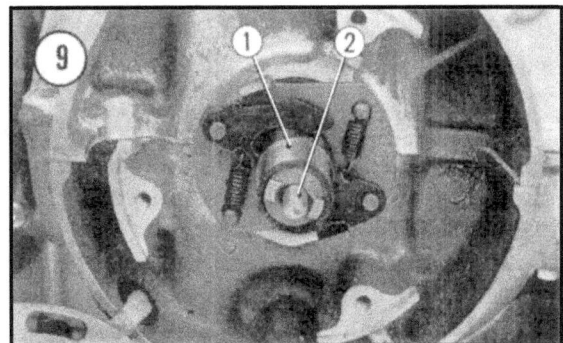

① Spark advancer   ② Spark advancer shaft

Inspection

1. Check the advancer spring for loss of tension, and replace if necessary.

2. Check the advancer shaft to make sure it is not bent or out-of-center. Turn the engine with the kickstarter while looking at the shaft. It should not wobble. A runout of .1mm or less is the permissible limit.

> NOTE: *The crankshaft hole for the advancer shaft is drilled slightly off-center. Thus, any advancer shaft, no matter how straight, will appear off center at rest.*

Reassembly

1. If necessary, install a new advancer shaft. The O-ring ridges are slightly oversize, and may have to be ground down about .1mm to fit.

2. Install the advancer mechanism, making sure the pin is inserted into the hole, **Figure 10**, at the end of the crankshaft.

3. Install the contact breaker assembly.

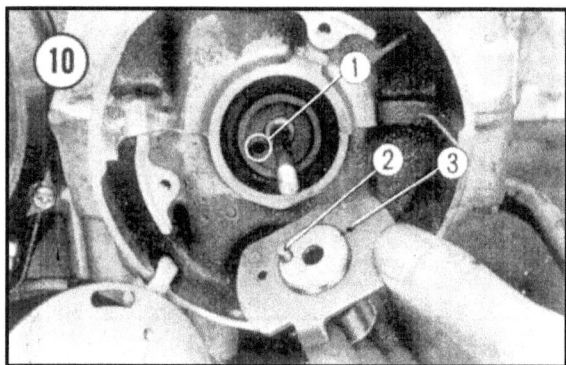

① Pin hole
② Spark advancer pin
③ Spark advancer

CHARGING SYSTEM

The alternator, voltage regulator, and rectifier comprise the charging system of a Honda 750.

This system is notably different from those in other Honda motorcycles, and is more similar to the type used in current model cars.

Unlike most alternators, the Honda 750 three-phase unit has stationary field and output windings with a soft iron rotor revolving between them. There are no brushes or slip rings.

The alternator field is excited, like those in automobiles. Control of the field current governs the alternator output, and thus the battery voltage.

The voltage regulator consists of a tapped resistor, a relay coil, and two sets of contacts. The upper set, farthest from the coil, is normally closed, and the lower one normally open.

There are only three variables that control alternator output voltage: alternator speed, field current, and the total alternator load.

Output voltage is raised by an increase in alternator speed or field current, or a decrease in alternator load. The voltage regulator controls the three modes of alternator operation.

Mode One

Figure 11 is a schematic of the current path when the battery voltage is below normal and the ignition switch is turned on.

Current flows from the battery through the closed upper armature contact of the regulator to the alternator field coil. The current through the relay coil does not produce a magnetic field strong enough to move the armature and open the upper set of contacts. The battery is connected directly to the field, causing maximum field current and alternator output.

Mode Two

Figure 12 schematically traces current path when the battery voltage is normal and the ignition is on. Current flows from the battery through a field resistor to the field. There is more field resistance, compared to Mode One, and so less current passes through the field. Consequently, there is reduced alternator output.

The current through the relay coil is greater than in the first mode, and does provide a magnetic field strong enough to break the upper contacts; but not strong enough, however, to close the lower contacts.

Mode Three

Figure 13 shows the current path when battery voltage is excessively high. In this mode, the current flows from the battery through the field resistor, then through the lower contacts in the regulator. No current flows to the field, and there is no output from the alternator.

Current through the relay coil is greater because of the high battery voltage. This produces a magnetic field in the relay coil strong enough to close the lower regulator contacts.

IGNITION AND CHARGING SYSTEMS

77

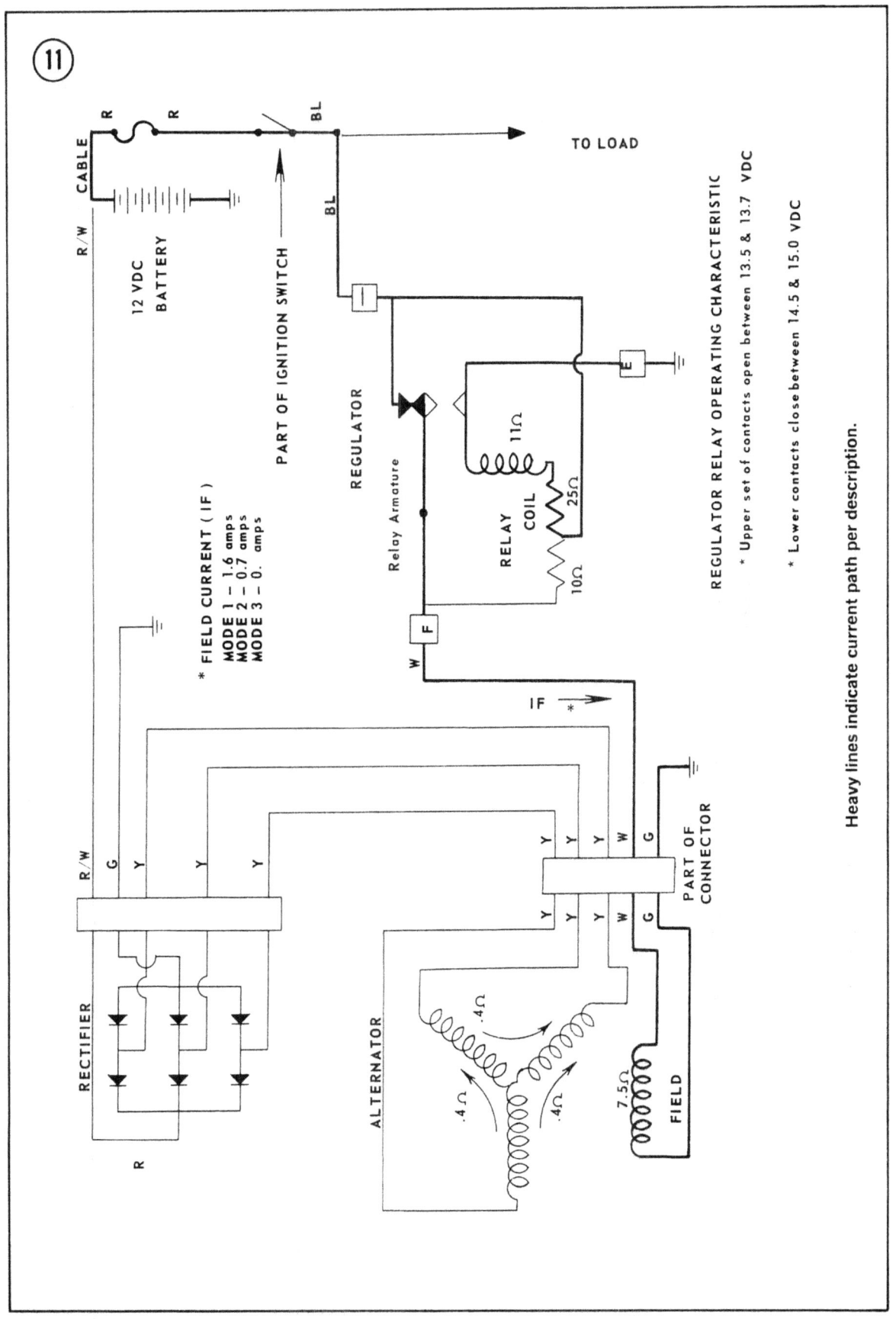

IGNITION AND CHARGING SYSTEMS

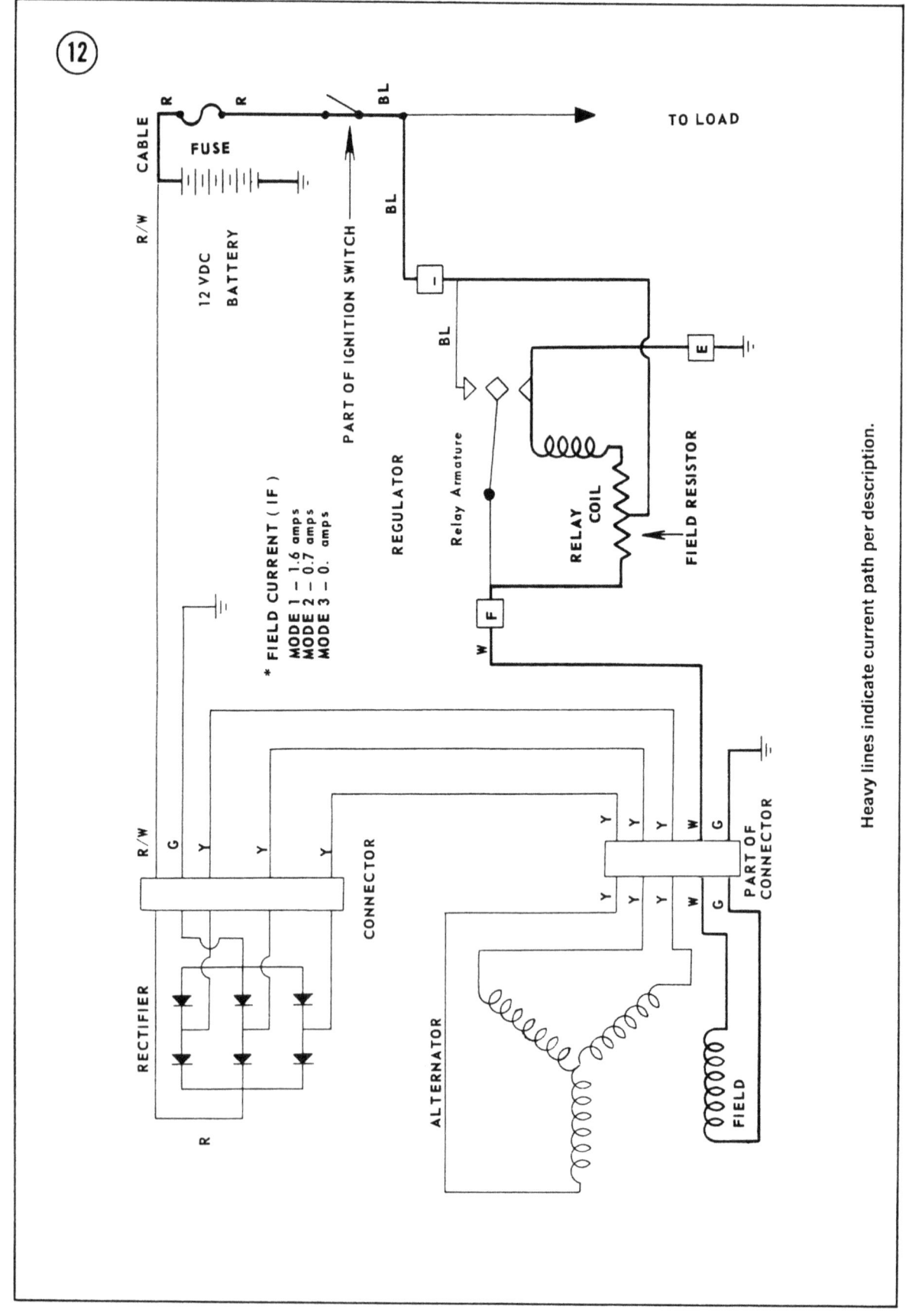

IGNITION AND CHARGING SYSTEMS

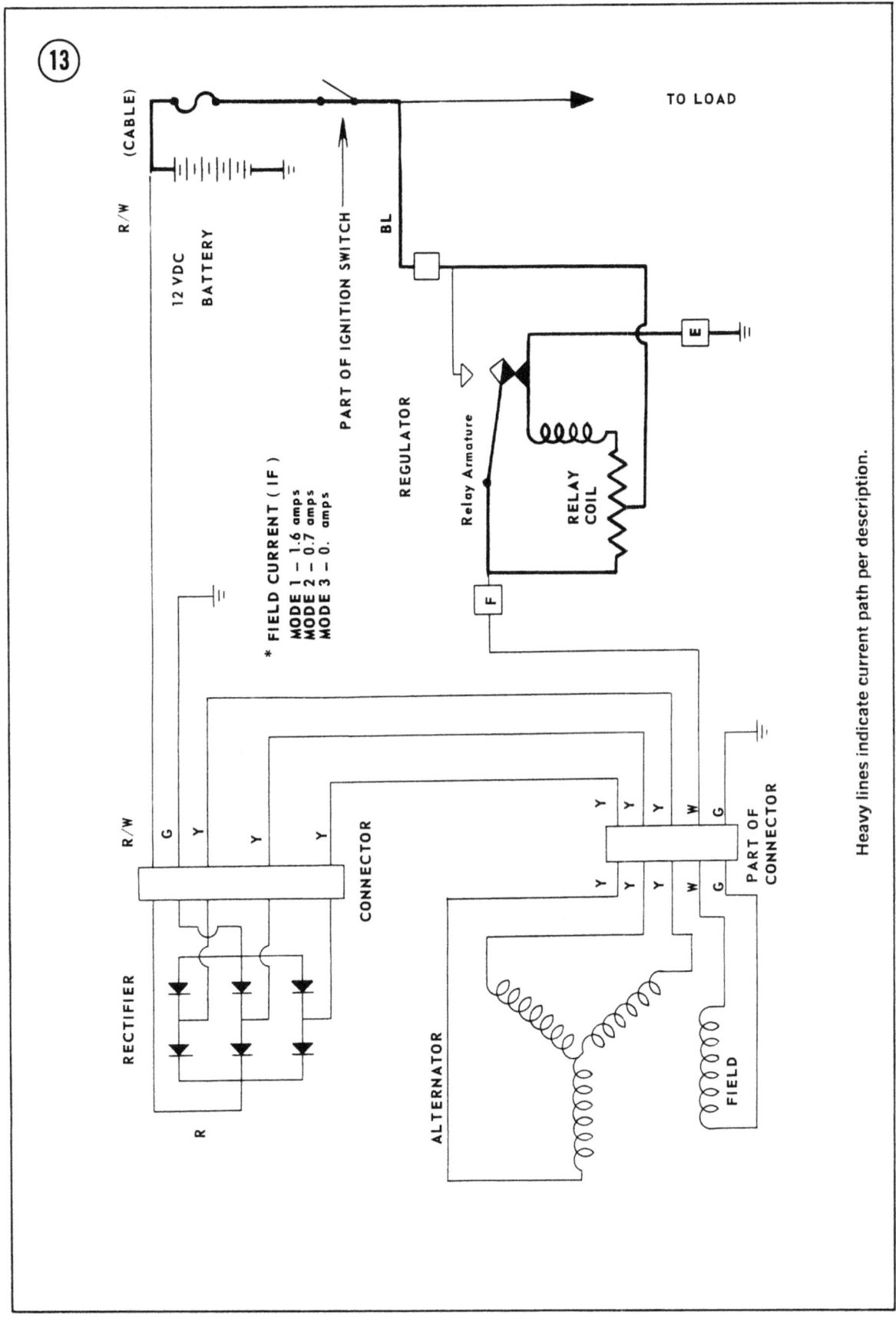

IGNITION AND CHARGING SYSTEMS

Testing Charging System

An ammeter is required to perform the test. Refer to the **Figure 14** schematic while following the operations.

1. Ensure that the battery voltage is normal. Measurement is described in the battery section of this chapter.
2. Locate the positive battery terminal and disconnect the red-white rectifier lead, and the red power lead. Connect both of these to the positive terminal of the ammeter.
3. Connect the positive terminal of the battery to the minus terminal of the ammeter with a wire.
4. Start the engine.
5. Referring to the **Figure 15** chart, operate the engine at the various speeds and check to see if the voltage measures up to the standard for night and day riding.

   Night riding: headlight high beam on.
   Day riding: turn signal and stop lights off.

ALTERNATOR

Figure 16 illustrates the components of the alternator: the field coil, stator coil, and the rotor. All the parts are shown in **Figure 17**.

NOTE: *The charge current read on the ammeter may fluctuate, depending on the condition of the battery.*

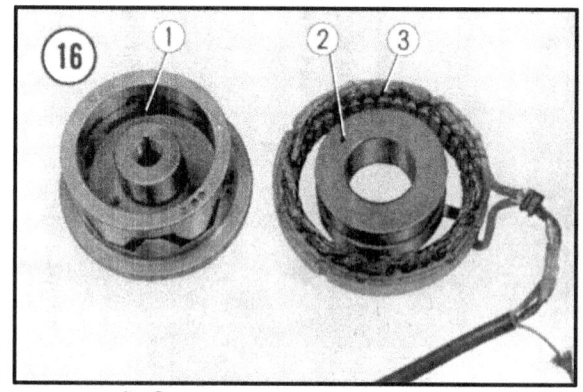

① Generator rotor
② Field coil   ③ Stator coil

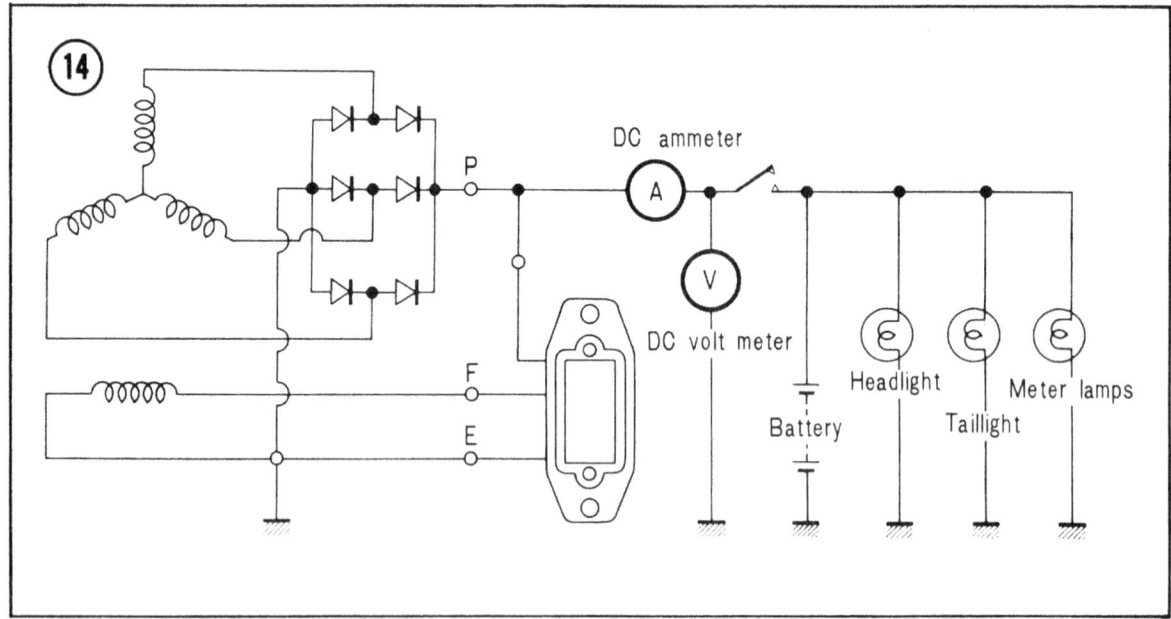

Engine (rpm) Charging current (A)	1,000	2,000	3,000	4,000	5,000	6,000	7,000	8,000
Night riding	6.5	0	2.4	1.3	1.0	1.0	0.8	0.6
Day riding	2—3	1	1	1	1	1	1	1
Battery terminal voltage (V)	12	12.4	13.2	14.5	14.5	14.5	14.5	14.5

IGNITION AND CHARGING SYSTEMS

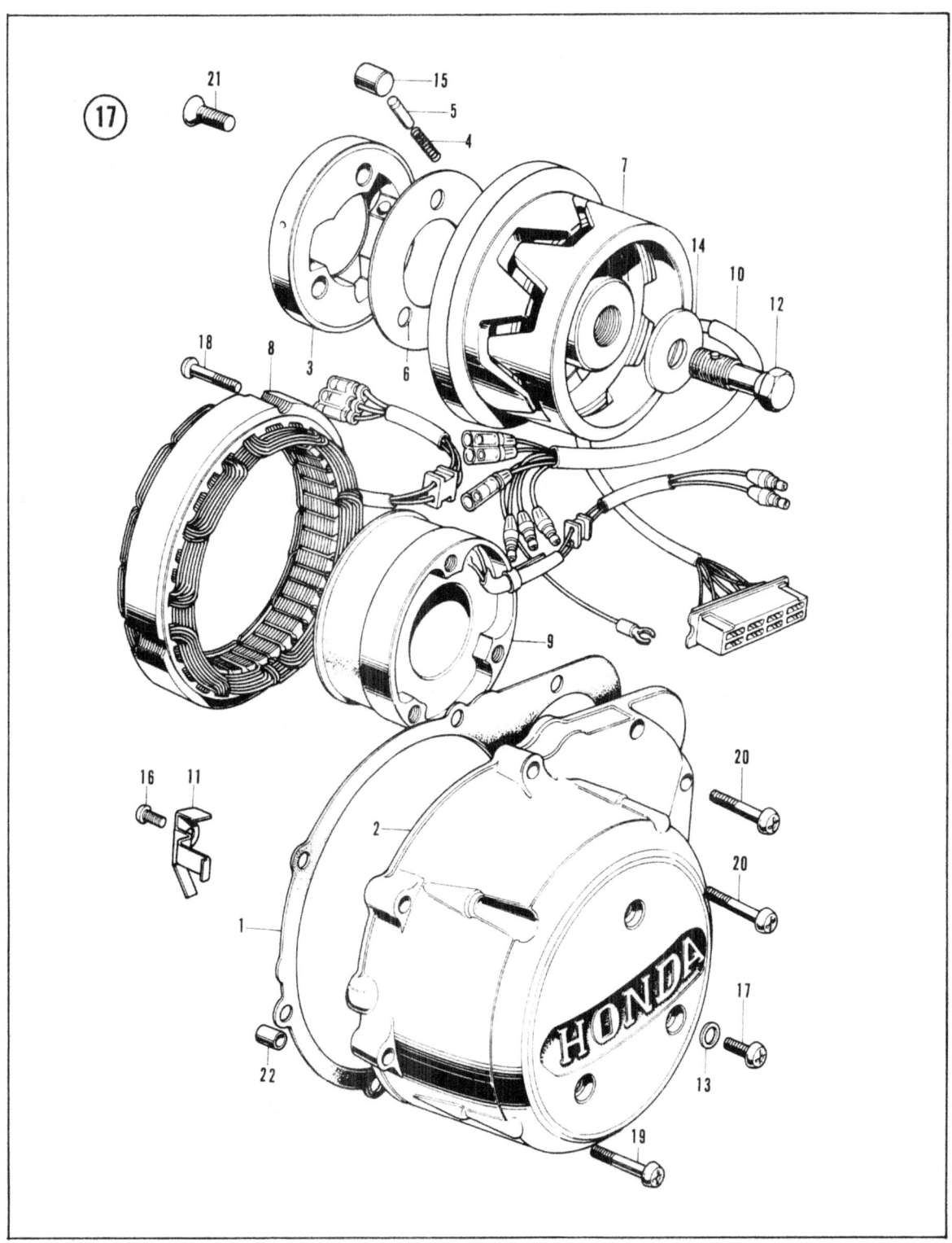

ALTERNATOR AND COVER

1. Dynamo cover gasket
2. Dynamo cover
3. Starting clutch
4. Starting clutch roller spring
5. Starting clutch roller spring cap
6. Starting clutch side plate
7. Rotor components
8. Stator components
9. Field coil components
10. A.C. generator wire harness
11. A.C. generator cord setting plate
12. Rotor set bolt
13. Washer
14. Washer
15. Roller
16. Pan screw
17. Pan screw
18. Pan screw
19. Pan screw
20. Pan screw
21. Flat screw
22. Dowel pin

IGNITION AND CHARGING SYSTEMS

Disassembly

1. Remove the dynamo cover and pull out the rotor. A special rotor puller, Honda tool No. 07011-30001, shown in **Figure 18**, is used for this operation.

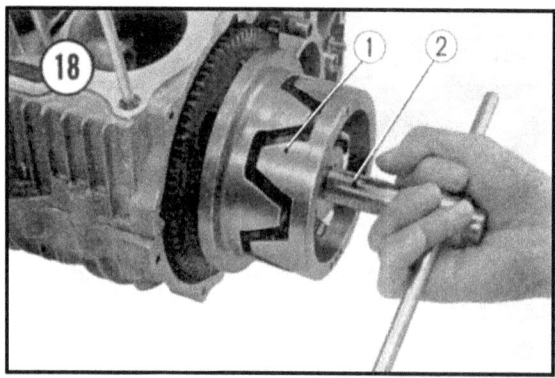

① A.C generator rotor
② Rotor puller

2. Referring to **Figure 19**, unscrew the four 6mm bolts and remove the stator coil from the dynamo cover.

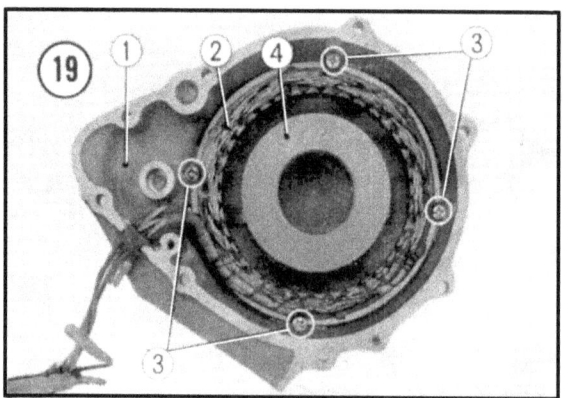

① Dynamo cover   ③ 6mm cross screws
② Stator coil   ④ Field coil

3. Remove the field coil from the cover by unscrewing the three 6mm Phillips screws, shown in **Figure 20**.

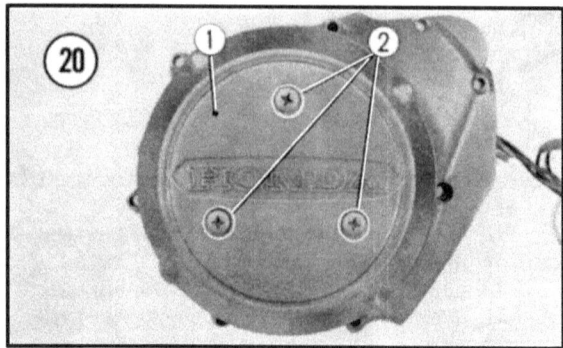

① Dynamo cover   ② 6mm cross screws

Testing Coil Continuity

A tester such as the one shown in **Figure 21** is required to check continuity.

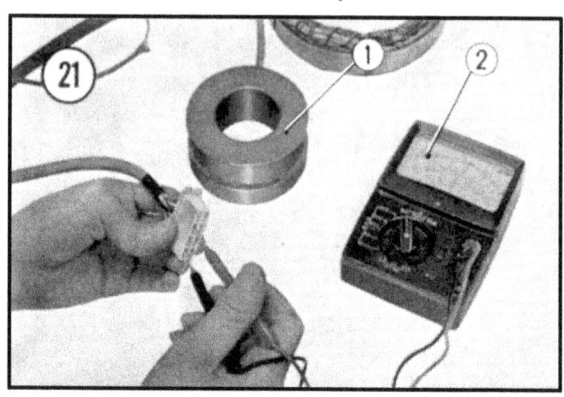

① Field coil   ② Tester

1. Hook the tester to the field coil according to the manufacturer's instructions. The rated resistance is 7.2 ohms. Replace the coil if there is continuity between the lead wires and the coil (grounded coil), or if there is no continuity between the wires (open circuit).

2. Check the continuity of the stator coil, **Figure 22**. The rated resistance is .2 ohms.

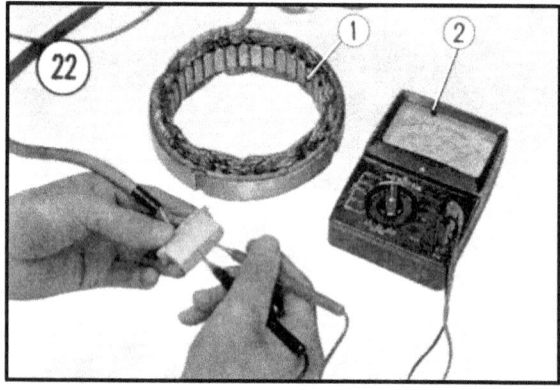

① Stator coil   ② Tester

REGULATOR

The dual contact voltage regulator is mounted inside the battery cover at the center of the frame. **Figure 23** shows its major parts.

Disassembly

1. Remove the battery cover and detach the regulator, **Figure 24**, by removing the two set bolts. Remove the cover by loosening the two screws.

IGNITION AND CHARGING SYSTEMS

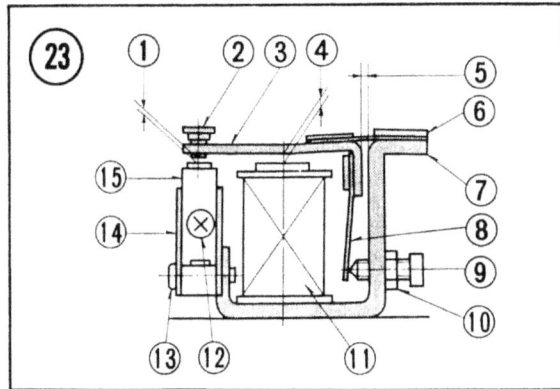

① Point gap
② Lower contact
③ Armature
④ Core gap
⑤ Yoke gap
⑥ Spring
⑦ Yoke
⑧ Adjusting spring
⑨ Voltage adjusting screw
⑩ Lock nut
⑪ Coil
⑫ Point gap adjusting screw
⑬ Core gap adjusting screw
⑭ Contact set
⑮ Upper contact

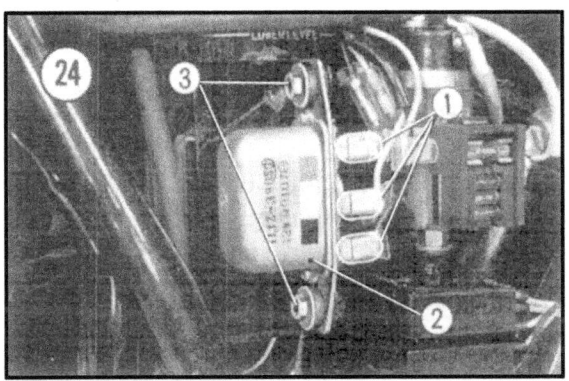

① Connectors
② Regulator
③ Regulator setting bolts

Inspection and Adjustment

The regulator must be adjusted if the charging system does not check out according to the test outlined earlier in this chapter.

1. **Figure 25** shows the location of the adjusting screw and its lock nut.

2. The circuit is normal if a voltmeter shows an output of from 14 to 15 volts at 5,000 rpm with no load. When the low speed contact circuit is broken and changes to the high speed contact circuit, there should be a .5 volt rise, as shown in **Figure 26**. If the increase is more than .5 volts, or if there is a drop, adjust the core gap (next procedure).

3. Refer to **Figure 27** for adjustment of the core gap. Clean the points with a point file, and check the gap with a feeler gauge. It should be

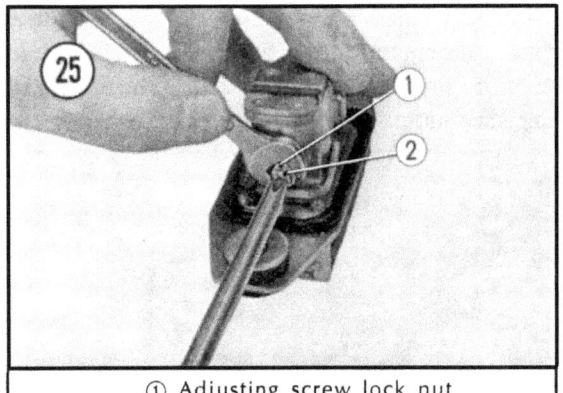

① Adjusting screw lock nut
② Adjusting screw

Low charging current or battery voltage:
Turn adjusting screw clockwise.
High charging current or battery voltage:
Turn adjusting screw counterclockwise.

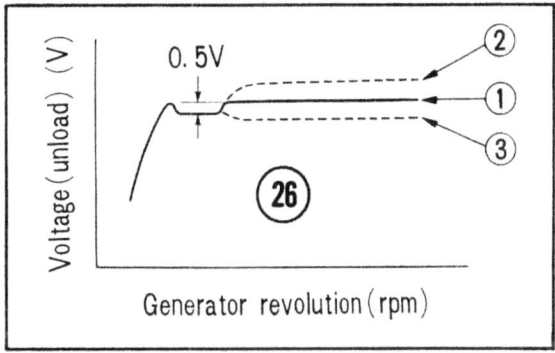

① Standard
② Wide core gap
③ Narrow core gap

① Thickness gauge
② Core gap adjusting screw

from .6mm to 1mm (.025 in to .04 in). If different, reset the gap with the adjusting screw.

4. Check the point gap with a feeler blade as shown in **Figure 28**. The standard gap is .3mm to .4mm (.12 in to .16 in). Loosen the lock screw to adjust.

RECTIFIER

Six silicon diodes rectify alternator current to

direct current. The assembly is attached away from the engine on the frame so it will remain cool. **Figure 29** shows its location in the charging schematic.

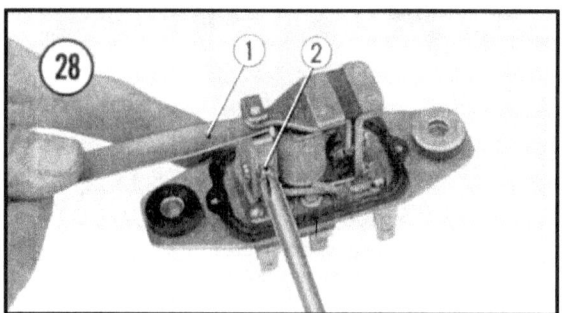

① Thickness gauge
② Point gap lock screw

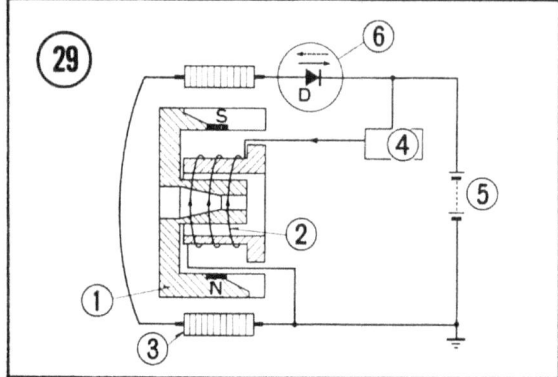

① Generator rotor ④ Regulator
② Field coil ⑤ Battery
③ Stator coil ⑥ Silicon rectifier

Disassembly

1. Remove the battery cover and unscrew the set nut, **Figure 30**, to detach the rectifier from the frame.

① Silicon rectifier ③ Connector
② Rectifier setting nut

Testing

Use a service tester, **Figure 31**, to check the continuity of the rectifier. A megger should not be used because the diodes could be damaged by high voltage. Be careful not to reverse the terminals when hooking the rectifier up to the tester. Also take care not to connect the testing battery in reverse polarity — the battery will short out and the rectifier will be damaged.

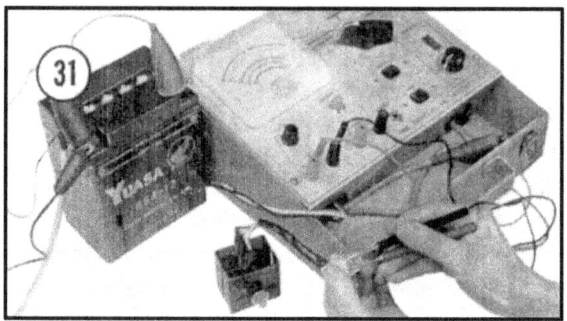

1. Test the rectifier in both directions.

2. Continuity in one direction indicates the rectifier is in good condition. Continuity in both directions or in neither direction indicates a defective unit.

BATTERY

The Honda 750's 12 volt, 14 ampere-hour battery is the heart of its electrical system. The electrolyte level should be checked regularly, especially in hot weather, as described in the tune-up section.

Disassembly

1. Raise the seat and remove the strap from the battery.

2. First, disconnect the ground, or negative cable. Then remove the positive cable. Their locations are pointed out in **Figure 32**.

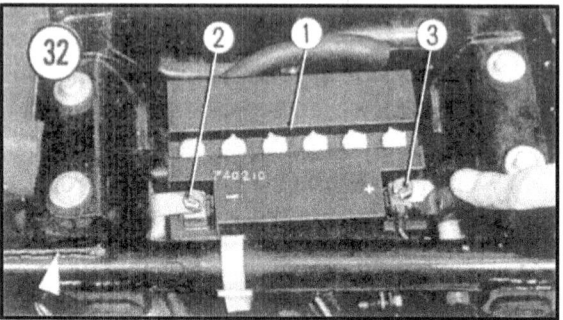

① Battery ② ⊖ terminal ③ ⊕ terminal

3. Lift the battery from the compartment. Be careful not to spill any of the corrosive acid electrolyte.

Inspection

1. Clean the terminals and clamps with a wire

IGNITION AND CHARGING SYSTEMS

brush on a baking soda and water solution. Corrosion causes current leaks.

2. Check the electrolyte level. It should be between the upper and lower marks shown in **Figure 33**. Top up the low cells only with distilled water.

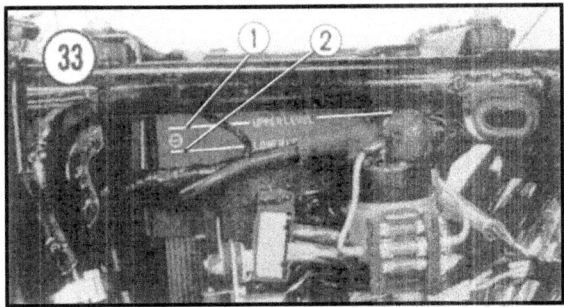

① Upper level mark   ② Lower level mark

3. Measure the specific gravity of the electrolyte with a hydrometer, reading it as shown in **Figure 34**. Generally, the specific gravity should be between 1.26 and 1.28. If the value is less than 1.189 at 20 degrees Centigrade (68°F), the battery is in poor condition and should be charged.

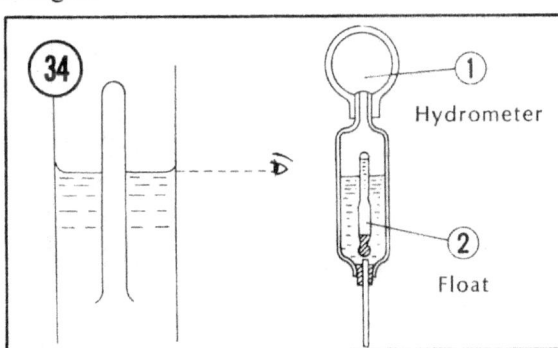

4. Specific gravity varies with the temperature. The chart in **Figure 35** should be used to correct hydrometer readings according to temperature conditions.

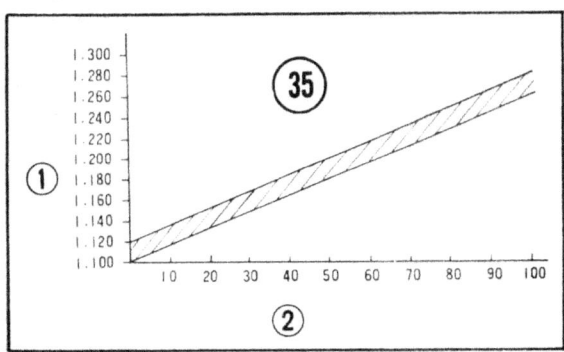

① Specific gravity (20°C)   ② Residual capacity (%)

Battery Charging

A "trickle" charger is recommended for restoring a low voltage battery. Most inexpensive automotive chargers have an output ranging from 2 to 6 amps.

So-called "quick" chargers should not be used on a fully discharged battery, and not used frequently to charge a low voltage battery because of the danger of overheating.

1. Connect the positive charger lead to the positive battery terminal, and the negative lead to the corresponding terminal. Remember, "positive to positive, negative to negative" or damage will result.

2. The electrolyte will begin bubbling, and highly explosive hydrogen gas will be released from the battery as it charges. Make sure the area is vented, and extinguish open flames.

3. Test with a hydrometer to see if the specific gravity is within the standard range of 1.26 to 1.28. If the reading is standard over an hour's time, the battery is charged.

4. If the charger is adjustable for current output, the chart in **Figure 36** shows the relationship between current and charging time.

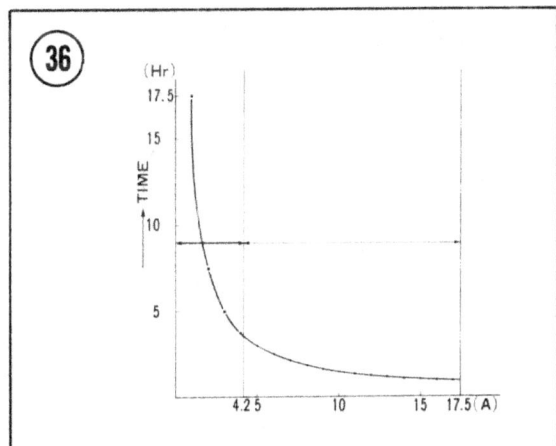

Reassembly

1. Make sure the battery terminals, cable clamps, and case are free of corrosion. Silicon spray can be applied to the terminals to retard decomposition of the lead.

2. Install the battery in reverse order of removal, being careful to route the vent tube so that it is not crimped. Connect the positive terminal first, then the negative one. Do not overtighten the clamps.

CHAPTER SIX

STARTER

STARTING MOTOR

The layout of the electric starting system is shown in **Figure 1.** When the starter button is pressed, it engages the magnetic switch that closes the circuit. About 120 amperes flow from the battery to operate the starting motor.

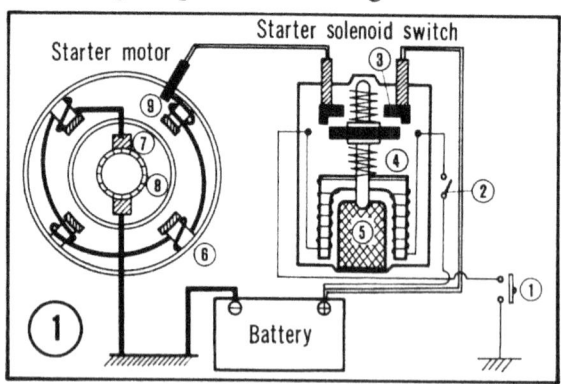

① Starter button switch
② Ignition switch
③ Contact unit
④ Excitation coil
⑤ Plunger
⑥ Pole
⑦ Brush
⑧ Armature
⑨ Field coil

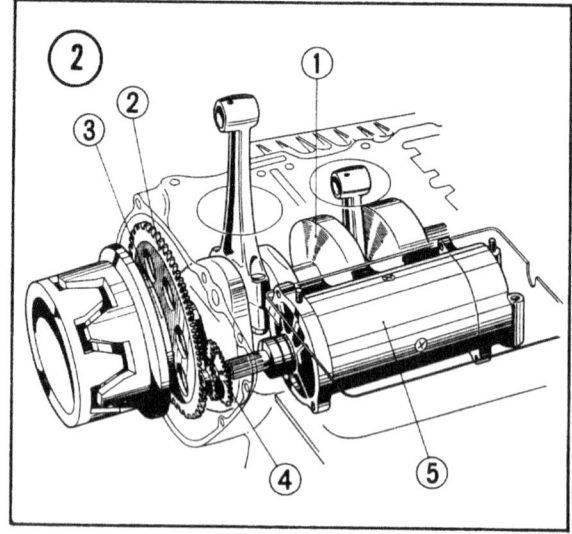

① Crankshaft
② Starting clutch gear
③ Starting clutch
④ Starting motor reduction gear
⑤ Starting motor

The kickstarter is covered in the engine section of this handbook. This chapter outlines servicing of the starter motor, its clutch, and the magnetic switch.

The motor turns between **11,000 and 22,000** rpm. A reduction gear and the clutch decrease this speed to a usable range. See **Figure 2.**

Disassembly

1. Take off the left side cover and disconnect the power cable, **Figure 3**, from the magnetic switch (solenoid).

2. Referring to **Figure 4**, remove the side cover and then detach the motor unit by unscrewing the set bolts. Remove the side cover from the motor.

STARTER

① Magnetic switch
② Starting motor cable

① Starting motor ② Motor setting bolts

3. Locate the brushes, **Figure 5**, and remove them from the holders by loosening the mounting screws.

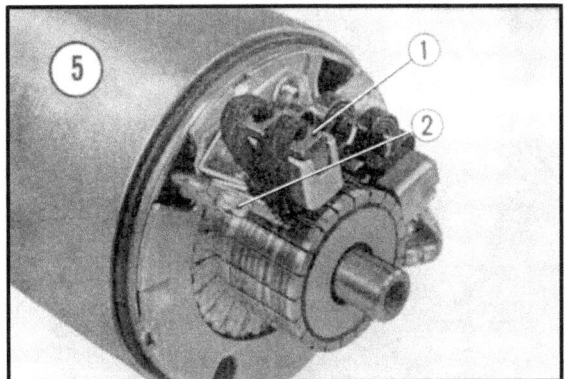

① Brush ② Brush mounting screw

Inspection and Adjustment

The overhaul of a starting motor is best left to an expert. This section shows how to determine if the unit is out of spec.

1. Use a vernier caliper, **Figure 6**, to measure the length of the brush. If it is worn beyond 5.5mm (.217 in), it should be replaced.

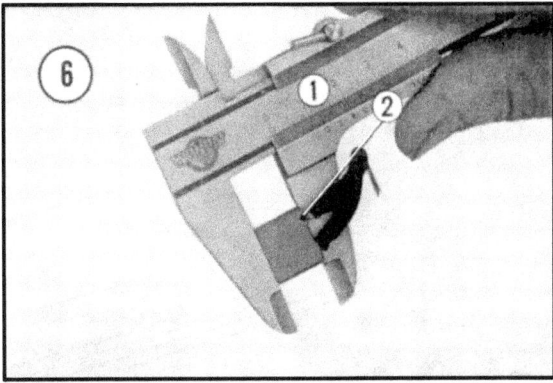

① Vernier caliper ② Carbon brush

2. Refer to **Figure 7** and measure the amount of mica undercut (the depth of the grooves). If the cut is less than .3mm (.012 in), the commutator should be repaired.

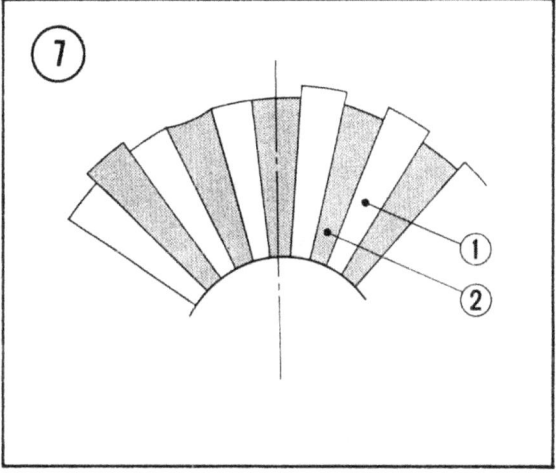

① Commutator
② Mica

3. Check the electrical continuity between the armature and the shaft mounting. If there is a short, the armature should be replaced.

4. Measure the amount of current drawn by the motor with a bench tester, using the external shunt setting. Without a load, the starting motor should draw a maximum of 35 amperes.

Reassembly

Refer to the exploded view of the starter, **Figure 8**, and reassemble in the reverse order of disassembly.

STARTING CLUTCH

Figure 9 shows major components involved in the operation of the clutch. The starting motor

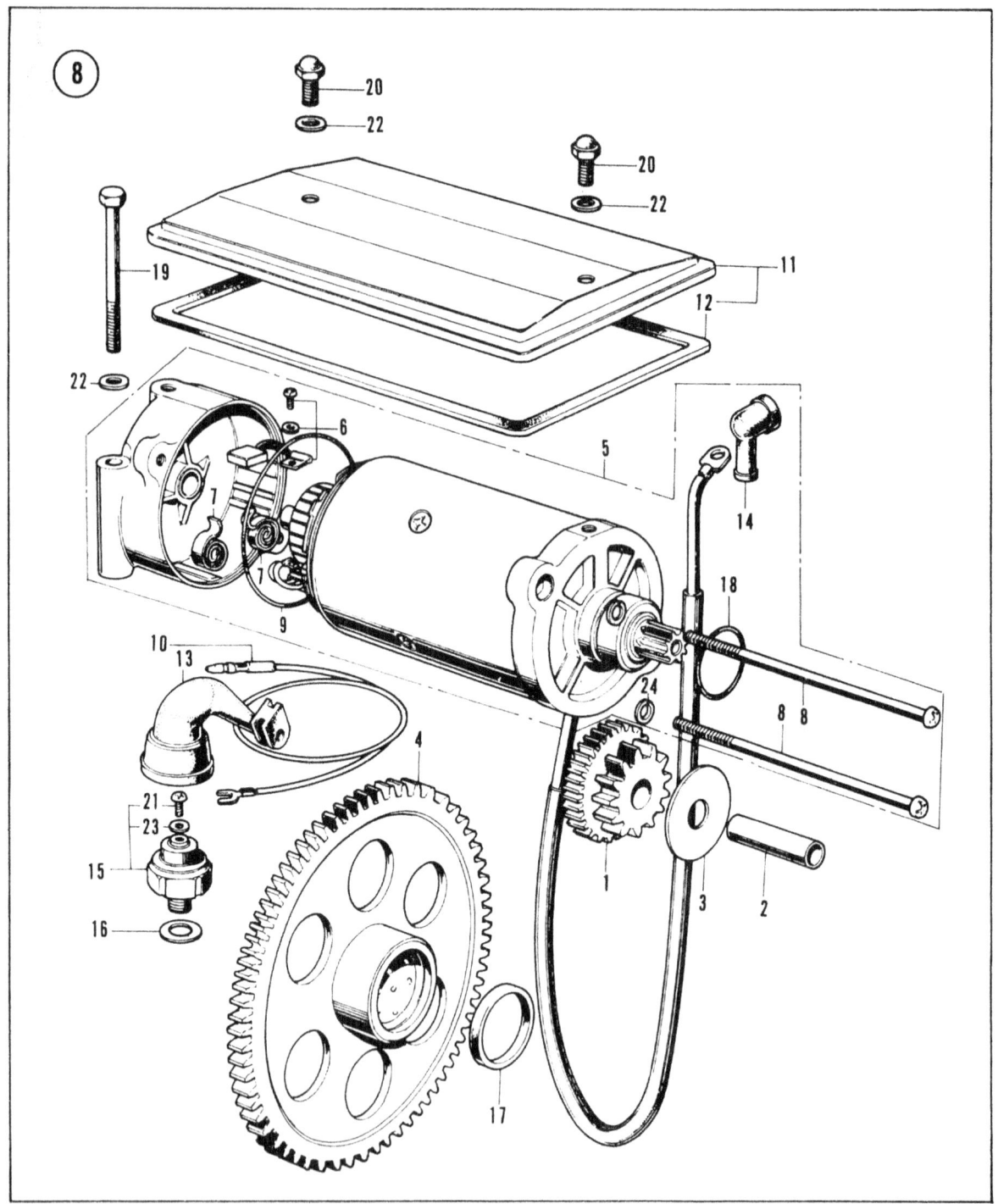

STARTING MOTOR

1. Starting motor reduction gear
2. Starter reduction gear shaft
3. Starting gear setting plate
4. Starting clutch gear components
5. Starting motor assembly
6. Carbon brush set
7. Carbon brush spring
8. Gear cover setting bolt
9. O-ring
10. Oil pressure switch cord assembly
11. Starting motor cover components
12. Starting motor cover gasket
13. Oil pressure switch cord grommet
14. Starting motor terminal cover
15. Oil pressure switch assembly
16. Oil bolt washer
17. Oil seal
18. O-ring
19. Hex bolt
20. Hex bolt
21. Pan screw
22. Plain washer
23. Spring washer
24. Spring washer

STARTER

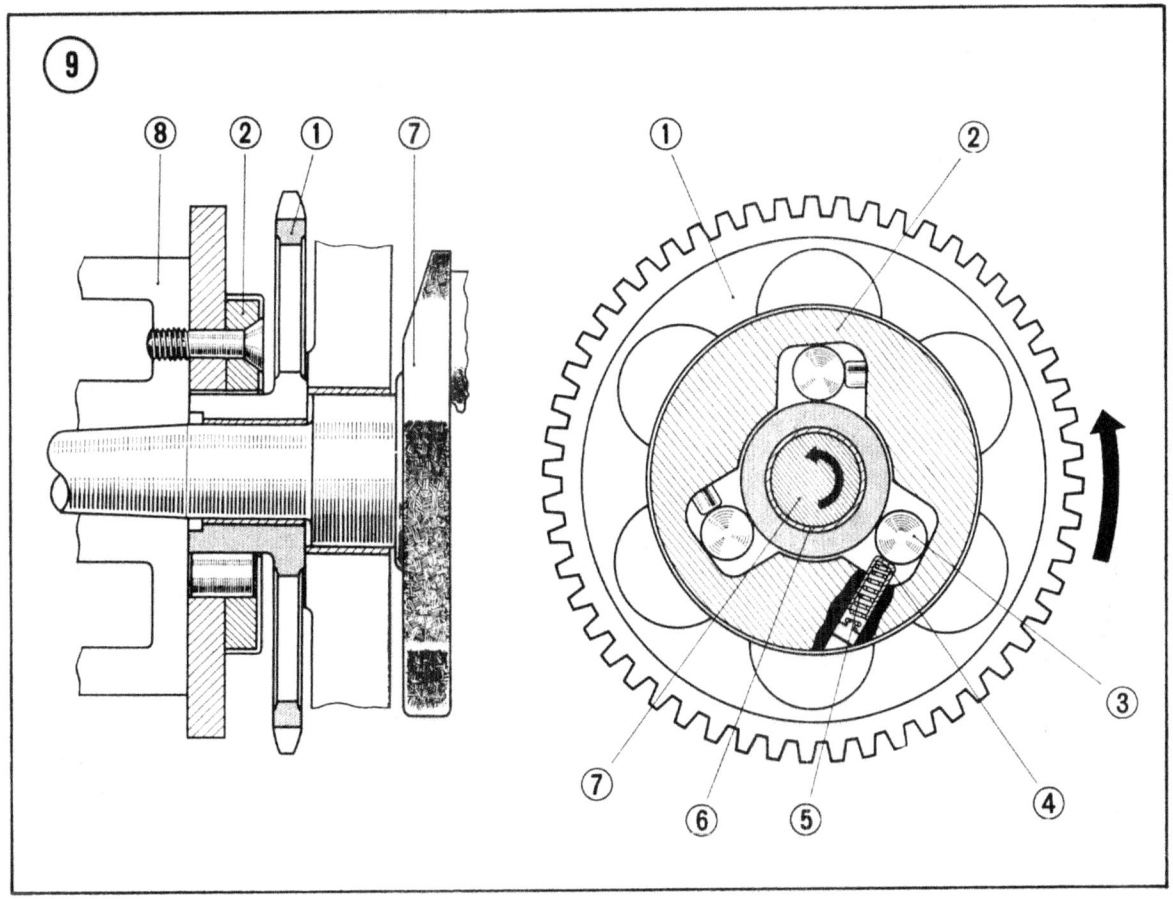

① Starting clutch gear
② Starting clutch
③ 15 mm × 13 roller
④ Roller spring cap
⑤ Roller spring
⑥ Bush
⑦ Crankshaft
⑧ AC generator rotor

rotates the clutch gear, and the rollers shift to the narrow portion of the slot against the spring. This action forces the clutch to engage. When the engine fires and crankshaft speed overtakes the speed of the clutch gear, centrifugal force moves the rollers to the wide section, and the springs disengage the starting clutch.

Disassembly

Gaining access to the starting clutch is a major operation involving removal of the cylinder head, cam chain tensioner, and generator. This operation is outlined in the crankshaft and connecting rod section of the Clutch and Transmission Chapter.

Inspection

Check the clutch roller to ensure it operates freely, and inspect the clutch for damage or wear.

Reassembly

Refer to the clutch and transmission section for reassembly steps.

MAGNETIC SWITCH

A solenoid switch is used to supply the heavy current for operating the starting motor. When the push button starting switch is pressed, the solenoid coil, **Figure 10**, is energized and becomes an electromagnet that draws the iron core to it. The circuit is completed when the contacts meet. A return spring pulls the iron core back to break the circuit when the push switch is released.

Disassembly

1. Remove the left side cover and disconnect the lead from the starting motor, **Figure 11**. Then remove the cover.

STARTER

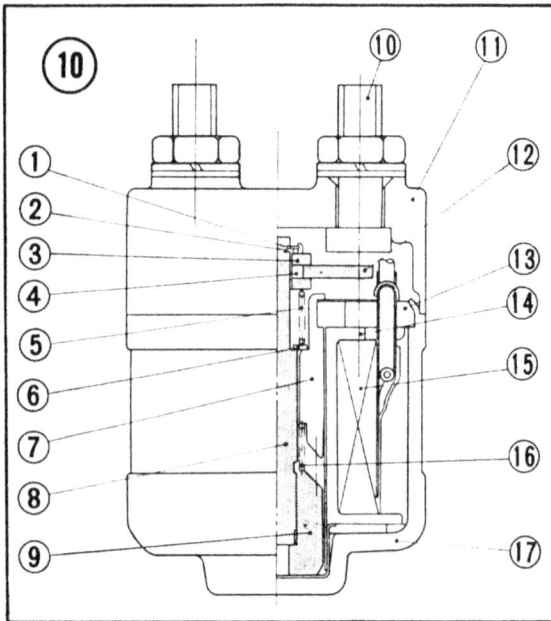

① Stopper
② Stopper holder
③ Insulation washer
④ Insulation collar A
⑤ Contact spring
⑥ Flat washer
⑦ Plunger holder
⑧ Plunger shaft
⑨ Plunger
⑩ Contact bolt
⑪ Case
⑫ Contact plate
⑬ Yoke
⑭ Coil bobbin
⑮ Coil complete
⑯ Return spring
⑰ Body

① Magnetic switch
② Starting motor cable

Inspection and Adjustment

1. Depress the starter switch and listen for the click of the iron core contacting the coil.

2. Check the condition of the contact points and dress with a point file if they are pitted or burned.

Reassembly

Reassemble in the reverse order of disassembly.

CHAPTER SEVEN

FRONT SUSPENSION AND STEERING

FRONT FORK

Changing Oil

The oil in the front fork should be changed every 10,000 kilometers (6,000 miles) to maintain good handling, and prolong the life of the damping mechanism. The following steps apply to all Honda 750's.

1. Drain the oil from the fork by removing the plug, **Figure 1**, at the bottom. Pump the unit up and down to force the oil out.

① Front fork drain plug

2. Replace the drain plug and remove the filler plug at the top, **Figure 2**.

3. Fill with a good quality, SAE 10W-30 weight oil. The fork holds 220cc to 230cc (7 oz to 7.3 oz) of oil. Replace the filler plug.

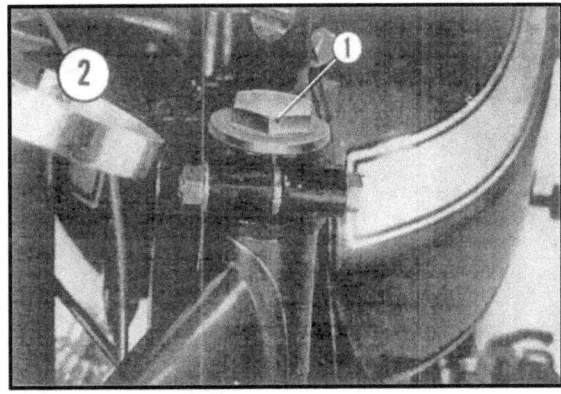

① Top filler plug

4. Lock the front brake and pump the fork up and down. Check for smooth action and for seepage around the seals.

Disassembly

Refer to the line drawing, **Figure 3**, for details of the telescoping, oil-damped front fork suspension.

1. Remove the front wheel according to the instructions in the wheel section. Drain the oil from the forks.

2. Refer to **Figure 4** and remove the three caliper set bolts and the adjuster nut. Then separate the caliper from the left fork.

3. Loosen the fork pipe mounting bolts on the top bridge, and the mounting bolts on the steer-

FRONT SUSPENSION AND STEERING

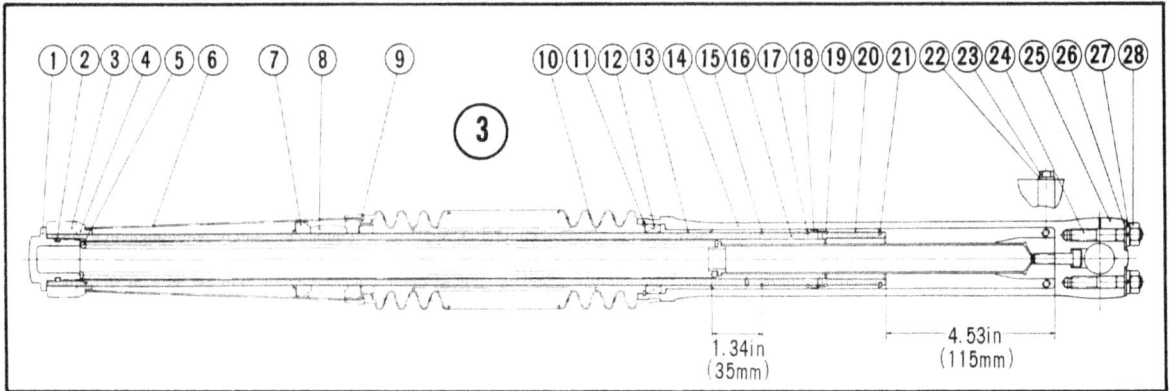

1. Front fork bolt
2. 23 × 2.8 "O" ring
3. Fork top bridge
4. Fork cover upper cushion
5. Front cushion spring
6. Front fork cover
7. Fork cover lower cushion
8. Steering stem
9. Front fork rib
10. Front fork boot
11. 47 mm circlip
12. 354611 oil seal
13. Front fork pipe guide
14. Front fork bottom case
15. Fork pipe stopper ring
16. Front fork pipe
17. Fork valve stopper ring
18. Front damper valve
19. Piston stopper ring
20. Front fork piston
21. Fork piston snap ring
22. Drain cock packing
23. 6 mm hex bolt
24. 8 mm stud bolt
25. Front axle holder
26. 8 mm flat washer
27. 8 mm spring washer
28. 8 mm hex nut

1. Caliper setting bolts
2. Caliper assembly
3. Adjuster nut

ing stem. Then gently pull the fork down and out, as in **Figure 5**.

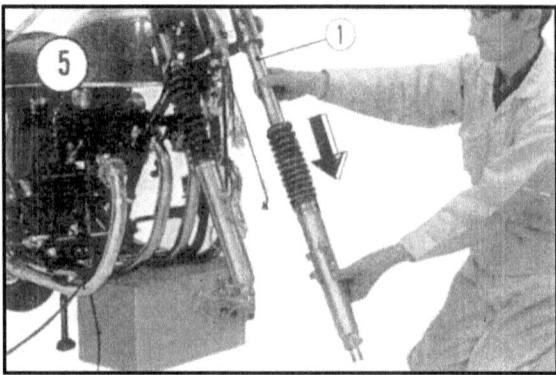

1. Front fork

4. Remove the internal clip, **Figure 6**, with circlip pliers and remove the pipe from the bottom case.

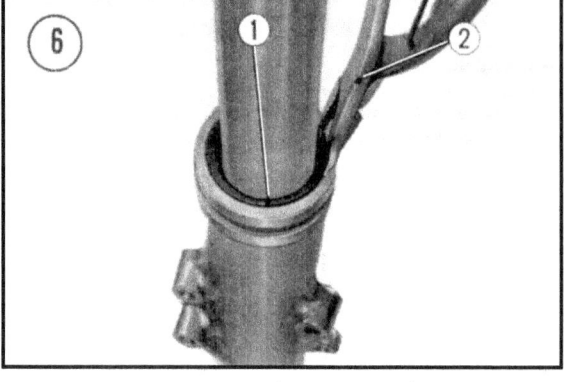

1. Internal circlip
2. Pliers

5. Refer to **Figure 7** and remove the snap ring and disassemble the piston and the damper valve.

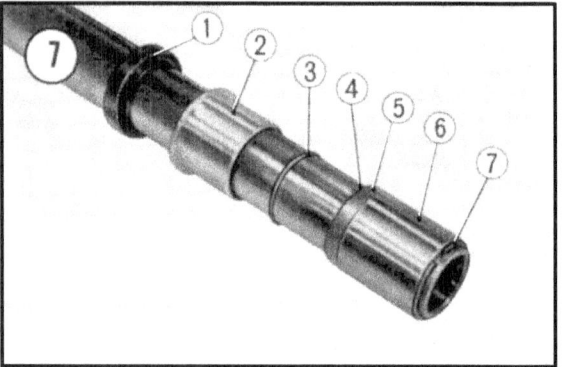

1. 354611 oil seal
2. Front fork pipe guide
3. Fork pipe stopper ring
4. Fork valve stopper ring
5. Front damper valve
6. Front fork piston
7. Fork piston snap ring

FRONT SUSPENSION AND STEERING

Inspection

1. Measure the piston diameter, **Figure 8**, with a micrometer. If its diameter is less than 39.4mm (1.551 in) the piston should be replaced.

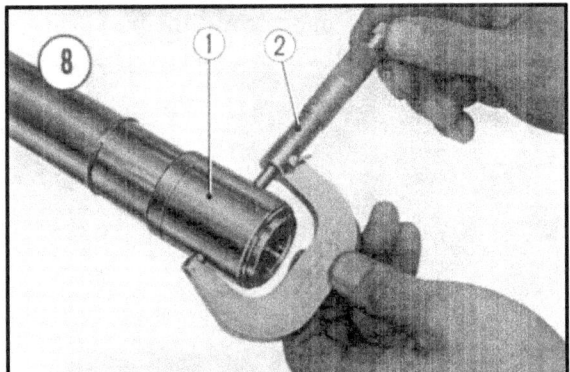

① Front fork piston
② Micrometer

2. Measure the inside diameter of the bottom case with a cylinder gauge, **Figure 9**. If the diameter is greater than 39.68mm (1.562 in), replace the case.

Reassembly

1. Clean all parts. Refer again to Figure 7, and assemble the parts in this order: pipe guide, stopper rings, damper valve, piston, and snap ring.

2. Insert the fork pipe into the bottom case, and install the oil seal. **Figure 10** shows the special tools needed for the operation: the driving guide (Honda tool No. 07054-30001) and the driving weight (Honda tool No. 07057-29201). Be careful not to damage the seal.

> NOTE: *In CB 750 K1 models, the outside diameter of the oil seal is 2mm (.08 in) greater than in earlier models, and the circlip diameter is 3mm greater. This was to correct the deformation of the seal and consequent oil leakage which occurred in some 750's.*

3. Refer again to Figure 6 and install the circlip.

4. Install the upper cover on the steering stem, above and below the cushion, and insert the fork pipe through the stem. Temporarily tighten with the 10mm set bolt.

5. Fill the fork with oil, as described in the oil change section of this chapter.

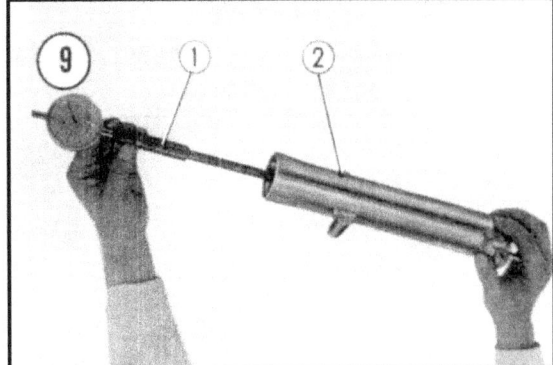

① Cylinder gauge ② Bottom case

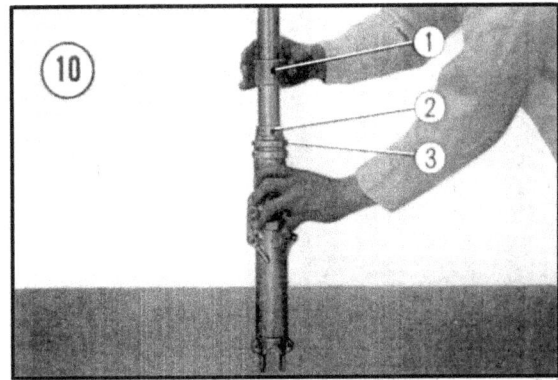

① Oil seal driving weight ③ Oil seal
② Oil seal driving guide

6. Tighten the 8mm and 10mm set bolts, referring to **Figure 11**.

7. Adjust the front brake according to the instructions in the brake section.

① Front fork assembling bar
② Front fork pipe setting bolt (8 mm)
③ Front fork pipe setting bolt (10 mm)

STEERING

Refer to the line drawing, **Figure 12**, for details of the steering assembly.

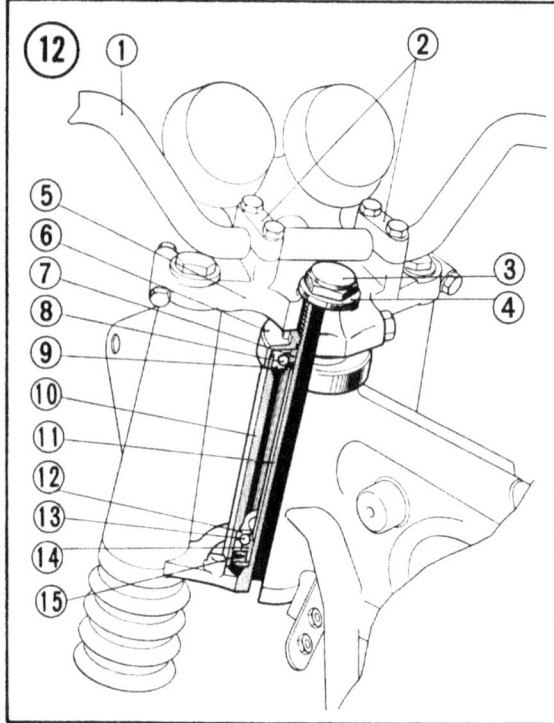

1. Handlebar
2. Handlebar clamps
3. Steering stem nut
4. Steering stem washer
5. Fork top bridge
6. Steering head top thread
7. Steering top cone race
8. Ball bearing
9. Steering top bearing race
10. Steering head
11. Steering stem
12. Stering bottom bearing race
13. Ball bearing
14. Steering bottom cone race
15. Steering head dust seal

Disassembly

1. Refer to **Figure 13** and remove the master brake cylinder unit by unscrewing the two mounting bolts. Disconnect the clutch cable at the lever.

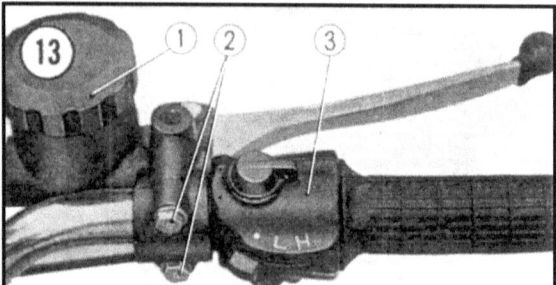

① Master cylinder body
② Cylinder body mounting bolts
③ Starter lighting ignition switch

2. Remove the ignition switch and disconnect the throttle cable at the grip.

3. Remove the headlight assembly from its case, and disconnect the wiring at the connectors.

4. Refer to **Figure 14**, and unscrew the two handlebar holders, and remove the bars.

① Upper handle holders
② Handle bar

5. Loosen the clamp that secures the speedometer and tachometer, and remove the instruments from the top bridge of the fork.

6. Refer to **Figure 15** and remove the top bridge by loosening the stem nut, two top bolts, and the three 8mm set bolts.

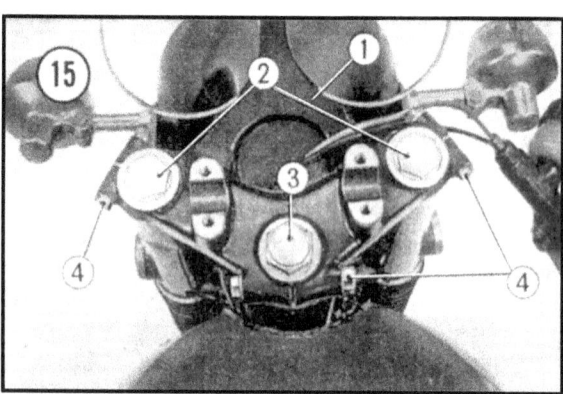

① Fork top bridge   ③ Stem nut
② Front fork top bolts   ④ 8mm setting bolts

7. Put a block under the front of the engine so that the front wheel is clear of the ground. Remove the front suspension as described earlier in the chapter.

8. Remove the steering stem thread. **Figure 16** shows a spanner wrench that will make the job easier. It is Honda tool No. 07072-20001.

9. Pull out the steering stem, being careful not to drop the ball bearings.

FRONT SUSPENSION AND STEERING

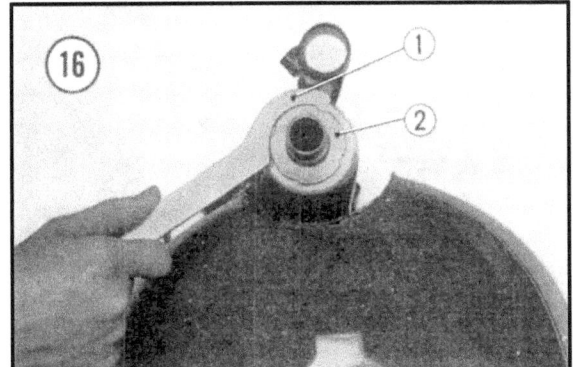

① Steering stem thread wrench
② Steering stem thread

Inspection

1. Check the handlebars for damage or bends.
2. Inspect the steering stem for distortion or cracks.
3. Check the bearings for wear.

Reassembly

1. Liberally grease the steering bearing races. Assemble the bearing, inserting 18 balls on the upper side, and 19 on the lower side. Refer to **Figure 17**.

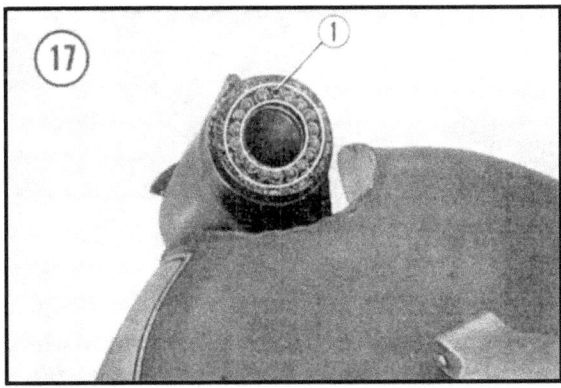

① Steel balls

2. Insert the stem into the head pipe, being careful not to lose any bearing balls.
3. Refer to **Figure 18**, and screw the thread down on the stem, so there is no clearance, and the assembly turns lightly through the entire arc.
4. Assemble the front suspension.
5. Install the speedometer and the tachometer.

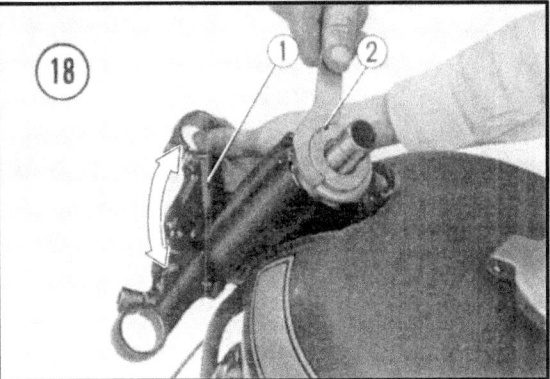

① Steering stem   ② Steering stem thread

6. Mount the handlebar and position it by aligning the punch marks on the bar with those on the holders, **Figure 19**.

① Punch marks

7. Connect the headlight wiring and install the light assembly.
8. Connect the throttle cable, clutch cable, and master cylinder, routing the hoses and wires as shown in **Figure 20**.

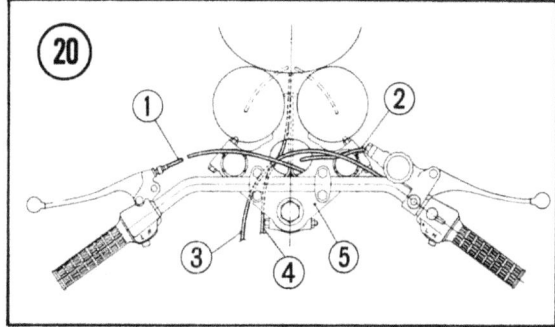

① Clutch cable   ④ Wire harness
② Front brake hose   ⑤ Fork top bridge
③ Throttle cable

CHAPTER EIGHT

REAR SUSPENSION

The rear suspension consists of a swing fork and De Carbon type shock absorbers containing compressed nitrogen. The adjustable shocks may be set for three spring ranges depending on operating conditions.

REAR SHOCKS

The rear shocks contain nitrogen gas under pressure and are sealed at the factory. They do not require routine servicing, and disassembly could be dangerous because of the compressed gas. **Figure 1** is an exploded view.

Disassembly

1. Refer to **Figure 2** and remove the cap nut and the bolt. Pull the unit from the frame.

① Rear cushion ② Cap nut ③ Setting bolt

2. Remove the spring with special Honda tool No. 07035-30001, shown in **Figure 3**.

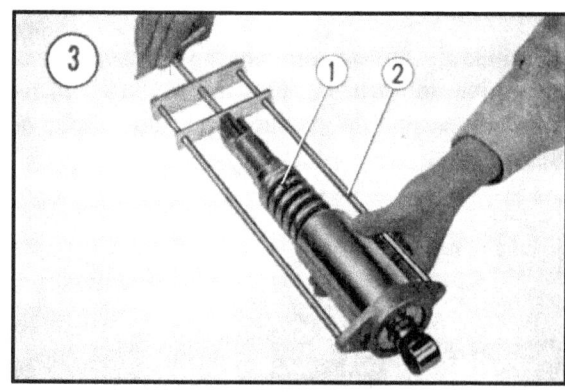

① Rear cushion spring
② Rear cushion disassembling tool

Inspection

1. Measure the free length of the spring with a vernier caliper, as in **Figure 4**. If the length is less than 460mm (18.11 in), replace the spring.

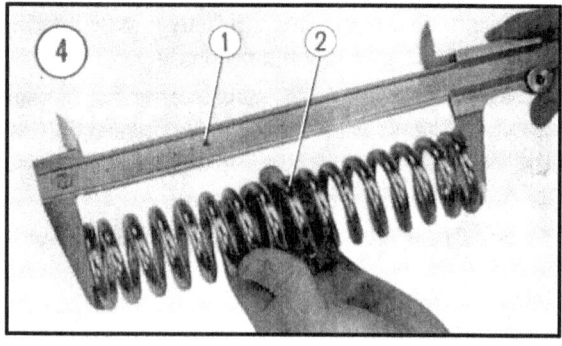

① Vernier caliper ② Rear cushion spring

REAR SUSPENSION

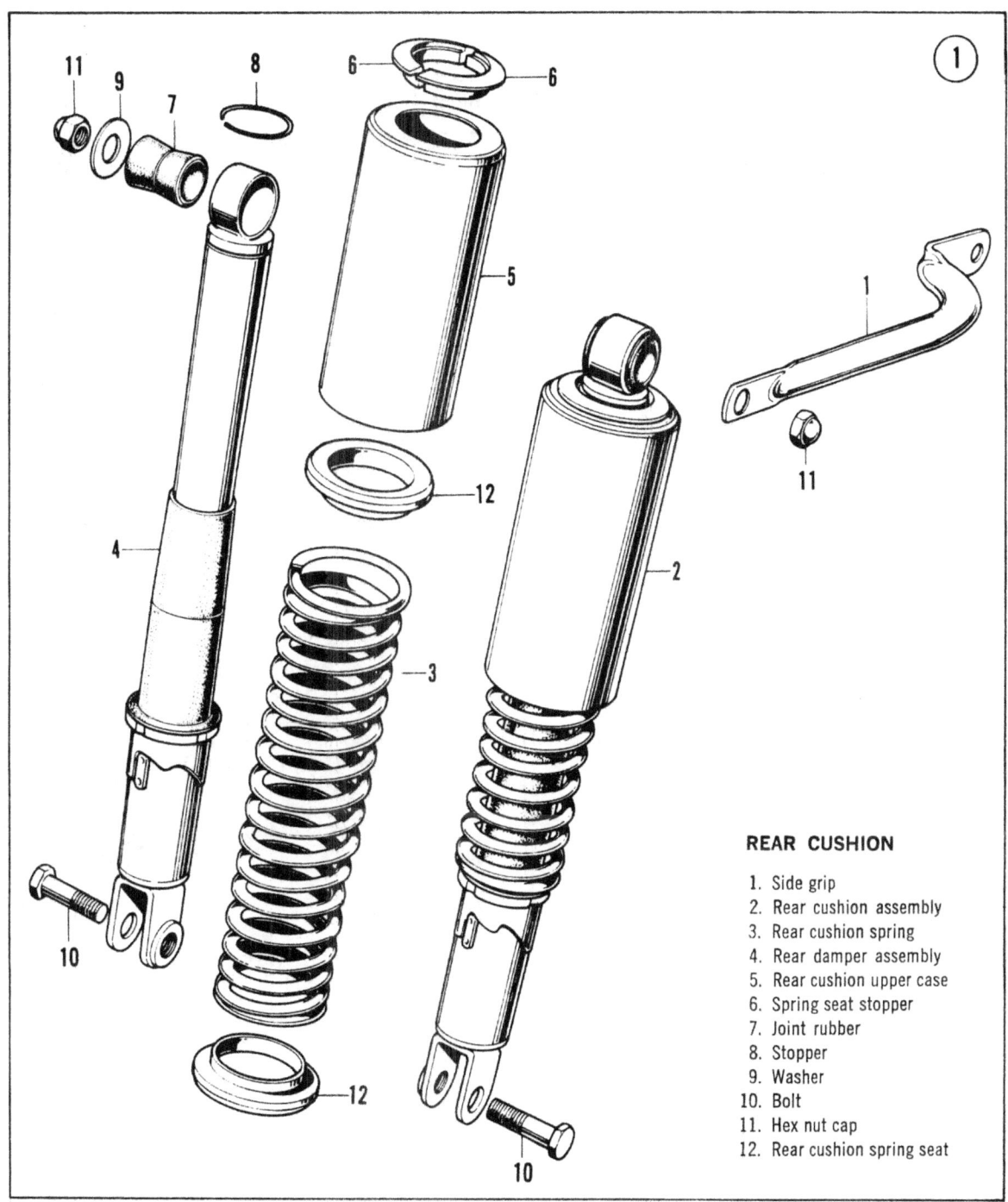

REAR CUSHION

1. Side grip
2. Rear cushion assembly
3. Rear cushion spring
4. Rear damper assembly
5. Rear cushion upper case
6. Spring seat stopper
7. Joint rubber
8. Stopper
9. Washer
10. Bolt
11. Hex nut cap
12. Rear cushion spring seat

2. Check the trueness of the spring by placing it on end on a flat surface and using a vernier caliper and a square to calculate the amount of tilt. If the tilt is more than 2.5 degrees, the assembly should be replaced.

3. Compress the unit by hand. There should be more resistance on the compression stroke than on the extension stroke.

4. Refer to **Figure 5** and inspect the damper for leakage, and check the case, rod, and stopper for damage or deformity.

Reassembly

On 750 K1 models, the dimensions of the stopper and the spring were changed from those on the earlier 750. The parts are not interchangeable between models.

1. Assemble the unit, Figure 5, using the special

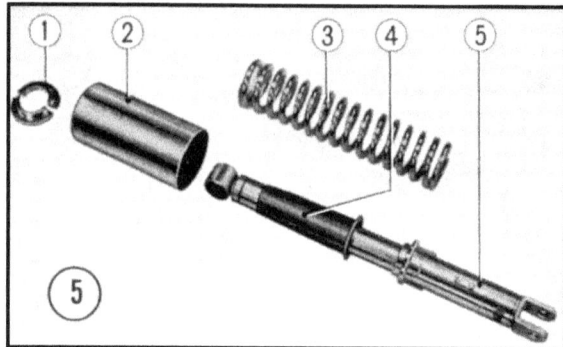

① Spring seat stopper
② Rear cushion upper case ③ Rear cushion spring
④ Rear cushion spring guide ⑤ Rear damper unit

tool to compress the spring and lock it in place with the stopper. Compress the unit by hand to make sure the parts are not binding.

2. Mount the shock on the frame with the cap nut and bolt, **Figure 6**.

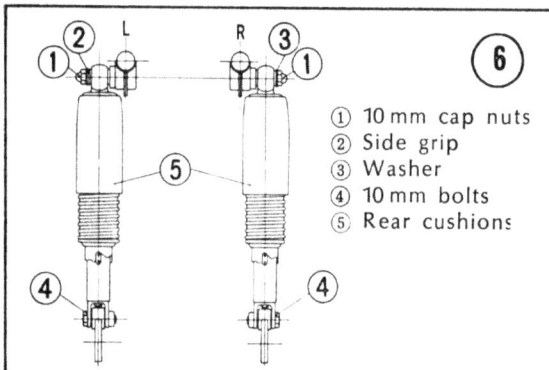

① 10 mm cap nuts
② Side grip
③ Washer
④ 10 mm bolts
⑤ Rear cushions

3. Check the alignment of the two cushions and the mounting bolts.

REAR FORK

The rear fork pivots the wheel in an arc on bounce and rebound of the suspension. The pivot point is close to the drive sprocket, however, so the action does not significantly affect chain tension. **Figure 7** shows the fork and its associated parts.

Disassembly

1. Remove the mufflers according to the steps in the frame section.

2. Remove the cotter pin from the axle, loosen the nut, and remove the drive chain.

3. Unscrew the adjuster nut for the rear brake, the torque bolt, and remove the axle and wheel. This operation is covered in more detail in the section on wheels and drive chain.

4. Refer to **Figure 8** and remove the fork pivot nut and bolt and remove the fork from the frame. Also remove the side washer and the pivot collar.

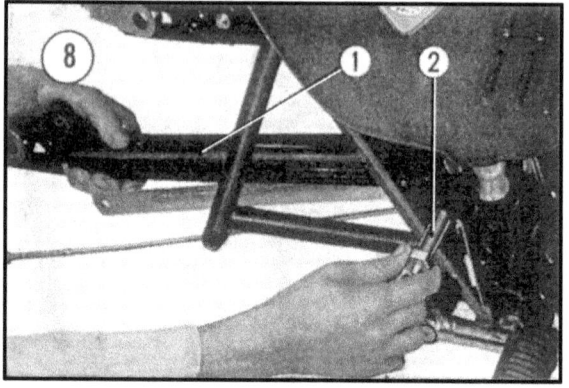

① Rear fork   ② Rear fork pivot bolt

Inspection

1. Check the fork for distortion or bends, and replace the unit if damage is excessive.

2. Measure the bores of the pivot bushing using a dial gauge, **Figure 9**. The serviceable inner diameter limit is 21.8mm (.858 in).

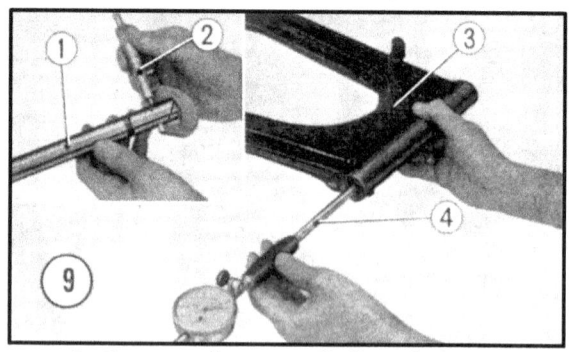

① Center collar   ③ Rear fork
② Micrometer   ④ Inner dial gauge

3. Measure the outside diameter of the center collar with a micrometer as shown in the illustration. The outside diameter serviceable limit is 21.4mm (.8452 in).

Reassembly

1. Grease the pivot collar liberally and insert it into the fork. Insert the pivot bolt from the right side. While holding the dust caps in place, tighten the nut.

2. Install the rear wheel and drive chain.

3. Adjust the rear brake pedal and drive chain tension. Instructions are in the appropriate sections.

REAR SUSPENSION

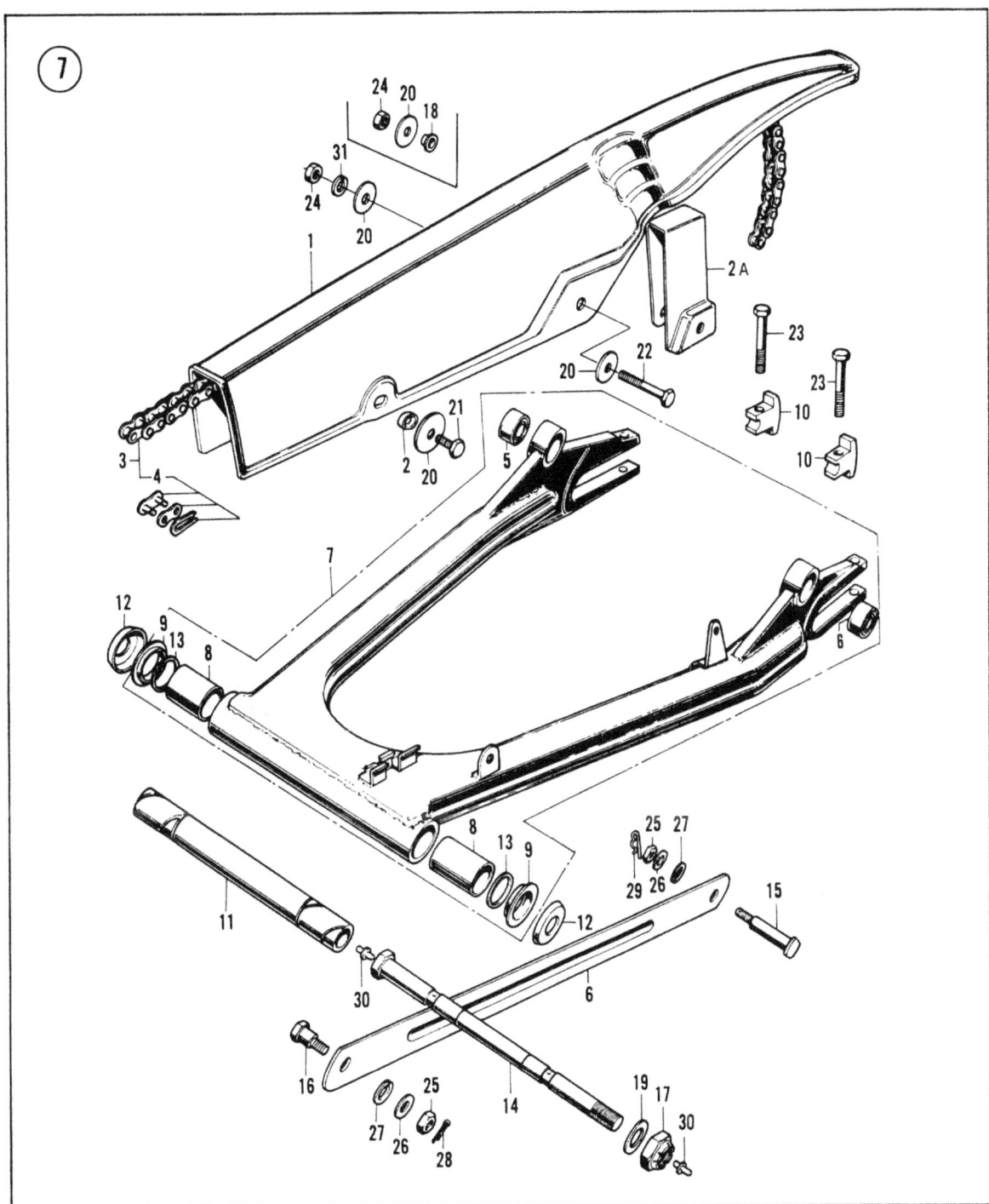

REAR FORK – CHAIN CASE

1. Drive chain case
2. Chain case collar
2A. Chain case plate
3. Drive chain
4. Joint drive chain
5. Rear cushion under rubber bushing
6. Rear brake stopper arm
7. Rear fork components
8. Rear fork pivot bushing
9. Rear fork pivot thrust bushing
10. Chain adjuster stopper
11. Rear fork center collar
12. Rear fork dust seal cap
13. Rear fork felt ring
14. Fork pivot bolt
15. Rear brake panel stopper bolt
16. Rear brake stopper arm bolt
17. Self lock nut
18. Washer
19. Rear fork pivot bolt washer
20. Washer
21. Hex bolt
22. Hex bolt
23. Hex bolt
24. Hex nut
25. Hex nut
26. Plain washer
27. Spring washer
28. Cotter pin
29. Lock pin
30. Grease nipple
31. Plain washer

CHAPTER NINE

WHEELS AND FINAL DRIVE

FRONT WHEEL

Refer to **Figure 1** for details of the front wheel assembly.

Disassembly

1. Place a block under the front of the engine so the wheel is raised clear of the ground.

2. Remove the speedometer cable, **Figure 2**, at the hub.

① Speedometer cable

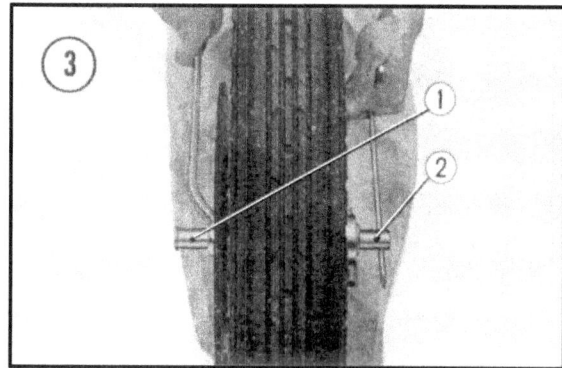

① Front axle nut ② Front axle

3. Loosen the axle holding nuts, and remove the wheel from the fork.

> NOTE: *Do not work the brake lever when the wheel is off the motorcycle, or the caliper piston will be forced out of the cylinder.*

4. Unscrew the axle nut, **Figure 3**, and remove the axle.

5. Remove the gear box for the speedometer.

6. Refer to **Figure 4** and remove the disc from the wheel by unlocking the washers and loosening the nuts.

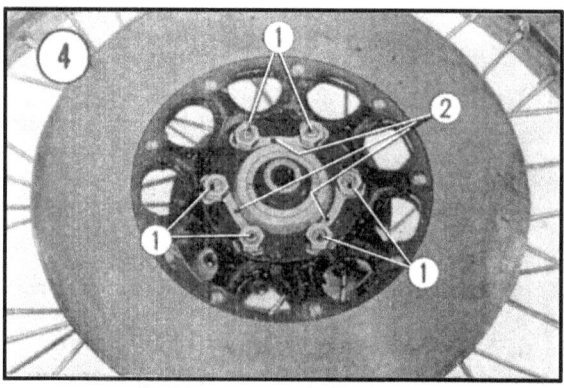

① Disc setting bolts & nuts
② Tongued washers

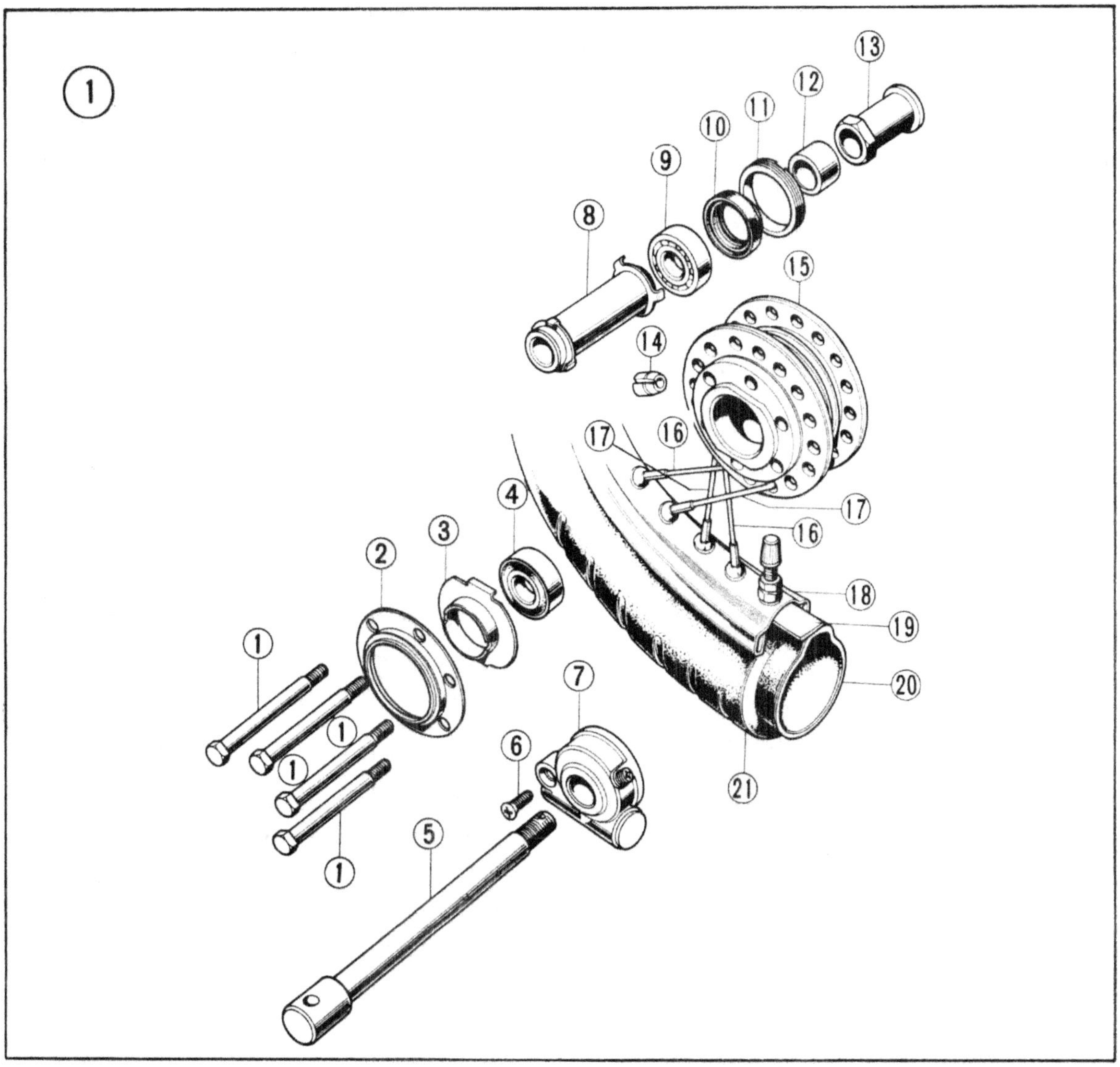

WHEELS AND FINAL DRIVE

① 8 × 10 mm bolt
② Gear box retainer cover
③ Gear box retainer
④ 6302 Z ball bearing
⑤ Front wheel axle
⑥ 5 × 15 mm oval screw
⑦ Speedometer gear box
⑧ Front axle distance collar
⑨ 6302 Z ball bearing
⑩ 22368 dust seal
⑪ Front wheel bearing retainer
⑫ Front wheel collar
⑬ Front wheel axle nut
⑭ Wheel balancer
⑮ Front wheel hub
⑯ Front spoke A
⑰ Front spoke B
⑱ Front wheel rim
⑲ Front tire flap
⑳ Front wheel tube
㉑ Front wheel tire

7. Remove the bearing retainer from the hub, **Figure 5**, and then remove the dust seal from the retainer.

8. Remove the bearing.

Tire Removal

This operation is necessary only if there is a puncture to be repaired or a new tire is to be installed on the wheel.

1. Lay the wheel on a soft surface to prevent damage to the hub.

① Front wheel bearing retainer   ② Dust seal

2. Check the tire and remove any sharp object that caused the puncture.

3. Remove the valve core and the valve stem retaining nut.

4. Break the bead free of the rim by stepping on it on both sides.

5. Insert two small tire irons four to six inches apart between the rim and the tire bead at the valve location.

6. Pry in and down with the irons, at the same time depressing the bead on the far side with the foot.

7. Work around the tire, moving only one iron at a time, until the bead is free of the rim all the way around.

8. Pull the inner tube out of the tire casing.

Inspection

1. Measure the flatness of the brake disc with a dial gauge as shown in **Figure 6**. The disc should be placed on a flat surface for this check. If the flatness varies by more than .3mm (.012 in), the disc should be replaced. If the thickness is less than 5.5mm (.217 in), the disc also should be replaced.

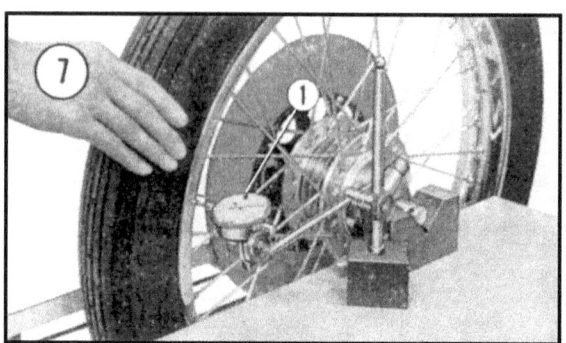

① Dial gauge

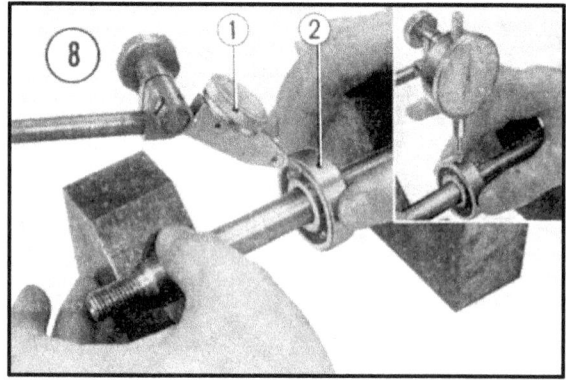

① Dial gauge   ② Ball bearing

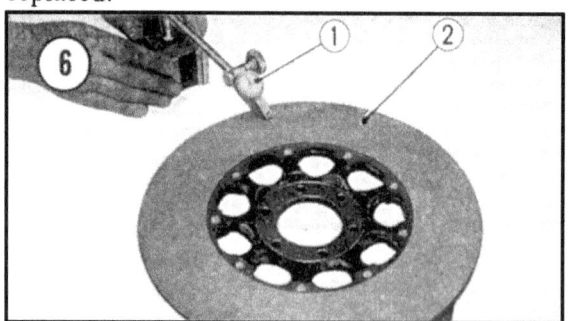

① Dial gauge   ② Front brake disc

2. Measure the runout of the wheel rim using a dial gauge. Mount the wheel on a horizontal shaft so it can turn freely, and measure according to **Figure 7**. Repair or replace the rim if the runout is more than 2mm (.080 in).

3. Refer to **Figure 8** and measure the axial and diametrical runout of the bearing with a dial gauge. Replace the unit if the axial runout is more than .1mm (.004 in) or if the diametrical value is more than .05mm (.002 in).

Tire Installation

1. Inflate the new inner tube slightly, leaving the valve core in place.

2. Make sure the inner strip that protects the tube is in good condition, and is centered over the spoke nipples.

3. Insert the tube into the tire casing with the valve stem aligned with the tire balance mark and with the hole in the rim.

4. Insert the valve stem through the hole in the rim, and partially tighten the retaining nut. Then remove the valve core.

5. Coat the bead surfaces and the edge of the rim with mounting solution. Liquid detergent can be used.

6. Push the tire into place with the feet. Start on the far side of the rim from the valve, and work in opposite directions around the wheel with the heels.

7. Force the last bit of bead into place with a soft-headed mallet. Do not use tire irons or screwdrivers that might damage the tube.

8. Insert the valve core, and overinflate the tire by 10 psi to seat the beads. Then deflate to the standard pressure and check for leaks.

Wheel Reassembly

1. Use a bearing driver to install the bearing into the wheel, **Figure 9**.

WHEELS AND FINAL DRIVE

① Bearing driver

2. Install the dust seal on the bearing retainer, and mount it into the hub.

3. Align the gear box retainer, **Figure 10**, to the cutout in the hub, and install it from above.

① Gear box retainer

4. Install the six disc mounting bolts, see note, then mount the disc on the opposite side and install the nuts.

> NOTE: *On CB 750 K1 models, the hub is 4mm (.157 in) thinner, and the mounting bolts were shortened by the same amount. Using the older, longer bolts on K1 models will result in the disc loosening during operation.*

When installing the disc, **Figure 11**, use new tongued washers, and bend the tabs so they will lock.

5. Insert the axle through the speedometer gear box, **Figure 12**, from the right side, and tighten the axle nut.

6. Mount the wheel on the forks, install the axle holders, and tighten the nuts.

7. Connect the speedometer cable to the gear box, **Figure 13**.

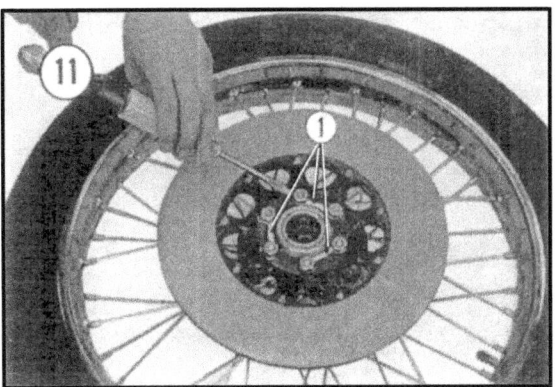

① Tongued washer

① Speedometer gear box
② Gear box retainer

① Speedometer cable   ② Setting screw

WHEEL BALANCING

These instructions cover static balancing. A special machine is required for dynamic balancing.

1. Raise the wheel off the ground and rotate.

2. When the wheel comes to rest, attach a weight to the spoke at the top of the wheel at rest. Weights are available in four sizes: 5 grams, 10 grams, 15 grams, and 20 grams.

3. Experiment with the weights until the wheel,

when spun, does not come to rest at the same position every time.

REAR WHEEL

Refer to **Figure 14** for details of the rear wheel and final drive.

Disassembly

1. Place the motorcycle on the main stand.

2. Remove the rear brake adjusting nut and rod from the drum, **Figure 15**.

① Rear brake arm
② Rear brake adjusting nut

3. Refer to **Figure 16** and remove the brake stopper arm lock pin, the nut, flat washer, spring washer, and bolt.

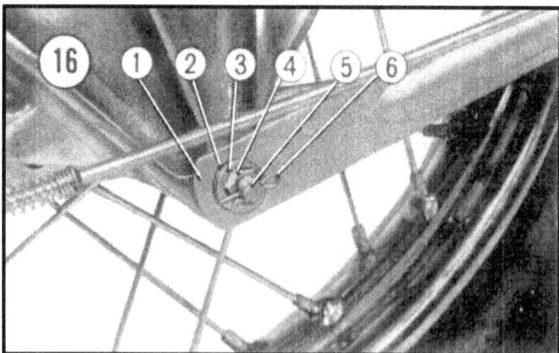

① Rear brake stopper arm
② 10 mm spring washer
③ 8 mm flat washer
④ 8 mm nut
⑤ Rear brake panel stopper bolt
⑥ Lock pin

4. Remove the cotter pin from the right side of the axle, and loosen the nut. See **Figure 17**.

5. Referring to Figure 17, loosen the lock nuts on the drive chain adjusting bolts, and then back out the bolts.

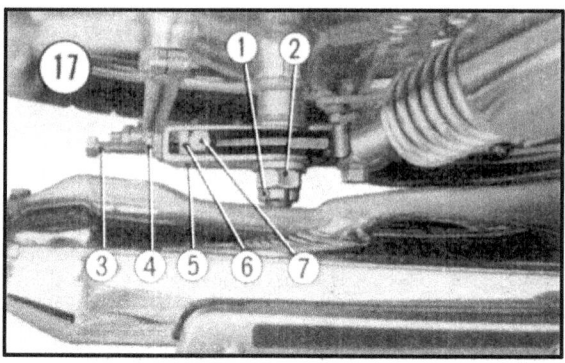

① Cotter pin   ⑤ Chain adjuster
② Rear axle nut   ⑥ Fork cap
③ Drive chain   ⑦ Fork cap fixing
   adjusting bolt   bolt
④ Lock nut

6. Turn down the chain adjusters and remove the fork cap fixing bolts and the caps.

7. Remove the wheel from the frame.

8. Refer to **Figure 18** and unlock the tongued washers, unscrew the nuts, and remove the sprocket.

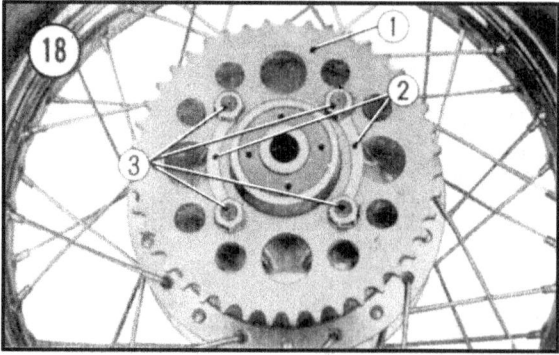

① Final driven sprocket ③ Sprocket setting bolts
② Tongued washers

9. Remove the bearing retainer, **Figure 19**, and the bearing.

> NOTE: *Inspection and disassembly procedures for the rear brakes will be found in Chapter Ten.*

Inspection

1. Measure the axial and diametrical runout of the bearing with a dial gauge. Replace the unit if the axial runout is more than .1mm (.004 in), or if the diametrical runout is more than .05mm (.002 in).

Reassembly

1. Assemble the hub parts in reverse order of disassembly, and mount the wheel on the forks.

WHEELS AND FINAL DRIVE

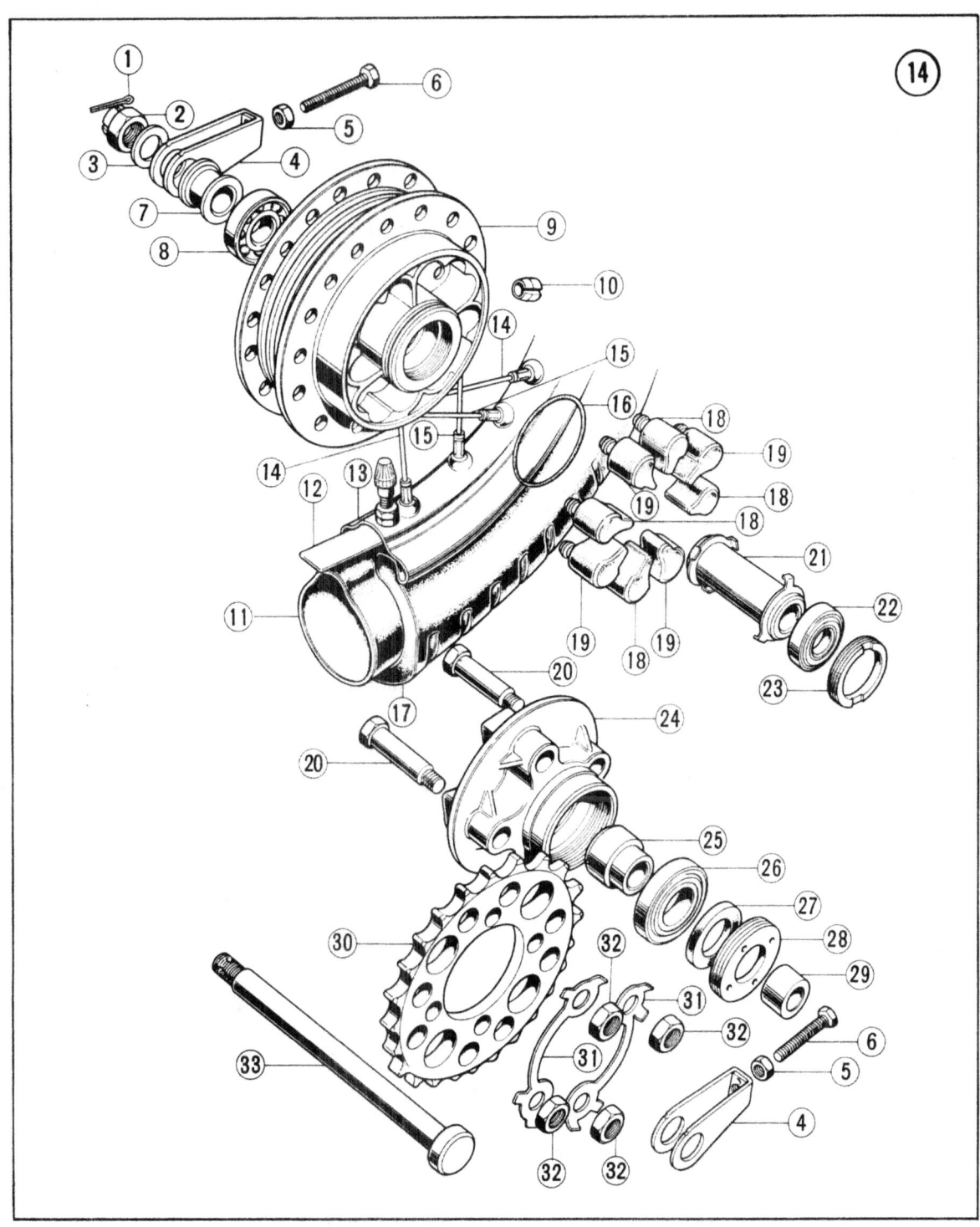

① 4×30 Cotter pin
② Rear axle nut
③ 18.5×34 washer
④ Chain adjuster
⑤ 8 mm hex nut
⑥ Chain adjusting bolt
⑦ Rear brake panel side collar
⑧ 6304 ball bearing
⑨ Rear wheel hub
⑩ Wheel balancer
⑪ Rear wheel tube
⑫ Rear tire flap
⑬ Rear wheel rim
⑭ Rear spoke B
⑮ Rear spoke A
⑯ 68×2.6 "O" ring
⑰ Rear wheel tire
⑱ Left rear wheel damper
⑲ Right rear wheel damper
⑳ Driven sprocket fixing bolt
㉑ Rear axle distance collar
㉒ 6304 ball bearing
㉓ Rear wheel bearing retainer
㉔ Final drive flange
㉕ Rear axle sleeve
㉖ 6305 ball bearing
㉗ 34×56×9 Oil seal
㉘ Rear wheel bearing retainer
㉙ Rear wheel side collar
㉚ Final driven sprocket
㉛ 12mm tongued washer
㉜ 12mm hex nut
㉝ Rear wheel axle

WHEELS AND FINAL DRIVE

① Rear wheel bearing retainer
② 6304 ball bearing

2. Adjust the drive chain tension with the adjustment bolt so there is a slack of 10mm to 20mm (.40 in to .80 in) at the center of the chain. See **Figure 20**. The final drive section of this chapter gives more details on the procedure.

3. Adjust the free play of the brake pedal according to instructions in Chapter Ten.

4. Balance the wheel according to the instructions for the front wheel in this chapter.

FINAL DRIVE

The CB 750 is equipped with one of two types of chains, the continuously staked type and the joint link type. A special tool, Honda tool No. 40531-300750, must be used to cut and join the staked type chain.

Disassembly

1. Remove the rear crankcase cover.
2. Break the chain. Depending on the type of link, remove the joint clip, or follow the instructions with the special tool for cutting a link.

Inspection

1. Measure drive chain wear by hanging the chain and attaching a 20 lb. to 40 lb. weight to the bottom end. This will ensure that the chain is fully extended. Service limits are 60 9/16 inches on the CB750 and 61 13/16 inches on the K1, measuring between first and last pins.

2. Inspect the chain for cracks, wear at the joints, and broken rollers.

Cleaning and Lubrication

1. Clean the chain in solvent, rinse in fresh solvent, and allow to dry.

2. Prepare a mixture of SAE 10W-30 oil and petroleum jelly in a 10:1 ratio. This could be one half quart of oil to five ounces of jelly. Immerse the chain and heat the mixture to between 66 degrees C and 100°C (150°F to 250°F) for about 10 minutes.

3. Remove the pan from the heat, and agitate the chain with a screwdriver to ensure that the lubricant penetrates all the joints. When cool, drain the chain and wipe off excess lubricant with a rag.

Reassembly and Adjustment

1. Route the chain through the sprockets, and position the two ends on the rear sprocket for joining.

2. Install the master link, taking care that the retaining clip faces in the direction of rotation, as in **Figure 21**. Use the special tool if the chain is the staked type.

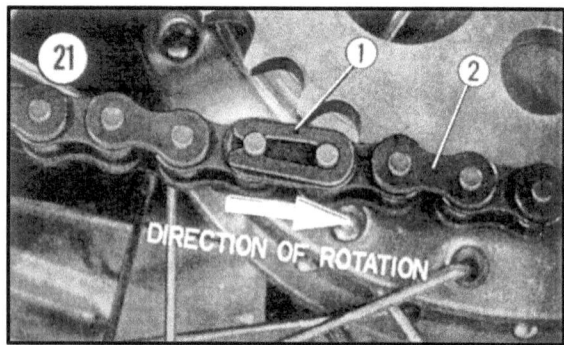

① Joint clip   ② Drive chain

3. Remove the rear axle nut cotter pin, and remove the nut. Then loosen the lock nuts on the adjusting bolts for the drive chain.

4. Adjust the slack to between 10mm and 20mm (.4 in to .8 in) at the center of the chain by rotating the adjusting bolts. Note the scales on both sides of the fork to aid in the alignment.

5. When the chain is adjusted, tighten the lock nuts down on the adjusting bolts to a torque of 8 kg-m to 10 kg-m (58 ft-lbs to 72 ft-lbs).

6. Install a new cotter pin when replacing the axle bolt.

CHAPTER TEN

BRAKES

FRONT BRAKE SYSTEM

Figure 1 shows major components of the hydraulic front disc brake. This type of brake operates better than a drum brake under heavy use.

The brake is self adjusting. As the pads wear down, more hydraulic fluid is taken into the system to compensate, and the lever travel remains constant.

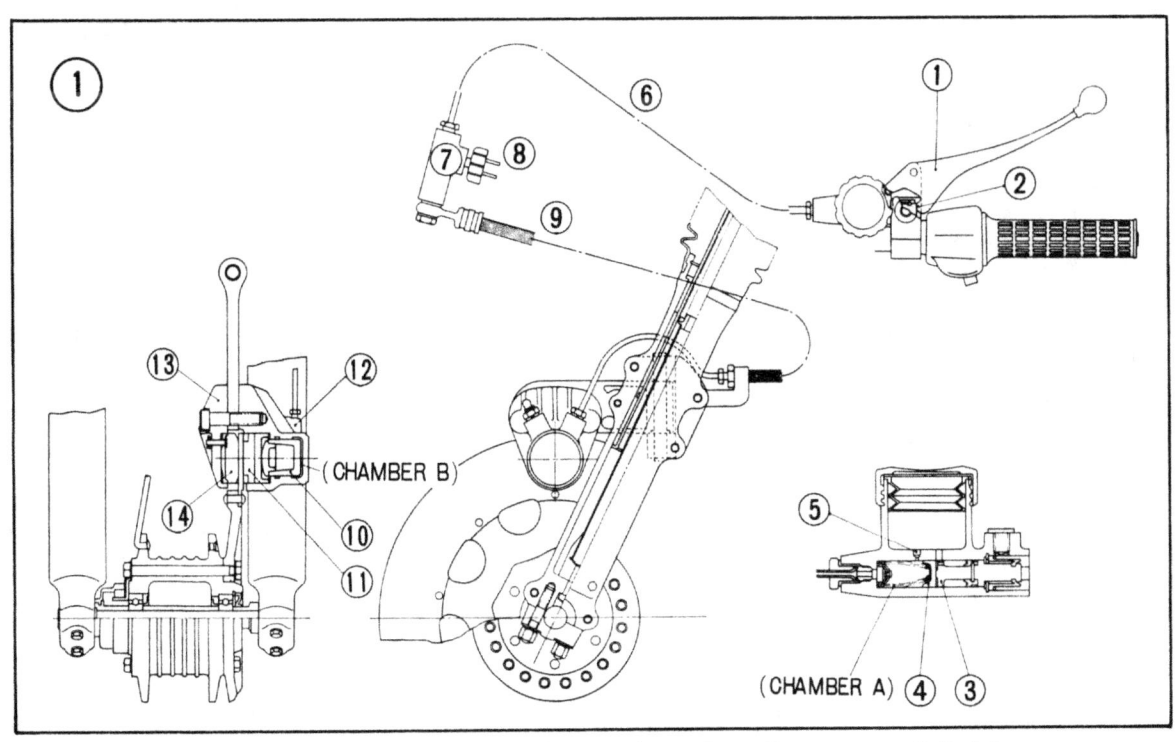

① Front brake lever
② Front brake lever cam
③ Master cylinder
④ Primary cup
⑤ Fluid passage
⑥ Front brake hose B
⑦ Three way joint
⑧ Stoplight switch
⑨ Front brake hose
⑩ Piston
⑪ Pad A
⑫ Caliper A
⑬ Caliper B
⑭ Pad B

Brake Wear

Wear of the pads is checked by measuring the clearance between the front of the caliper and the disc face using a feeler gauge as in **Figure 2**. If the clearance is less than 2mm (.08 in), the pads should be replaced as a set. The front wheel and the caliper assembly must be removed to perform this operation.

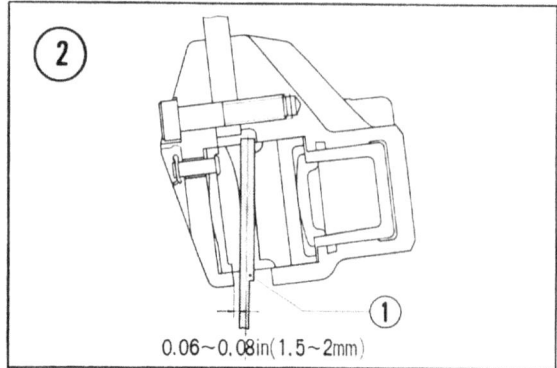

① Brake disc

Disassembly

1. Remove the front wheel according to the instructions in the previous chapter.

2. Refer to **Figure 3** and disconnect the front hose by removing the bolt at the joint.

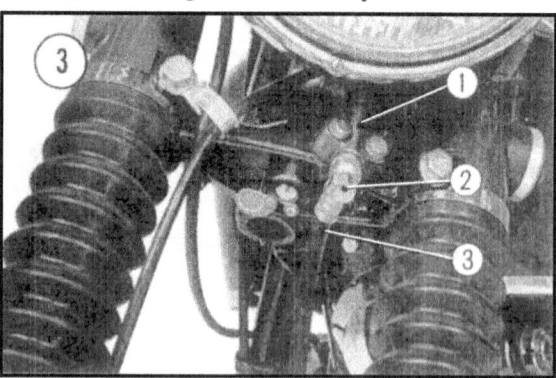

① Joint ③ Oil hose
② Oil bolt

3. Remove the caliper assembly, **Figure 4**, by unscrewing the three mounting bolts. Remove the two set bolts with an Allen wrench, and separate the two calipers.

4. Remove the **A** pad from the **A** caliper and then take out the cylinder and piston, shown in **Figure 5**. Remove the **B** pad from the **B** caliper by taking out the cotter pin.

5. The master hydraulic cylinder is attached to the handlebars near the front brake lever. Un-

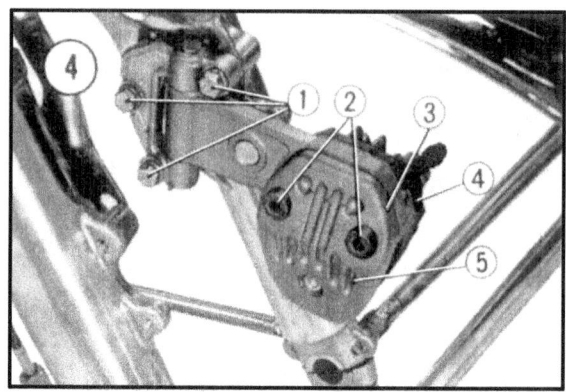

① Caliper mounting bolts
② Hollow head set bolts
③ Caliper   ⑤ Caliper B
④ Caliper A

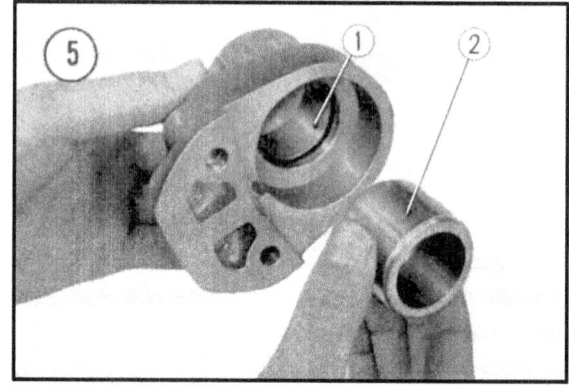

① Caliper A   ② Piston

screw the oil bolt, **Figure 6**, and the two set bolts, then remove the assembly from the grip.

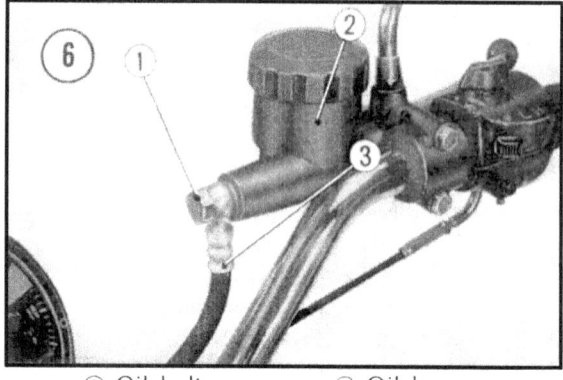

① Oil bolt   ③ Oil hose
② Master cylinder

6. Referring to the exploded view in **Figure 7**, remove the stopper washer and boot from the body.

7. Remove the circlip from the body, using circlip pliers as shown in **Figure 8**.

8. Remove the 10.5mm washer, piston, secondary cup, primary cup, spring, and check valve shown in Figure 7.

BRAKES

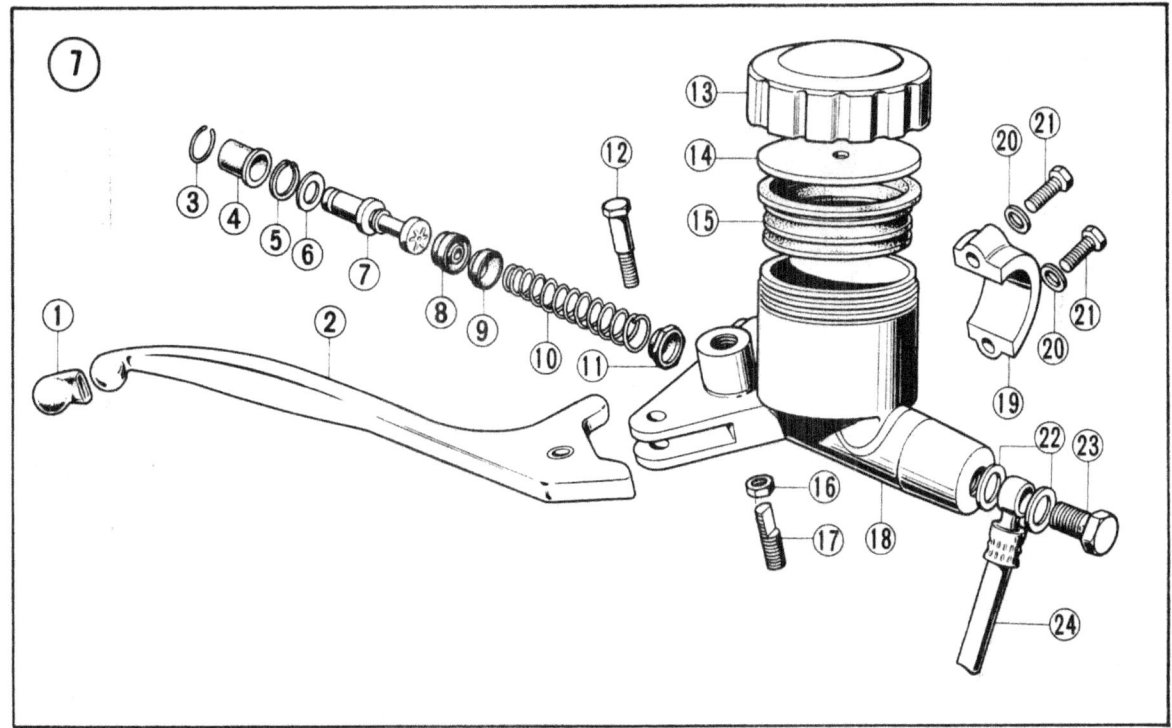

① Brake lever cap
② Brake lever
③ Stopper washer
④ Boot
⑤ 18 mm internal circlip
⑥ 10.5 mm washer
⑦ Piston
⑧ Secondary cap
⑨ Primary cap
⑩ Spring
⑪ Check valve
⑫ Handle lever pivot bolt
⑬ Oil cup cap
⑭ Master cylinder plate
⑮ Diaphragm
⑯ 8 mm hex nut
⑰ Lever adjusting bolt
⑱ Master cylinder body
⑲ Master cylinder holder
⑳ 6 mm spring washer
㉑ 6 mm hex bolt
㉒ Oil bolt washer
㉓ Oil bolt
㉔ Front brake hose

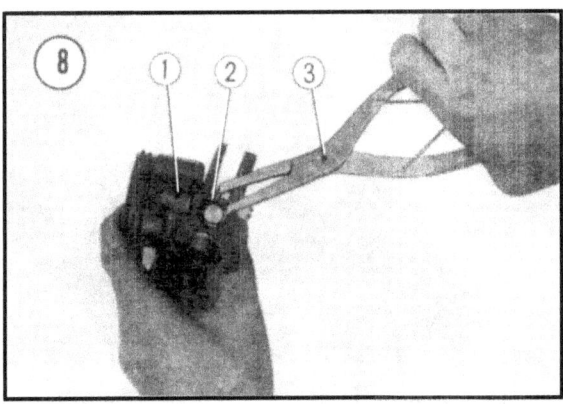

① Master cylinder body ③ Special pliers
② Circlip

Inspection

1. Measure the inner diameter of the caliper cylinder with a dial gauge, **Figure 9**, and the outer diameter of the piston with a micrometer. Compute the clearance by subtraction. If the difference is more than .11mm (.004 in), the parts should be replaced.

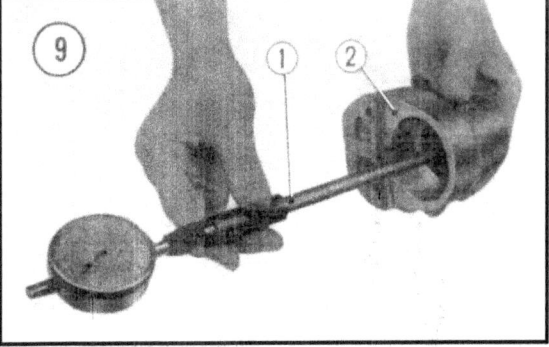

① Cylinder gauge ② Caliper cylinder

2. Perform the same measurements for the master cylinder, **Figure 10**, and its piston. Replace if the clearance is more than .115mm (.0045 in).

3. Check the caliper piston seal, and replace if it is damaged.

4. Check the hose for damage, and replace if necessary.

Reassembly

All parts of the braking system should be

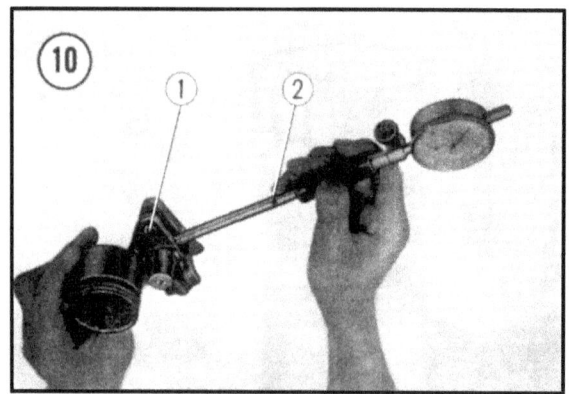

① Master cylinder body
② Inside dial gauge

absolutely clean before reassembly. Assemble in reverse order of disassembly, noting the following.

1. Before mounting the pads, apply a small amount of silicon sealing grease, not molybdenum brake grease, at the points shown in **Figure 11**. Be careful not to get grease on the pad surfaces.

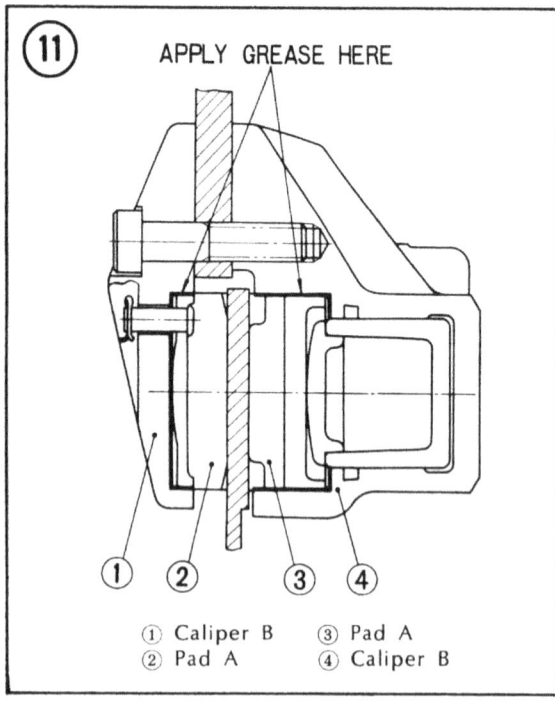

① Caliper B ③ Pad A
② Pad A ④ Caliper B

2. Adjust the free play of the brake lever, if required, according to the instructions in Chapter One.

Bleeding the Front Brake

Air should be bled from the brake system whenever it has been worked on. In addition, there is probably air in the system if travel of the lever increases markedly, or if the action is spongy.

Use only fresh, SAE 70 R3 heavy duty brake fluid. Be careful not to spill any on painted surfaces, because the fluid will leave a mark.

The bleeding operation is easier when performed by two persons, with one pumping the lever, and the other monitoring the bleeding valve.

1. If the system has been drained, remove the master cylinder reservoir cap and fill with fluid, **Figure 12**.

2. Attach a hose to the bleeder valve, **Figure 13**.

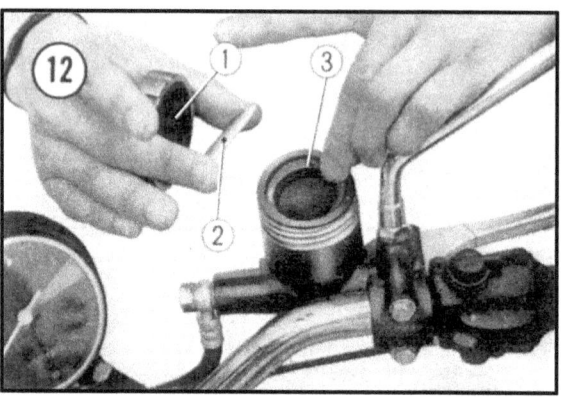

① Reservoir cap ③ Diaphragm
② Washer

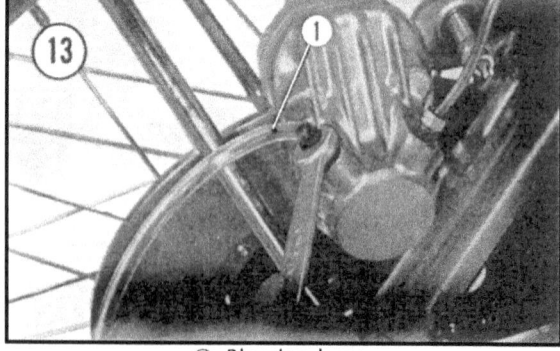

① Bleeder hose

3. Open the bleeder valve one-half turn, squeeze the brake lever, close the valve, and release the lever.

4. Repeat the procedure until hydraulic fluid flows from the end of the bleeder hose. Replenish the fluid in the reservoir as the level decreases. Then proceed to the actual bleeding operation.

5. Immerse the free end of the bleeder hose in a cup of brake fluid.

BRAKES

6. Open the bleeder valve one-half turn and squeeze the brake lever. Close the valve and then release the lever. Top up the reservoir with fluid if necessary. No air should enter the system from the top.

7. Repeat the bleeding operation until no air bubbles come from the tip of the hose.

8. Remove the hose and replace the dust cap. Replace the reservoir cap after checking the fluid level one last time.

9. Squeeze the brake lever, and check for pressure leaks and seepage.

Front Brake Adjustment

1. Raise the front wheel off the ground by inserting a prop under the engine.

2. Refer to **Figure 14** and loosen the lock nut on the stopper bolt.

① Brake caliper ③ Stopper bolt lock nut
② Friction pads ④ Stopper bolt

3. Turn the stopper bolt in the direction of **A** until the pad contacts the disc. The wheel should drag slightly when it is turned.

4. Rotate the front wheel and slowly back off the stopper bolt in the direction of **B**, Figure 14, until the wheel turns freely without drag.

5. Back off the stopper bolt one-eighth to one-quarter turn more, and tighten down the lock nut.

REAR BRAKE

The rear brake is a mechanically-operated drum system which does not work as hard as the front disc because of weight transfer to the front wheel during braking.

Disassembly

Figure 15 shows details of the rear brake pedal and the linkage.

1. Remove the pedal by unscrewing the mounting bolt and disconnecting the stop switch spring.

2. Remove the brake adjuster nut, and pull the rod from the arm.

3. Unhook the brake return spring, **Figure 16**, and remove the shaft.

① Rear brake return spring
② Rear brake shaft

4. Remove the rear wheel according to the instructions in Chapter Nine.

5. Referring to **Figure 17**, remove the two cotter pins and washer, then pull the shoes from the panel.

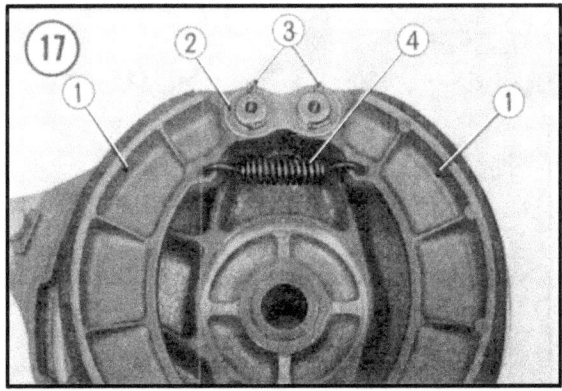

① Rear brake shoes ③ 2.5 × 20 cotter pin
② Anchor pin washer ④ Brake shoe spring

Inspection

1. Measure the diameter of the drum with a vernier caliper, as shown in **Figure 18**. If the diameter is more than 183mm (7.205 in), the rear wheel should be replaced. Severe score marks, or grooves, in the drum, also indicate wheel replacement.

2. Measure shoe thicknes with a vernier caliper, **Figure 19**. If the reading is less than 2mm (.08

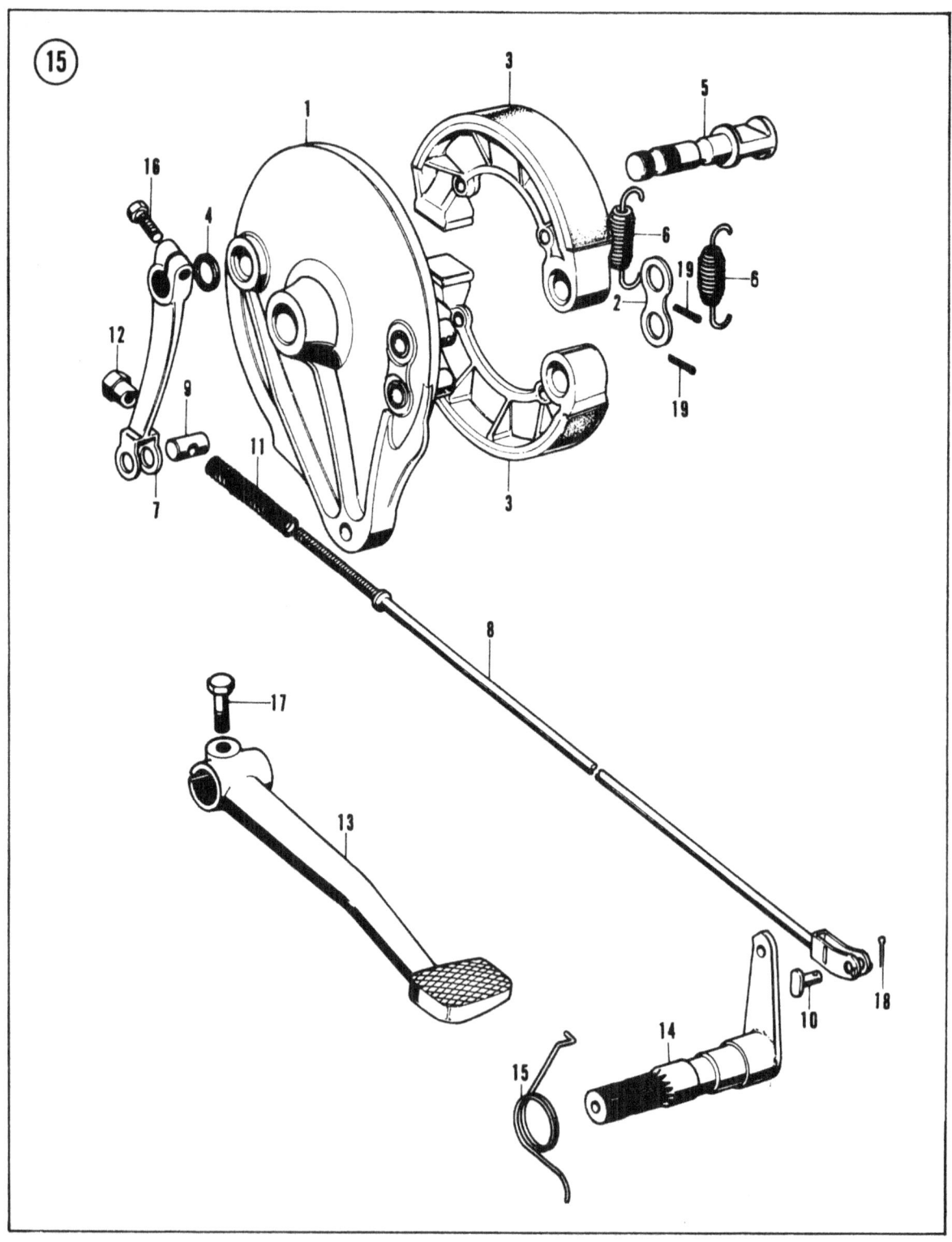

REAR BRAKE PEDAL—PANEL

1. Rear brake panel
2. Rear brake anchor pin washer
3. Rear brake shoe components
4. Brake cover dust seal
5. Rear brake cam
6. Brake shoe spring
7. Rear brake arm
8. Rear brake rod components
9. Rear brake arm joint
10. Brake rod joint pin
11. Rear brake rod spring
12. Rear brake adjusting nut
13. Rear brake pedal
14. Rear brake spindle components
15. Brake pedal spring
16. Hex bolt
17. Hex bolt
18. Cotter pin
19. Cotter pin

BRAKES

① Vernier caliper

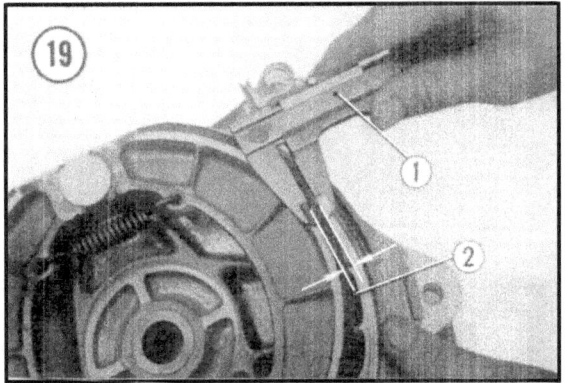

① Vernier caliper
② Rear brake shoe

in), the part should be replaced. If the lining is worn unevenly, the shoe also should be replaced.

Reassembly

Reassemble in reverse order of disassembly, referring to the exploded illustration (Figure 15).

Adjusting Rear Brake

1. Place the motorcycle on the main stand to lift the rear wheel clear of the ground.
2. Check free travel of the brake pedal by rotating the rear wheel and noting the distance the pedal moves before the brake takes hold. The distance should be measured at the point shown in **Figure 20**.

① Rear brake pedal
② Rear brake pedal free travel

3. Adjust, if necessary, with the adjusting nut, **Figure 21**, so that free travel is about 25mm (1 in). Turn the nut clockwise for less travel, counterclockwise for more.

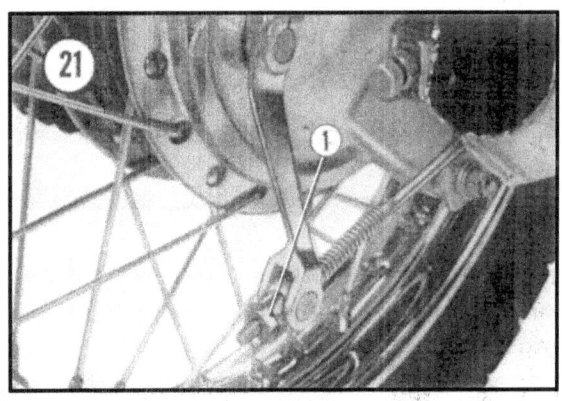

① Rear brake adjusting nut

4. Check to see that the cutout on the nut is seated on the arm pin after the final adjustment.

CHAPTER ELEVEN

FRAME

STRIPPING THE FRAME

1. Remove the engine. See Chapter Two.
2. Remove the steering assembly. See Chapter Seven.
3. Remove the wheels. See Chapter Nine.
4. Remove the suspension. See Chapters Seven and Eight.
5. Remove electrical components. See Chapter Twelve.
6. See **Figure 1** and remove the main stand cotter pin from the shaft collar, then remove the two mounting bolts.

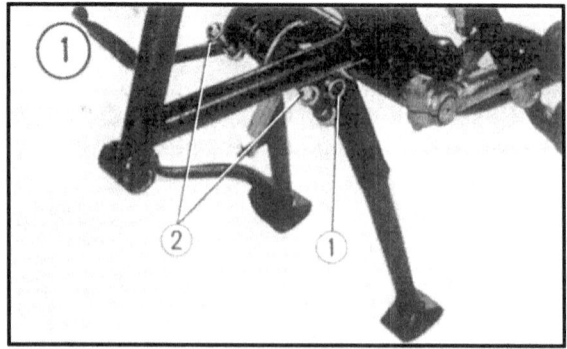

① Cotter pin ② Main stand mounting bolts

7. Unhook the spring and remove the main stand.
8. Remove the two seat hinge bars, **Figure 2**, and pull the seat from the frame.

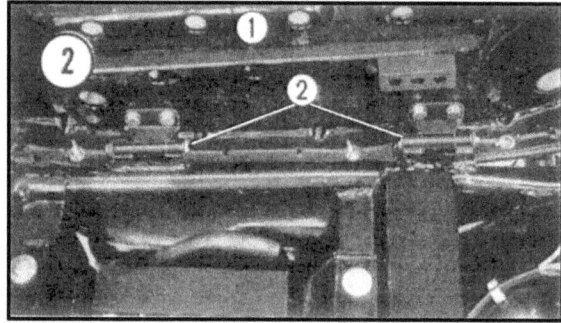

① Seat ② Seat hinge bars

9. Remove the rear fender by unscrewing the two 6mm and two 8mm bolts.
10. Refer to **Figure 3** and drive out the upper and lower ball bearing races from the steering head. Use a wooden drift to avoid damaging the races.

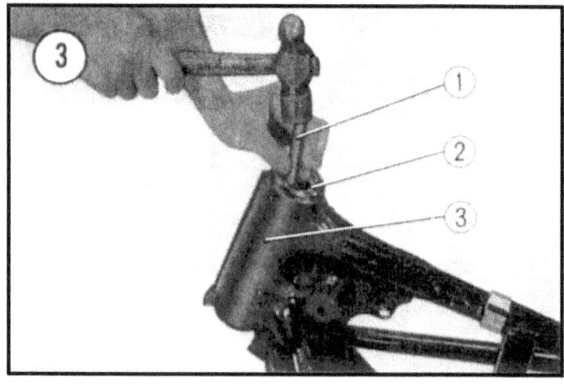

① Wooden drift ② Ball race ③ Head pipe

FRAME

Inspection

1. **Figure 4** shows the standard dimensions of the frame. The frame should be straightened in a press if the specs are off. This is a job for an expert.
2. Check the steering bearing races for damage.
3. Inspect the main stand for cracks or bends.

Reassembly

Reassemble the machine in reverse of disassembly, noting the following:

1. Do not overtighten the main stand mounting bolts.
2. Install a new cotter pin and lock.

OIL TANK

The oil tank, **Figure 5**, receives oil from the engine sump under pressure and supplies lubricant to the engine through a separate hose.

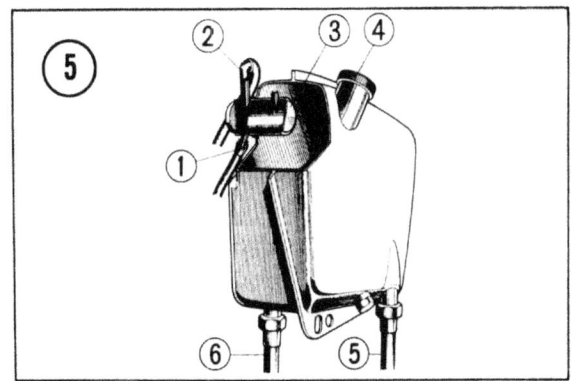

① Breather tube A
② Oil tank breather pipe
③ Breather chamber
④ Oil filter cap
⑤ Oil hose B (scavenge side)
⑥ Oil hose A (delivery side)

The oil tank on the later model CB 750 K1 is narrower in width than the tank on the earlier CB 750. Oil tank covers are not interchangeable between the two models.

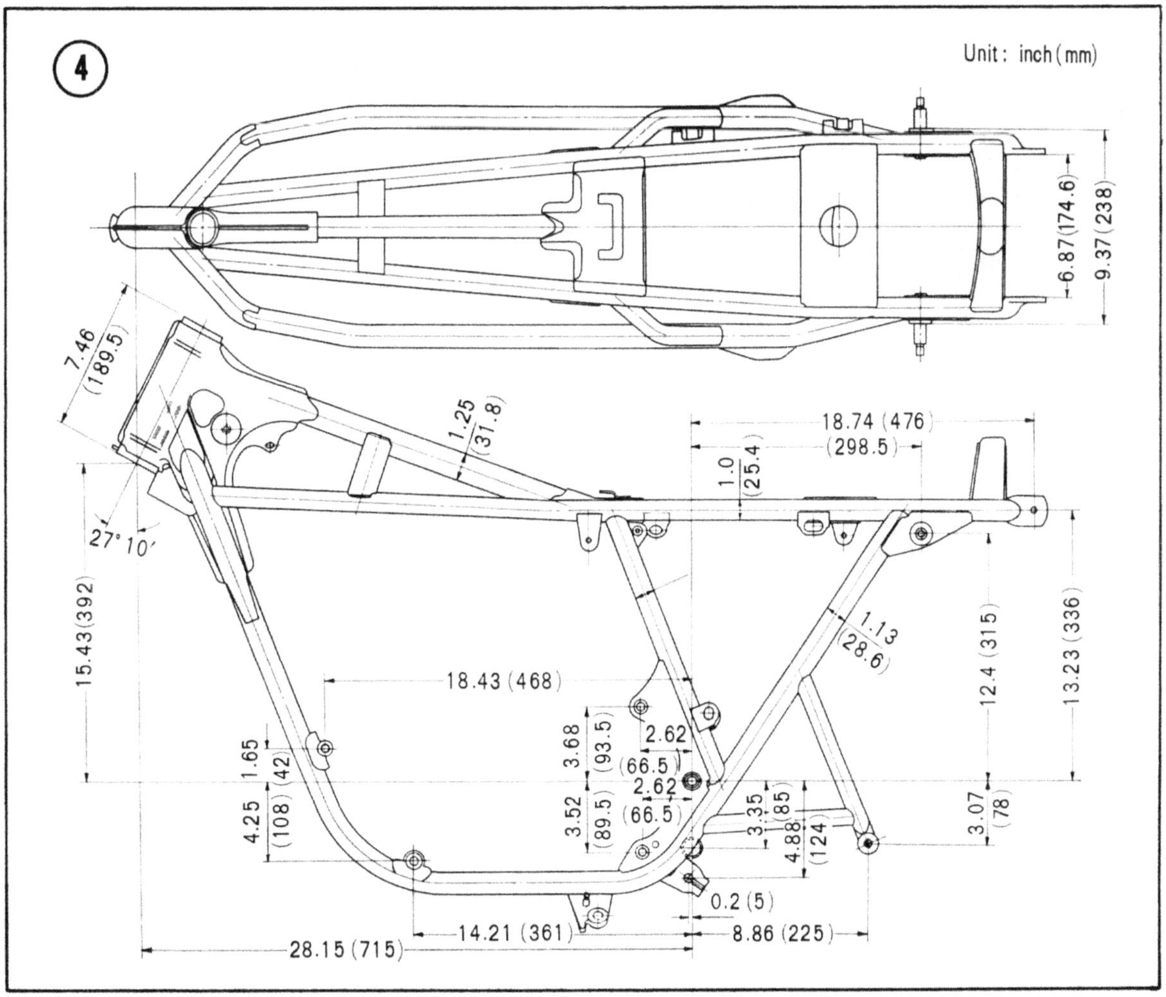

Disassembly

1. Remove the cover from the tank.

2. Remove the drain plugs from the crankcase and the oil tank, and drain the oil. See Chapter One.

3. Disconnect the two oil hoses at the fittings, **Figure 6**.

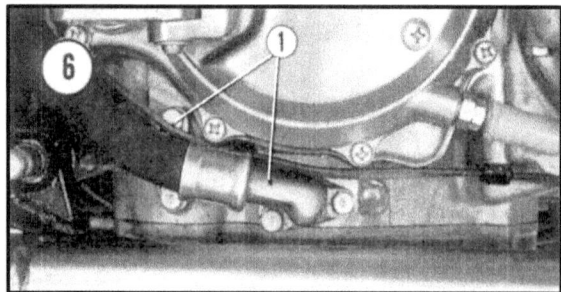

① Engine oil hoses

4. Remove the three mounting bolts, **Figure 7**, and remove the tank.

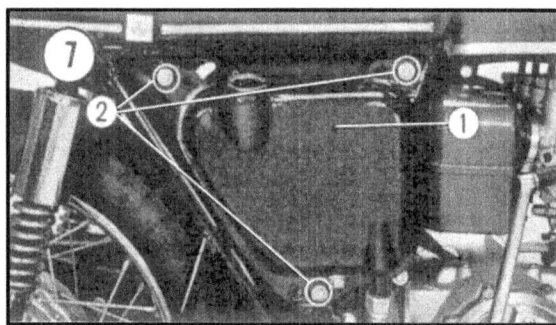

① Oil tank   ② Oil tank mounting bolts

Inspection

1. Check the tank for damage or leaks.

2. Check the oil hoses for tightness and wear.

Reassembly

Reassemble in reverse order of disassembly, referring to **Figure 8** and noting the following:

1. Do not accidentally switch the scavenge and delivery hoses when installing.

2. Make sure the tank is set correctly on its rubber mounts.

3. Remember the 15mm O-ring when installing the hoses on the engine.

EXHAUST

The Honda 750 mufflers are joined on each side by a connecting tube, **Figure 9**, that increases silencing without causing the buildup of

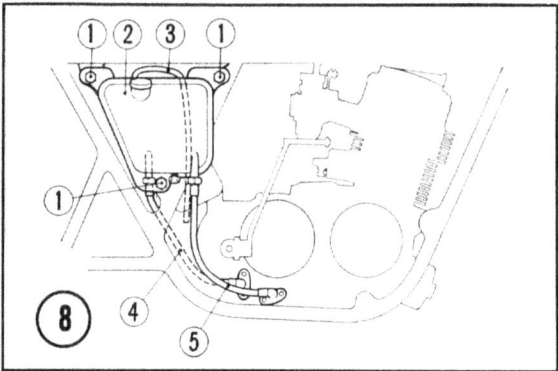

① 6 mm bolts   ④ Oil hose A (delivery side)
② Oil tank   ⑤ Oil hose B (scavenge side)
③ Breather tube A

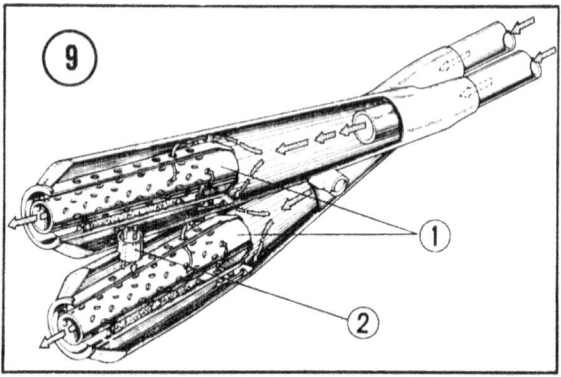

① Muffler connecting tube   ② Exhaust muffler

back pressure which would result from a larger expansion chamber. **Figure 10** shows details of the exhaust system.

Disassembly

1. Loosen the 8mm bolt on the exhaust joint, and remove the pillion step bolt on both sides.

2. Loosen the muffler connecting band and remove the mufflers.

Inspection

1. Check the gaskets for damage.

2. Inspect mufflers for cracks, dents or other damage.

Reassembly

1. Install the gasket on the cylinder head and mount the exhaust flange with the two 8mm screws.

2. Install the joint on the flange and mount the muffler to the frame. Check to make sure that the connecting tube is in place between the upper and lower muffler on each side.

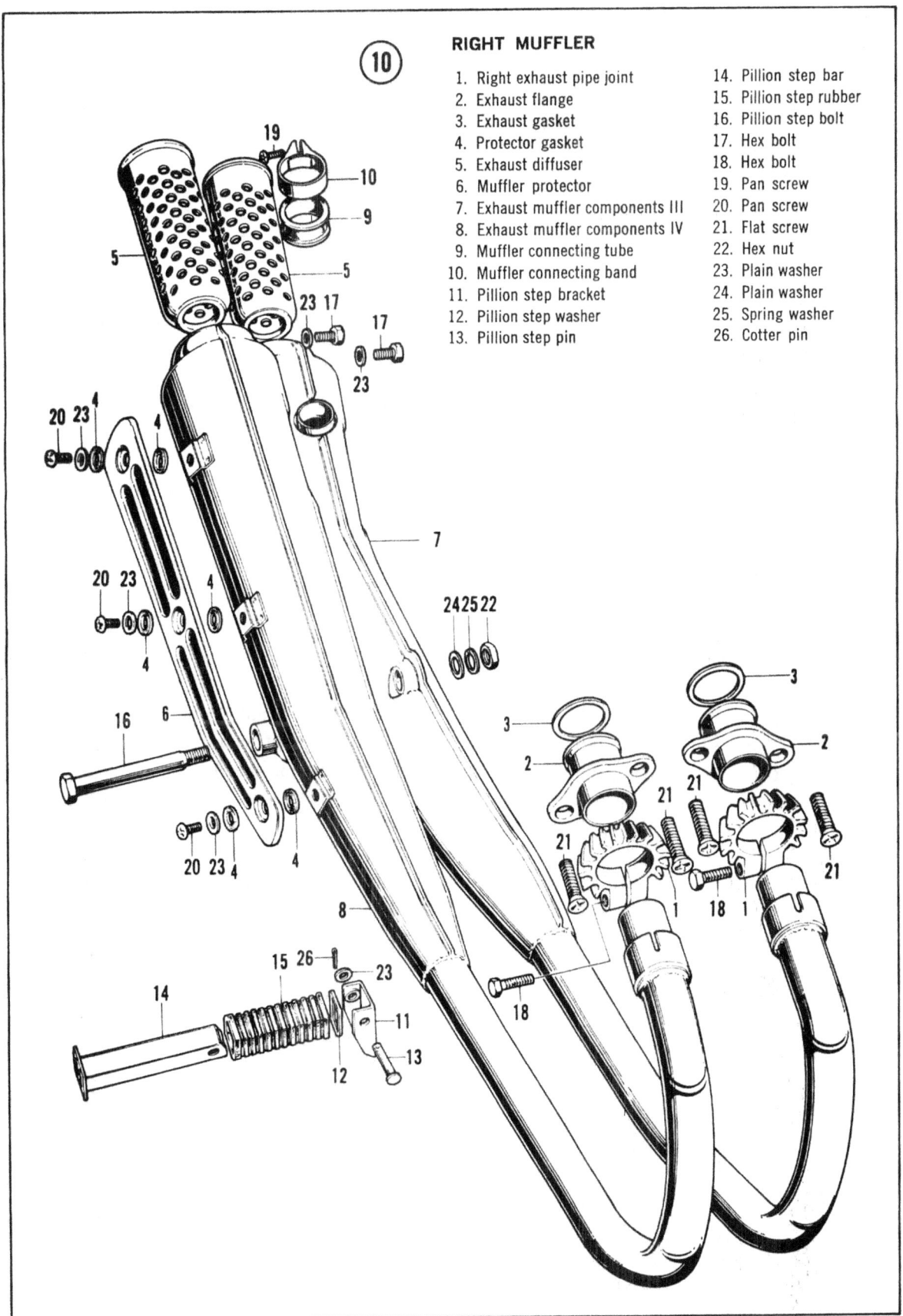

CHAPTER TWELVE

LIGHTING, WIRING, AND INSTRUMENTS

This chapter covers the warning and running lights, the switches that activate them, and the instrument group. Wiring schematics for American, French, and German models are at the end of the manual. Except when noted, reassembly is in reverse order of disassembly.

INSTRUMENT GROUP

The speedometer and tachometer are driven by separate, flexible shafts. Repairs should only be attempted by an expert. Details of the instruments are shown in **Figure 1**.

Starting with the CB 750 K1 models, the instrument cases were painted flat black to prevent reflection. The previous acrylic resin windows were changed to glass for better resistance against brake fluid spills.

Disassembly

1. Remove the headlight unit, according to the instructions in that section of this chapter.

2. Disconnect the speedometer and tachometer cables from the backs of the instruments.

3. Remove the set screw, **Figure 2**, and dismount the instruments.

4. Unscrew the two cross screws and remove the underplate. Remove the bulbs.

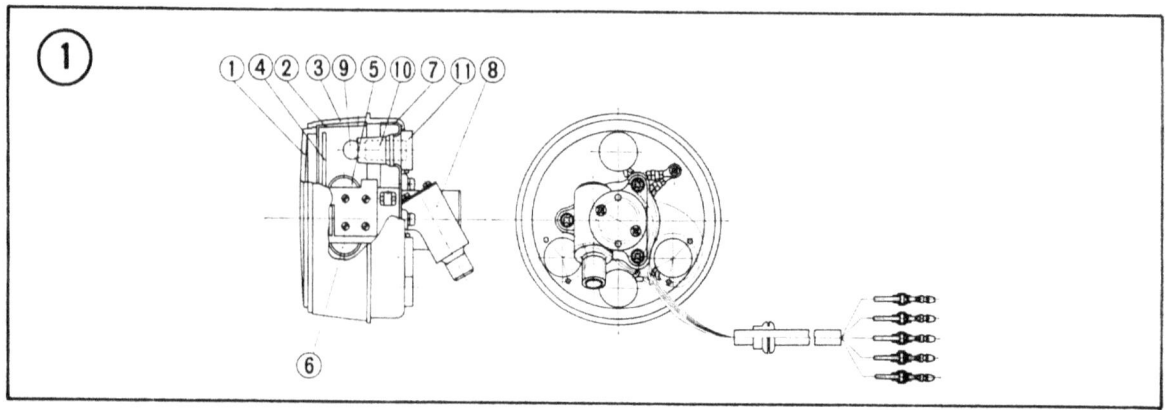

① window glass
② window plate
③ Case
④ Division plate
⑤ Trip counter
⑥ Total counter
⑦ Lower case
⑧ Gear box
⑨ Lamp bulb
⑩ Socket
⑪ Socket cover

LIGHTING, WIRING, AND INSTRUMENTS

① Tachometer   ③ Setting screw
② Speedometer

HEADLIGHT

Refer to **Figure 3** for construction of the sealed beam headlight.

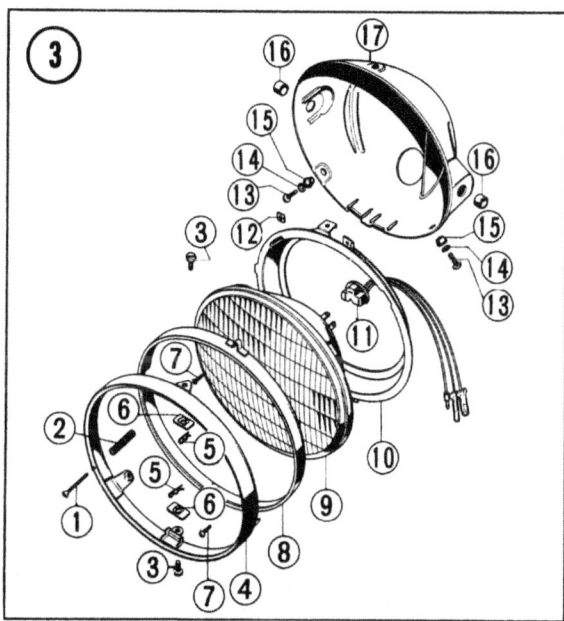

① Beam adjusting screw   ⑩ Mounting ring
② Beam adjusting spring ⑪ Headlight cord socket
③ Unit holder screw   ⑫ Beam adjusting nut
④ Headlight rim   ⑬ 5 mm cross screw
⑤ 5 mm cotter pin   ⑭ 5 mm spring washer
⑥ Unit holder nut   ⑮ Headlight setting collar
⑦ 3 mm cross screw   ⑯ Headlight case collar
⑧ Retaining ring   ⑰ Headlight case
⑨ Sealed beam unit

Disassembly

1. Loosen the three mounting screws and remove the light unit from the case.

2. Disconnect the electrical leads, **Figure 4**.

3. Referring to **Figure 5**, remove the two set screws and the beam adjusting screw. Then remove the light from the rim.

① Headlight socket   ② Headlight unit

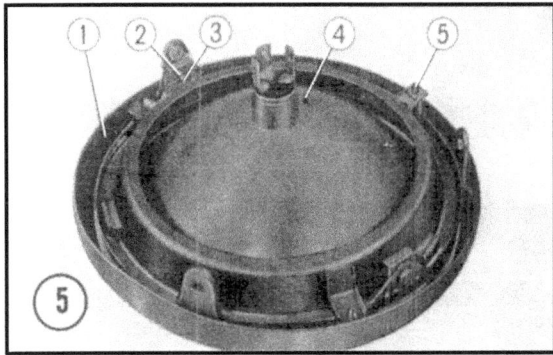

① Headlight rim   ④ Headlight beam unit
② Cotter pin   ⑤ Adjusting screw
③ Headlight beam unit screw

4. Remove the beam unit by loosening the two headlight screws.

Inspection

1. Test or check visually for a broken filament, and replace the unit if necessary.

2. Inspect the wiring for corrosion or fraying.

TAIL AND STOP LIGHTS

The double-duty assembly uses a bulb with two filaments, as in **Figure 6**.

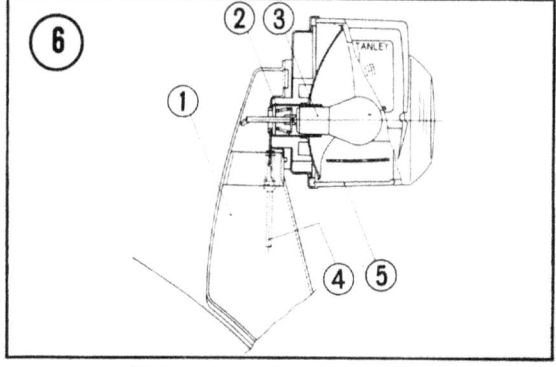

① Number plate bracket
② Taillight socket   ④ Taillight ground cord
③ Taillight bulb   ⑤ Taillight lens

Disassembly

1. Disconnect the electrical leads, **Figure 7**, and remove the bracket by loosening the two screws.
2. Remove the lens and then the bulb, **Figure 8**.

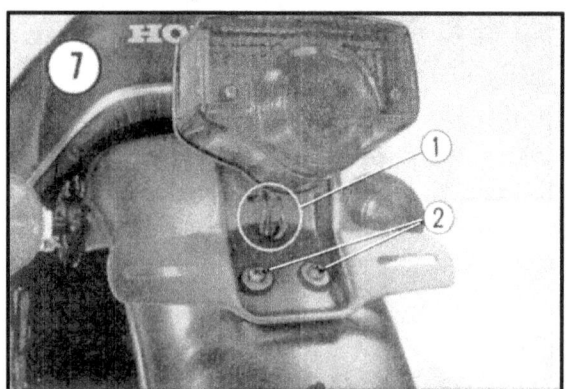

① Lead connectors
② Taillight bracket screws

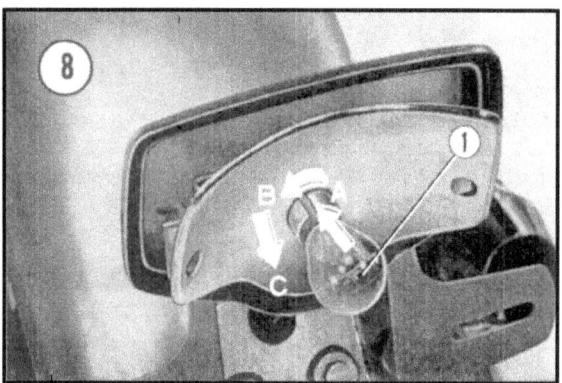

① Tail/stoplight bulb

Inspection

1. Inspect the bulb for broken filaments.
2. Check the wiring for fraying.

Reassembly

Reassemble in reverse order. Make sure not to overtighten the screws when installing the lens, or it may crack.

TURN SIGNAL

Figure 9 shows the parts of the turn signal.

Disassembly

Disassembly is the same as the tail/stoplight.

Inspection

1. Check the bulb for a broken filament.
2. Check the wiring for loose connections or fraying.

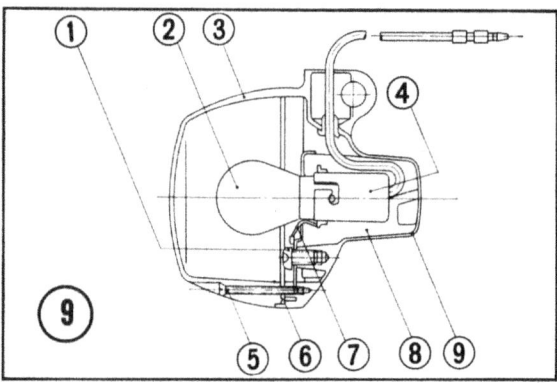

① Cross screw
② Turn signal light bulb
③ Turn signal light lens
④ Turn signal light socket
⑤ Oval screw
⑥ Lens packing
⑦ Socket holder
⑧ Socket cushion
⑨ Turn signal light base

FLASHER RELAY

Figure 10 shows the wiring schematic of the single-stat relay. It is located near the battery, **Figure 11**.

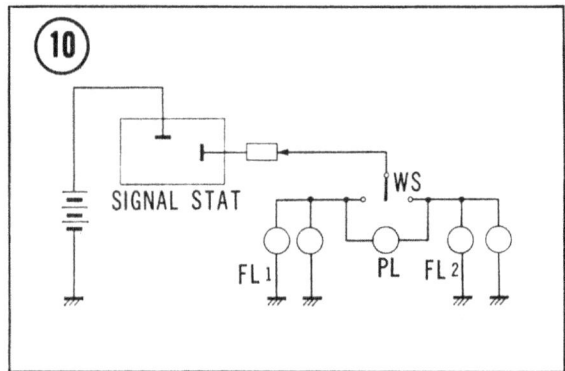

① Signal stat

Disassembly

1. Remove the battery cover.
2. Disconnect the electrical leads from the stat, and remove the unit.

LIGHTING, WIRING, AND INSTRUMENTS

Inspection

1. If the flashing rate is abnormal, check the turn signal bulb rating. The rate is affected by the wrong bulb.

2. Check the rate by connecting the relay unit to a 12 volt, 25 watt bulb, and grounding the circuit. The bulb should flash from 65 to 90 times per minute.

IGNITION SWITCH

This key switch controls all electrical circuits of the motorcycle.

Disassembly

1. Remove the fuel tank.

2. Refer to **Figure 12** and unscrew the lock nut. Then disconnect wires at the junction and remove the unit.

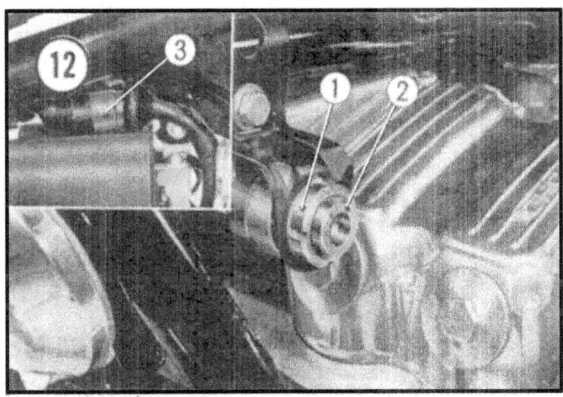

① Lock nut
② Main ignition key switch
③ Connector

Inspection

1. Run a continuity test on the switch circuit with a bench tester. Use the X terminal of the tester and turn the switch to the "on" position with the key. **Figure 13** shows the various phases of the switch. If the continuity lamp lights up, the circuit is good. If not, the circuit is open and the switch should be repaired or replaced.

STARTER, LIGHTING, AND IGNITION SWITCH

Disassembly

1. Loosen the two mounting screws on the right handlebar, and remove the switch bracket.

2. Refer to **Figure 14** and disconnect the throttle cable, then remove the connector from the lower side of the switch.

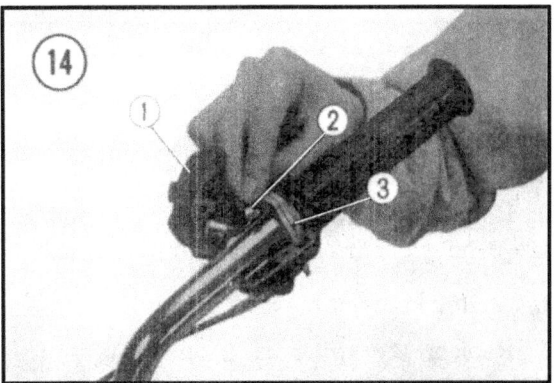

① Starter lighting ignition switch assembly
② Throttle cable
③ Throttle control

3. Disconnect the wiring at the headlight case and remove the switch unit.

Inspection

1. If the switch is malfunctioning, it should be replaced as a unit.

Reassembly

Assemble in reverse order. When installing the lower half of the switch on the handlebar, make sure the pin is inserted into the stopper hole on the bar and is tightened with the upper half.

⑬	BAT (red)	IG (black)	TL 1 (brown/white)	TL 2 (brown)	Function	With Key:
OFF					Electrical equipment inoperative; engine cannot be started.	Removed
I	O—-—O		O—-—-—O		Electrical equipment operative; engine can be started.	In place
II	O—-—-—-—-—-—-—-—O				Parking light operative; engine cannot be started.	Removed

TURN SIGNAL AND HORN SWITCH

Figure 15 shows the construction of this switch, which is mounted on the left handlebar.

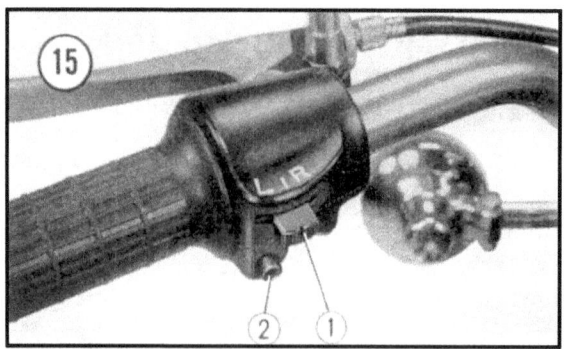

① Turn signal switch ② Horn button

Disassembly

1. Remove the headlight and disconnect the wiring at the case.
2. Remove the two mounting screws and remove the upper and lower halves of the switch.

Inspection

1. Replace the switch as a unit if it is malfunctioning.

Reassembly

Assemble in reverse order. Make sure the pin on the lower half of the switch is inserted into the stopper hole on the handlebar. Tighten the lower half together with the upper half.

HORN

Figure 16 shows construction of the horn. An electromagnet excites a metal diaphragm that vibrates to produce the noise.

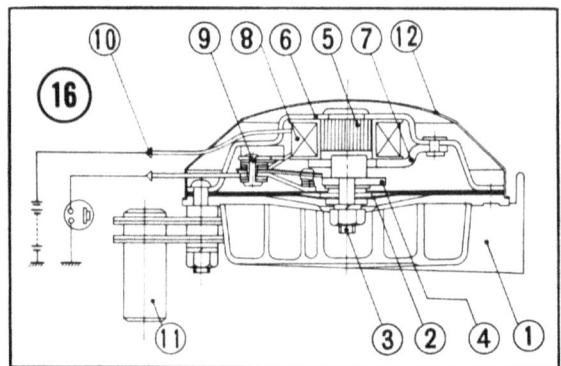

① Curling horn ⑤ Pole A ⑨ Contacts
② Diaphragm ⑥ Case ⑩ Coupler (black)
③ Pole B ⑦ Core plate ⑪ Horn clamp
④ Armature ⑧ Coil ⑫ Cover

Disassembly

1. Disconnect the electrical leads at the connections, **Figure 17**.

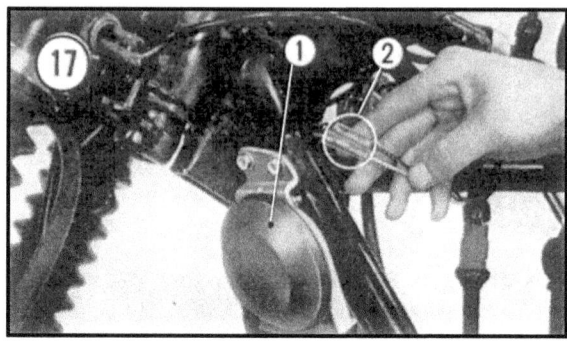

① Horn ② Lead connectors

2. Unscrew the two mounting bolts and remove the horn unit.

Inspection

1. The volume of the horn can be increased by turning the adjusting screw, **Figure 18**, to the right.

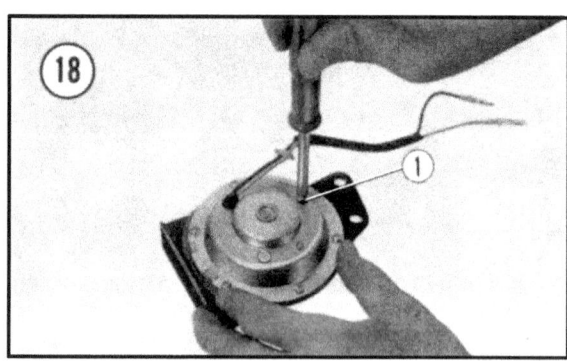

① Adjusting screw

FRONT STOP SWITCH

The switch is activated by pressure in the brake hose and is located next to it. (**Figure 19**).

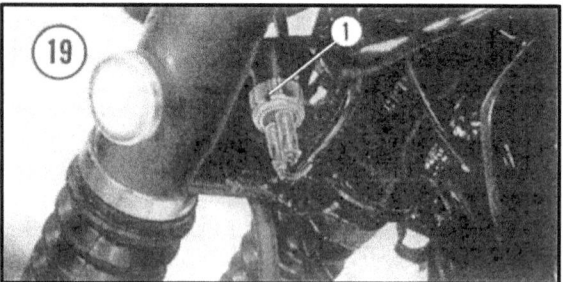

① Stop switch

Disassembly

1. Disconnect the electrical leads.

LIGHTING, WIRING, AND INSTRUMENTS

2. Loosen the mounting bolts, **Figure 20**, and remove the switch from the joint.

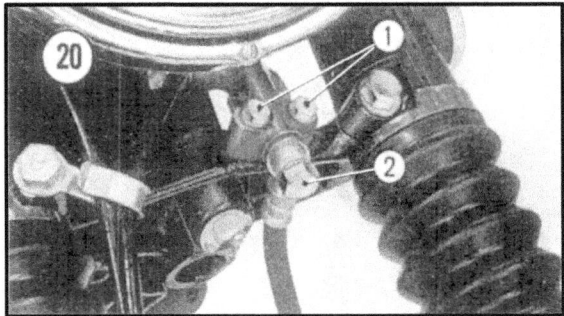

① Joint mounting bolt ② Joint bolt

Inspection

1. Replace the switch as a unit if it is malfunctioning.

REAR STOP SWITCH

The rear switch is activated by the brake pedal, **Figure 21**.

① Stop light switch ③ Leads connectors
② Stop switch spring

Disassembly

1. Disconnect the electrical leads, and remove the switch from the bracket.

Inspection

1. Adjust the brake pedal, according to the instructions in Chapter Ten.
2. The switch should function at the point where the rear brake just starts to take hold. Screw in the lock nut to make the light turn on earlier, screw it out to make the light come on later.

OIL PRESSURE SWITCH

The switch is mounted on the upper crankcase behind the block. It functions when the oil pressure is greater than 4 kg-cm^2 to 6 kg-cm^2 (56.9 lbs-in^2 to 85.3 lbs-in^2).

Disassembly

1. Remove the switch from the crankcase, **Figure 22**, and disconnect the electrical lead.

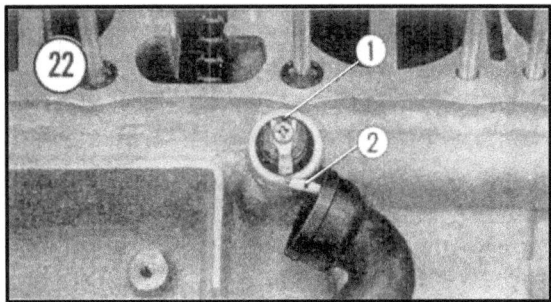

① Oil pressure switch ② Electrical lead

Inspection

1. Replace the unit if defective.

NEUTRAL SWITCH

The neutral switch is mounted under the lower crankcase, as shown in **Figure 23**, and operates the neutral indicator bulb.

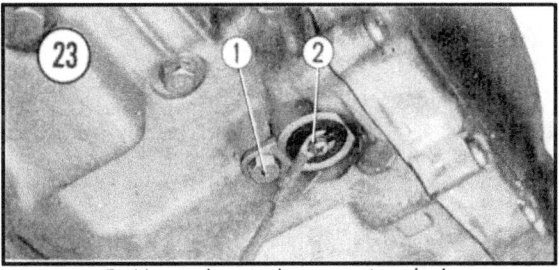

① Neutral switch mounting bolt
② Neutral switch

Disassembly

1. Disconnect the electrical lead, remove the mounting bolt, and remove the switch.

Inspection

1. Replace the switch if defective.

WIRING HARNESS

The wiring harness is color coded according to the **Figure 24** chart.

Disassembly

1. Remove the fuel tank.
2. Remove the headlight and disconnect the leads at the case.

LIGHTING, WIRING, AND INSTRUMENTS

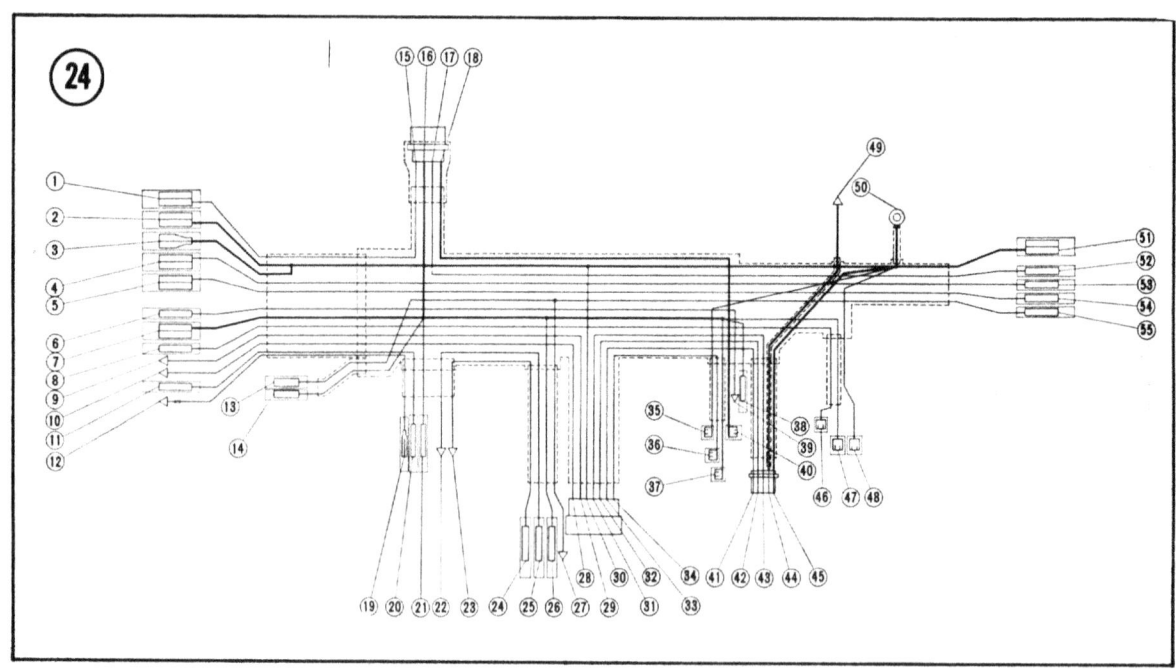

No.	Lead color	Connection
①	Brown/White	Speedometer lamp, Beam selector switch, Tachometer lamp
②	Green	Headlight, Speedometer, Tachometer
③	Green	R.L front turn signal light
④	Light blue	R. front turn signal light, starter switch, turn signal pilot lamp
⑤	Orange	Turn signal pilot lamp, L. front turn single light, Starter/turn signal switch
⑥	Yellow/Red	Starter/turn signal switch
⑦	Black	Neutral pilot lamp, Oil pressure lamp, Head light beam selector switch, ignition switch
⑧	Grey (white tube)	Starter switch, Turn signal switch
⑨	Blue/Red	Oil pressure lamp
⑩	Light green/Red	Neutral pilot lamp
⑪	Light green	Horn switch, Beam selector switch
⑫	Black/White	Ignition switch
⑬	Green/Yellow	Front stop switch
⑭	Black	Front stop switch
⑮	Brown/White	Main key switch
⑯	Black	〃
⑰	Brown	〃
⑱	Red	〃
⑲	Black/White	Ignition coil
⑳	Light green	Horn
㉑	Black	Horn. ignition coil
㉒	Blue	Ignition coil
㉓	Yellow	Ignition coil

No.	Lead color	Connection
㉔	Yellow	Contact breaker
㉕	Blue	〃
㉖	Black	〃
㉗	Green/Yellow	Stop switch
㉘	Light green/Red	Neutral switch
㉙	Blue/Red	Oil pressure switch
㉚	Green	A.C generator
㉛	Yellow	〃
㉜	〃	〃
㉝	〃	〃
㉞	White	〃
㉟	Green	Regulator
㊱	White	〃
㊲	Black	〃
㊳	Black	Starter magnetic switch
㊴	Yellow/Red	〃
㊵	Red	Fuse
㊶	Yellow	Silicon rectifier
㊷	〃	〃
㊸	〃	〃
㊹	Red/White	〃
㊺	Green	〃
㊻	Grey	Winker relay
㊼	Black	〃
㊽	Green	—
㊾	Red/White	Starter magnetic switch
㊿	Green	Frame body
51	Green	Tail/stop light, turn signal light
52	Brown	Tail light
53	Light blue	R. rear turn signal light
54	Orange	L. rear turn signal light
55	Green/Yellow	Stop light

LIGHTING, WIRING, AND INSTRUMENTS

3. In order, disconnect the leads for the ignition coil, horn, front stop switch, main key switch, generator contact breaker, and stop switch.

4. Take off the battery cover and remove the regulator, starter magnetic switch (solenoid), rectifier connector, fuse case, and turn signal relay. **Figure 25** shows the various components.

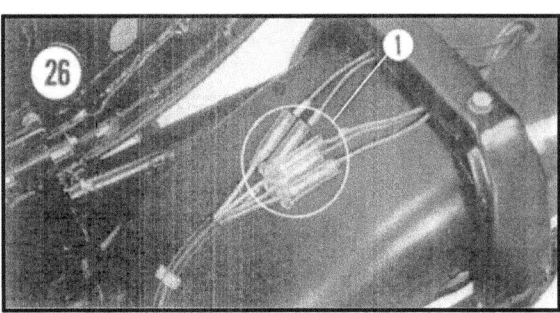

① Electric leads

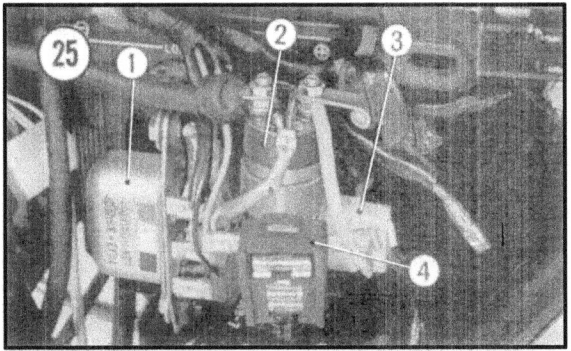

① Regulator ③ Rectifier connector
② Starter magnetic switch ④ Fuse case

5. Refer to **Figure 26** and disconnect the leads over the rear fender.

6. Remove the harness bands and then pull the wiring from the frame.

Inspection

1. Refer to the color code chart and perform continuity tests on any suspect circuits.

2. Replace the harness tape if torn or deteriorated.

Reassembly

Reassemble in reverse order, routing the harness as shown in **Figure 27**.

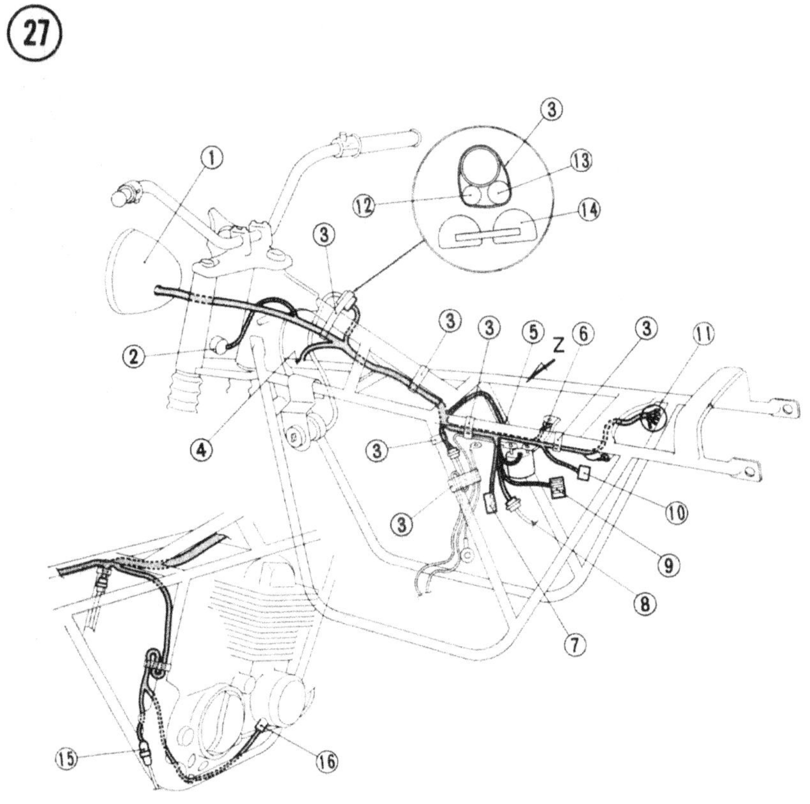

1. Headlight
2. Stop switch (front)
3. Wire harness band
4. To horn and ignition coil
5. To stop switch and contact breaker
6. To battery
7. To regulator
8. To rectifier
9. To fuse
10. To flasher relay
11. To tail/stop light and turn signal light
12. Wire harness
13. Main key switch coupler
14. Ignition coil
15. Stop switch (rear)
16. To contact breaker points

CHAPTER THIRTEEN

SUPPLEMENT TO CB750K1~K4
GROUP 20

COMPARISON OF CB750K1 to CB750

ENGINE MECHANICAL

LUBRICATION SYSTEM

DRIVE CHAIN OILER

The oil which lubricates the chain is fed from the center of the shaft, through the porous sintered oil reserve element ⑦, along the outer surface of the rubber orifice ⑤, out the oil passage ④ and along the surface of the drive sprocket.

To simplify the procedure for regulating the feed of the lubricant, it is performed by the adjusting screw ① in the chain oiler. Turning the screw clockwise (A direction) will force the rubber orifice against the oil reserve element, causing it to expand and restricting the flow of oil around the rubber orifice. Turning the adjusting screw counter clockwise (B direction) will permit the rubber orifice to shrink toward its normal size and allow greater oil flow. In other words, the change in the diameter of the rubber orifice regulates the amount of oil to lubricate the drive chain.

Fig. 20-1 ① Drive chain
② Oil guide

ADJUSTMENT PROCEDURE

1. Remove the rear crankcase.
2. Wipe the oil on the drive chain thoroughly with a rag.
3. The adjusting screw is adjusted to maximum oil flow on all motorcycles leaving the factory. After riding for a short period, if excessive oil is noticed by indication of chain oil on the rim, fender, spokes etc., turn the adjusting screw about 1/4 turn in the clockwise direction and recheck the oil flow condition after riding for one minute at 50~70 mph (80~110 kph). The adjustment is proper if the chain link plates and rollers are

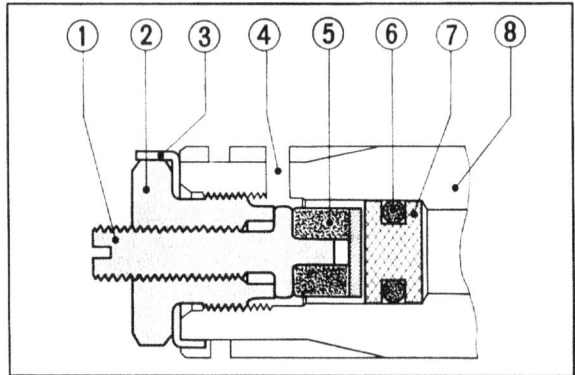

Fig. 20-2 ① Adjusting screw
② Final shaft plug
③ 14 mm lock washer
④ Oil passage
⑤ Rubber orifice
⑥ 6.5×3 O-Ring
⑦ Oil reserve element
⑧ Final driven shaft

20. SUPPLEMENT TO CB750K1~K4

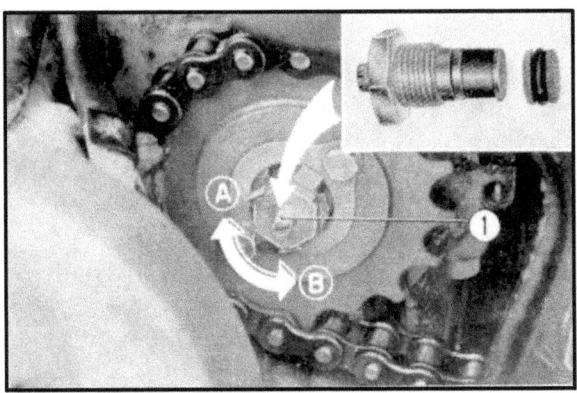

Fig. 20-3 ① Adjusting screw

Fig. 20-4 Point cam position at 15° ATDC

wet with oil and the other areas are free from excessive oil.
4. Readjust the screw if necessary until the proper oiling condition is obtained.

SUPPLEMENT LUBRICATION

Drive chain rollers and side plates must be properly lubricated at all times. Sustained high-speed driving or improper adjustment of the chain oiler may cause inadequate lubrication. If the rollers or side plates are dry or show evidence of rust, apply a high-quality chain lubricant according to the manufacturer's instructions.

CAM CHAIN TENSIONER

A loose cam chain causes a loud clattering noise. It may also affect valve timing, resulting in performance loss.
A recommended crankshaft position for adjusting the cam chain tensioner is that when the crankshaft is rotated to 15° ATDC of cylinders #1 and #4, immediately after cylinder #1 has fired.

Adjustment

1. Remove the tappet covers from the #1 cylinder.
2. Remove the point cover, and use a 23 mm box wrench to rotate the crankshaft to the "T" position for cylinders #1 and #4 (1.4).
3. Check the both valves of #1 cylinder. If both valves are free, proceed to next step: if either or both of the valves are tight, rotate the crankshaft 360°, and then proceed with the next step.
4. Rotate the crankshaft clockwise until the spring peg on the advancer assembly at the 1.4 position is just to the right of a line from the timing index (Fig. 20-4). This position is 15° ATDC 1.4.
   At this point, the slack in the cam chain will be on the tensioner side, thus assuring effective tensioner operation.
5. Loosen the cam chain tensioner lock nut, and back out the setting screw until the tensioner arm is released and moves in to take up the slack.

Note: The tensioner is automatic. Do not use additional pressure to remove the tensioner arm.

6. Retighten the setting screw and lock nut, re-install point cover and tappet covers.

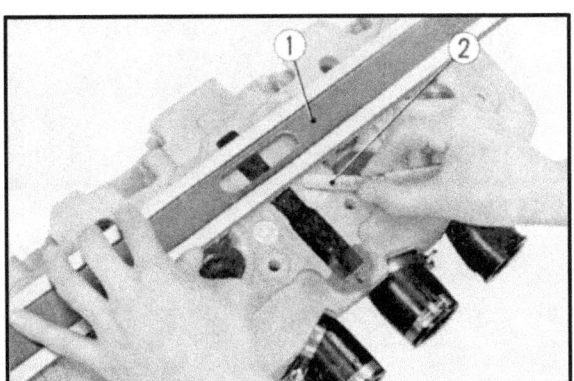

Fig. 20-5 ① Stretch
② Tickness gauge

CYLINDER HEAD

When measuring the flatness of the cylinder head, place a straight across the measuring surface of the cylinder head.
Check the clearance with a thickness gauge at several points and make sure the head not to be warped.

Item	Standard value	Serviceable limit
Clearance	0.002 in. (0.05 mm max.)	0.009 in. (0.25 mm max.)

Rework the cylinder head or replace with new one if beyond the serviceable limit

FUEL SYSTEM

CARBURETOR (link type)

The quadruple piston type carburetors are mounted on the cylinder head with a stay plate. Choke lever is a link type which operates all four choke valves simultaneously.
To simlify the idle adjustment and synchronization of the carburetors, the throttle cables from the four carburetors are joined to operate from a single linkage.
Fig. 20-6 shows the construction details of the carburetor.

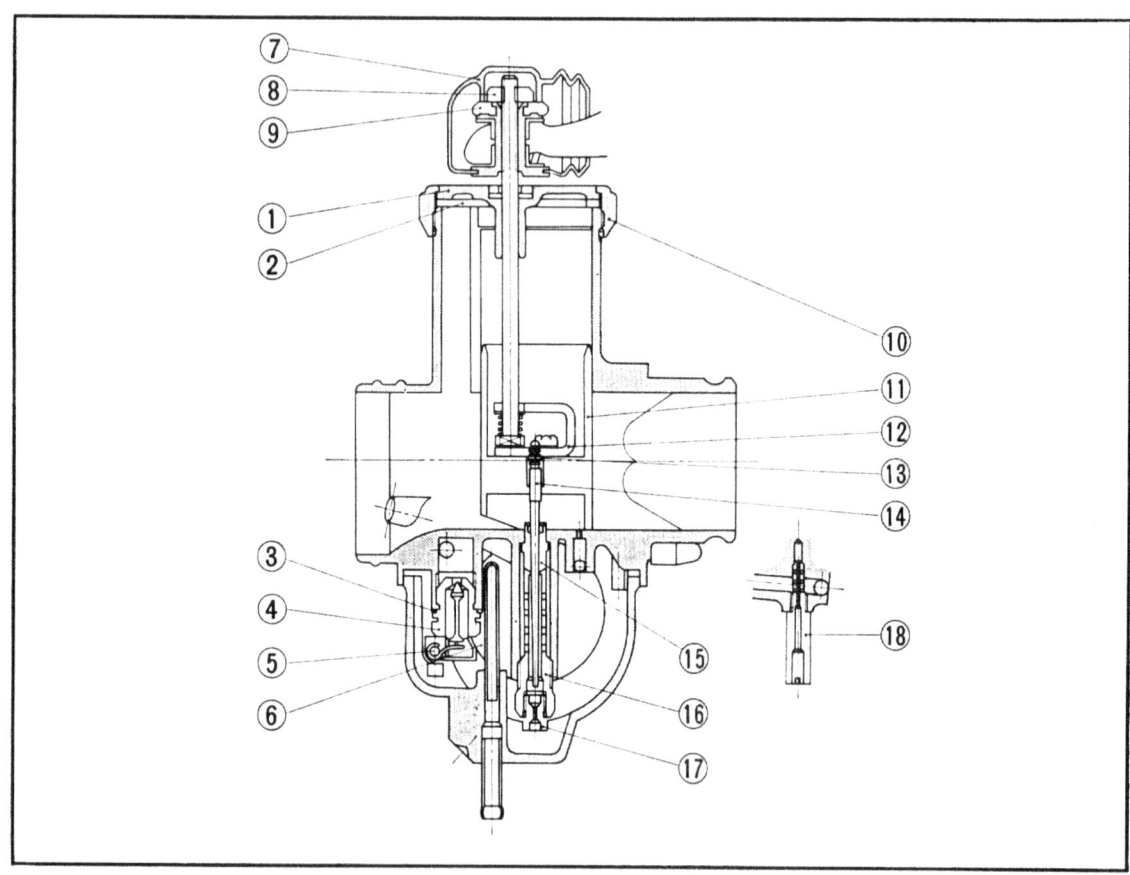

Fig. 20-6

① Carburetor top
② Top washer
③ Flat washer
④ Valve seat
⑤ Float arm pin
⑥ Float
⑦ Rubber cap
⑧ Lock nut
⑨ Adjuster screw
⑩ Cap
⑪ Throttle valve
⑫ Needle set plate
⑬ Clip
⑭ Jet needle
⑮ Needle jet
⑯ Needle jet holder
⑰ Main jet
⑱ Slow jet

20. SUPPLEMENT TO CB750K1~K4

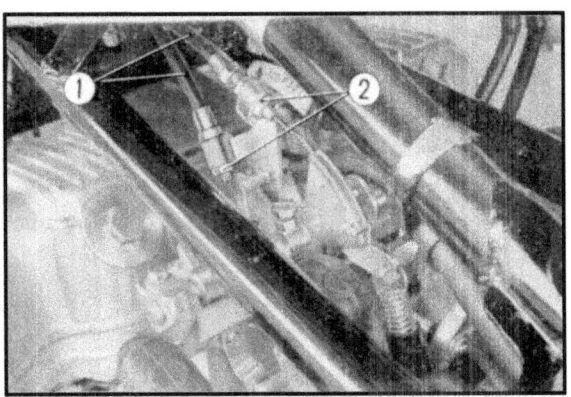

Fig. 20-7 ① Throttle cable
② Lock nuts

Fig. 20-8 ① Air cleaner connecting band
② Carburetor insulator band

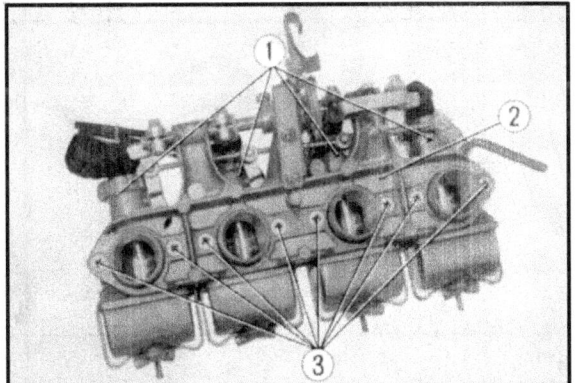

Fig. 20-9 ① Carburetor   ③ Setting screws
② Carburetor stay plate

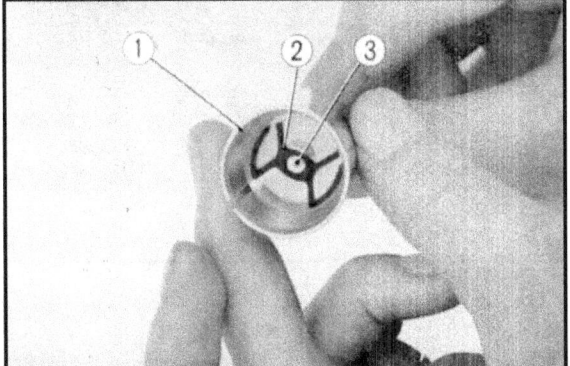

Fig. 20-10 ① Throttle valve   ③ Jet needle
② Needle set plate

DISASSEMBLY

1. Turn the fuel tank valve to the "STOP" position, remove the fuel lines from the fuel valve body, raise the seat and pull the rear tank rubber mounting away from the rear tank mount. Remove the fuel tank.

2. Disconnect the throttle cables from the link lever, loosen the air cleaner connecting tube and insulator bands and then remove the carburetors as an assembly.

3. Unscrew two 6 mm screws and dismount the respective carburetor from the stay plate. Disconnect the individual choke rod and separate the carburetors.

4. In order to remove the needle jet from the throttle valve, remove the needle set plate.

5. Remove the float chamber retightening clip and remove the following carburetor components with a small screwdriver.
   * Slow jet
   * Main jet
   * Needle jet holder
   * Float
   * Float valve set

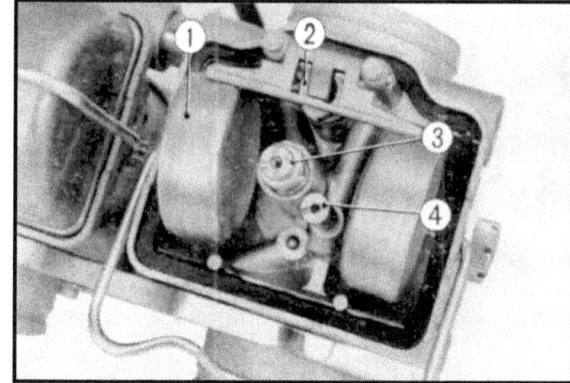

Fig. 20-11 ① Float
② Float valve set
③ Main jet
④ Slow jet

INSPECTION

1. Carburetor adju tment should be made in accordance with the description on pages 17 & 67.
2. Fuel level check
   Remove the float chamber and set the float arm as shown in the **Fig. 20-12** so that it just barely touches the valve and in this position, check the position of the float with the gauge set vertically. At a standard setting, the float should just barely come in contact with the gauge. If there is clearance between the gauge and float or if the float is interfering with the gauge, adjustment should be made. The height of float above the carburetor body, which should be **1.023 in. (26 mm)** can be adjusted by bending the float arm using a narrow screwdriver.
3. Jet needle, float valve
   The jet needle is constantly moving and if it is found to be excessively worn, it should be replaced. Further, check the wear of the valve and the valve seat and if it is defective, part should be replaced. **(Fig. 20-13)**
4. The clogging of the respective jet should be cleaned by blowing out the jets with compressed air followed by properly torquing the jets.

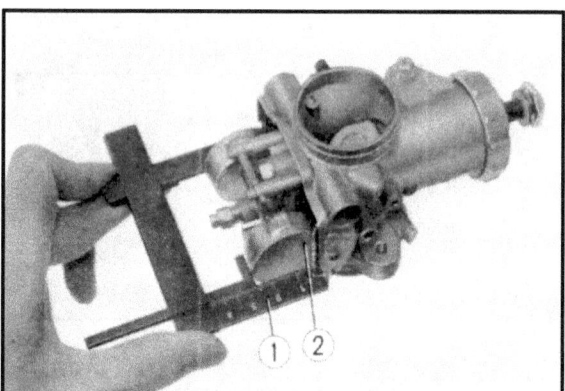

Fig. 20-12 ① Float level gauge
② Float

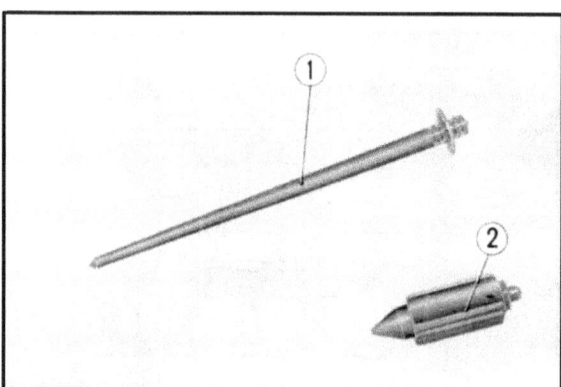

Fig. 20-13 ① Jet needle
② Float valve

20. SUPPLEMENT TO CB750K1~K4

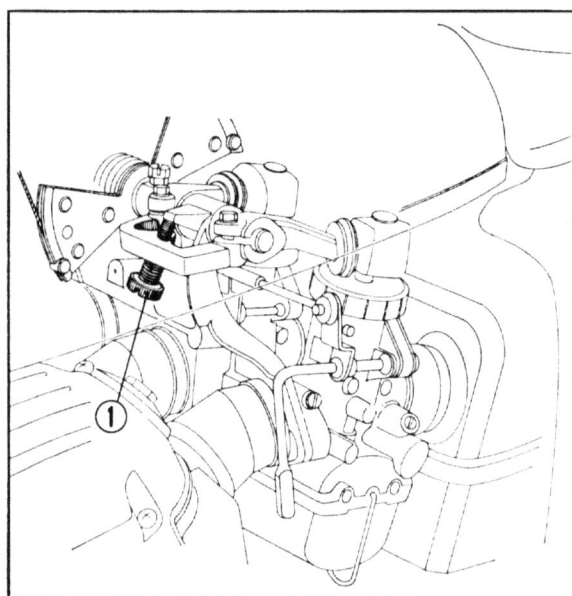

Fig. 20-14 Idle adjustment
① Throttle stop screw

ADJUSTMENT

Adjustment is normally performed after the engine has been warmed up to operating oil temperature of 140° to 157°F (60 to 70°C).

Idle adjustment

Set the engine idle speed to 900-1,000 rpm with the throttle stop screw. **(Fig. 20-14)**

* Turning the stop screw in the clockwise direction will decrease the idle speed.
* Turning in the counter clockwise direction will increase the idle speed.

Carburetor synchronization

1. Remove the fuel tank from the frame and position it approximately 20 in. (50 cm) higher than motorcycle, and then reconnect the tank and the carburetor system with a rubber tube.
2. Remove the rubber boot from the link arm.
3. Connect up the vacuum gauges. Remove the carburetor plugs and connect the longer size adapters to the two inside carburetors, and the shorter size adapters to the outside carburetors.

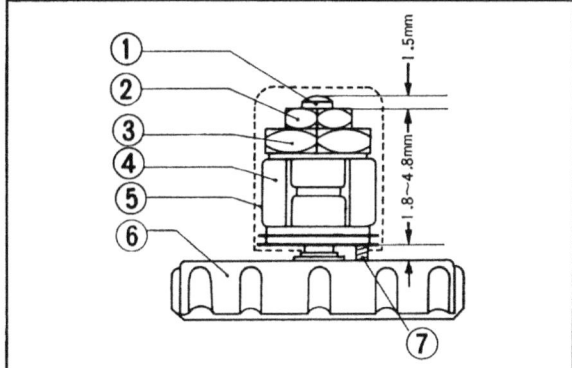

Fig. 20-15 Link component
① Rod
② Lock nut
③ Adjuster screw
④ Link arm
⑤ Rubber boot
⑥ Top
⑦ Gauge

4. Start the engine, loosen the adjuster screw lock nut and turn the adjuster screws so that the vacuum gauges connected to the carburetors are all indicating uniformly (within **3.0 cmHg**) between **16 to 24 cmHg. (Fig. 20-15)**
   ○ Turning the adjuster screw in the clockwise direction will raise the vacuum pressure.
   ○ Turning the screw in the counter clockwise direction will lower the vacuum pressure.

Note:

Before synchronizing the carburetor with the vacuum gauge, make sure that all the rods are extending at least one thread above the lock nut. (Fig. 20-16)

If there is insufficient thread extension, the following preadjustment must be made before adjusting the synchronization.

① Turn the throttle stop screw until there is a slight clearance between the stopper and the screw.

② Adjust the adjuster screw so that there is a **0.070–0.189 in. (1.8–4.8 mm)** clearance between the adjuster screw and the top. **(Fig. 20-15)**

③ Turn the throttle stop screw in the counter clockwise direction back to the original position.

5. When all the carburetors are indicating uniform vacuum pressure, adjust the throttle stop screw to obtain the specified idle speed.

6. Snap the throttle several times to verify the idle stability before tightening the lock nut.
   Torque lock nut to: **0.86–1.44 ft-lbs (12–20 kg-cm)**

Carburetor air screw adjustment

Adjust the respective air screw so that the engine rpm is smoothest with maximum vacuum pressure. The standard adjustment which gives best performance is **3/4 to 1¼** turns open from the full close position.

Note:

After the adjustment is completed, make sure that the rubber boots is not pinched or rolled under.

Overcross stop adjustment

Loosen the lock nut and turn the eccentric link pin to provide a clearance of **0.08–0.12 in. (2–3 mm)** between the throttle lever and link pin. **(Fig. 20-17, 20-18)**

Fig. 20-16 Lock nut

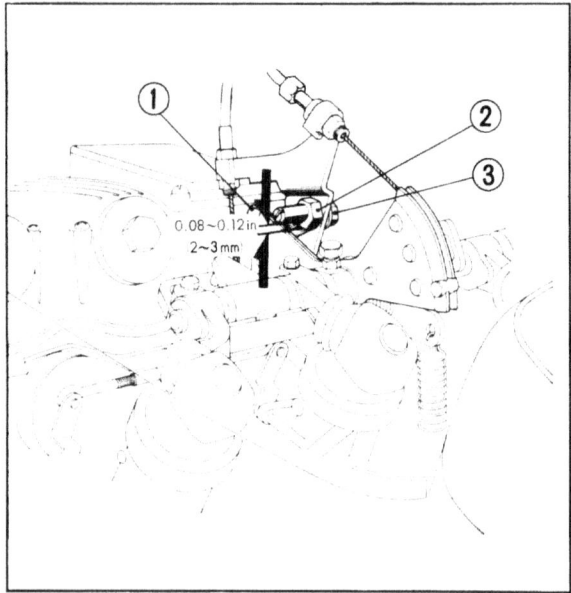

Fig. 20-17 Overcross stop adjustment
① Throttle lever   ③ Lock nut
② Eccentric link pin

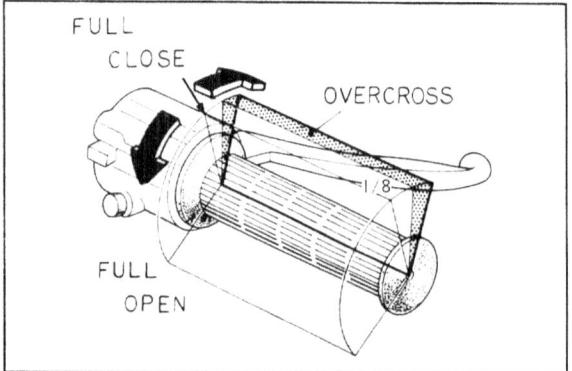

Fig. 20-18 Overcross part

20. SUPPLEMENT TO CB750K1~K4

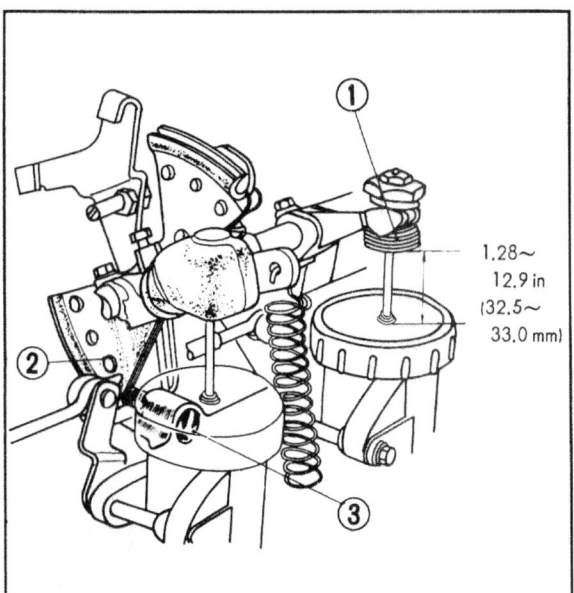

Fig. 20-19 Full open stopper adjustment
① Adjuster screw
② Throttle lever
③ Full open stopper screw

Full open stopper adjustment

Adjust the stopper screw so that there will be a distance of **1.28-1.29 in. (32.5-33.0 mm)** between the top and the adjuster screw with the throttle grip in the full open position. **(Fig. 20-19)**

Throttle cable adjustment

1. Turn the adjuster counter clockwise on the handle end to increase the play in the cable. To permit fine adjustment with the adjuster screw, leave about a **0.12 in. (3 mm)** play in the cable.
2. Turn the adjuster nut at the carburetor end to provide a **0.12-0.16 in. (3-4 mm)** play at the grip flange. **(Fig. 20-20)**

Note:
The throttle lever should hit the link pin when the grip is forced to the full close position.
If this does not occur, the throttle cable must be replaced.

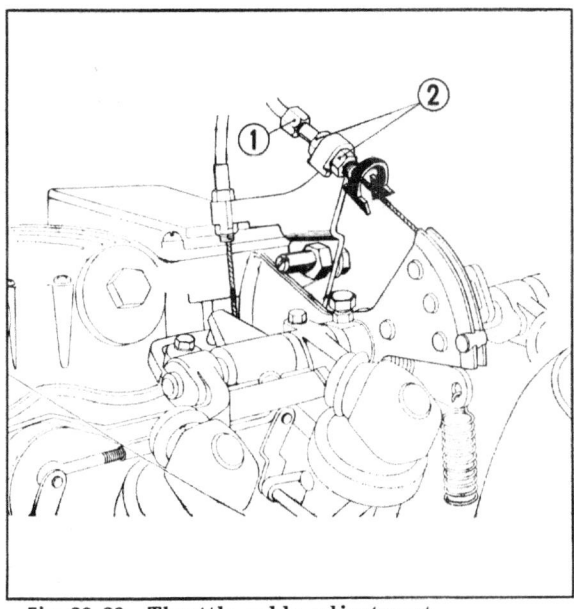

Fig. 20-20 Throttle cable adjustment
① Adjust nut
② Lock nut

STEERING AND FRONT SUSPENSION

FRONT SUSPESION

The front fork is assembled into a complete unit by the fork bottom bridge, axle and the fork top bridge and their respective mounting bolts. This three-point mounting design provides a highly rigid unit for good stability. The front suspension is a telescoping oil damper type with an aluminum fork bottom case used for lightness.

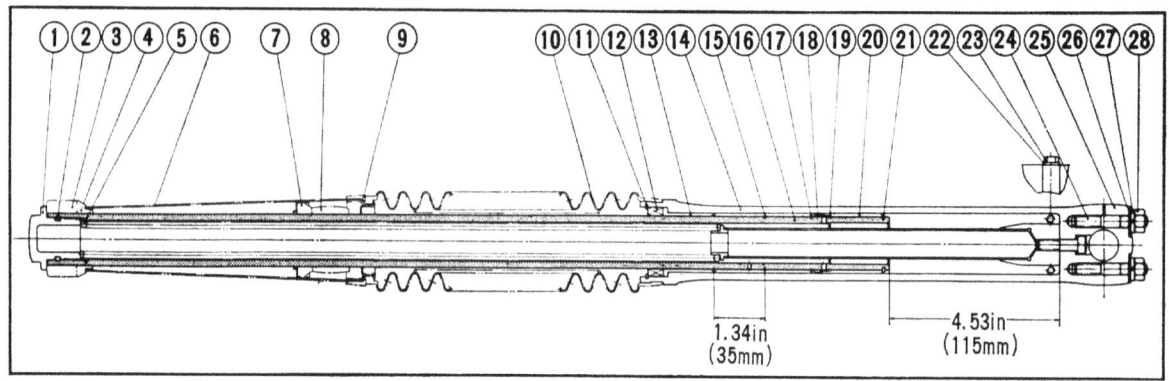

Fig. 20-21

① Front fork bolt
② 23×28 "O" ring
③ Fork top dridge
④ Fork cover upper cushion
⑤ Front cushion spring
⑥ Front fork cover
⑦ Fork cover lower cushion
⑧ Steering stem
⑨ Front fork rib
⑩ Front fork boot
⑪ 50 mm circlip
⑫ 354811 oil seal
⑬ Front fork pipe guide
⑭ Front fork bottom case
⑮ Fork pipe stoper ring
⑯ Front fork pipe
⑰ Fork valve stopper ring
⑱ Front damper valve
⑲ Piston stopper ring
⑳ Front fork piston
㉑ Fork piston snap ring
㉒ Drani cock packing
㉓ 6 mm hex bolt
㉔ 8 mm stud bolt
㉕ Front axle holder
㉖ 8 mm flat washer
㉗ 8 mm spring washer
㉘ 8 mm hex nut

As the outside diameter of oil seal 354811 is 0.08 in. (2 mm) larger than previous model to prevent the deformation of oil seal and oil leakage, the diameter (50 mm) of circlip is also larger than previous one (47 mm).

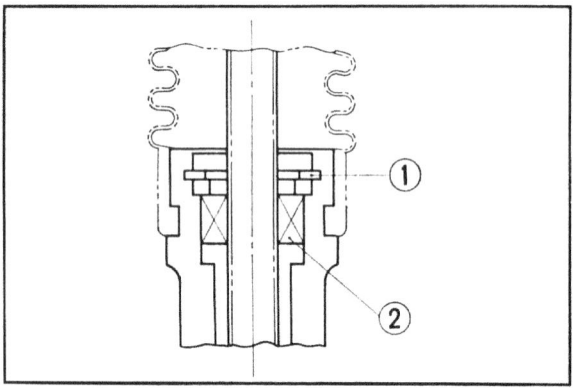

Fig. 20-22 ① 50 mm circlip
② 354811 oil seal

REAR SUSPENSION

REAR SHOCK ABSORBER

A De Carbon type damper containing nitrogen gas under high pressure is contained within the cylinder to maintain a pressure against the oil. This prevents the bubbles from being produced in the oil during compression. It assures positive damping action. The spring force can be adjusted to the three positions according to carring load and riding condition. The stroke of the rear shock absorber is **3.4 in. (87 mm)**.

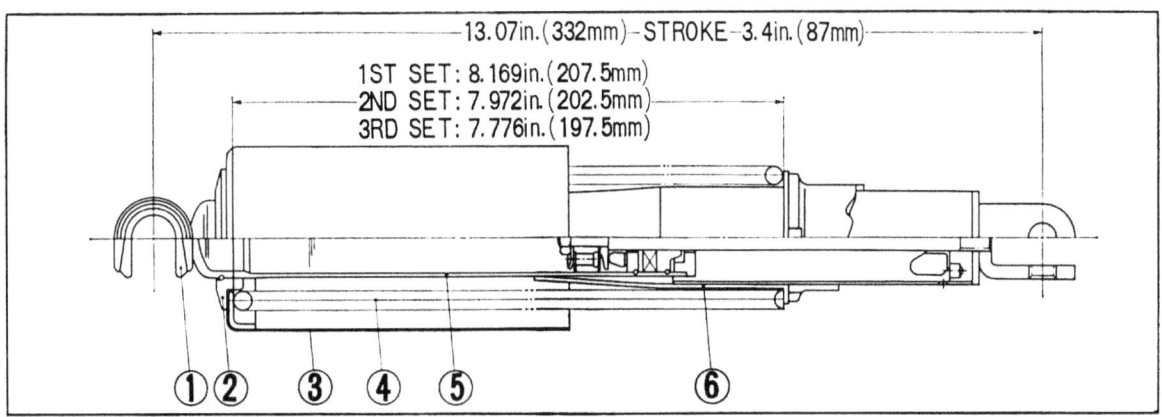

Fig. 20-23
① Joint rubber
② Spring seat stopper
③ Rear cushion upper cover
④ Rear cushion spring
⑤ Rear damper assembly
⑥ Rear cushion spring guide

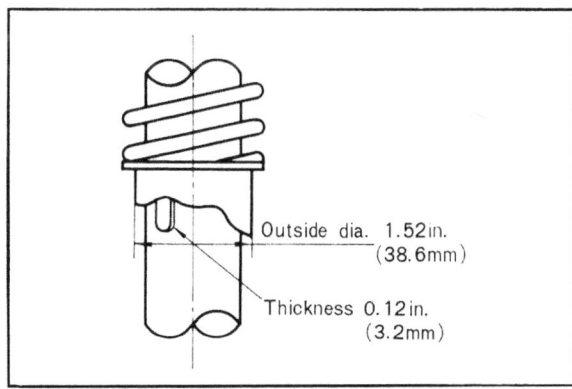

Fig. 20-24

The stopper was changed 0.09 in. (2.3 mm) to 0.12 in. (3.2 mm) thickness and the outside diameter 1.52 in. (38.6 mm) of shock absorber is 0.08 in. (2 mm) larger than previous one. Consequntly, the spring diameter is 0.15 in. (4mm) larger than previous model.

Inspection

Damping force cannot be measured therefore, the test is performed by compressing the shock absorber unit by hand. Normal operating condition is indicated by a greater resistance on the extension stroke than on the compression stroke.

When replacing the shock absorber spring, note that the new and previous spring are not interchangeable.

Item	Standard value	Serviceable limit
Shock absorber spring		
Spring inner diameter	1.56~1.86 in. (39.7~40.3 mm)	—
Free length	8.58 in. 218 mm	8.346 in.(212 mm)
Coil diameter	(0.276 in. 7 mm)	—
Installation load	7.98 in./66.6 lbs (202.9mm/30.2kg)	—
Tilt	within 1.5°	Over 2.5°

WHEELS, TIRES AND FINAL DRIVE

FRONT WHEEL HUB AND MOUNTING BOLTS

As the width of the front wheel hub was made 0.157 in. (4 mm) narrow in width, the length of the mounting bolts was changed from 4.17 to 4.02 in. (106 to 102 mm) shortened by 0.157 in. (4 mm).

Whenever replacing these parts, make sure that the proper length bolts are used. Using the old longer bolts on the new hub will cause the disc plate to loosen during riding. When the front hub is replaced, the associated parts corresponding to this hub must be replaced in set. Old and new parts are not interchangeable.

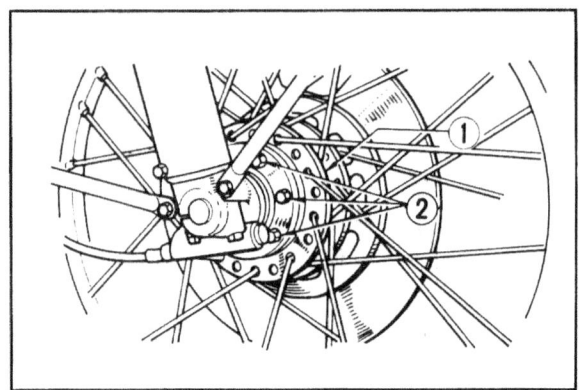

Fig. 20-25 ① Front wheel hub
② Disc plate mounting bolts

REAR WHEEL DAMPER

The shape of both side wheel dampers which was changed as shown in figure, absorb the shock when the rear wheel was turned by the drive chain and it prolongs the drive chain service life.

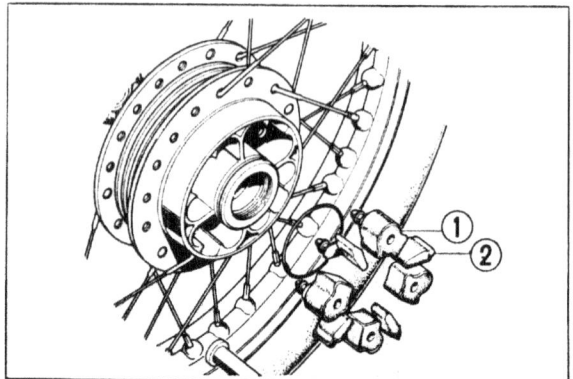

Fig. 20-26 ① R. rear wheel damper
② L. rear wheel damber

BODY, OIL TANK, AIR CLEANER AND EXHAUST SYSTEM

OIL TANK AND OIL COVER

The oil tank mounted on the right side center of the motorcycle is connected to the engine with two oil hoses. Since the oil tank was made narrow in width, the oil tank cover was designed sporty shape and narrow in width.

Note:
Both new and old are not interchangeable.

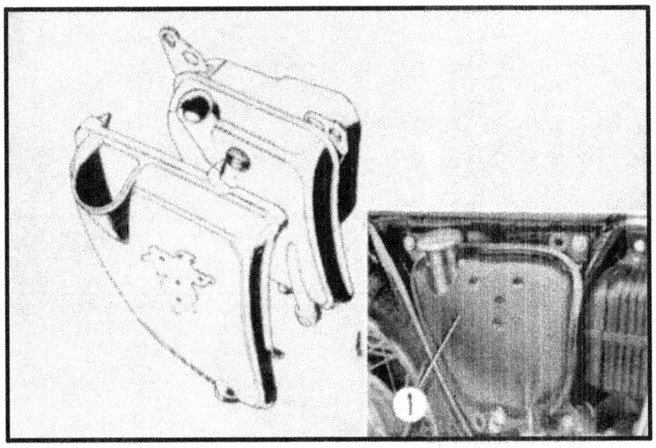

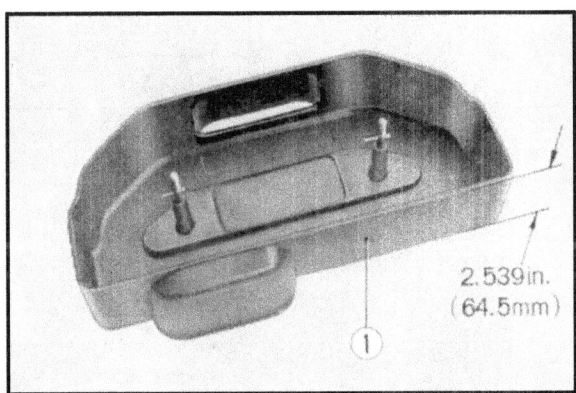

Fig. 20-27 ① Oil tank

AIR CLEANER COVER, SEPARATOR CASE AND CLEANER CASE

The air cleaner mounted at the center of the motorcycle under the fuel tank which was made narrow in width and the material was improved against chemical reaction and vibration shock when travelling on rough roads. The air cleaner cover was designed 0.08 in. (2 mm) narrow in width with concave parts on both side of it. The height of knobs on separator case was made 0.13 in. (3.5 mm) higher and the air cleaner case was designed as shown in Fig. 20-29.

Note:
If the air cleaner cover, separator case, cleaner cover and battery cover are replaced in set, new and old are interchangeable.

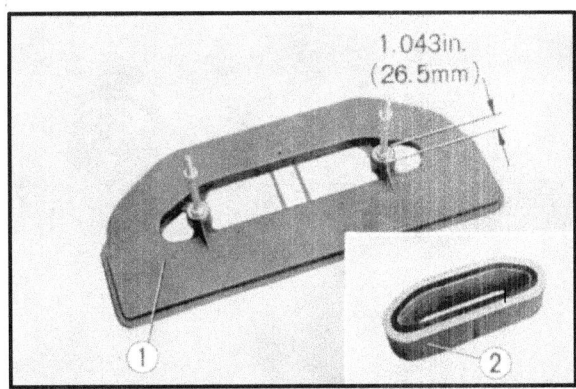

Fig. 20-28 ① Air cleaner cover

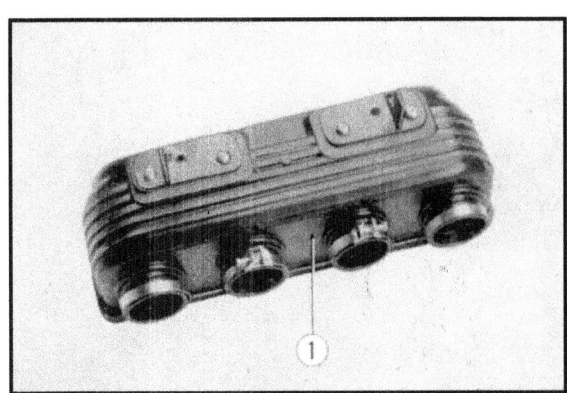

Fig. 20-29 ① Air cleaner separator case
② Air cleaner element

Fig. 20-30 ① Air cleaner case

BATTERY COVER

The battery cover was narrowed in width and its shape was designed sporty looking with alluring emblems. Therefore, they are not interchangeable.

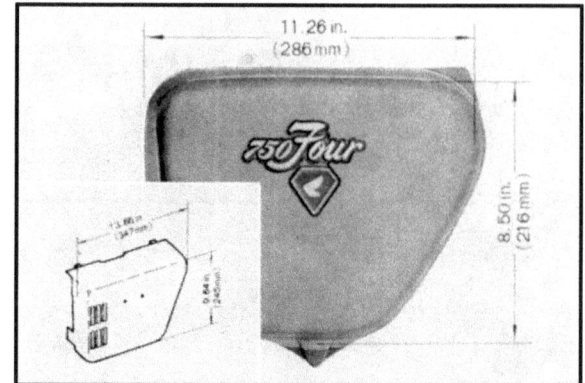

Fig. 20-31

SEAT AND SEAT LATCH

The front part of the seat was made narrow and the seat was designed into the double seat type covered with vinyl leather.
A seat latch of flip motion type was equipped to simply lock or unlock the seat.
Note:
If the seat latch, hook and seat are replaced at the same time, new and old are interchangeable.

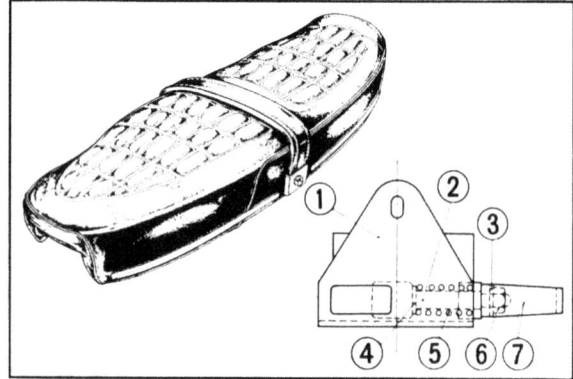

Fig. 20-32
① Seat catch plate
② Seat catch slider
③ 6 mm, washer
④ 8 mm, washer
⑤ Seat catch spring
⑥ 6 mm nut
⑦ Seat catch lever

MAIN STAND

The welded metal sheet shown in Fig. 51 was made 0.4 in. (10 mm) wider for providing the stability when the main stand was operated.

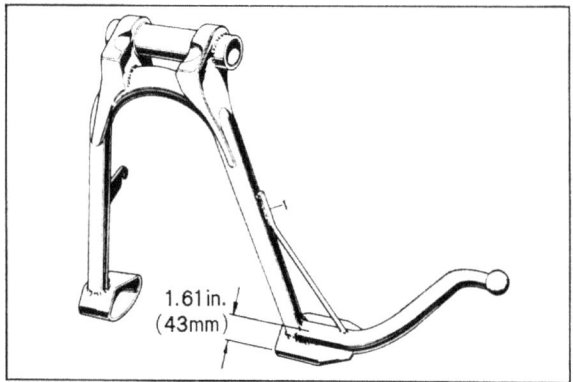

Fig. 20-33

BODY ELECTRICAL AND INSTRUMENTS

Fig. 20-34 ① Speedometer
② Tachometer
③ Red zone

SPEEDO/TACHOMETER

The speedometer and tachometer cases were painted flat black to prevent annoying reflection. Further, to provide the superior quality against the brake fluid reaction, the material of both windows was changed to the glass from the acrycic resin, and the tachometer red zone is 8,000~9,500 rpm.

DRIVE CHAIN CONNECTOR AND DISCONNECTOR OPERATION

On the models CB 750, it is necessary to to cut the endless chains. To cut the chains, proceed as follows:

A. Disconnection of Drive Chain

1. Position chain link pin to be cut on chain holder in place as shown in Fig. 20-35 Screw in pressure bolt until pressure holder holds chain in position. Back off adjuster bolt so that it does not interfere with chain.

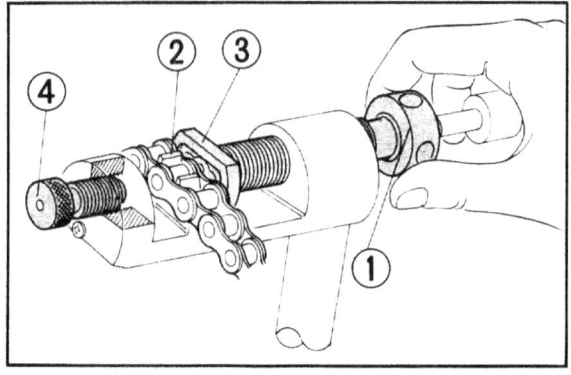

Fig. 20-35 ① Pressure bolt ③ Pressure holder
② Chain holder ④ Adjuster bolt

2. By use of handlebar, screw in pressure bolt B until before joint pin is just pushed off joint plate.

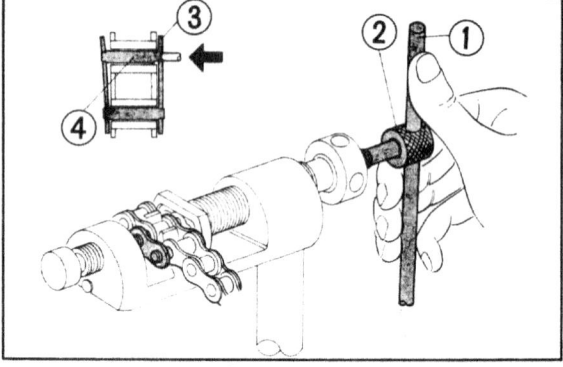

Fig. 20-36 ① Handlever ③ Joint plate
② Pressure bolt B ④ Joint pin

3. Position adjacent chain link pin on chain holder and repeat step 1 and 2 screw in pressure bolt B until joint pin is completely pushed off joint plate.
4. Reposition original chain link pin on chain holder and disconnect chain by pushing off joint pin in the same way as in step 3.

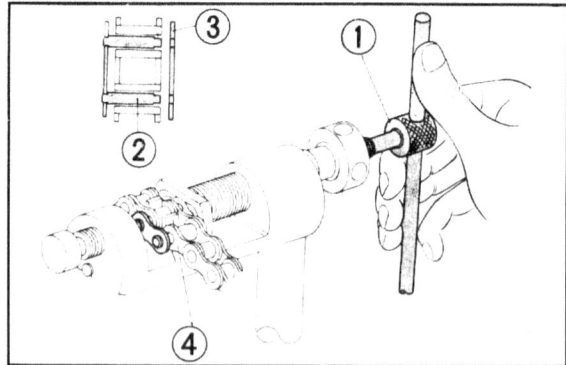

Fig. 20-37 ① Pressure bolt B ③ Joint plate
② Joint pin ④ Chain holder

B. Press-in Connection of Drive Chain

Newly improved chain joints and plates are of a pressfitted type. Only press-fitted type chain joint and plate require this procedue.

1. Join new drive chain by inserting joint pin.

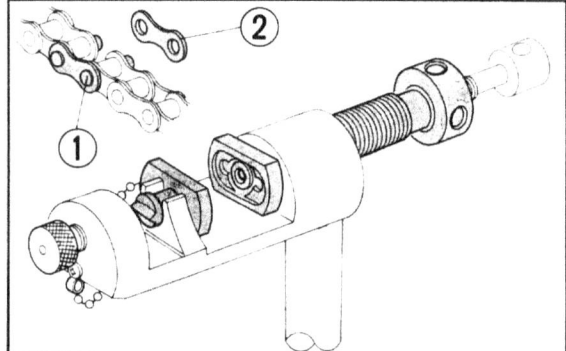

Fig. 20-38 ① Joint pin
② Joint plate

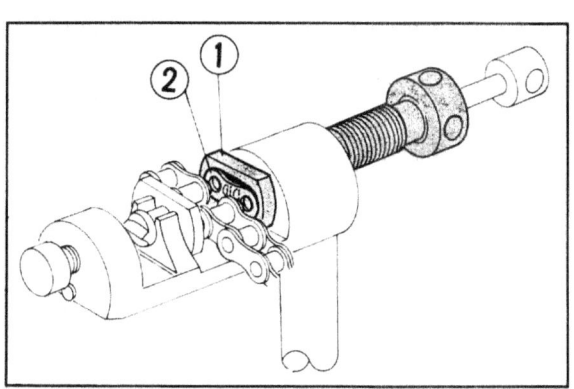

Fig. 20-39 ① Pressure holder
② Joint plate

2. Apply a thin coat of grease in recess of pressure holder. Set joint plate in recess of pressure holder with chamfered side (side with chain code stamped on it) inward, exercising care not to drop it.

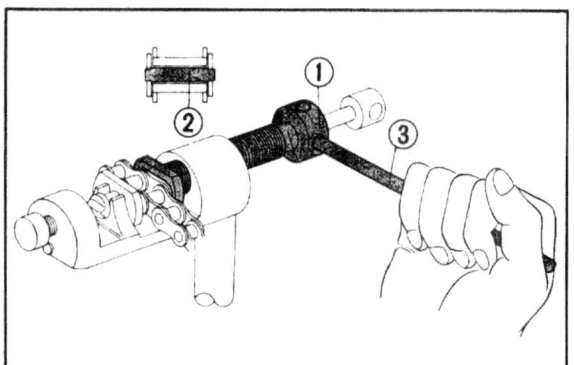

Fig. 20-40 ① Pressure bolt A
② Joint pin   ③ Handle bar

3. Position chain portion to be connected between chain holder and pressure holder. Hold chain in position by screwing in pressure bolt A. After making sure that two pins of joint pin align with corresponding two holes in joint plate. By turning in pressure bolt A with handlebar, press-fit until it goes no longer because of steps on pins.

4. Measure distance between two joint plates to make sure if correctly press-fitted.
   Specified distance between two plates:
   DID50HDS··········19.7mm
   DID50DS ··········19.0mm
   If reading exceeds specifications as above, repeat steps.

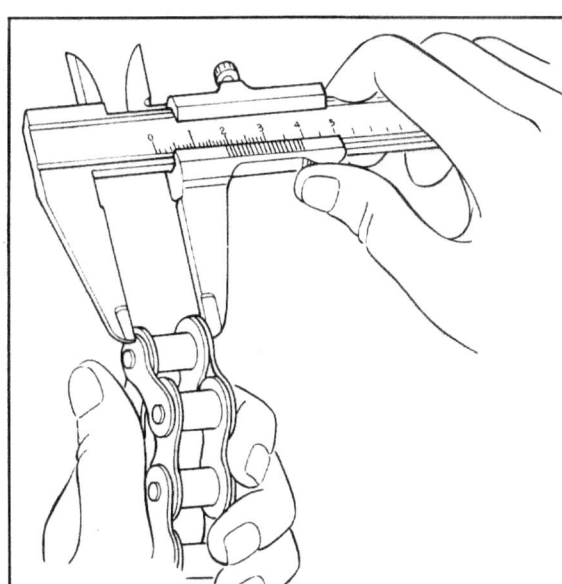

Fig. 20-41

C. Staking of Drive Chain

1. Position drive chain joint portion to be staked on chain holder in place and also place wedge holder between chain holder and pressure holder as shown in Fig. 20-42. So that tip of wedge is in line with center of joint pin.
   By tightening finger-tight, move forward pressure bolt A until it stops.

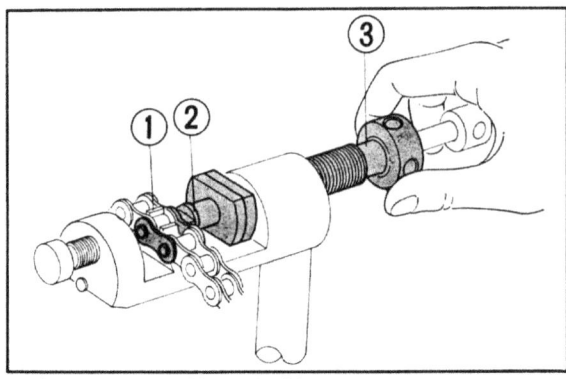

Fig. 20-42 ① Chain holder
② Joint pin
③ Pressure bolt A

2. Screw in adjuster bolt until opposite end of joint pin is forced against it.
   NOTE:
   Screw in adjuster bolt until finger-tight.

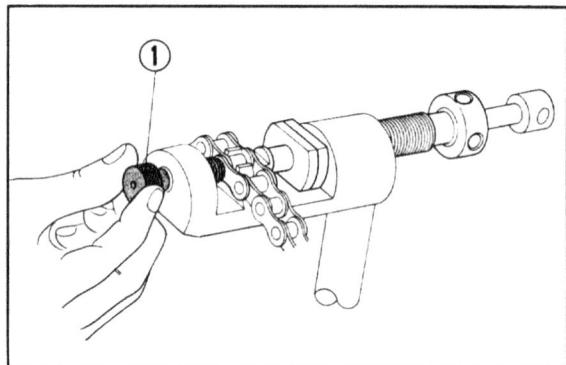

Fig. 20-43 ① Adjuster bolt

3. By use of handlebar, stake end of joint pin by turning pressure bolt B 3/4 turn.
   NOTE:
   Never exceed 3/4 turn.

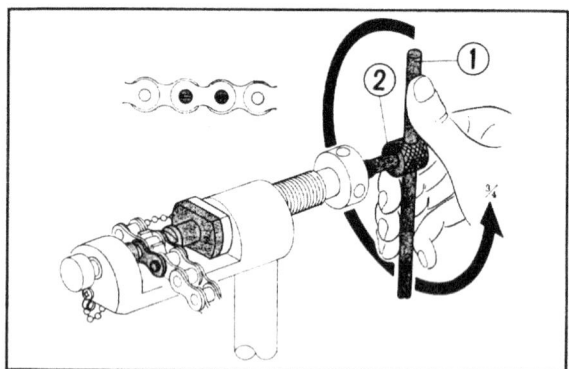

Fig. 20-44 ① Handle bar
② Pressure bolt B

4. After backing off pressure bolt A approx. two turns, back off wedge pin 1/4 turn (90 degrees) and repeat steps 1 thru 3 so that end of joint pin is staked in a cross pattern. Repeat entire steps on opposite end.
   NOTE:
   Be sure that cross patterned stakings are performed at 90° angles.

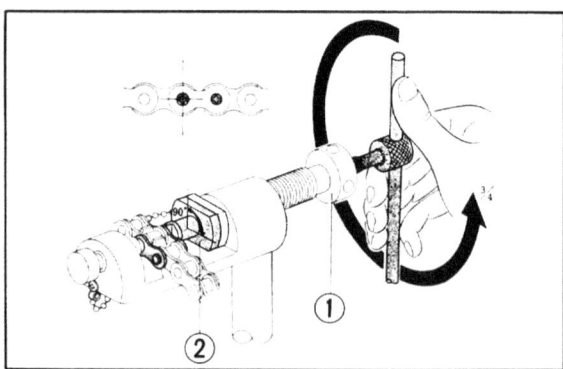

Fig. 20-45 ① Pressure bolt A
② Wedge pin

SUPPLEMENT TO CB750K1~K4

K2

COMPARISON OF CB750K2 TO CB750K1

Part of item	CB 750 K1	CB 750 K2	Modified part
seat seat catch seat lock	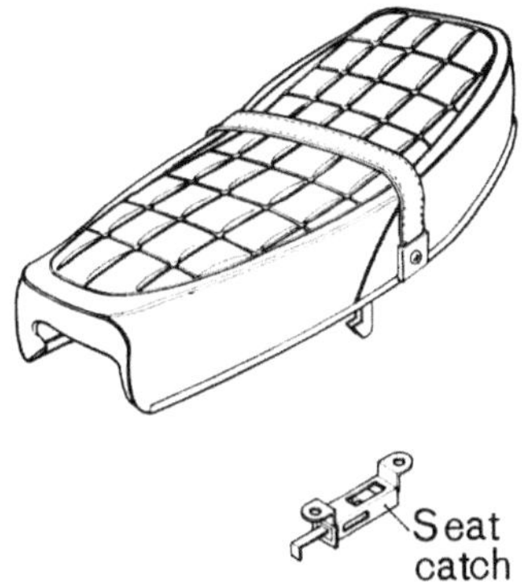 Fig. 20-46 — Seat catch	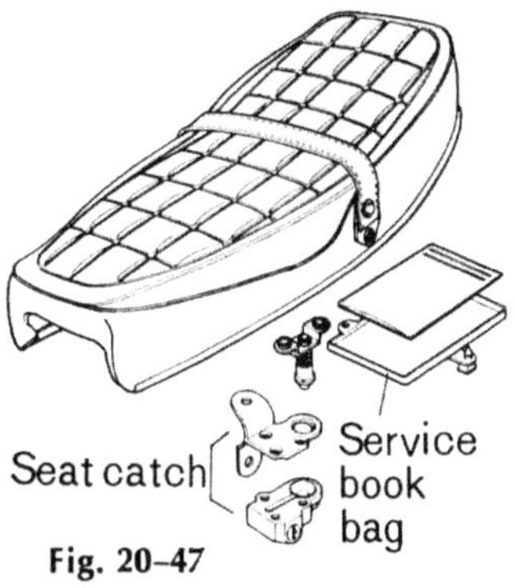 Fig. 20-47 — Seat catch, Service book bag. The seat was changed in pattern and partially in shape. The seat catch was changed as shown.	seat catch seat lock
brake pedal	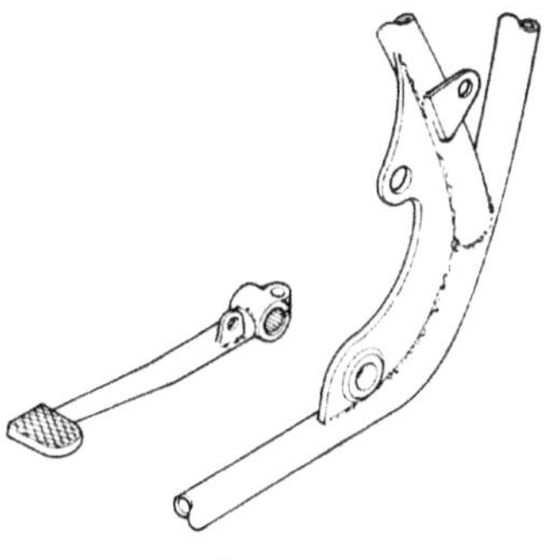 Fig. 20-48	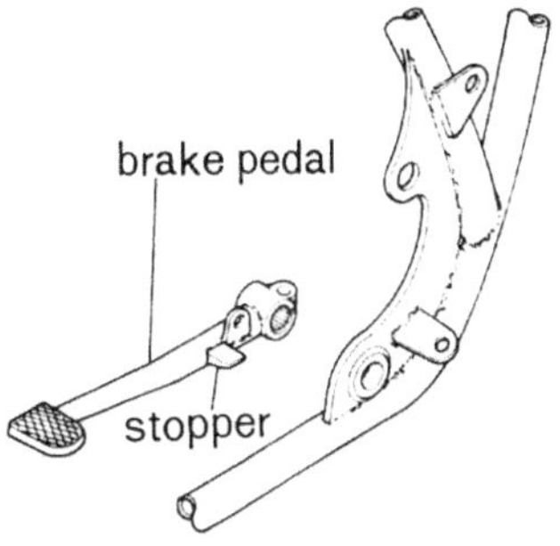 Fig. 20-49 — brake pedal, stopper. A stop was added to the brake pedal returning the pedal properly.	
driven flange	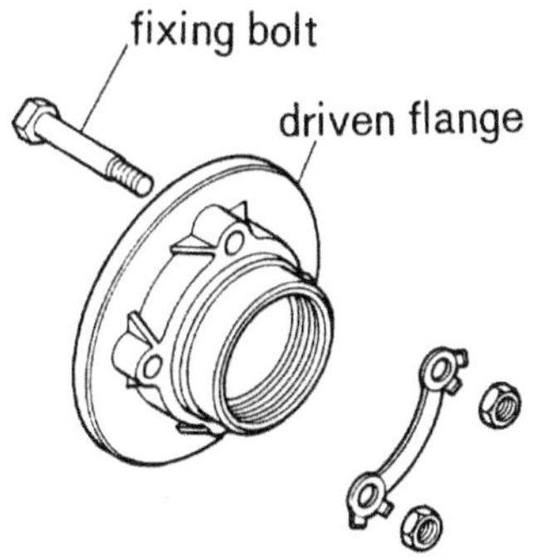 Fig. 20-50 — fixing bolt, driven flange	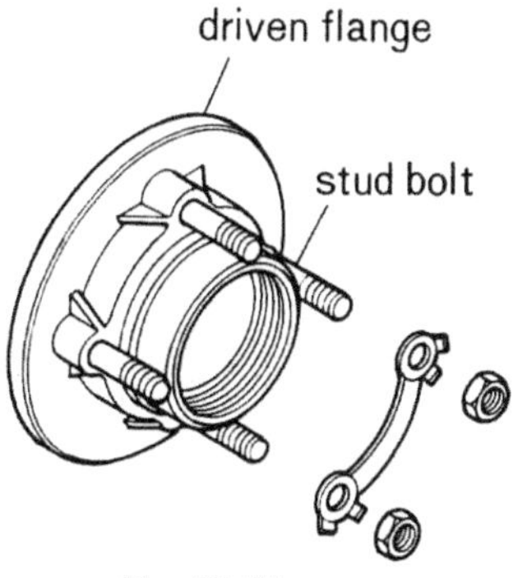 Fig. 20-51 — driven flange, stud bolt. The fixing bolt was changed from the removable type to the press-in type.	

20. SUPPLEMENT TO CB750K1~K4

Part of item	CB 750 K1	CB 750 K2	Modified part
turn signal Buzzer swich	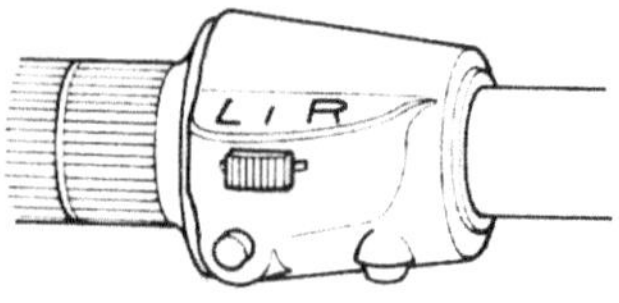 Fig. 20-52	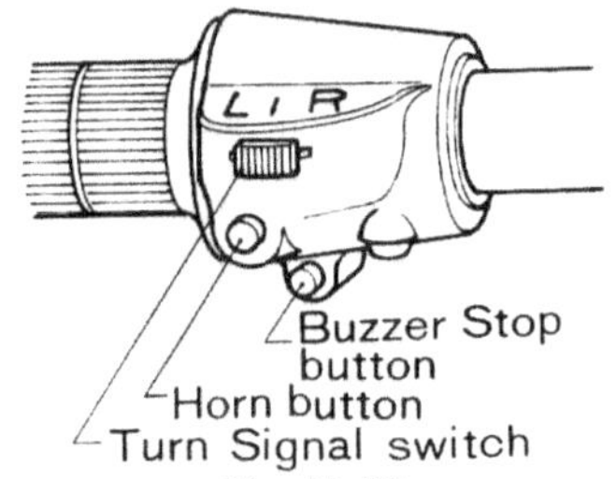 Buzzer Stop button / Horn button / Turn Signal switch — Fig. 20-53 A turn signal buzzer was newly installed. Correspondingly a buzzer stop button was provided and the operation is described below. A warning buzzer which starts sounding when the switch is moved to either position is provided to prevent a rider from forgetting to return the switch after completing a turn. When a turn signal has to be kept flashing for any length of time at a crossing or the like, the buzzer can be stopped by pushing the buzzer stop button.	• Buzzer stop switch • Turn signal buzzer
Wire harness and rectifier coupler lock	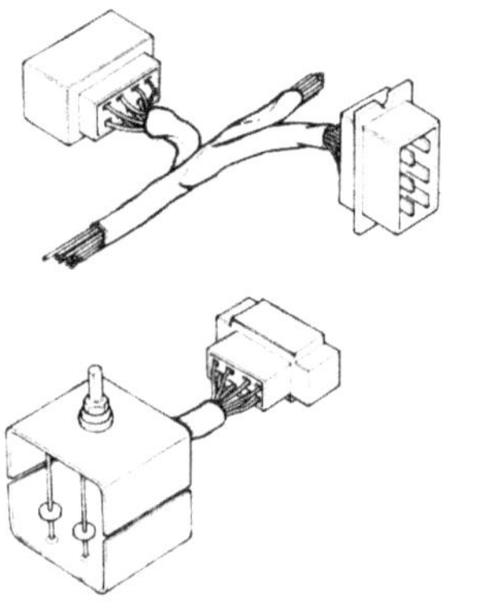 Fig. 20-54	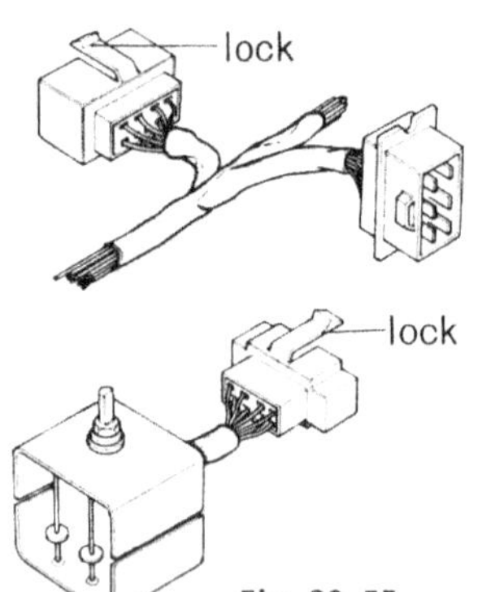 lock ... lock — Fig. 20-55 The employment of a coupler lock assures a complete locking.	
Indicator panel	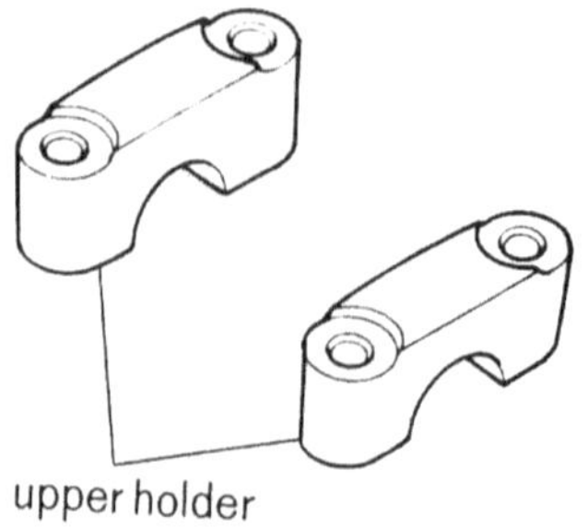 upper holder — Fig. 20-56	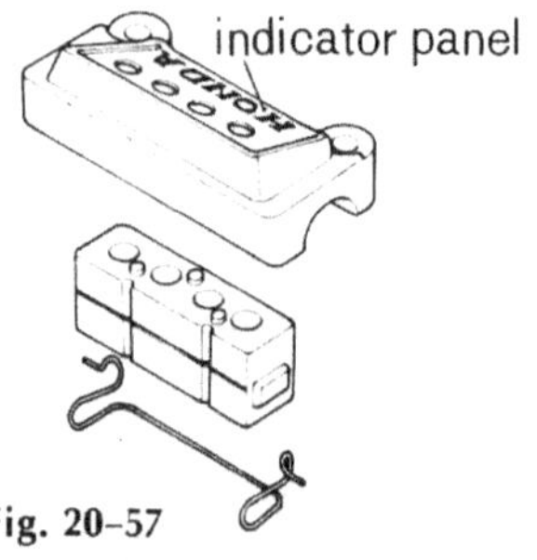 indicator panel — Fig. 20-57 An indicator panel of the same type used in the model CB 500 was employed, grouping various control lamps for improved serviceability.	

20. SUPPLEMENT TO CB750K1~K4   145

K3

COMPARISON OF CB 750 K3 TO CB 750 K2

Part of item	CB 750 K2	CB 750 K3	Modified part
Rear shock absorbers	(Cross valves) Number of rear shock absorber adjusting positions increased	(One-way valves)	• Shape of valves
	Shock absorber spring adjusting positions: 3	Shock absorber spring adjusting positions: 5 The valves were changed from the cross type to the one-way type. For the details see page 150.	
	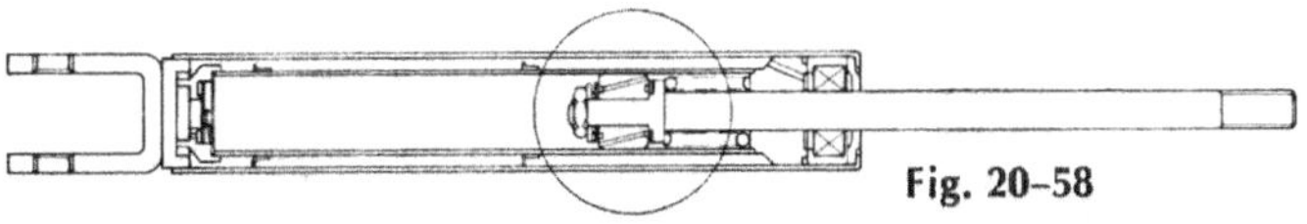 Fig. 20-58 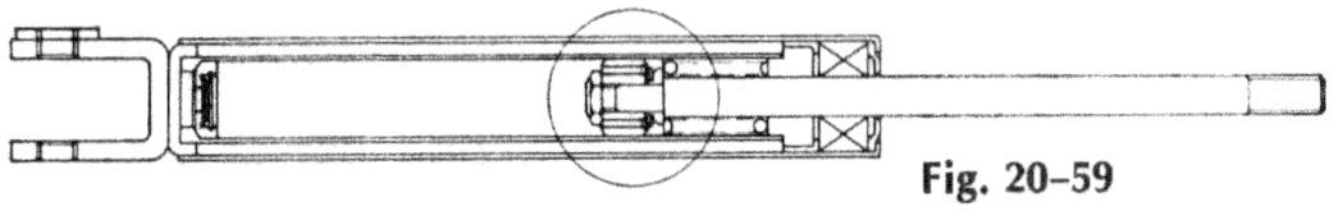		
	Fig. 20-59		
Front forks	Valve in front shock absorber and its specifications changed		
	Piston type valve	Free valve	
	Specifications		
	Damping force: 39.5-40.5 Kg/0.5 m/sec. Stroke: 143 mm Oil capacity: 220-230 cc	Damping force: 34-46 Kg/0.5 m/sec. Stroke: 141.5 mm Oil capacity: 155-160 cc The valves were changed from the piston type to the free type. For the construction and function see page 149.	
Disc cover	Disc cover newly installed		
	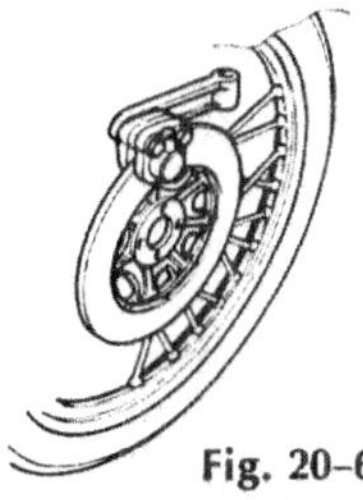 Fig. 20-60	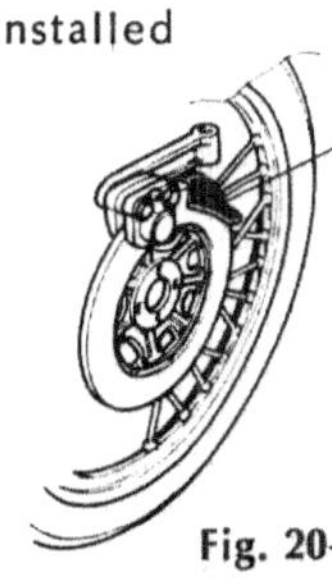 Disc cover Fig. 20-61	
Fuses		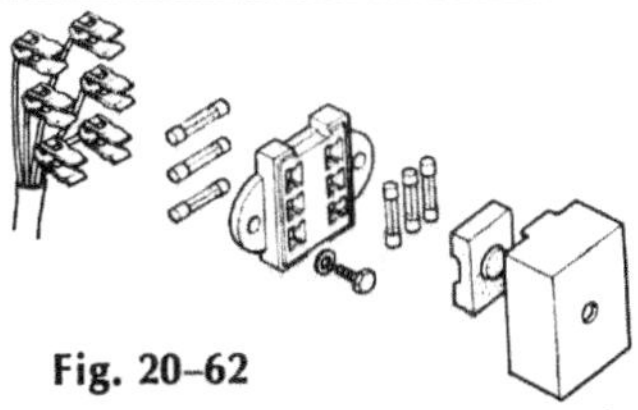 Fig. 20-62 The fuses were installed separately for lights such as headlight, taillight, etc. for a quick troubleshooting.	

20. SUPPLEMENT TO CB750K1~K4

Part of item	CB 750 K2	CB 750 K3	Modified part
Safety unit Clutch switch	none	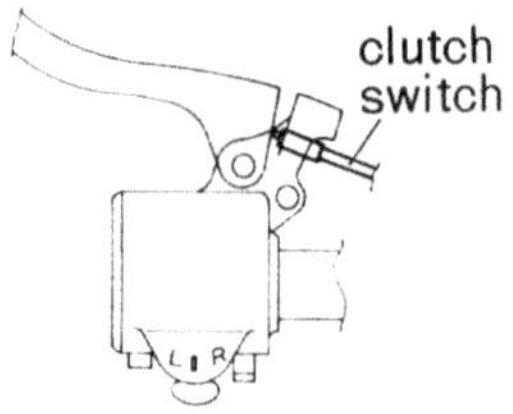 Fig. 20-63 A safety unit and a clutch switch were added to prevent the motorcycle from running out as soon as the engine starts. For the operation see page 152.	
Lighting kill switch	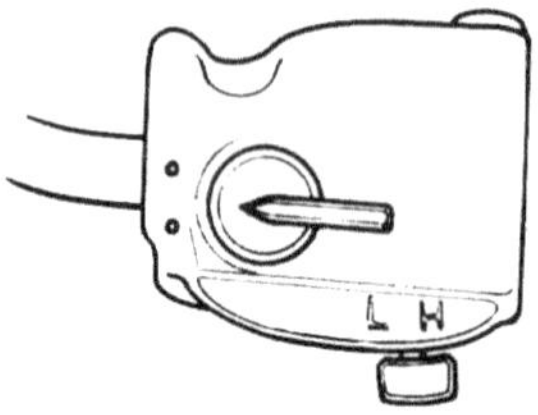 Fig. 20-64	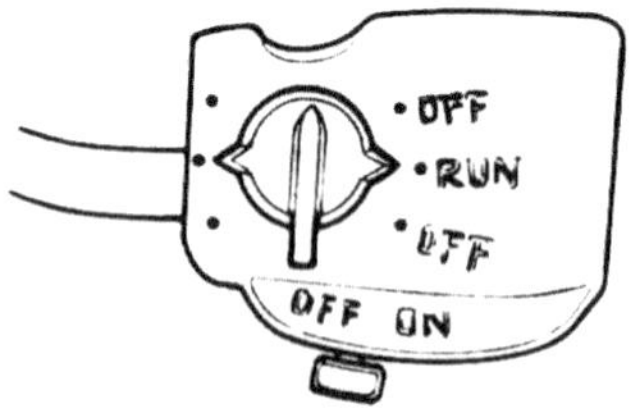 Fig. 20-65 The kill switch was changed in operating pattern from the up-down motion to the right-left motion.	
Horn switch Dimmer switch	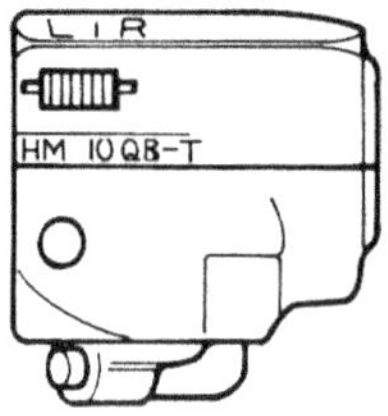 Fig. 20-66	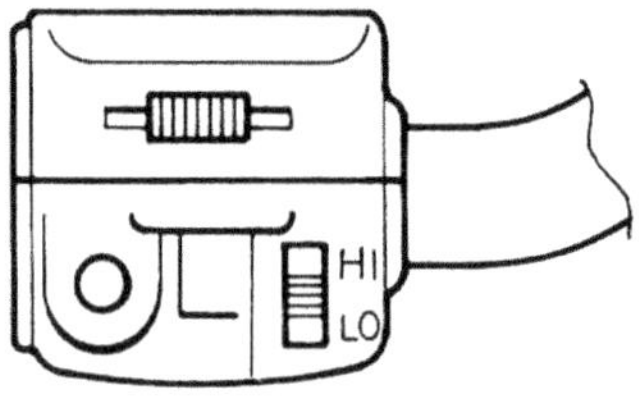 Fig. 20-67 The switches were changed in shape and installation positions. The turn signal knob is of an automatic return type.	
Oil ring	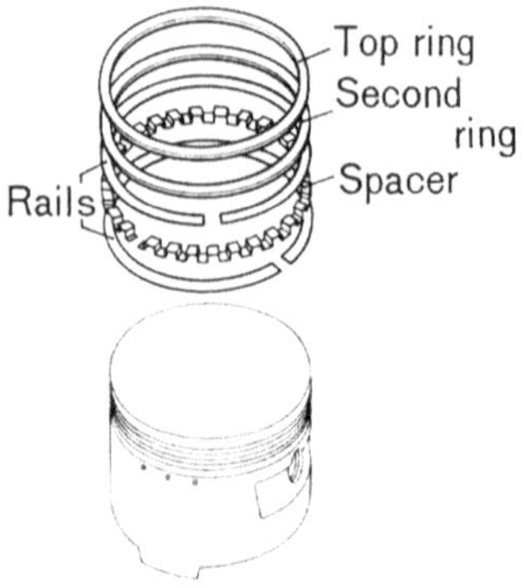 Fig. 20-68	The three-piece type oil ring was changed. • The key points of assembling procedure are described below. a. When installing the oil ring, first place the spacer and then the rails in position. b. The spacer and rail gaps must be staggered 2~3 cm (0.787~1.18 in.).	• Rails • Spacer

20. SUPPLEMENT TO CB750K1~K4

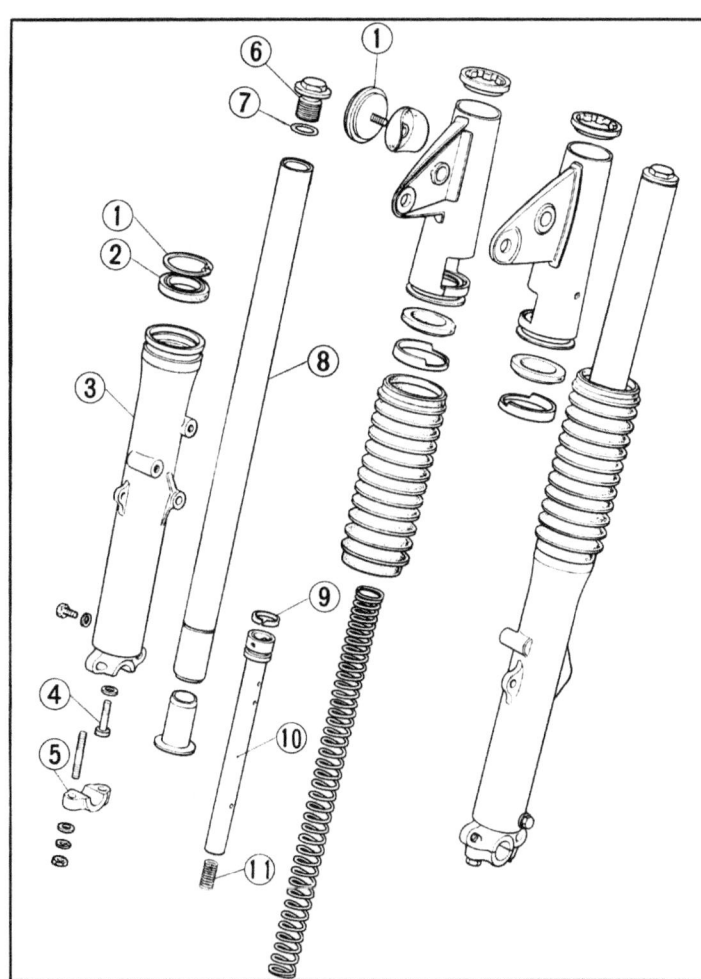

In the model CB750K3 front shock absorbers, the valves were changed to free valves.

As its damping force can be adjusted by changing its stroke to meet a driver's preference of conditions of a road or surfaces, it always provides a comfortable ride even under severe driving conditions.

The disassembly and operation are as follows:

Fig. 20-69
① 48 mm Internal circlip
② 354811 oil seal
③ Front fork bottom case
④ 8 mm socket bolt
⑤ Front axle holder
⑥ Front fork bolt
⑦ 23×2.3 O ring
⑧ Front fork pipe
⑨ Piston ring
⑩ Bottom pipe
⑪ Front rebound spring

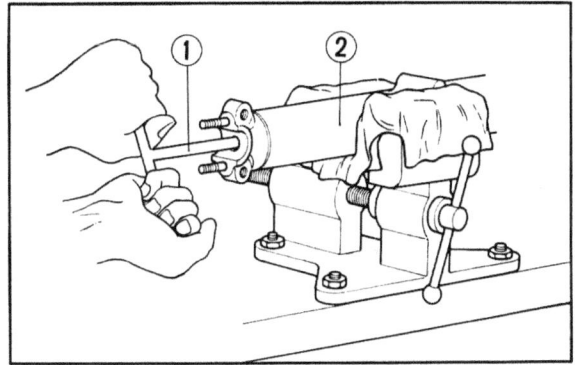

Fig. 20-70 ① Allen head wrench
② Front fork bottom case

Disassembly

To disassemble the front forks, see page 91.
1. Remove the front forks by referring to page 91.
2. Remove the front fork bolts and drain front shock absorber oil.
3. With each front fork bottom pipe held in a vice, remove the socket bolt using the Allen head wrench (Tool No. 0717-3230000) and separate the pipe from the bottom base.

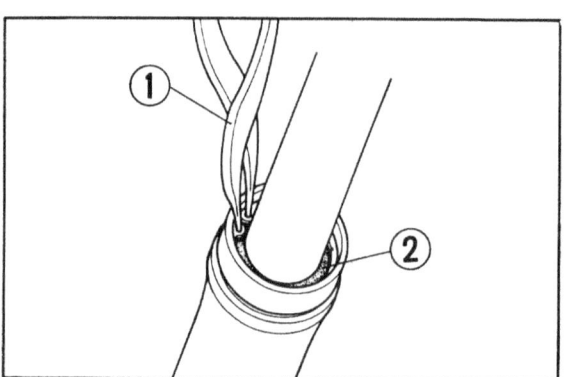

Fig. 20-71 ① 48 mm internal snap ring
② dust seal

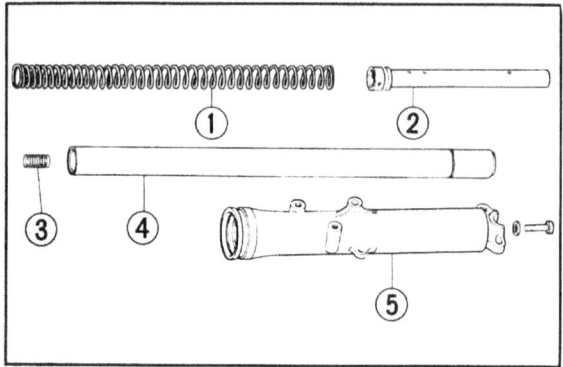

Fig. 20-72 ① Front suspension ② Bottom pipe
③ Front rebound spring
④ Front fork pipe
⑤ Front bottom case

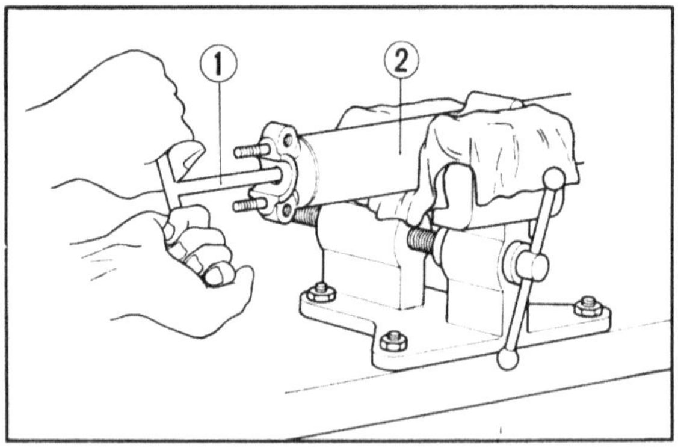

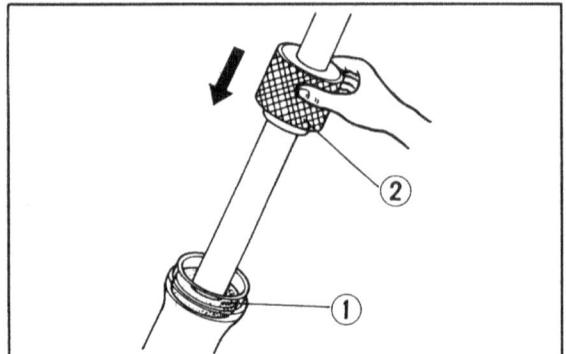

Fig. 20-73 ① Allen head wrench
② Front fork bottom case

Fig. 20-74 ① Oil seal ② Fork seal driver

4. Remove the front fork dust seal, 48 mm internal circlip and oil seal.

Inspection
1. Measure the front shock absorber spring free length. Check the spring tension.
2. Check the front fork piston rings for wear.
3. Check the front fork pipe-to-bottom case clearance.
4. Check the oil seals for scores, scratches or breakage.
5. Check the sliding surfaces of the front fork pipes for scores or scratches.

Assembly
To assemble, reverse the disassembly procedures, paying attention to the following:
1. Position each fork pipe in the bottom case. Apply a coat of locking sealant to the socket bolt and tighten it with the Allen head wrench used at the time of disassembly.

2. Apply a coat of high quality ATF to the inside and outside circumferences of the oil seal and install it using the fork seal driver (Tool No. 07947-3330000).
   Note:
   Use a new oil seal.

3. Fill the fork pipes with high quality ATF up to the specified level.
   Capacity (each fork pipe):
   150~155 cc (5.3~5.5 ozs.) at the time of fork disassembly.

Operation

- When the wheel meets holes or bumps in the road, it moves up and down. This up-and-down movemement of the wheel is transmitted to the bottom leg.
  Since the bottom leg is integrated with a pipe, the pipe also moves up and down. With either action, two springs on the pipe flux and rebound, absorbing the road to the motorcycle.
  In this case, oil in the chamber Ⓑ pushes up the free valve and flows into the space Ⓐ freely.
  At the same time, oil in the chamber Ⓑ also flows through orifices in the lower end of the spring under seat into the space Ⓒ by the amount by which the pipe is moved up.

- Extension
  As the wheel has passed the bump or hole, it moves down. To eliminate excessive up-and-down motion of the spring and wheel, there will be a restraint on the spring and wheel action
  In operation, as the wheel moves down, the free valve is closed, introducing high pressure in the space Ⓐ. This high pressure then forces the oil out and into the space Ⓒ through the orifices in the spring under seat.
  Since the oil encounters a restraint as it passes through the orifices, excessive wheel and spring movement as well as spring oscillation are prevented.

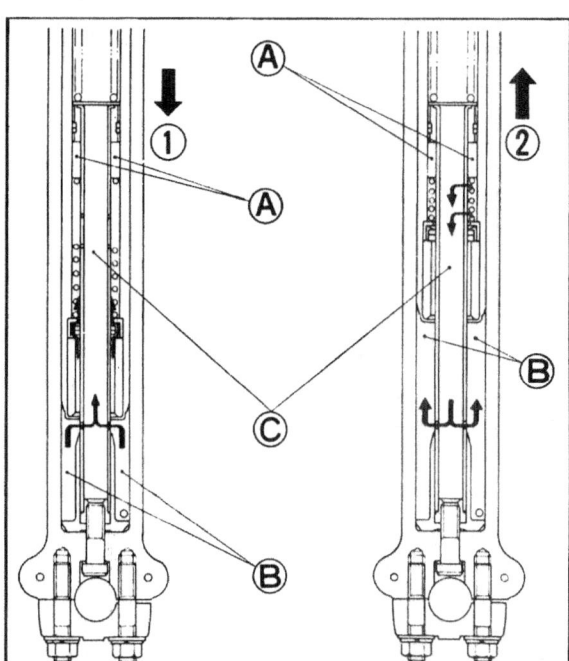

Fig. 20-75 ① Compression ② Extension

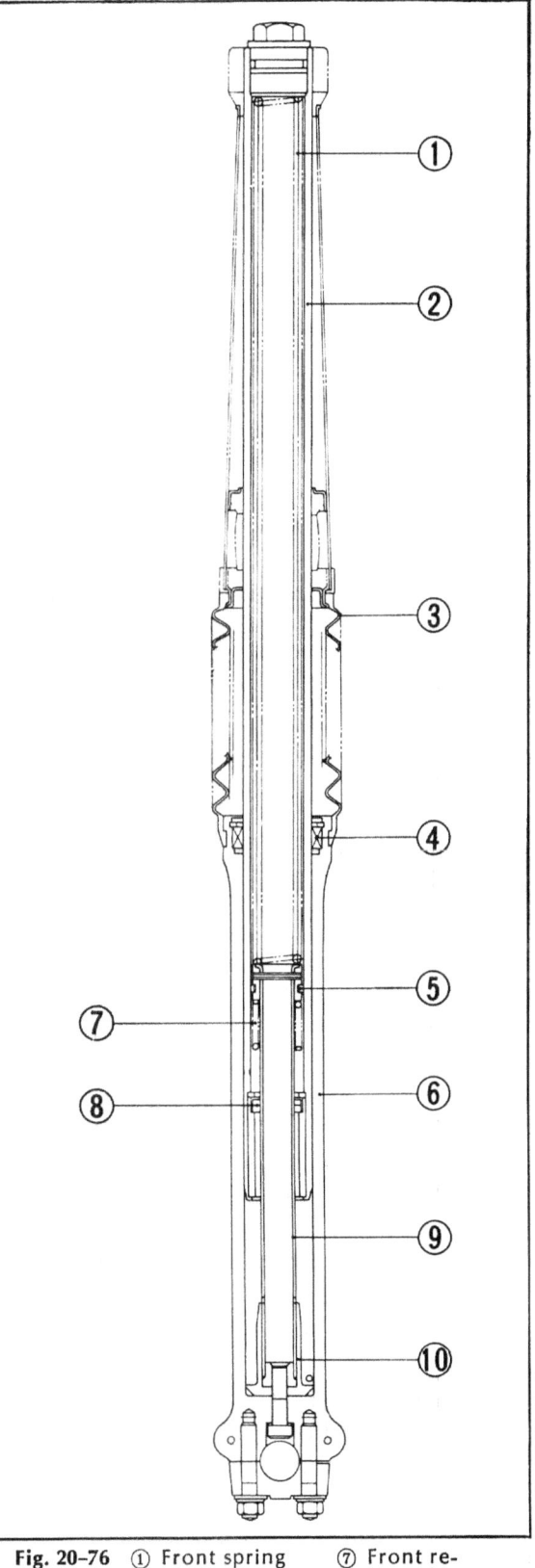

Fig. 20-76
① Front spring
② Front fork pipe
③ Front fork dust seal
④ Oil seal
⑤ Piston ring
⑥ Front fork bottom leg
⑦ Front rebound spring
⑧ Free valve
⑨ Bottom pipe
⑩ Oil lock piece

Rear Shock Absorbers (cross valve)

Each rear shock absorber uses a double-cylinder, cross type oil damper a bottom valve, preventing occurrence of air bubbles to provide a constant damping force. On both the extension and compression sides, the characteristic of damping force is excellent and the damping efficiency is higher.

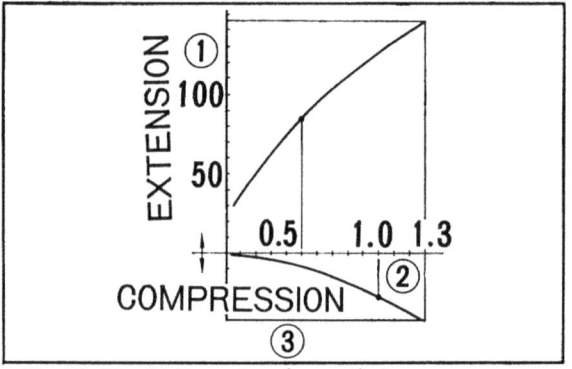

Fig. 20-77
① Damping force (kg)
② Piston speed (m/s)
③ Characteristic of damping force

Operation

Each oil damper is equipped with piston valves A and B and a bottom valve. The damping force is provided by means of the valve A on the extension side, and the resistances on the bottom valve side and in the passage II on the compression side.

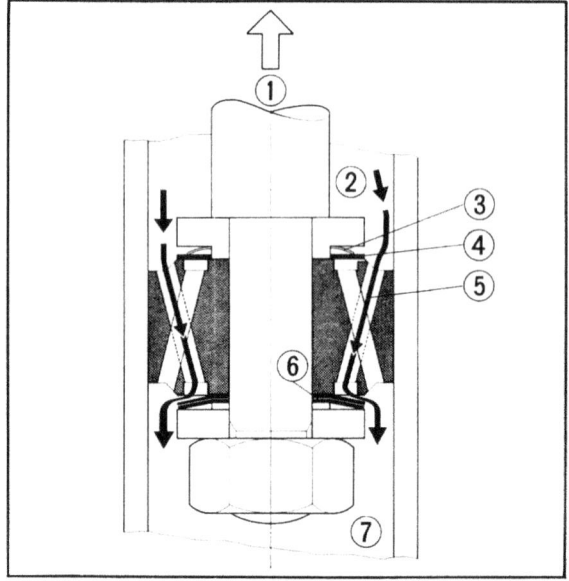

Fig. 20-78
① Extension side　⑤ Passage I
② Chamber "a"　　⑥ Valve B
③ Valve spring　　⑦ Chamber "b"
④ Valve B

- Extension side

When oil attempts to flow from the chamber "a" to the chamber "b", the valve B is closed. Then the oil passes through the passage I to force the valve A to open, and the damping force is provided by the resistance of the valve. (Fig. 20-79) At this time the bottom valve is open, and the oil passes through the chamber "c" and passage III to lift up the bottom valve spring and flows into the chamber "b" from the bottom of the valve. (Fig. 20-81)

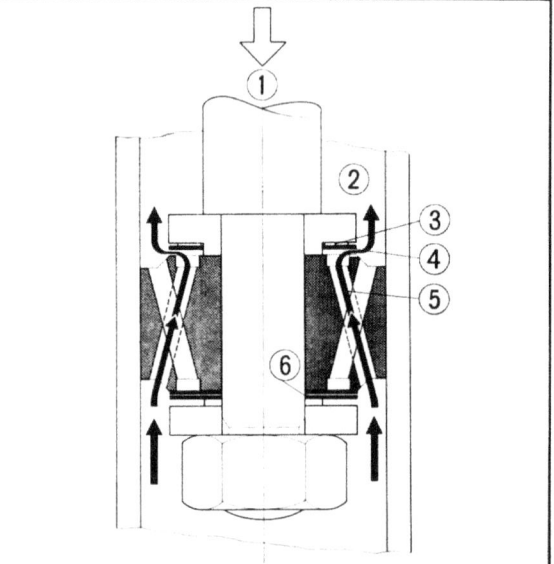

Fig. 20-79
① Compression side　④ Valve B
② Chamber "a"　　　⑤ Passage II
③ Valve spring　　　⑥ Valve A

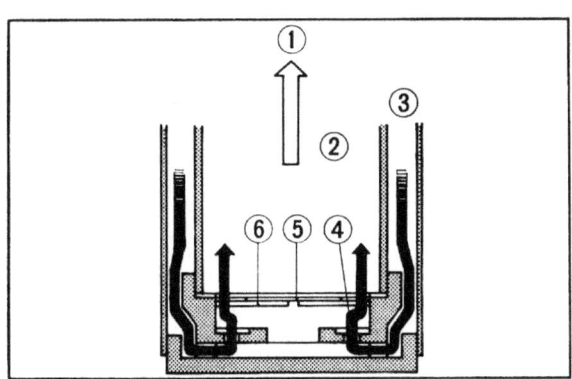

Fig. 20-80
① Extension side
② Chamber "b"
③ Chamber "c"
④ Passage III
⑤ Bottom valve spring
⑥ Bottom valve

- Compression side
When oil attempts to flow from the chamber "b" to the chamber "a", the valve A is closed. Then the oil passes through the passage II to cause the valve B to lift up the valve spring and flows into the chamber "a" from the bottom of the valve. (Fig. 20-80)

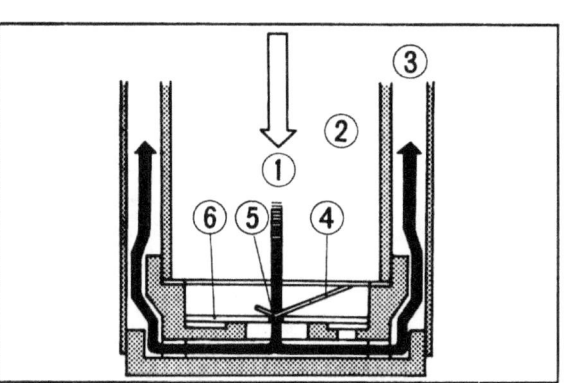

Fig. 20-81
① Compression side
② Chamber "b"
③ Chamber "c"
④ Bottom valve spring
⑤ Orifice
⑥ Bottom valve

A small qvantity of damping force may be provided by the resistance of the valve spring, but a large quantity of the force can be provided by the resistance on the bottom valve side. The oil in the chamber "b" flows by the amount corresponding to the volume of rod into the chamber "c" through the orifice I and the damping force is provided by the resistance at this time. (Fig. 20-81)

2. STARTING MOTOR SAFETY UNIT

- Description

The starting motor safety unit operates in the way that the starting motor functions only when the transmission is in neutral or while the clutch lever is being squeezed in any gear position, assuring rider safety and preventing damage of the motor and transmission gears.

- Circuits and operations

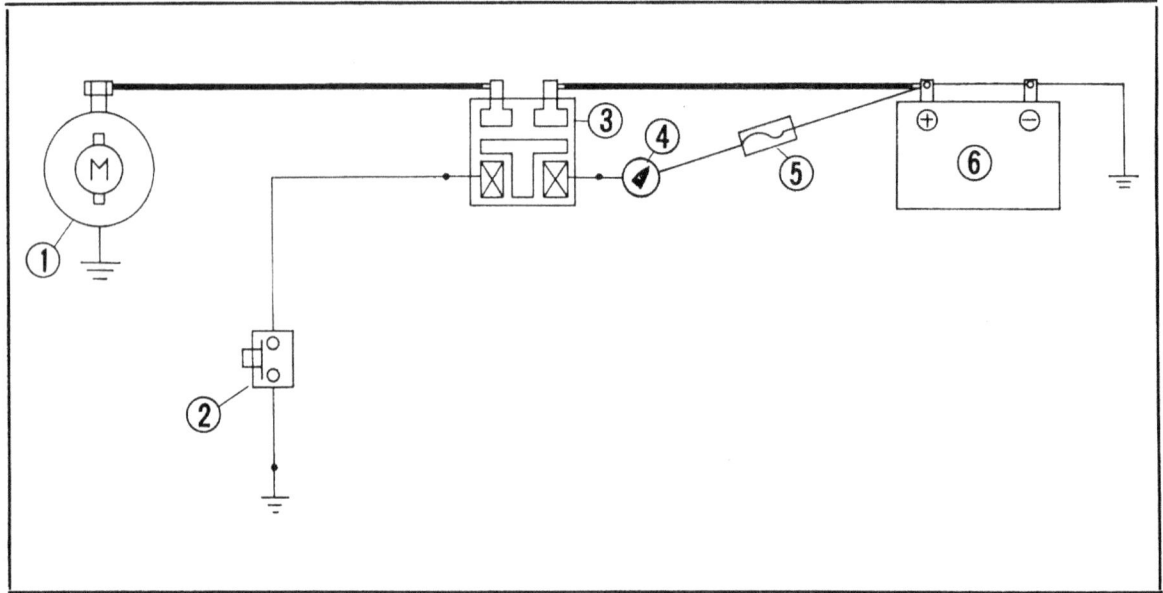

Fig. 20-82 Circuit of models without safety unit
① Starting motor   ④ Main switch
② Starter button switch   ⑤ Fuse
③ Starter magnetic switch ⑥ Battery

When the engine switch is turned on, some amount of electricity is usually applied to the starter magnetic switch coil. If the starter button switch is then turned on, the starter magnetic switch will operate to cause the starting motor to turn. In other words, the motorcycle begines to move when the main switch and starter button switch are turned on with the transmission in gear.

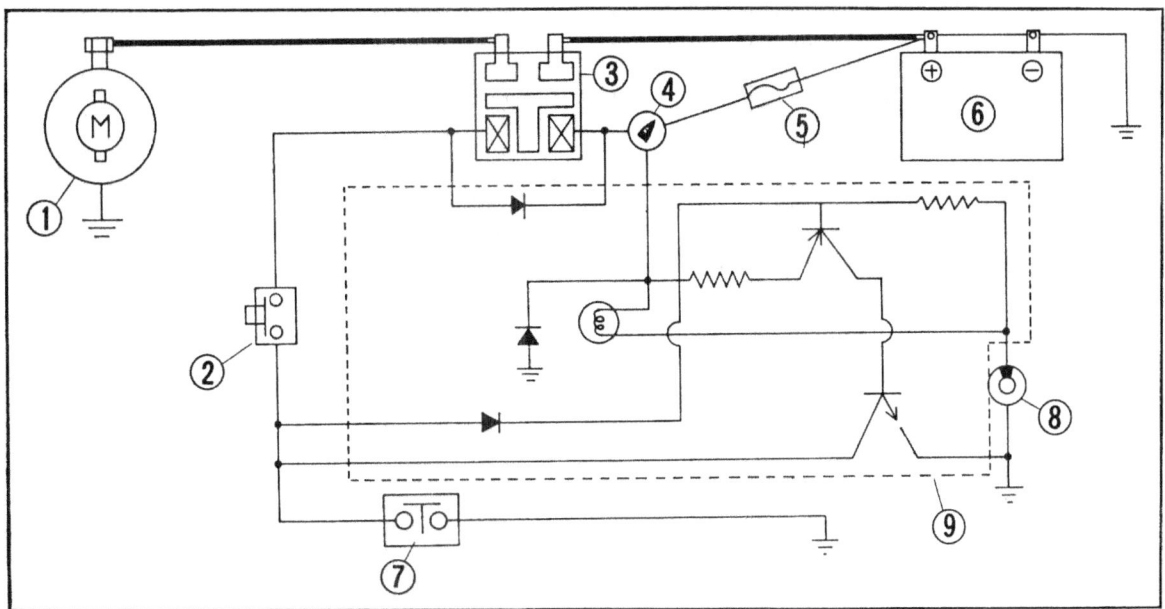

Fig. 20-83 Circuit of model (CB 750) with safety unit
① Starting motor
② Starter button Switch
③ Starter magnetic switch
④ Main switch
⑤ Fuse
⑥ Battery
⑦ Clutch lever switch
⑧ Neutral switch
⑨ Safety unit

The ground side of the starter button switch is connected to the body through the clutch lever switch and neutral switch. When the clutch lever switch or the neutral switch is turned on the starter magnetic switch will operate to cause the starting motor to turn.

(1) Clutch lever switch

The cluch lever switch is designed to be tuned on when the clutch lever is squeezed to cause the clutch to be disengaged only. (This switch has the same construction and function as those of the front stop switch.)

3. 3-CIRCUIT FUSES

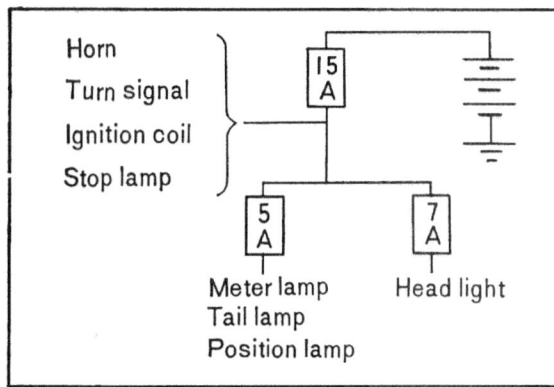

Fig. 20-84

In a conventional 1-circuit fuse, if it burns out, the engine cannot be started.

The 3-circuit fuses contain a 15A main fuse and two 7A and 5A subfuses, one for the headlight and the other for the position lamp, taillight and meter lamp. Even if the 7A fuse or 5A fuse or both burn out, the horn, turn signals, ignition switch and stoplight operate properly. However, it is wise to locate the cause of trouble and replace a damaged fuse with new one as soon as possible. The fuses are set in the fuse box which is taken out by opening the seat.

4. BRAKE LINING WEAR INDICATOR

Discription

The brake lining wear indicator is provided to check the wear condition of the brake linings visually from outside. As shown in the figure below, the indicator plate is attached to the brake cam. As the brake linings wear the brake cam moves excessively. Such a movement of the cam is checked by the arrow on the periphery of the indicator. Further the brake panel cam boss is provided with the "wear limit" mark to make it possible to check the service limit (replacement time) of the lining easiy with the brake panel installed.

Descriptive illustration

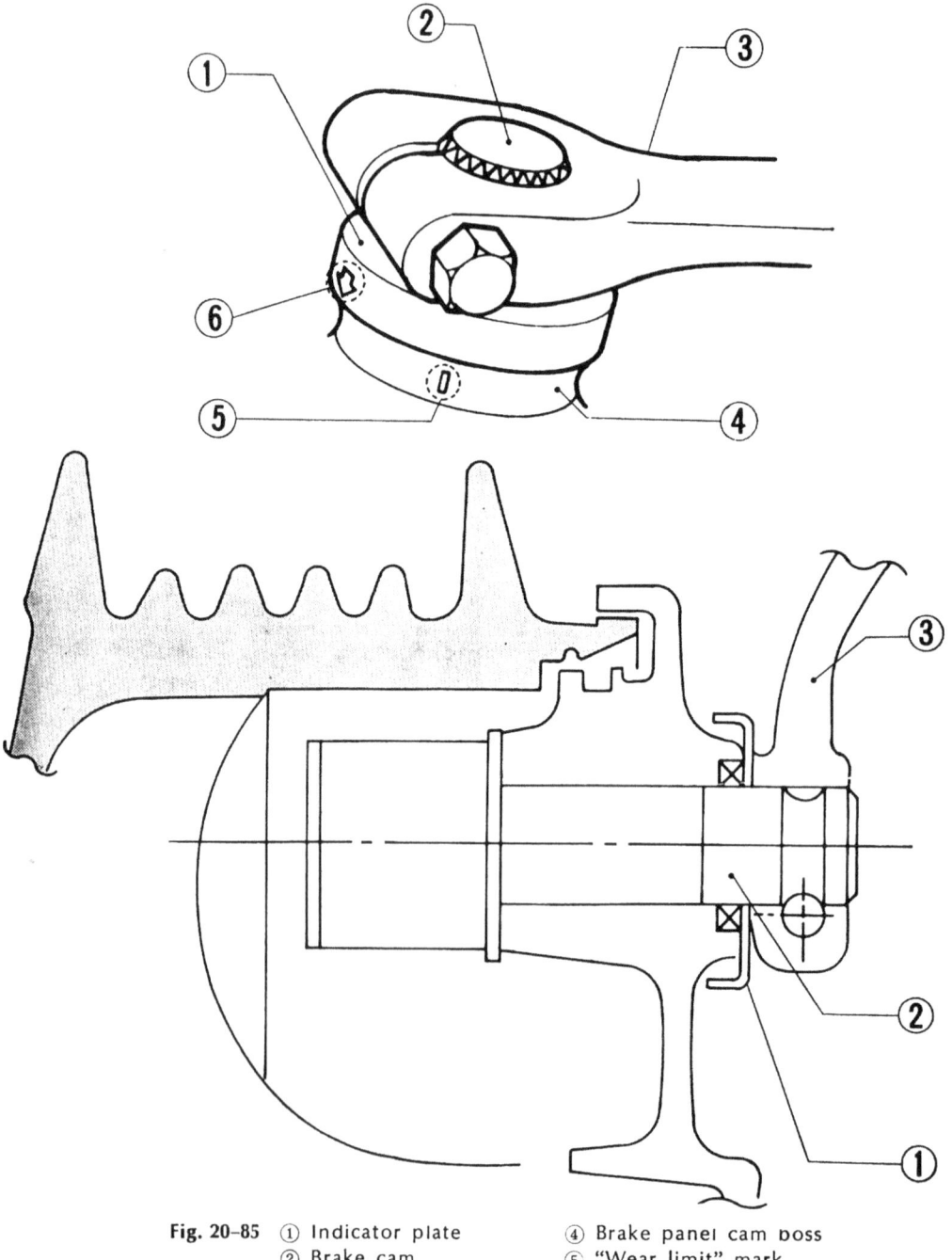

Fig. 20-85
① Indicator plate
② Brake cam
③ Brake arm
④ Brake panel cam boss
⑤ "Wear limit" mark
⑥ Arrow

5. REAR SHOCK ABSORBER ASSEMBLIES
(K2 to K4 model)

The rear shock absorber assemblies feature the telescopic type oil dampers with bottom valve to give an optimum damping performance under all bump and rebound conditions. The damping performance on the extension side is well matched with that on the compression side, providing maximum damping.
Stroke of rear shock absorber: **86.3 mm (3.39 in.)**

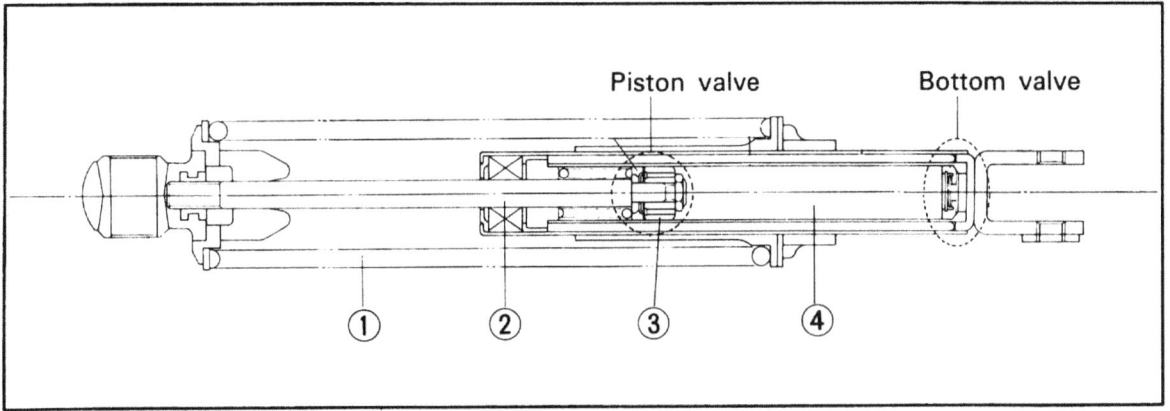

Fig. 20-86 ① Rear shock absorber spring ② Damper rod
③ Damper piston ④ Damper cylinder

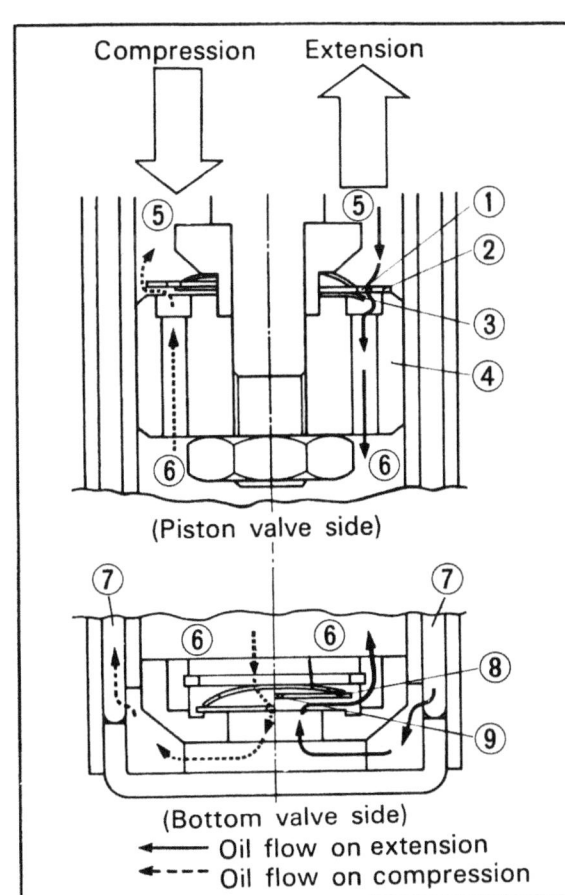

Fig. 20-87 ① Orifice (I) ② Valve "A"
③ Valve "B" ④ Piston
⑤ Chamber "a" ⑥ Chamber "b"
⑦ Chamber "c" ⑧ Bottom valve
⑨ Orifice (II)

Operation

Each oil damper is equipped with the piston valves A and B and bottom valve. On the extension side, the damping action is provided by means of the piston valves. While, on the compression side, the damping action is provided by means of the bottom valve.

On extension side:

The oil in the chamber [a] flows into the chamber [b] through the orifice (I) in the valve A (sheet metal). By the resisting force of this oil, the damping action is provided. The valve A is overlapped with the valve B (leaf spring) which covers the half of the orifice. The damping action is regulated by the deflection of the valve B. Under such a condition, the bottom valve is opened and the oil in the chamber [c] flows into the chamber [b] smoothly to prevent air bubbles from being produced.

On compression side:

The oil in the chamber [b] flows by amount of oil equivalent to the volume of damper rod into the chamber [c] through the orifice in the bottom valve. By the resisting force of this oil, the damping action is provided. At this time the piston valves are opened and the oil flows from the chamber [b] into the chamber [a] smoothly.

K4

COMPARISON OF CB 750 K3 TO CB 750 K4

Part of item	CB 750 K3	CB 750 K4	Modified part
		The stripes on the fuel tank are changed.	

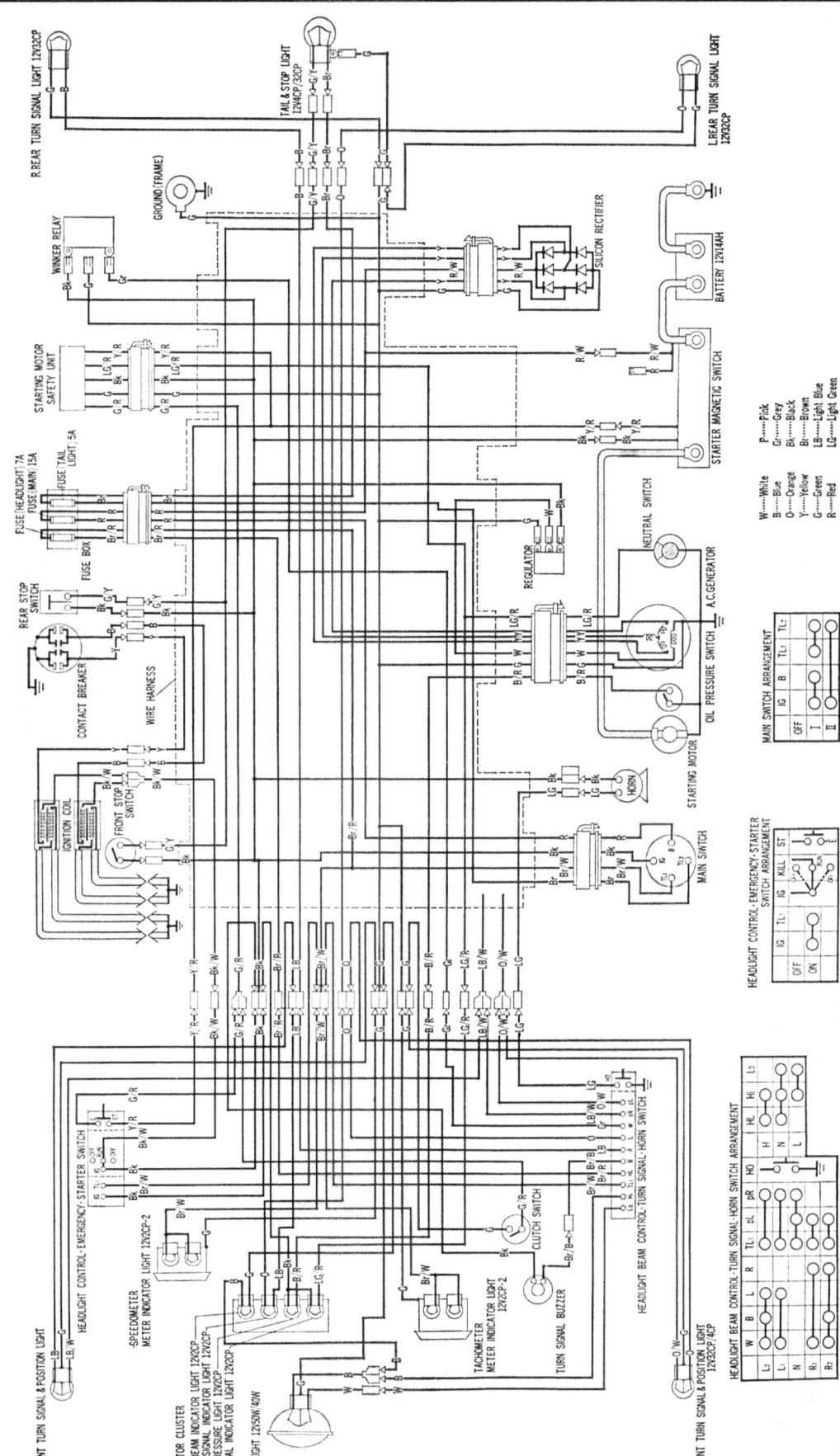

SUPPLEMENT TO CB750 K5

GROUP 21

1. FUEL COCK

The fuel cock is new for the revised model. Concurrent with this change, the indication marks and their positions on fuel cock was changed. It was also relocated from the right to the left side of the fuel tank.

Inspection and cleaning

1. Place the fuel lever in the "OFF" position; disconnect the fuel tube. Take out the fuel tank.
2. Drain the fuel tank thoroughly.
3. Loosen the fuel cock fixing nut and then remove the fuel cock and fuel filter from the fuel tank.
4. Check the gasket to see if it is not damaged. Replace with a new one, if found to be damaged too badly beyond use.
5. Wash the fuel filter in solvent and dry with compressed air. Any slightest damage cannot be tolerated here. Also replace the filter with a new one if found to be clogged.
6. Install the fuel filter to the fuel cock with the fixing nut. Do not forget to install the gasket into the groove of the fixing nut.
7. Install the fuel cock to the fuel tank with the fixing nut.
8. Install the fuel tank in place on the frame; connect tube and secure with the clip.
9. Fill the tank with fuel. With the fuel cock lever in the "ON" position, check for any leakage past the tube joints or connections.

Fig. K5-1　① Fuel cock　③ Fuel cock fixing nut
② Lever

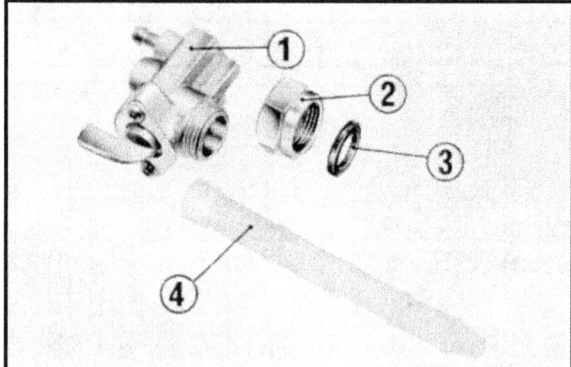

Fig. K5-2　① Fuel cock　③ Gasket
② Fixing nut　④ Fuel filter

2. THROTTLE GRIP

The throttle grip adjuster, **Fig. K5-3**, hitherto offered, was discontinued.

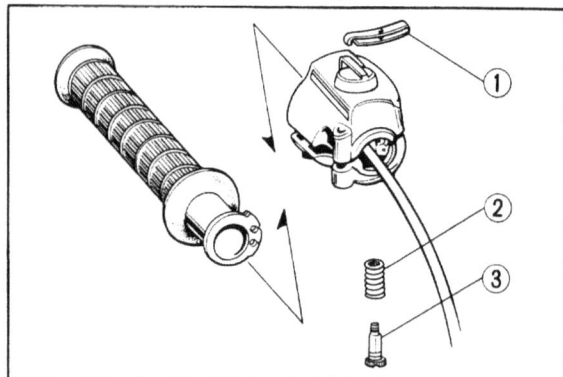

Fig. K5-3　① Throttle grip adjuster
② Spring　③ Adjusting bolt

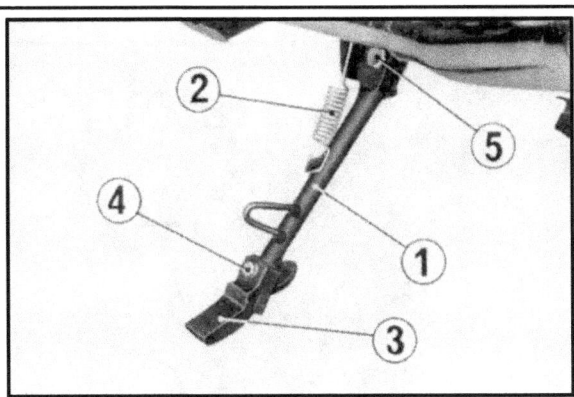

Fig. K5-4
① Side stand bar
② Spring
③ Rubber pad
④ 6 mm bolt
⑤ Side stand pivot bolt

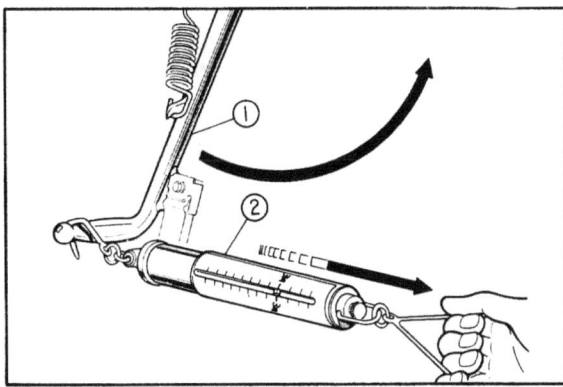

Fig. K5-5
① Side stand bar
② Spring scale

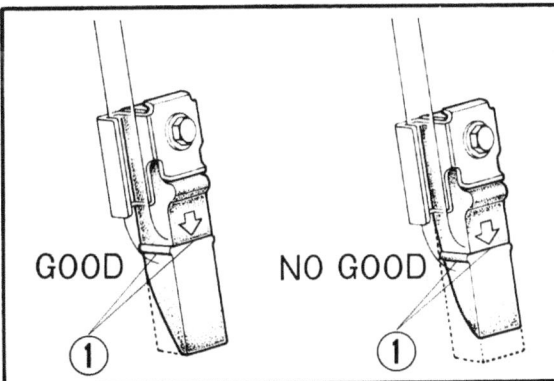

Fig. K5-6 ① Wear line

Fig. K5-7
① Rubber pad
② Collar

3. SIDE STAND

The side stand was changed to a new type with a shock absorbing rubber pad. The stand must be inspected periodically to determine that it is in good condition.

Inspection

1. Check the entire stand assembly (side stand bar, bracket and rubber pad) for installation, deformation or otherwise excessive damage.
2. Check the spring for freedom from damage or other defects.
3. Check the side stand for proper return operation:
   a. With the side stand applied, raise the stand off the ground by using the main stand.
   b. Attach a spring scale to the lower end of the stand and measure the force with which the stand is returned to its original position.
   c. The stand condition is correct if the measurement falls within **2–3 kg (4.4–6.6 lbs.)**.

   If the stand requires force exceeding the above limit, this might be due to neglected lubrication, overtightened side stand pivot bolt, worn stand bar or bracket, or otherwise excessive tension. Repair as necessary.
4. Check the rubber pad for deterioration or wear.
   When the rubber pad wear is excessive so that it is worn down to the wear line, replace it with a new one.

Rubber pad replacement

1. Remove the 6 mm bolt; separate the rubber pad from the bracket at the side stand.
2. After making sure the collar is installed, put a new rubber pad in place in the bracket with the arrow mark out.

NOTE: Use rubber pad having the mark "OVER 260 lbs. ONLY".

3. Secure the rubber pad with the 6 mm bolt.

4. TURN SIGNAL LIGHT

The front and rear turn signal lights were changed to new, larger types See **Figs. K5-8** and **K5-9**.

Fig. K5-8 ① Front turn signal light

Fig. K5-9 ① Rear turn signal light

5. MAINTENANCE SCHEDULE

Some additions occured in the MAINTENANCE SCHEDULE, of which details are as shown immediately below:

MAINTENANCE SCHEDULE This maintenance schedule is based upon average riding conditions. Machines subjected to severe use, or ridden in unusually dusty areas, require more frequent servicing.	INITIAL SERVICE PERIOD	REGULAR SERVICE PERIOD Perform at every indicated month or mileage interval, whichever occures first.			
		1 month	3 months	6 months	12 months
	500 miles	500 miles	1,500 miles	3,000 miles	6,000 miles
*SIDE STAND—Check installation, operation, deformation, damage and wear.				○	

Items marked * should be serviced by an authorized Honda dealer, unless the owner has proper tools and is mechanically proficient. Other maintenance items are simple to perform and may be serviced by the owner.

21. SUPPLEMENT TO CB750K5

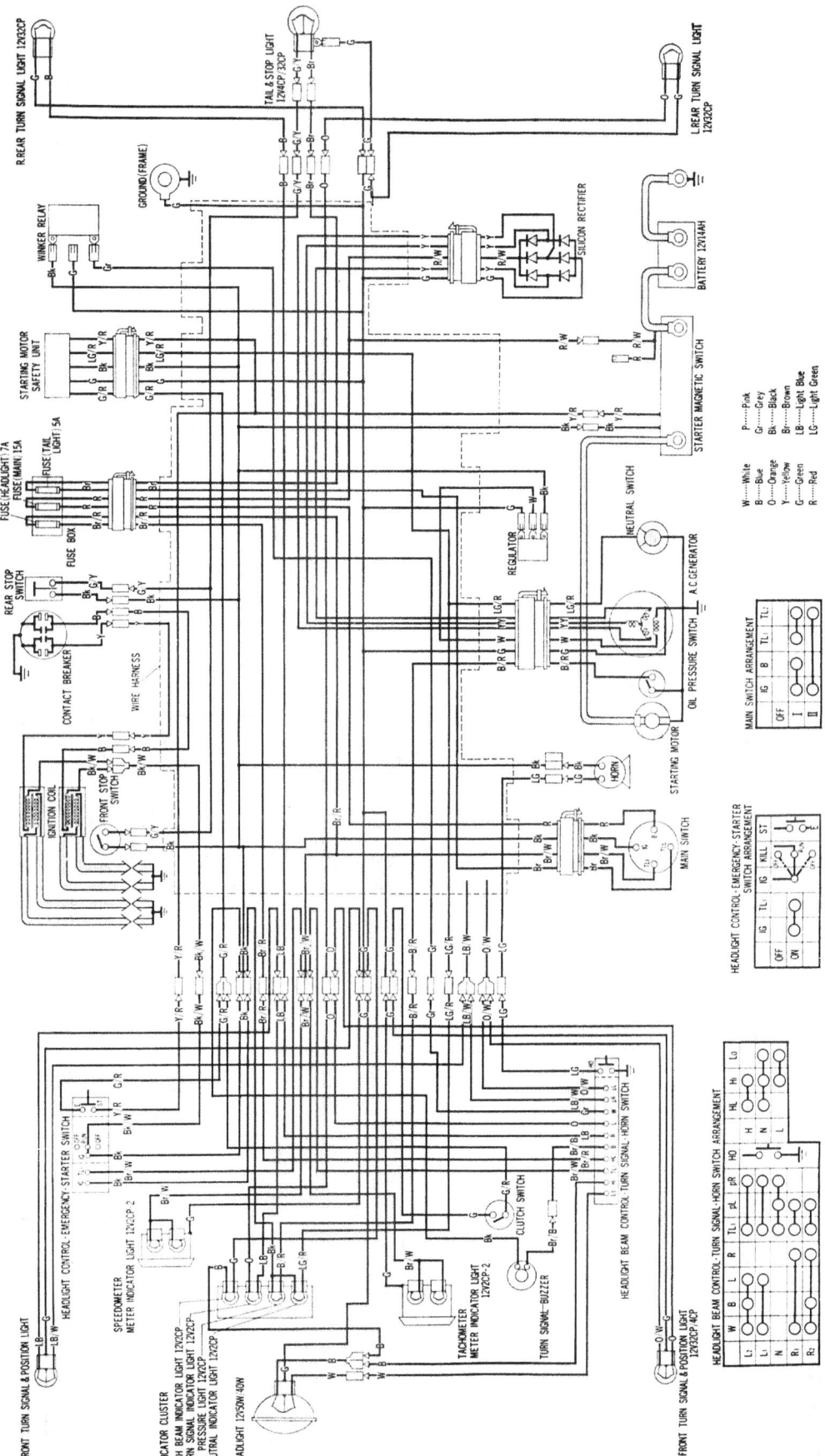

6. WIRING DIAGRAM

SUPPLEMENT TO CB750F

GROUP 22

1. Carburetor Setting:

Item	CB750F
Setting mark	CB750F
Venturi dia.	28⌀mm
Main jet	105
Air jet	120
Slow jet	40
Air screw opening	1±3/8
Cutaway	2.5
Valve seat dia.	2.0 mm
Fuel level	26 mm
Jet needle setting	Third notch

MUFFLER

Disassembly

1. Remove the two bolts ① securing the muffler in position.
2. Remove the eight joint nuts and take out the exhaust pipe joint, joint collar and muffler as an assembled unit.
3. Loosen the muffler band clamp bolt and remove the two exhaust pipes and sealing gaskets off the muffler.

Inspection

1. Check the muffler for damage or other defects.
2. Check the exhaust pipe gasket for condition.
3. Examine if the muffler sealing gasket is in good condition and is not damaged or broken.

Fig. 1 ①

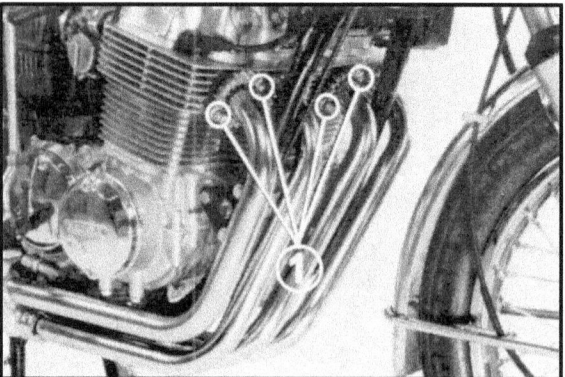

Fig. 2 ① Joint nuts

22. SUPPLEMENT TO CB750F

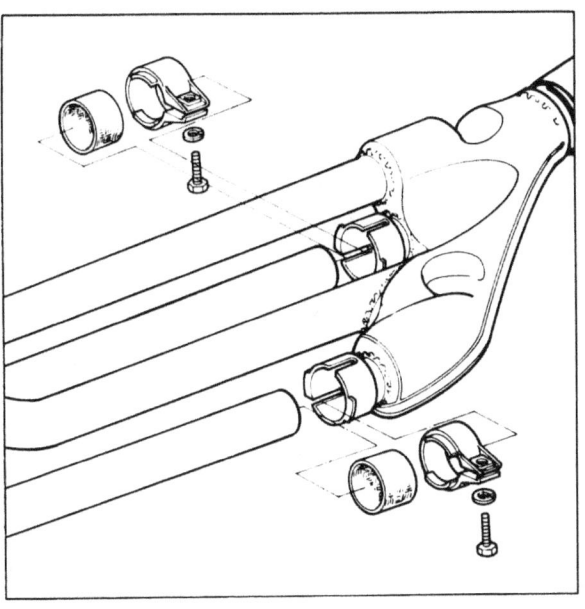

Fig. 3

Assembly

1. Install the muffler before attaching the two exhaust pipes.
2. Put the sealing gasket on the exhaust pipe, and then assemble the pipe to the muffler.
3. Fasten the exhaust pipe to the cylinder with the joint and joint collar in between.
4. Install the muffler band so that the band clamping bolt is exactly down on the muffler.

Fig. 4 ① Air cleanting mounting bolt
② Air cleaner lower case

Air Cleaner Maintenance

1. Remove the two air cleaner mounting bolts ① and remove the air cleaner lower case ②.

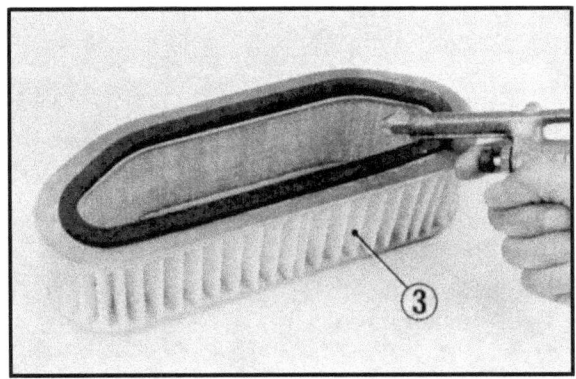

Fig. 5 ③ Air cleaner element

2. Clean the air cleaner element by tapping it lightly to loosen dust.
   The remaining dust can be brushed from the outer element surface or blown away by applying compressed air from the inside of the element.

22. SUPPLEMENT TO CB750F

3. Remove the 6 mm breather element case mounting bolt ④ and remove the breather element.
4. Remove the two screws ⑥ and pull out the breather element ⑦ from the breather element case.
5. Wash the breather element ⑦ in clean solvent.
   Squeeze out excess solvent and then dry the element thoroughly.

WARING: Gasoline or low flash point solvents are highly flammable and must not be used to clean the breather element.

6. To reinstall the air cleaner, reverse the removal procedure.

Fig. 6 ④ Breather element case mounting bolt
⑤ Breather element case ⑥ Screws

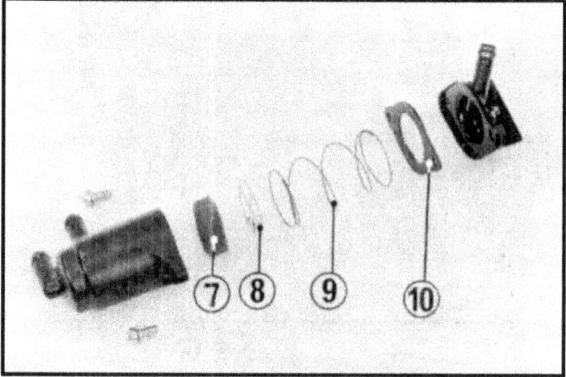

Fig. 7 ⑦ Breather element
⑧ Element retaining plate
⑨ Spring ⑩ Cover gasket

FRONT BRAKE

Disassembly

Caliper

1. Remove the caliper as an assembled unit.
2. To separate the calipers A and B, remove the caliper setting bolts.
   To service the calipers mounted on the motorcycle, remove the oil pipe from the caliper beforehand.

Fig. 8 ① Oil pipe ③ Caliper A
② Caliper setting ④ Caliper B

With the wheel bearing in place insert the axle shaft through the bearing. Place the axle shaft on V blocks, holding the wheel vertical. Check carefully for runout while rotating the wheel by hand.

	Standard value	Service limit
Surface runout	0.5 mm max.	2.0 mm min.
Radial runout	0.5 mm max.	2.0 mm min.

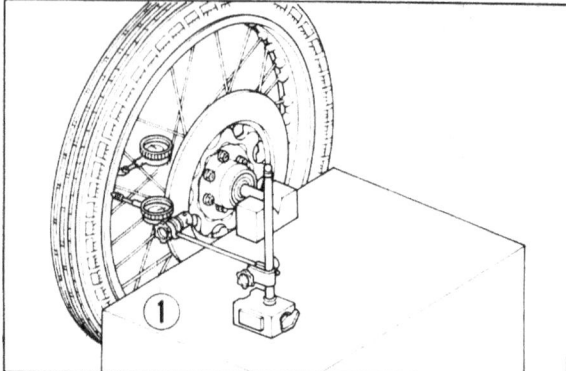

Fig. 9 ① Dial gauge

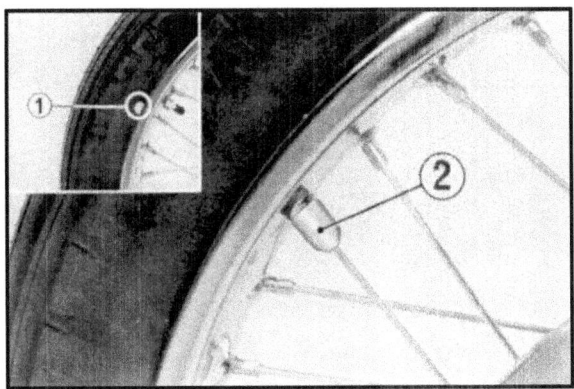

Fig. 10   1 Balancing mark
             2 Balancing weight

Balancing the Front Wheel

1. Remove the front wheel.
2. Remove the speedometer gear box.
3. Remove the front wheel collars.
4. Remove the front brake disc.
5. Insert the axle shaft through the wheel and place the shaft on V blocks.
6. Make three chalk marks on the wheel and spin by hand, allowing the heavy part to roll to the bottom.
7. Attach compensating weights to the top section, and again spin the wheel to check the result.
8. The weights should be installed to the spoke. The following four weights are available: 5 g, 10 g, 15 g and 20 g.

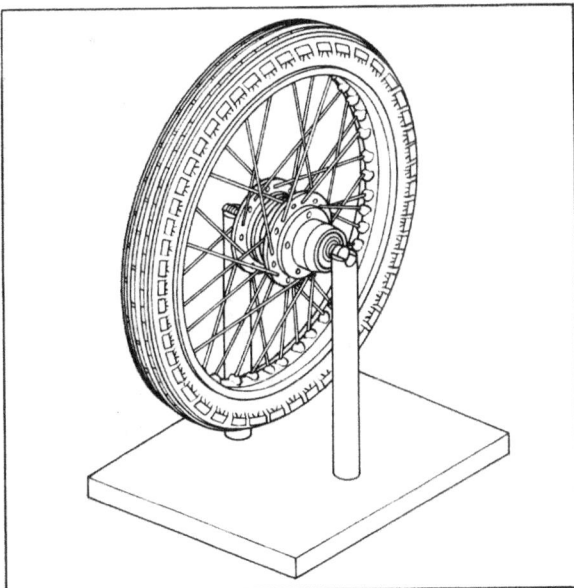

Fig. 11

22. SUPPLEMENT TO CB750F

REAR FORK

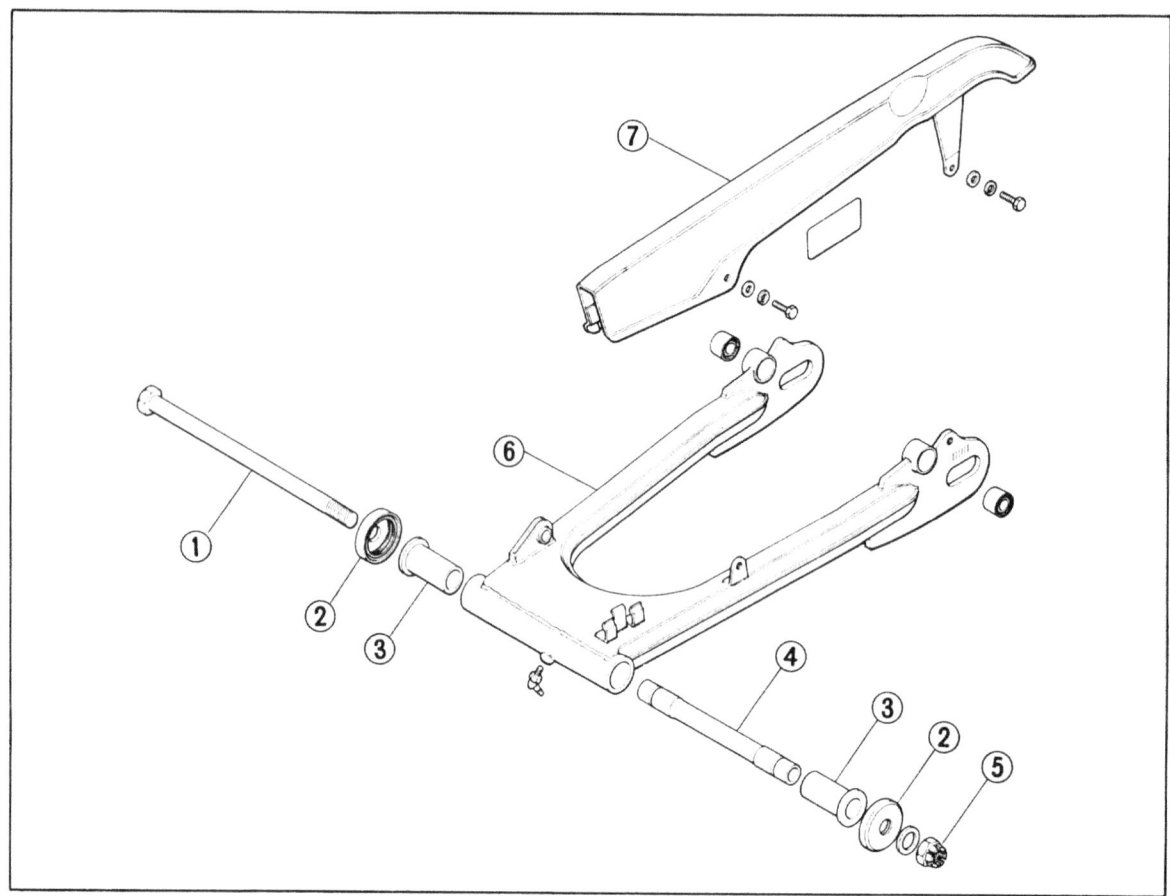

Fig. 12
① Rear fork pivot bolt
② Dust seal cap
③ Rear fork pivot bushing
④ Rear fork center collar
⑤ 14 mm self-locking nut
⑥ Rear fork
⑦ Chain case

Disassembly

1. Remove the rear shock absorber mounting nut ②.
2. Remove the bolt ④ to remove the rear shock absorber.
3. Remove the torque link from the rear brake.

Fig. 13
① Rear shock absorber
② Rear shock absorber mounting nut

22. SUPPLEMENT TO CB750F

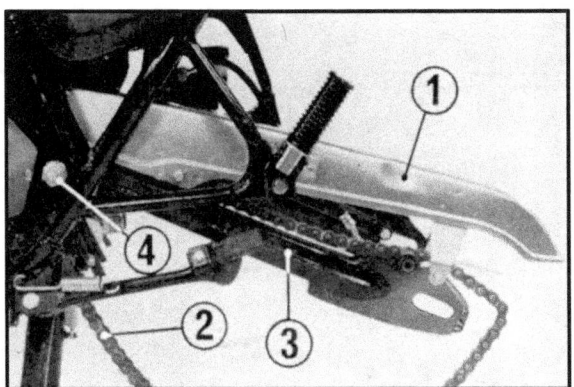

Fig. 14 ① Drive chain case   ③ Rear fork
        ② Drive chain   ④ Self-locking nut

Fig. 15 ① Rear fork pivot bolt

Fig. 16 ① Grease nipple

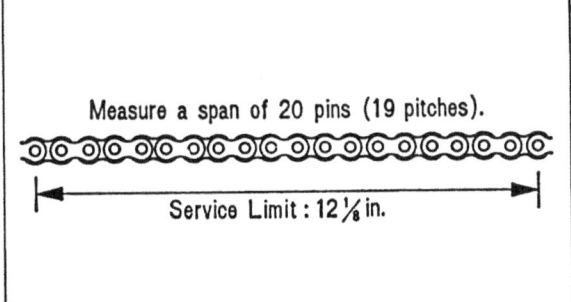

Fig. 17

4. Remove the chain case.
5. Remove the self-locking nut, pull off the rear fork pivot bolt and take the rear fork off the frame.
6. Remove the dust seal cap, pivot bushing and center collar from the rear fork.

Inspection

1. Check the rear fork for deformation, damage or other defects.
2. Check the rear fork center collar and bushing for excessive looseness.
3. Check the pivot shaft for bending along its entire length.
4. Check the axle holes in the rear fork ends for alignment.

Assembly

Assembly is the reverse order of the disassembly.

1. Apply a coating of grease to the rear fork center collar before installing the rear fork to the frame.
2. Coat the sealing lip of the dust seal with grease when assembling the dust seal cap.
3. Insert the rear fork pivot bolt from the right side with the end through the fork; install the self-locking nut on the end and tighten to correct torque.
4. Pump grease through the grease fitting at the rear fork.

Measuring drive chain wears

Measure a section of drive chain to determine whether the chain is worn beyond its service limit. Put the transmission in gear, then turn the rear wheel forward until the lower section of the chain is pulled taut. With the chain held taut and any stiff joints straightened measure the distance between a span of 20 pins, from pin center to pin center. In will measure $11^7/_8$ in. (each pitch=$^5/_8$ in.) If the distance exceeds $12^1/_8$ in. the chain is worn out and must be replaced. After the chain is measured, shift the transmission into neutral again before proceeding with inspection and service.

Engine oil change

Fill the oil tank with approximately 2.6 quarts of premium quality, SE, SEA 10W-40 oil. Start the engine and operate for a few minutes. Stop the engine, refill the tank with approximately 1.1 quarts of oil and check the oil level with the filler cap dipstick.

Fuel tank over flow tube inspection

1. Inspect the fuel tank over flow tube for defects.
2. Squeeze lower end of the over flow tube, and remove any oil or water which may have accumulated.

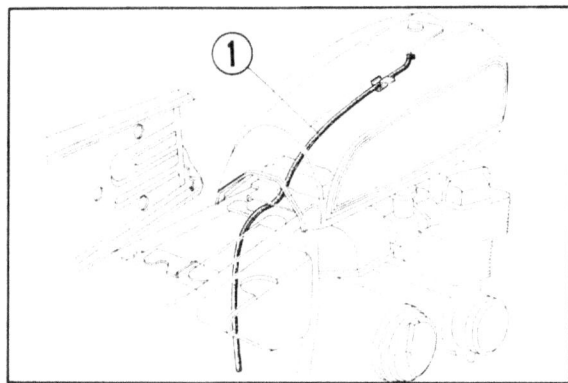

Fig. 18 ① Over flow tube

FRONT SUSPENSION

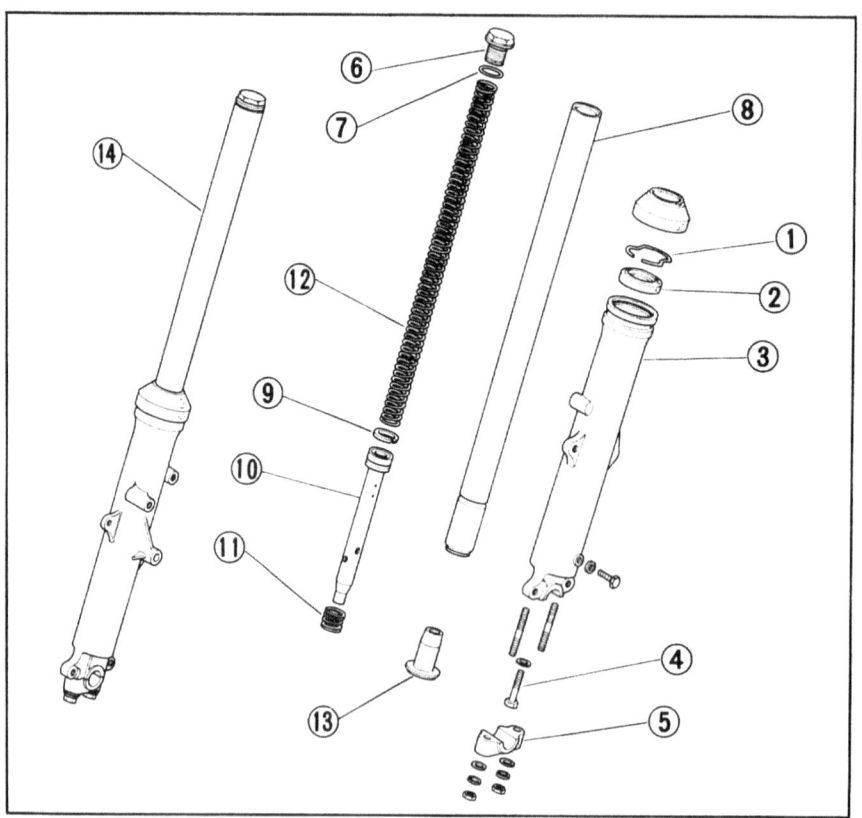

Fig. 19
① Oil seal stop
② Oil seal
③ Bottom case
④ Socket bolt
⑤ Front axle holder
⑥ Fork bolt
⑦ O-ring
⑧ Front fork pipe
⑨ Piston ring
⑩ Bottom pipe
⑪ Rebound spring
⑫ Front shock absorber spring
⑬ Oil lock piece
⑭ Front shock absorber assembly

22. SUPPLEMENT TO CB750F

REAR SUSPENSION

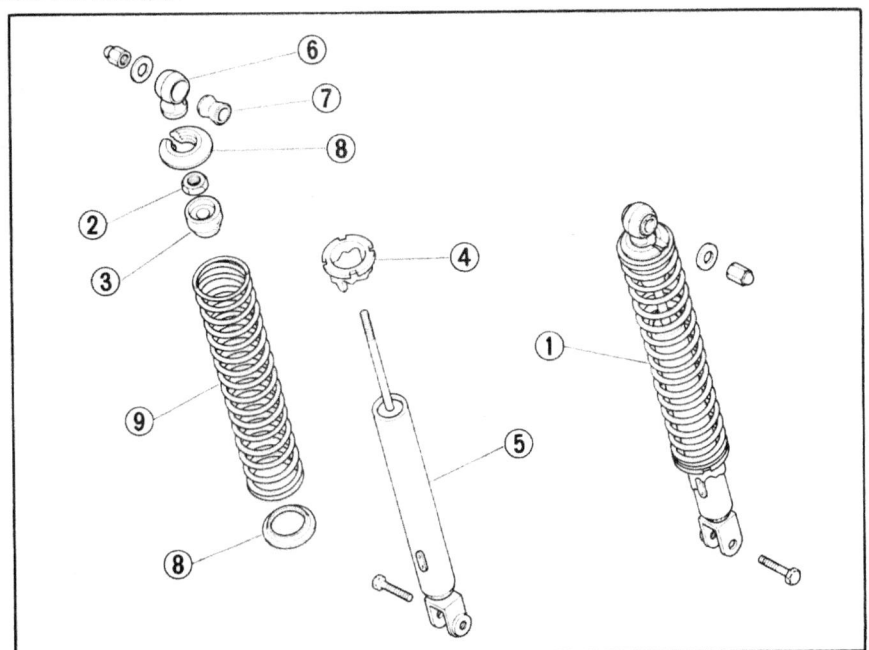

Fig. 20
① Rear shock absorber assembly
② Lock nut (10 mm)
③ Stop rubber
④ Spring adjuster
⑤ Rear damper
⑥ Upper joint
⑦ Joint rubber
⑧ Spring seat stop
⑨ Rear shock absorber spring

REAR BRAKE

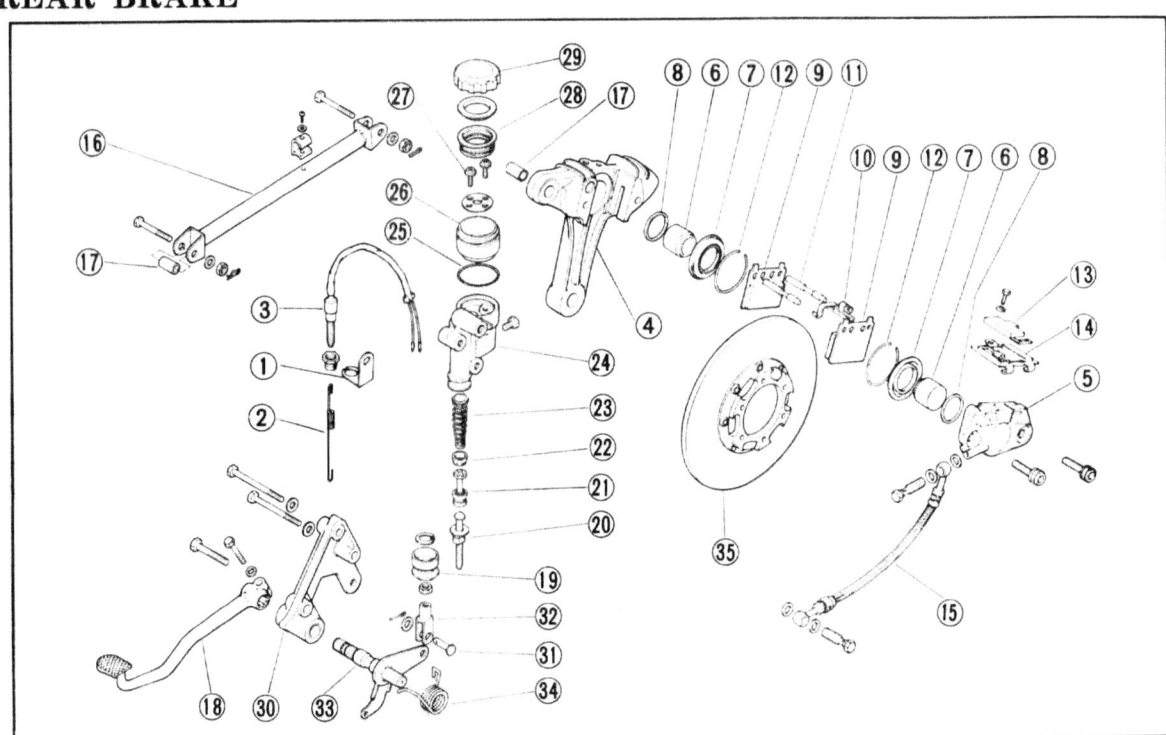

Fig. 21
① Stop switch bracket
② Stop switch spring
③ Stop light switch
④ Caliper A
⑤ Caliper B
⑥ Piston
⑦ Dust cover
⑧ Piston seal
⑨ Pad
⑩ Spring pad set
⑪ Pad pin
⑫ Dust cover, clip
⑬ Indicator cover
⑭ Pad cover
⑮ Rear brake hose
⑯ Torque link
⑰ Link collar
⑱ Rear brake pedal
⑲ Master cylinder, boot
⑳ Push rod
㉑ Piston
㉒ Primary cup
㉓ Spring
㉔ Rear master cylinder
㉕ O-ring
㉖ Oil cup
㉗ Oil cup screw
㉘ Diaphragm
㉙ Oil cup, cap
㉚ Rear master cylinder holder
㉛ Brake rod pin
㉜ Brake rod joint
㉝ Rear brake shaft
㉞ Brake pedal spring
㉟ Rear brake disk

Removal of Caliper

1. Drain the brake system by loosening the caliper bleeder valve.
2. Remove the bolts from the caliper and take out the torque link.

Fig. 22 ① Bleeder valve   ② Torque link

3. Pry off the cotter pin, loosen off the axle nut, and remove the axle shaft.

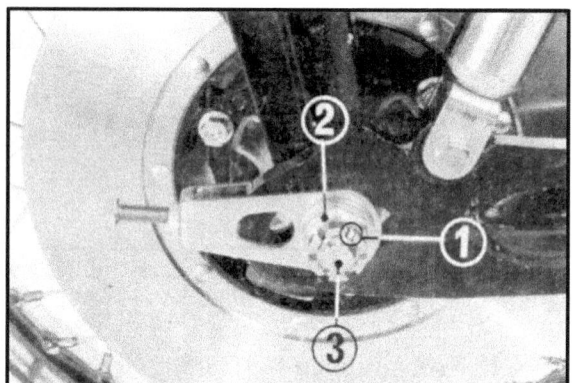

Fig. 23 ① Cotter pin   ③ Axle shaft
         ② Axle nut

4. Remove the oil bolt and pull off the brake hose. Take out the caliper as an assembled unit.

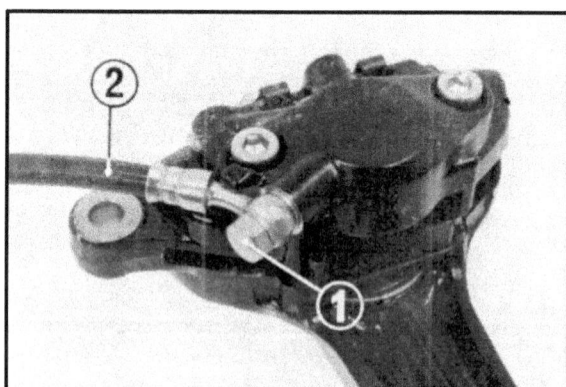

Fig. 24 ① Oil bolt   ② Brake hose

Removal of Master Cylinder

1. Remove the rear brake hose off the caliper. Drain the brake system by pumping the brake pedal.
2. Using a suitable pair of pliers, pull off the cotter pin and then remove the brake rod pin.

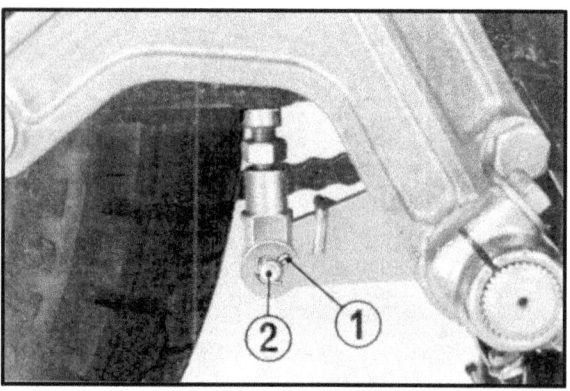

Fig. 25 ① Cotter pin   ② Brake rod

22. SUPPLEMENT TO CB750F

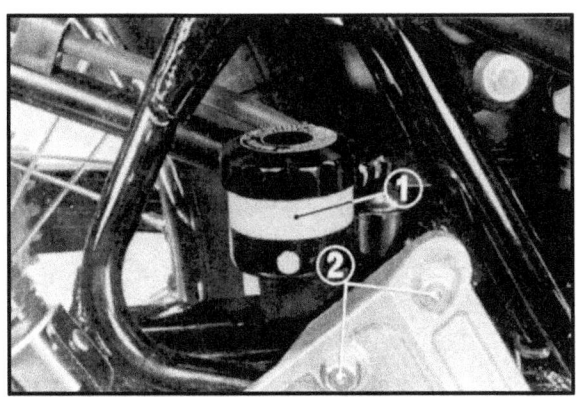

Fig. 26 ① Master cylinder

3. The rear brake master cylinder will be taken out easily by removing the bolts ②.

NOTE:
- Handle the master cylinder with care to avoid damaging the brake hose.
- Avoid getting grease on the friction surfaces of the pad and disc since a trace of oil or grease on the friction surface may cause erratic braking performance.
- Do not spil brake oil onto the tire.

Caliper

1. Disconnect the brake pipe from the master cylinder as per the instruction given in perceding paragraph.
2. Remove the caliper off the rear fork following the procedure under Removal of rear fork.
3. Disconnect the brake hose from the caliper.

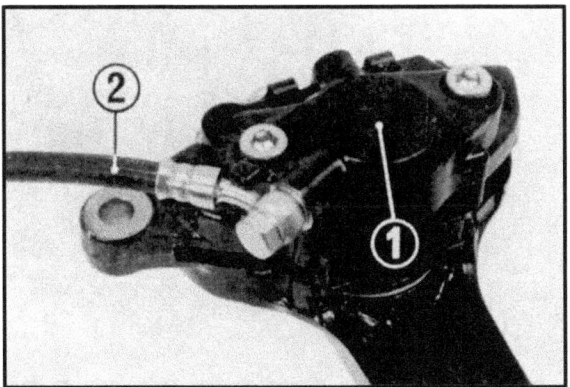

Fig. 27 ① Caliper ② Brake hose

Replacement of brake pad (rear)

1. Remove the 5mm bolts securing the pad cover to the caliper.

Fig. 28 ① Pad cover ② 5mm bolt

2. Press down on the brake pad set spring; without disturbing the above setup, withdraw the upper pin from the pad.

Fig. 29 ① Brake pad set spring
② Brake pad pin

3. Assembly is the reverse order of the disassembly. The pad pin has a step. Hook the pad set spring over the pin at a point where the diameter is reduced.

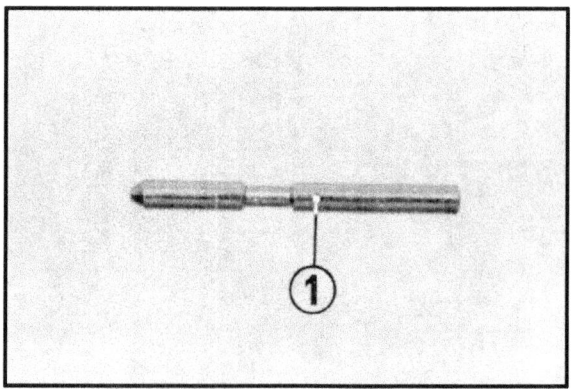

Fig. 30 ① Pad pin

Disassembly

Master cylinder

1. Disconnect the brake rod joint from the push rod by loosening the 8mm nut.
2. Remove the 8mm nut and take out the boot.

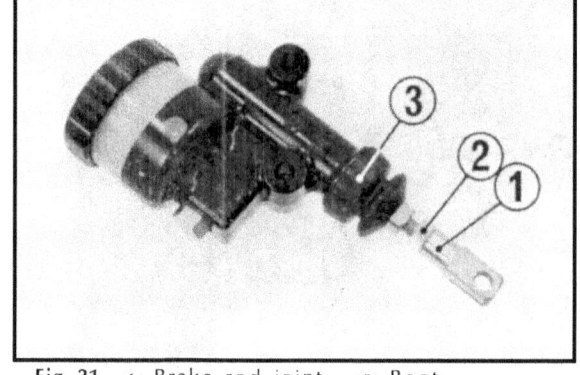

Fig. 31 ① Brake rod joint ③ Boot
② 8mm nut

3. Using tool "Snap Ring Pliers" (Tool No. 07914-3230000), remove the internal snap ring. The push rod can then be taken out.

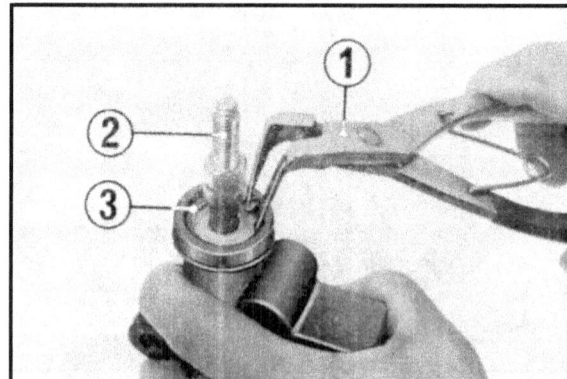

Fig. 32 ① Snap ring pliers ③ Snap ring
② Push rod

4. Remove the piston together with the secondary cup.
5. Remove the primary cup.
6. Remove the spring.
7. Remove the check valve.
8. Remove the oil cup cap diaphragm in the order listed.

Fig. 33 ① Piston ② Secondary cup

22. SUPPLEMENT TO CB750F

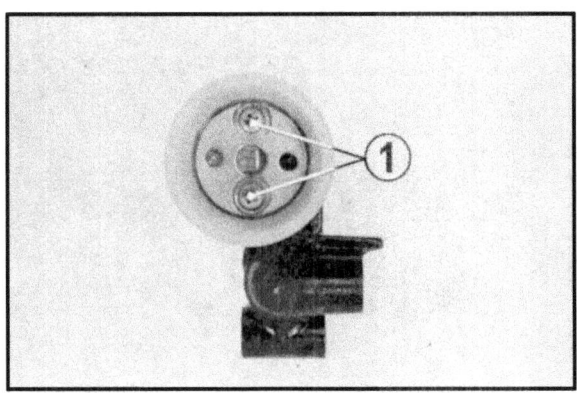

Fig. 34　① Oil cup screw

9. Remove the oil cup screw and take out the oil cup plate.
10. Pull the oil cup off the master cylinder body.
11. Remove the O-ring.

Note: Above steps No. 9 thru. 11 describe the disassembly procedures for separate type master clinder oil cup (up to Frame No. CB750F-1010686). For machines on and after 1010687, the oil cup is integrated with the master cylinder body.

Caliper

1. Remove the 5mm bolt securing the pad cover to the caliper. The wear indicator cover will then be removed together with the pad cover.
2. With help of a 8mm Allen wrench, unscrew the caliper set bolt. Separate the calipers A and B.

Fig. 35　① Caliper set bolt　② Caliper B

3. Remove the pads, pad pins and pad springs.
4. Remove the joint seal.

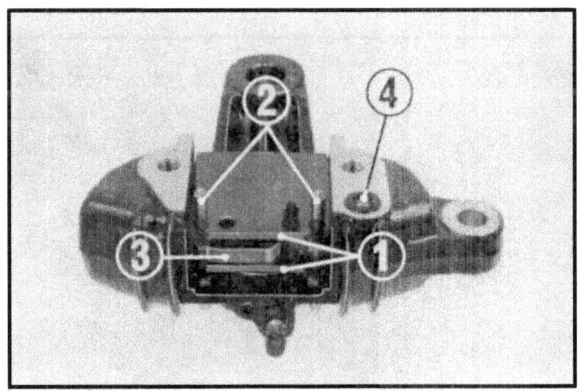

Fig. 36　① Pad　③ Pad set spring
　　　　② Pad pin　④ Joint seal

5. Remove the dust seal clip to remove the dust seal.

Fig. 37　① Dust seal clip　② Dust seal

22. SUPPLEMENT TO CB750F

6. Force the piston out of the bore in the caliper by applying compressed air in the oil hole.
7. Take out the piston seal.

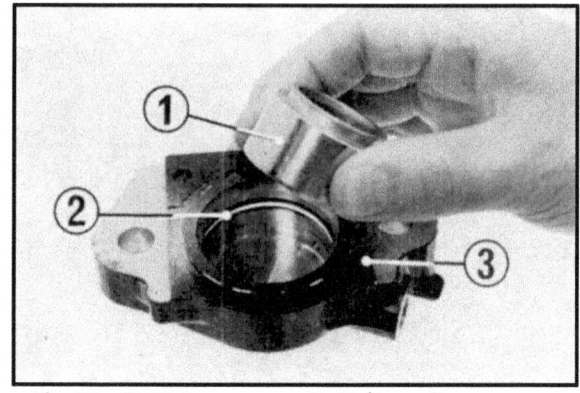

Fig. 38 ① Piston ③ Caliper B
② Piston seal

Inspection

Master Cylinder

1. Measure the ID of the master cylinder to see if it is held within the specified limits. Replace the old cylinder with a new one if it is worn excessively or that the service limit is exceeded. Use a cylinder gauge to measure the cylinder bore.

   Standard value   Service limit
   14.000~14.043 mm   14.055 mm

2. With the use of a micrometer, measure the OD of the piston. If wear is too great, replace with a new one.

   Standard value   Service limit
   13.957~13.980 mm   13.940 mm

3. Check to make sure that the primary and secondary cups are in good condition and are not scored or scratched on their sliding surfaces. Replace the cups with new ones if found to be scored or scratched too badly beyond use.

4. Check the oil for freedom from dust, dirt or any other foreign particles. If necessary, drain oil thoroughly and refill with clean oil up to the correct level.

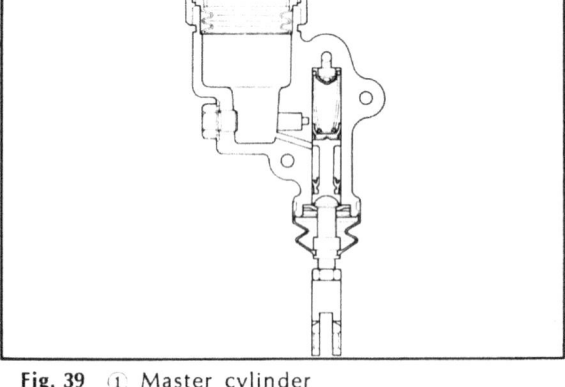

Fig. 39 ① Master cylinder

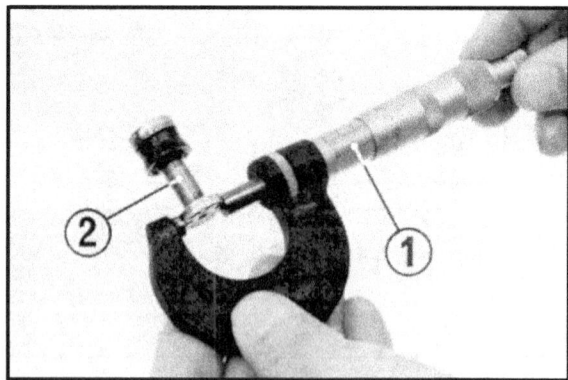

Fig. 40 ① Micrometer ② Piston

Caliper

1. Measure the bore in the caliper using a cylinder gauge. Where wear is too great, replace as necessary.

   Standard value   Service limit
   38.18~38.28 mm   38.245 mm

2. Measure the OD of the piston with a micrometer. If the service limit is exceeded, the piston should be replaced with a new one.

   Standard value   Service limit
   3.1115~38.148 mm   38.105 mm

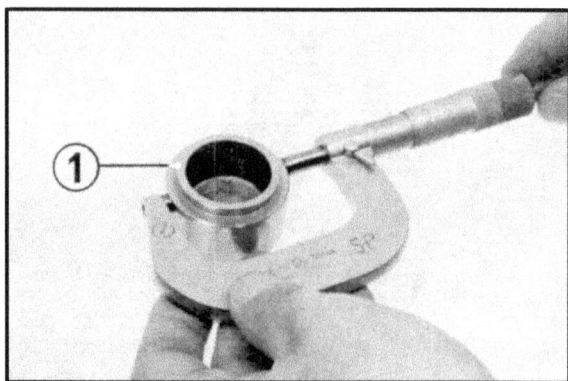

Fig. 41 ① Piston

Fig. 42　② Right brake pad　④ Red mark
　　　　③ Left brake pad

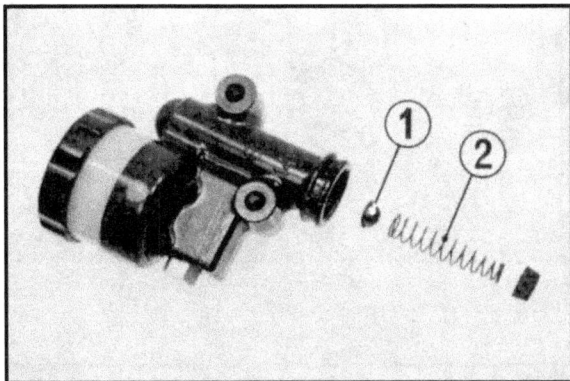

Fig. 43　① Check valve　② Spring

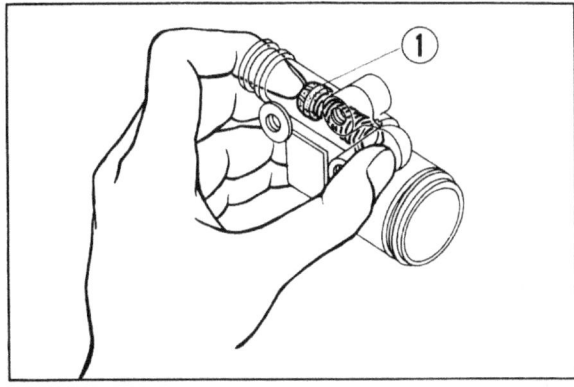

Fig. 44　① Primary cup

3. Check the piston seal for deterieration or other defects and replace if necessary.
4. Brake pad wear should be checked with the caliper mounted on the frame.
5. Replace both brake pads when the right ② or left ③ pad is worn to the red mark ④ on the caliper.

Brake Hose

1. Check the brake hose for damage, breakage or other defects.
2. Examine if the brake fluid is free from dust, dirt or any other foreign materials. If necessary, drain oil thoroughly and refill with clean oil up to the proper level.

Assembly

Master Cylinder

1. Dip the cylinder, piston and primary and secondary cups in clean brake fluid before they can be assembled.
2. When the check valve is to be installed in the master cylinder, assemble the valve with the valve spring first so that they can be inserted into place in the cylinder easily. Be careful not to install the valve in the reverse direction.
3. Install the primary cup so that the cupped side is toward the spring. Make sure it is square in the bore in the cylinder and is not tilted.
4. After installing the 18 mm internal snap ring, check to make sure that it is seated in the groove properly.

Caliper

1. Check to make sure that the piston seal is seated in the groove in the caliper properly.
2. Apply a thin coating of silicone grease to the inner wall of the cylinder and piston seal.
3. Tighten the caliper set bolt to the following torque:
   Specified tightening torque:
   　　　　　　　　250~300 kg-cm

Rear Brake

1. After air has been bled out thoroughly, raise the rear wheel off the ground and make sure that the wheel does not drag by rotating it by hand. Slight dragging can be tolerated here.
2. Before installing the brake pedal, apply grease to the pivot portion.

Brake pedal height adjustment

1. Hold the hex nut ② with a wrench and loosen the lock nut ③.
2. Remove the cotter pin ⑤ and pull out the rear brake pedal pin ⑦.
3. Turning the brake rod ④ in direction Ⓐ will decrease the pedal height and turning it in direction Ⓑ will increase the pedal height.
   Clearance between the brake pedal arm and the footrest should be not less then 0.9 inches' (5 mm). After adjusting, secure the brake rod to the pedal with the pedal pin ⑦ plain washer ⑥ and cotter pin ⑤ Always use a new cotter pin and bend the ends of the pin.

Bleeding the Brake System

When the entire system has been overhauled, when the pedal is soft or spongy or when there is any reason to believe that air has been drawn into the system, the system must be bled throughly. Also note that the master cylinder does not function if the fluid level is too low, and this will also introduce air into the system and the system must be bled.

To bleed air from the brake system, proceed as follow:

1. Fill the master cylinder reservoir with brake fluid. Install the diaphragm to prevent fluid from spilling out of the reservoir.
2. Slip a bleeder pipe on the caliper bleeder valve. Place the lower end of the pipe into a clean glass jar.
3. Depress the brake pedal a full stroke until resistance is felt, and then allow it to return slowly. Repeat this procedure several times, finally holding the pedal fully depressed. Loosed the bleeder valve, and then tighten it immediately after the pedal is depressed to the frame body.
4. Repeat the step 3 several times until the fluid flows from the bleeder pipe without bubbles. Close the bleeder valve.
5. Fill the master cylinder reservoir with brake fluid up to the correct level.

NOTE: Allowing the master cylinder reservoir to empty will cause air to be drawn into the system. During the step 3 above, check the master cylinder frequently to make sure that it contains enough fluid.

6. Bleeder valve tightening torque: Specified torque: 70~90 kg-cm

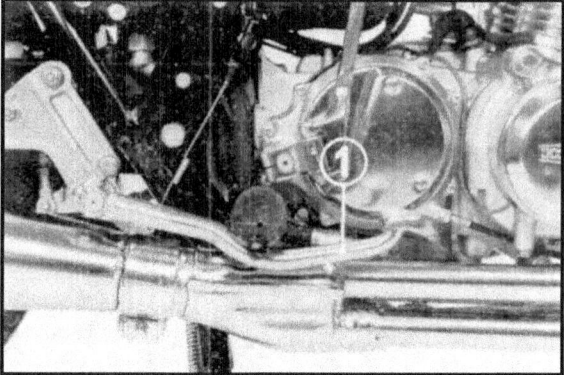

Fig. 45　① Rear brake pedal

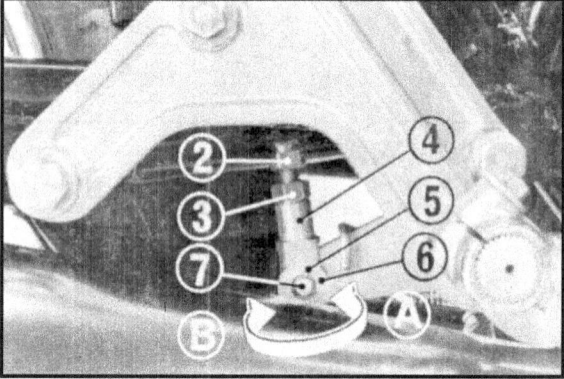

Fig. 46　② Hex nut　　⑤ Cotter pin
　　　　③ Lock nut　　⑥ Plain washer
　　　　④ Brake rod　　⑦ Pedal pin

Fig. 47　① Master cylinder　② Diaphragm

Fig. 48　① Bleeder valve　② Pipe

REAR WHEEL

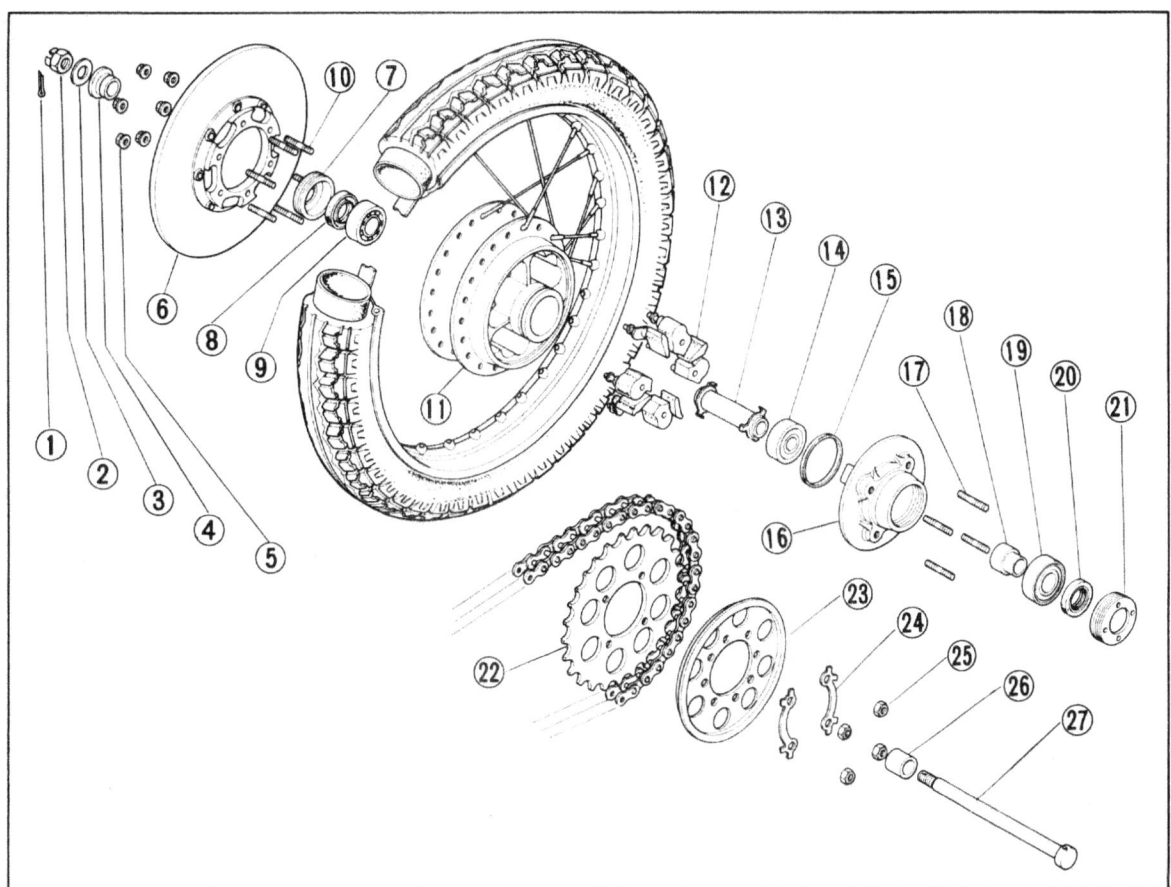

Fig. 49

① Cotter pin
② Rear axle nut
③ 18.5×34 washer
④ Side collar
⑤ Disc nut
⑥ Disc
⑦ Bearing retainer
⑧ Oil seal
⑨ 6304 bearing
⑩ Stud bolt
⑪ Rear wheel hub
⑫ Rear wheel damper
⑬ Distance collar
⑭ 6304 bearing
⑮ O-ring
⑯ Final drive flange
⑰ Stud bolt
⑱ Axle sleeve
⑲ 6305 bearing
⑳ Oil seal
㉑ Bearing retainer
㉒ Drive sprocket
㉓ Plate sprocket side
㉔ Lock washer
㉕ Hex Nut
㉖ Side collar
㉗ Rear wheel axle

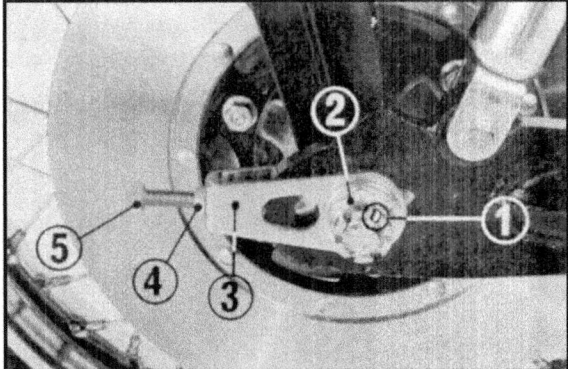

Fig. 50
① Cotter pin
② Axle nut
③ Drive chain adjuster
④ Lock nut
⑤ Chain adjusting bolt

Disassembly

1. Loosen the drive chain adjusting bolt and lock nut. Pry the cotter pin off the axle shaft and remove the axle nut.

22. SUPPLEMENT TO CB750F

2. Remove the drive chain from the final driven sprocket; take out the wheel.
3. Remove the disc nuts and remove the disc from the wheel.

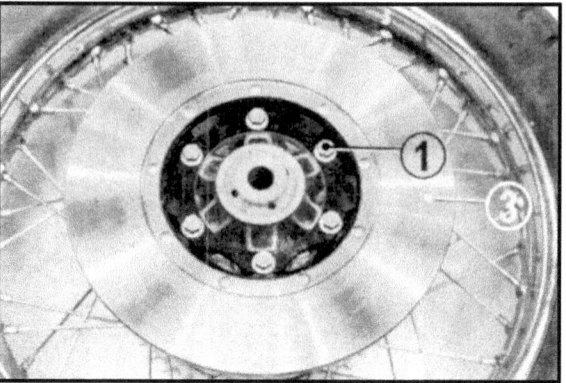

Fig. 51　① Disc nut
　　　　　③ Disc

Inspection

1. Wear of disc
   Inspect the brake disc for wear. This can be made with a dial gauge and by placing it on a surfaceplate as shown. If the dial gauge reading exceeds the service limit, replace the disc.

Standard value	Service limit
0~0.1 mm	0.3 mm

2. Surface runout of disc
   With the brake disc in place on the wheel, check carefully for runout by placing the axle shaft in V blocks. Replace the disc if the runout is excessive.

Standard value	Service limit
0~0.1 mm	0.3 mm

3. Thichness of disc
   Measure the thickness of the brake disc to make sure that it is held within the specified limits. Discs that are worn excessively beyond the service limit must be replaced.

Standard value	Service limit
0.05 mm	0.3 mm

4. Wear on rear wheel hub
   Visually check the rear wheel hub rubber dampers fer excessive wear or deterioation.

5. Surface and axial runouts of rear wheel rim
   With the wheel bearing in place, insert the wheel axle shaft. Place the shaft on V blocks, holding the wheel vertical. Measure the rim for runout while rotating it by hand carefully. Replace the rim if found to be damaged excessively beyond use.

Standard value	Service limit
Surface runont	
0.5 mm max.	2.0 mm min.
Axial runout	
0.5mm max.	2.0 mm min.

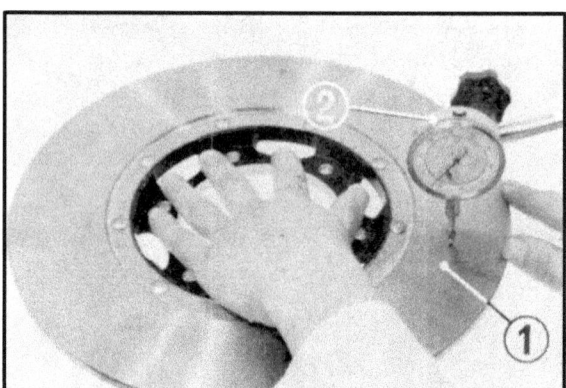

Fig. 52　① Brake disc
　　　　　② Dial gauge

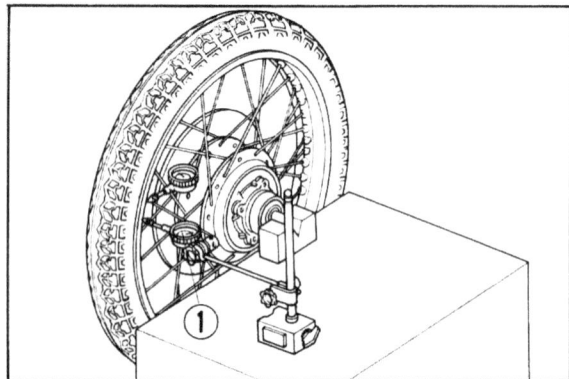

Fig. 53

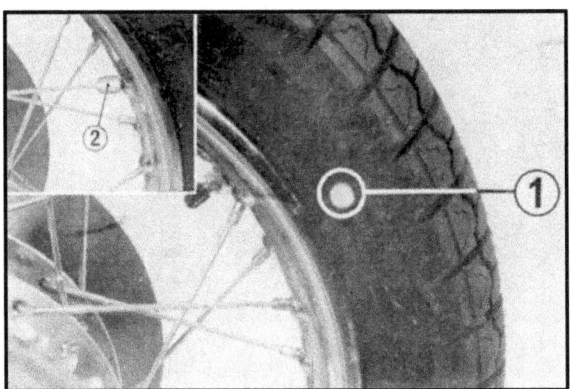

Fig. 54 ① Balancing mark
② Balancing weight

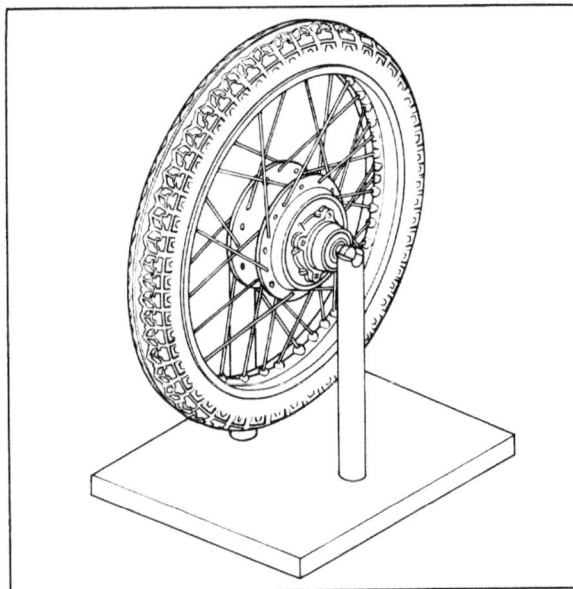

Fig. 55

6. Balancing the Rear Wheel
a. Remove the rear wheel.
b. Remove the side collars from both sides of the wheel.
c. Remove the rear brake disc.
d. Insert the axle shaft through the rear wheel and place the shaft V blocks, holding the wheel vertical.
e. Make three chalk marks on the wheel and spin by hand, allowing the heavy part to roll to the bottom.
f. Attach compensating weights to the top section, and again spin the wheel to check the result.
g. The weights should be installed to the spoke. The following four weights are available: 5 g, 10 g, 15 g and 20 g.

Assembly

1. Assembly is the reverse order of the removal.

NOTE: Make sure your hands and tools are free of dust and abrasives as they may ruin the bearing if allowed inside.

2. Install the wheel axle shaft from the left side.
3. After assembling, check the tension of the drive chain and the operation of the brake and adjust as necessary.

WIRING

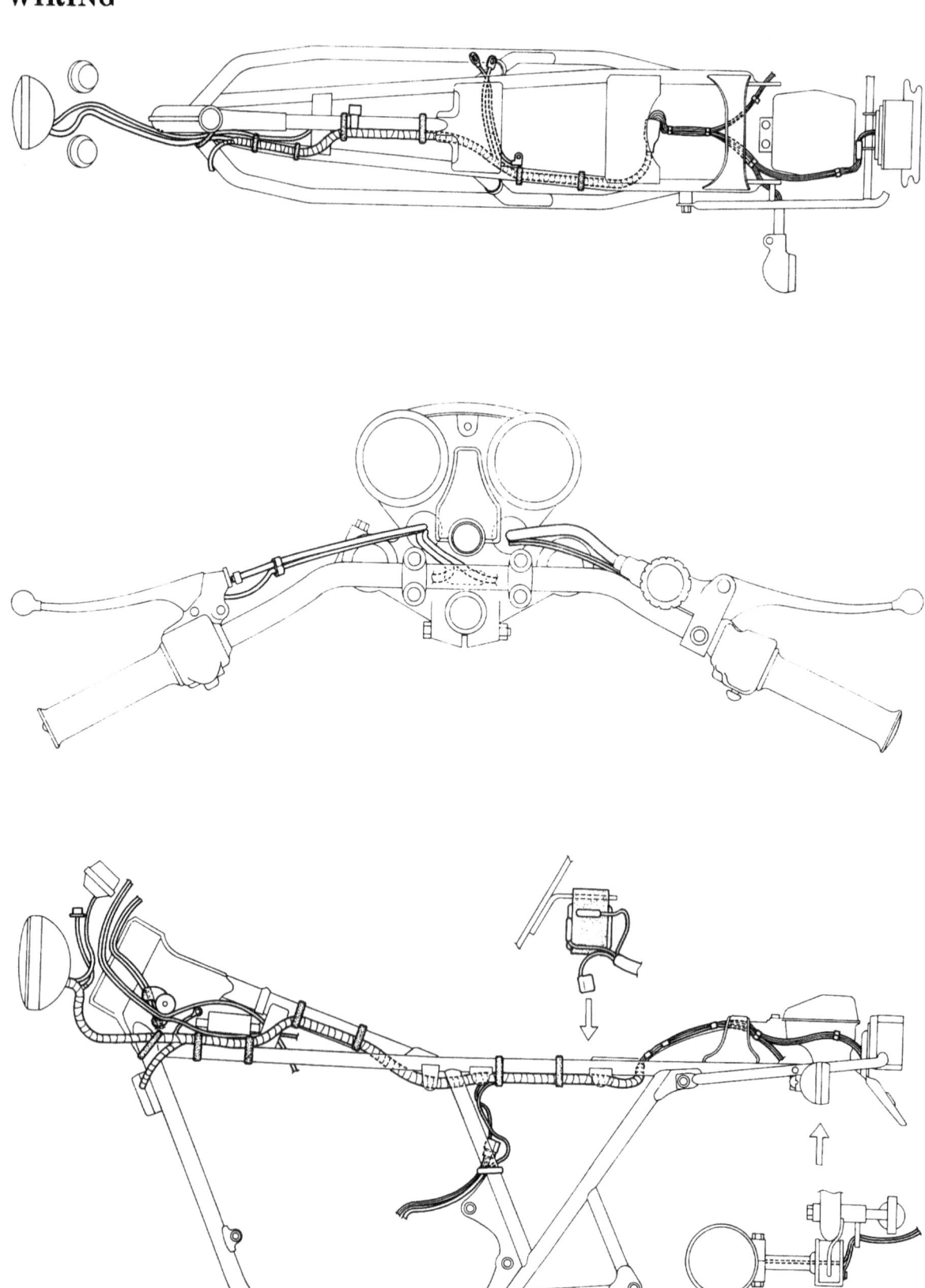

22. SUPPLEMENT TO CB 750 F

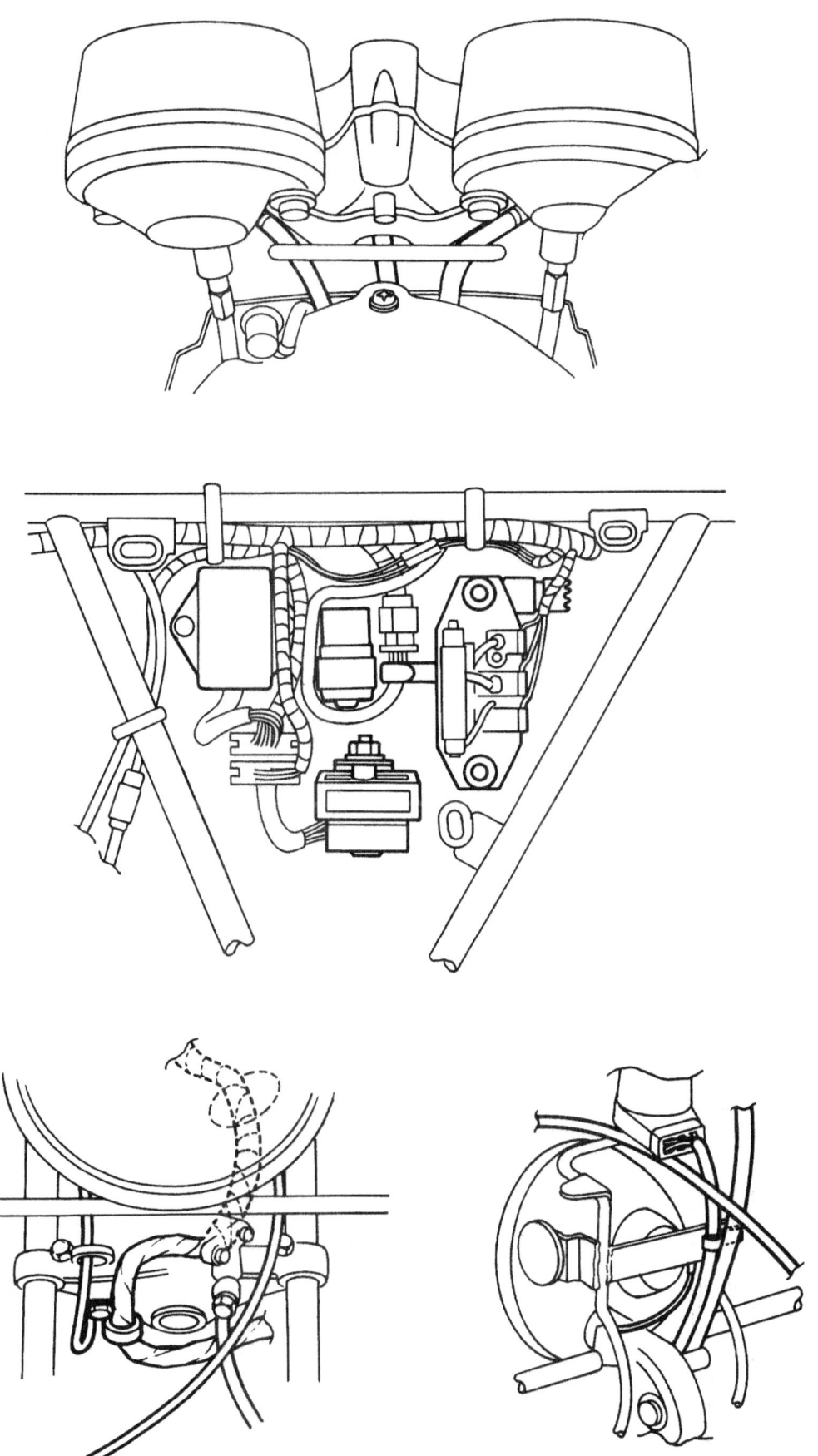

TIGHTENING TORQUE STANDARD

No.	Tightening point	Torque values	
		kg-m	lbs-ft
1	Tappet adjusting nut	1.5 ~ 1.8	10.8 ~ 13.0
2	Cam sprocket lock bolt, 7×12	1.6 ~ 2.0	11.6 ~ 14.5
3	Cylinder head nut, 8 mm	2.0 ~ 2.5	14.5 ~ 18.1
4	A.C. generator rotor set bolt	8.0 ~ 9.0	57.9 ~ 65.2
5	Starting clutch screw 6×18	2.0 ~ 2.5	14.5 ~ 18.1
6	Connecting rod nut	1.8 ~ 2.2	10.8 ~ 15.9
7	Oil pressure switch	1.4 ~ 1.8	10.1 ~ 10.8
8	Oil filter center bolt	2.8 ~ 3.2	16.6 ~ 23.1
9	Spark plug	1.2 ~ 1.6	8.6 ~ 11.6
10	Oil drain bolt	3.5 ~ 4.0	25.3 ~ 28.9
11	Tappet hole cap	1.0 ~ 1.4	7.2 ~ 10.1
12	Oil path cap	1.0 ~ 1.4	7.2 ~ 10.2
13	Drive sproket	1.1 ~ 1.5	5.1 ~ 10.8

No.	Tightening point	Torque values	
		kg-m	lbs-ft
1	Foot peg nut	4.5 ~ 5.5	32.5 ~ 39.8
2	Rear fork pivot nut	5.5 ~ 7.0	32.5 ~ 50.6
3	Oil bolt	3.0 ~ 4.0	21.7 ~ 28.9
4	Front fork bolt	4.5 ~ 5.5	32.5 ~ 39.8
5	Steering stem nut	8.0 ~ 12.0	57.9 ~ 86.8
6	Rear wheel axle nut	8.0 ~ 10.0	57.8 ~ 72.3
7	Front wheel axle nut	5.5 ~ 6.5	39.8 ~ 47.0
8	Final driven sprocket	4.5 ~ 5.5	32.5 ~ 39.8
9	Front stop switch	3.0 ~ 4.0	21.7 ~ 28.9

Standard parts

	Torque values			Torque values	
	kg-m	lbs-ft		kg-m	lbs-ft
SCREW pan 5 mm	0.35 ~ 0.5	2.5 ~ 3.6	BOLT hex. NUT hex 10 mm	3.0 ~ 4.0	21.7 ~ 28.9
SCREW pan 6 mm	0.7 ~ 1.1	5.1 ~ 8.0	BOLT hex. NUT hex 12 mm	5.0 ~ 6.0	36.2 ~ 43.4
BOLT hex. NUT hex 5 mm	0.45 ~ 0.6	3.2 ~ 4.4	BOLT flange 6 mm	1.0 ~ 1.4	7.2 ~ 10.1
BOLT hex. NUT hex 6 mm	0.8 ~ 1.2	5.8 ~ 8.7	BOLT flange 8 mm	2.4 ~ 3.0	17.2 ~ 21.7
BOLT hex. NUT hex 8 mm	1.8 ~ 2.5	10.1 ~ 18.1	BOLT flange 10 mm	3.0 ~ 4.0	21.7 ~ 28.9

22. SUPPLEMENT TO CB 750 F

SPECIFICATIONS CB 750 F

	Item	Metric	English
Dimension	Overall length	2,200 mm	86.6 in
	Overall width	860 mm	33.9 in
	Overall height	1,160 mm	45.7 in
	Wheelbase	1,470 mm	57.9 in
	Seat height	810 mm	31.9 in
	Foot peg height	320 mm	12.6 in
	Ground clearance	135 mm	5.3 in
	Dry weight	227 kg	499 lb
Frame	Type	Double cradle	
	F. suspension, travel	Telescopic fork, travel 141.5 mm 5.6 in	
	R. suspension, travel	Swing arm , travel 86.3 mm 4.0 in	
	F. tire size, pressure	3.25 H-19-4 PR Rib pattern, tire air pressure 2.25 kg/cm^2 32 psi	
	R. tire size, pressure	4.00 H-18-4 PR Block pattern, tire air pressure 2.80 kg/cm^2 40 psi	
	F. brake, lining area	Disk Brake, lining swept area 685.2 cm^2 106.2 sq. in	
	R. brake, lining area	Disk Brake, lining swept area 672.3 cm^2 104.2 sq. in	
	Fuel capacity	18 lit	4.3 U.S. gal 4.0 Imp. gal
	Fuel reserve capacity	5 lit	1.3 U.S. gal 1.1 Imp. gal
	Caster angle	62°	
	Trail length	115 mm	4.5 in
	Front fork oil capacity	145~155 cc	—
Engine	Type	Air cooled 4 stroke OHC engine	
	Cylinder arrangement	4 cylinder in line	
	Bore and stroke	61.0×63.0 mm	2.402×2.480 in
	Displacement	736 cc	44.91 cu. in
	Compression ratio	9.2 : 1	
	Valve train	Chain driven type	
	Oil capacity	3.5 lit	3.7 U.S. qt 3.1 Imp. qt
	Lubrication system	Forced pressure and dry sump	
	Cylinder head compression pressure	12 kg/cm^2 (170.7 psi)	
	Intake valve — Open	At 5° (before top dead center)	
	Intake valve — Close	At 35° (after bottom dead center)	
	Exhaust valve — Open	At 35° (before bottom dead center)	
	Exhaust valve — Close	At 5° (after top dead center)	
	Valve tappet clearance	IN: 0.05 Ex: 0.08 mm	IN: 0.002 Ex: 0.003 in
	Idle speed	1000 rpm	

	Item	Metric	English
Carburetor	Type	28 mm venturi dia - Piston valve type	
	Setting mark	064 A	
	Main jet	♯ 105	
	Slow jet	♯ 40	
	Air screw opening	1 ± 3/8 turns	
	Float height	26 mm	0.866 in
Drive train	Clutch	Wet mulit plate type	
	Transmission	5 speed constant mesh	
	Primary reduction	1.985	
	Gear ratio I	2.500	
	Gear ratio II	1.708	
	Gear ratio III	1.333	
	Gear ratio VI	1.133	
	Gear ratio V	0.969	
	Final reduction	2.824, drive sprocket 17 T, driven sprocket 48 T	
	Gear shift pattern	left foot operated return system	
Electrical	Ignition	Battery and Ignition coil	
	Starting system	starter motor or kick starter	
	Alternator	Three phase A.C. generator 12 V 0.21 kW 5,000 rpm	
	Battery capacity	12 V – 14 AH	
	Spark plug	NGK D8ES-L	ND X 24ES
	Headlight	Low/High 12 V 40/50 watt	
	Tail/stoplight	Tail/stop 12 V 3/32 CP	
	Turn signal-light	Front/Rere 12 V 32/32 Cp	
	Speedometer light	12 V	2 CP
	Tachometer light	12 V	2 CP
	Neutral indicator light	22 V	2 CP
	Turn signal indicator light	12 V	2 CP
	High beam indicator	12 V	2 CP
	Position Light	12 V	3 Cp

22. SUPPLEMENT TO CB750F

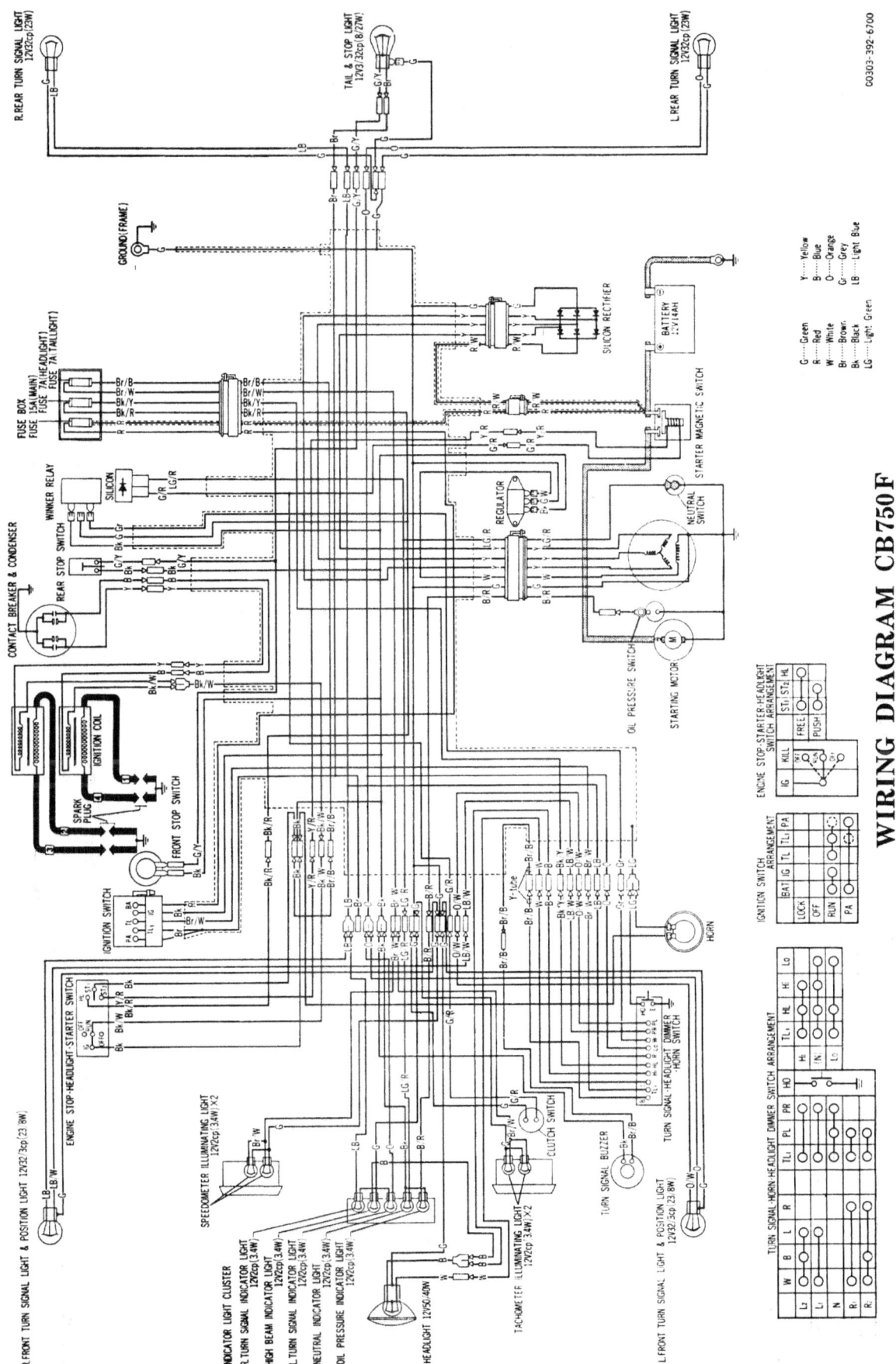

SUPPLEMENT TO CB750K6 ('76)

GROUP 23

1. LUBRICATION SYSTEM

The drive chain lubricating mechanism, page 126, was discontinued. Concurrent with this change, the final drive system will incorporate a new, modified drive shaft as shown.

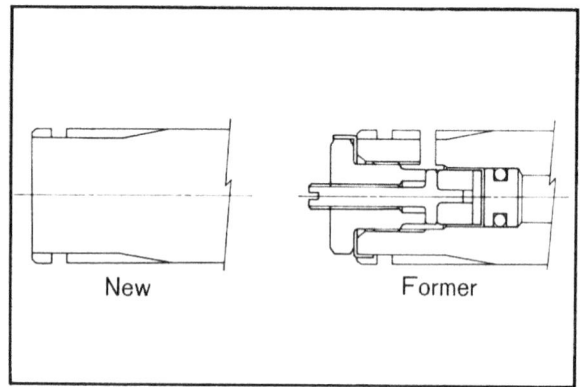

Fig. K6-1 Final drive shaft

2. CLUTCH

Effective with the subject machine serial number, all CB750 will include a 40mm snap ring to retain the clutch outer on the primary driven sprocket.

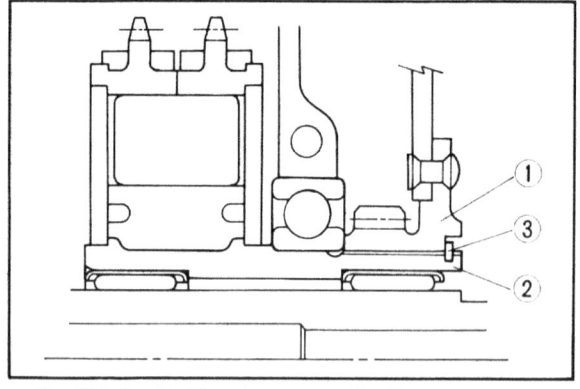

Fig. K6-2 ① Clutch outer ③ 40mm snap ring
② Primary driven sprocket

3. CARBURETOR

The carburetor will be a continuation from the previous type with the exception that the throttle stop screw is relocated from the left to the right side. Specifications of the revised carburetor are as shown immediately below:

Setting No.	086 A
Main jet	#105
Slow jet	#40
Air screw opening	1 ± 1/8
Float height	26 mm (1,024 in.)

Fig. K6-3 ① Throttle stop screw

23. SUPPLEMENT TO CB750K6 ('76)

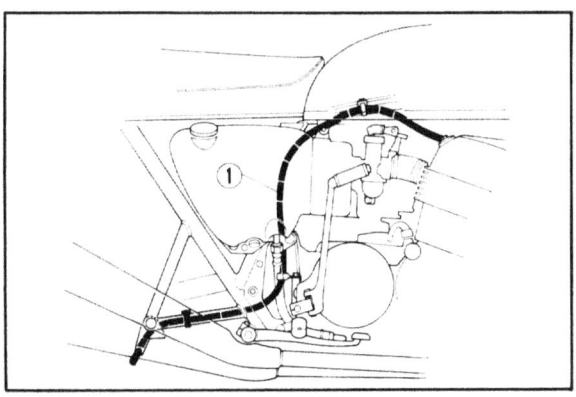

Fig. K6-4 ① Breather tube

4. BREATHER TUBE

The breather tube has been rerouted. The tube will extend down along the right rear fork arm as shown. The end of the tube will be kept more than 50 mm (2 in.) away from the rear wheel.

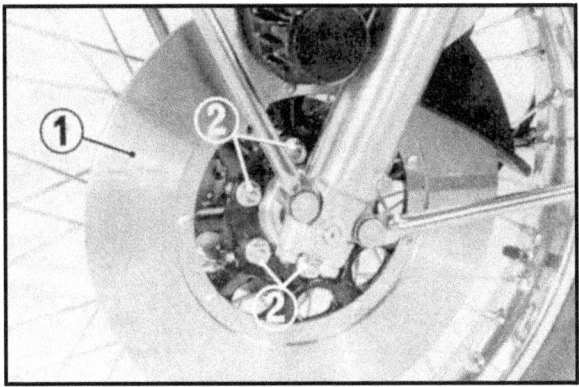

Fig. K6-5 ① Front brake disc
② UBS nut

5. FRONT WHEEL

The front brake will no longer use the tanged washer and nut arrangement for the attachment of the brake disc to the wheel hub. The disc is now tightened with UBS nuts.

Tightening torque: 270–230 kg-cm
(20–24 lbs-ft)

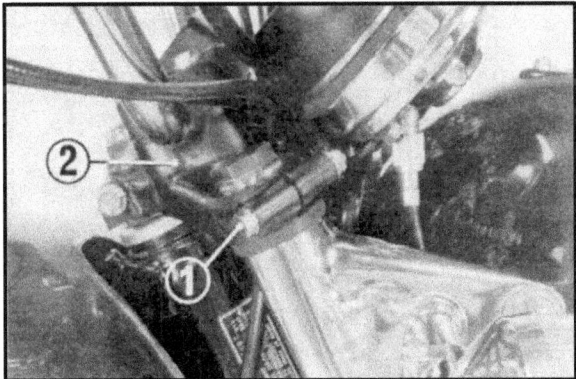

Fig. K6-6 ① 7 mm flange bolt
② Fork top bridge

6. FORK TOP BRIDGE

The flanged bolts used for tightening the fork top bridge will be changed in size from 8 mm to 7 mm.

Tightening torque: 180–250 kg-cm
(13–18 lks-ft)

7. DRIVE CHAIN

CB750 now use a new, improved drive chain in place of the one formerly used. For maintenance tips, see pages 106, 140 & 167. Use new Drive Chain Joint Tool Set (Tool No. 07975-3000002) when replacing the drive chain.

8. REAR FORK

The rear fork pivot pipe now has a grease nipple at its center. The grease nipples formerly located at both ends of the rear fork pivot bolt were discontinued.

Fig. K6-7 ① Grease nipple

9. SPECIFICATIONS (CB 750 '76)

Item	
DIMENSION	
Overall Length	2,175 mm (85.6 in.)
Overall Width	870 mm (34.3 in.)
Overall Height	1,170 mm (46.1 in.)
Wheel Base	1,455 mm (57.3 in.)
Seat Height	810 mm (31.9 in.)
Foot Peg Height	310 mm (12.2 in.)
Ground Clearance	140 mm (5.5 in.)
Dry Weight	218 kg (479 lb.)
FRAME	
Type	Double Cradle
F. Suspension, Travel	Telescpic fork , travel 143 mm (5.6 in.)
R. Suspension, Travel	Swing arm , travel 85 mm (3.3 in.)
F. Tire Size, Type	3.25–19–4 PR Rib , tire air pressure 2.0/2.25 kg/cm² (28/32 psi)
R. Tire Size, Type	4.00–18–4 PR Block , tire air pressure 2.0/2.8 kg/cm² (28/40 psi)
F. Brake	Disk Brake
R. Brake	Internal expanding shoe
Fuel Capacity	17 lit. (4.5 U.S. gal. 3.7 Imp. gal.)
Fuel Reserve Capacity	5 lit. (1.3 U.S. gal. 1.1 Imp. gal.)
Caster Angle	63°
Trail Length	95 mm (3.7 in.)
Front Fork Oil Capacity	155~160 cc (5.3–5.4 ozs.)
ENGINE	
Type	Air cooled 4 stroke O.H.C. engine
Cylinder Arrangement	4 cylinder in line
Bore and Stroke	61.0×63.0 mm (2.402×2.480 in.)
Displacement	736 cc (44.9 cu in.)
Compression Ratio	9.0 : 1
Carburetor, Venturi Dia.	Four piston valve type, venturi dia. 28 mm (1.102 in.)
Valve Train	chain driven over head cam shaft
Oil Capacity	3.5 lit. (3.7 U.S. qt 3.1 Imp. qt)
Lubrication System	Forced pressure and dry sump
Fuel Required	Low-lead gasoline with 91 octane number or higher
Air Filtration	Paper filter
Valve Tappet Clearance	IN 0.05 EX 0.08 mm (IN: 0.002, EX 0.003 in.)
Air Screw Opening	1
Idle Speed	950 rpm
DRIVE TRAIN	
Clutch	wet multi plate type
Transmission	5-speed constant mesh
Primary Reduction	1.708
Gear Rrtio I	2.500
II	1.708
III	1.333
IV	1.097
V	0.939
Final Reduction	2.667, drive sprocket 18 T, driven sprocket 48 T
Gear Shift Pattern	Left foot operated return system
ELECTRICAL	
Ignition	Battry and ignition coil
Starting System	Starting motor or kick starter
Alternator	Three phase AC Generator 0.21 kw/5,000 rpm
Battery Capacity	12 V–14 AH
Fuse Capacity	15 amp.
Spark plug	NGK D8ES-L NDX 24ES

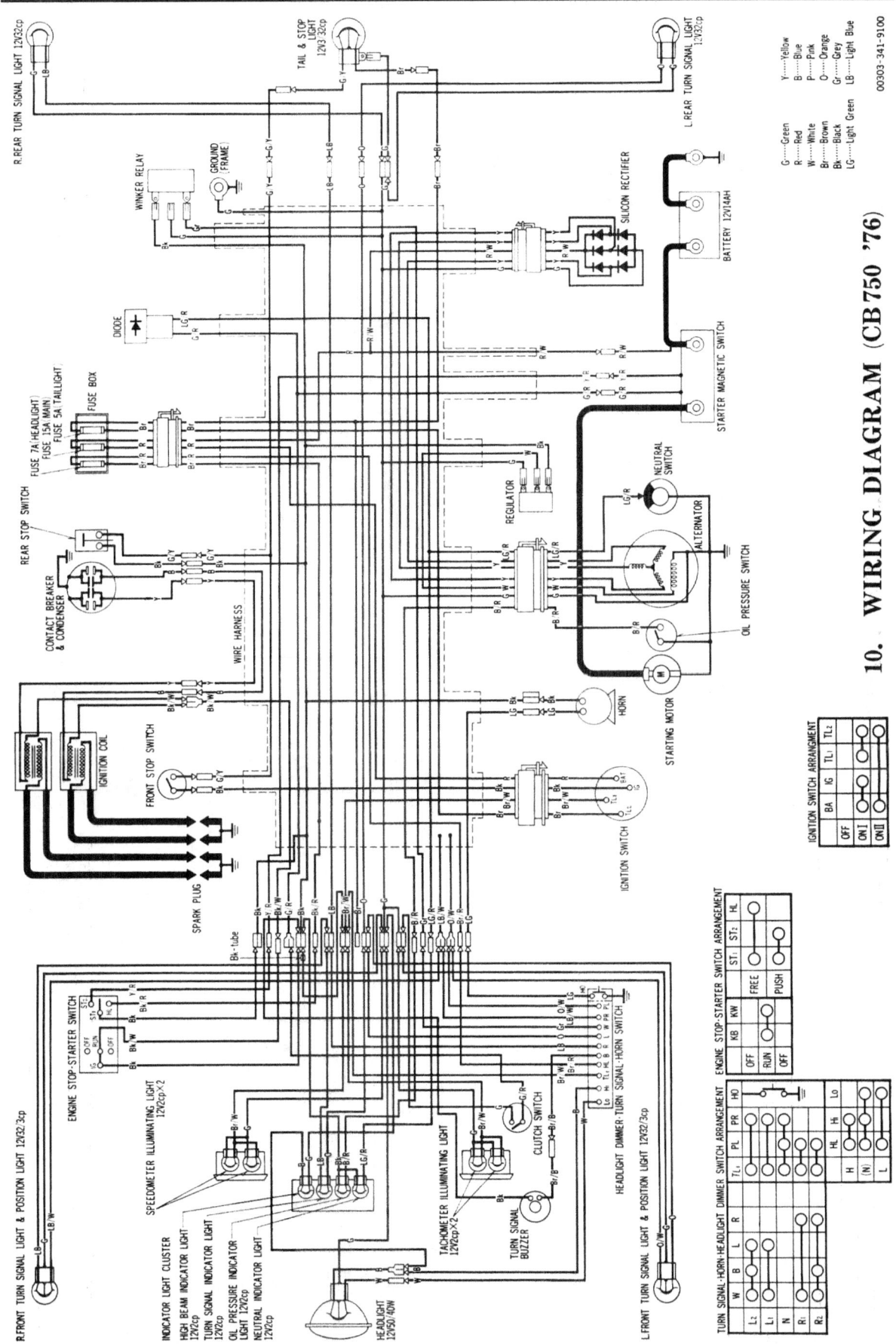

SUPPLEMENT TO CB 750 K7 ('77)

Engine No. CB 750 E—2700001 and subsequent
Frame No. CB 750—2700002 and subsequent

GROUP 24

1. CARBURETOR

A. Removal and installation

1. Turn the fuel valve lever to the "OFF" position and disconnect the fuel tube at the fuel valve.
2. Open the seat and remove the fuel tank.
3. Remove the air cleaner lower case by loosening the two mounting bolts. Loosen the air cleaner connecting bands and remove the two air cleaner hanger bolts. Remove the air cleaner upper case from the carburetors.

Fig. K7-1 ① Air cleaner mounting bolt
② Lower case
③ Hanger bolt
④ Connecting band

4. Remove the throttle and choke cables from the cable holder and disconnect them from the shaft levers.

Fig. K7-2 ① Throttle cable
② Choke cable
③ Cable holder

5. Loosen the carburetor insulator bands and take out the carburetor assembly.
6. To install the carburetor assembly, reverse the removal procedure.

Fig. K7-3 ① Carburetor insulator band

24. SUPPLEMENT TO CB 750 K7 ('77)

Fig. K7-4 ① Bolt   ③ Choke relief spring
② Rear stay   ④ Choke lever

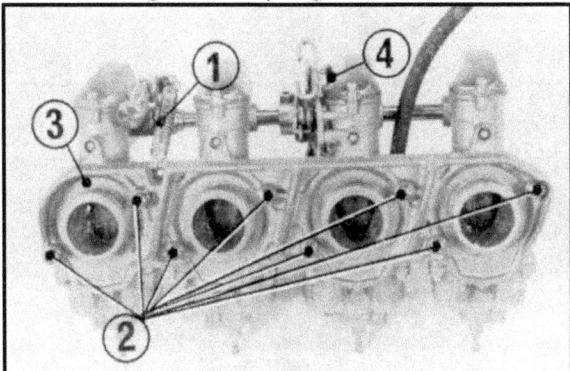

Fig. K7-5 ① Throttle return spring
② Screw
③ Stay plate
④ Accelerator pump spring

Fig. K7-6 ① Link arm fixing screw
② Set screw   ③ Lock nut

Fig. K7-7 ① Screws   ③ Tube
② Choke valve

B. Disassembly

Carburetor, throttle valve and jet needle:

1. Remove the carburetor assembly from the engine.
2. Remove the rear stay from the carburetor assembly by loosening the four bolts.

3. Unhook the throttle return spring from the stopper arm. Remove the stay plate by loosening the eight screws.
Remove the accelerater pump spring. Unhook the choke relief spring at the choke lever.

4. Remove the carburetor top by loosening the two screws.
5. Loosen the link arm fixing screw.
Loosen the lock nut and remove the throttle lever set screw.

6. Remove the choke valve from the choke shaft by loosening the two screws.
Remove the accelerator pump fuel tubes.
7. Separate the carburetors.

8. Remove the link arm assembly from the carburetor.
9. Loosen the two screws and remove the throttle valve and jet needle from the link arm.

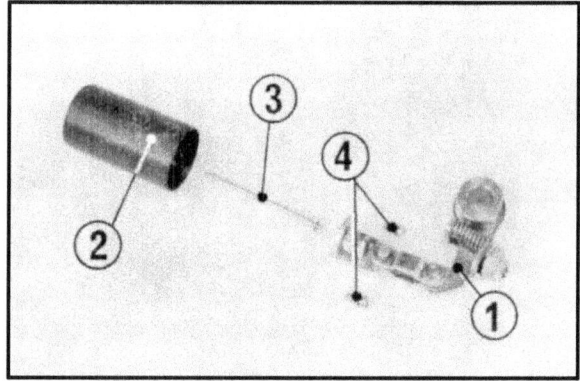

Fig. K7-8
① Link arm
② Throttle valve
③ Jet needle
④ Screw

Float, main jet, slow jet and accelerator pump:
1. Remove the carburetor assembly from the engine.
2. Remove the float chamber body from the carburetor by loosening the three screws.
3. Pull out the float arm pin and remove the float.
4. Remove the main jet and slow jet.

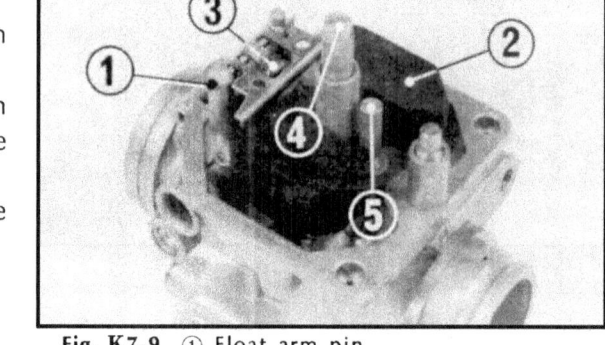

Fig. K7-9
① Float arm pin
② Float
③ Float valve
④ Main jet
⑤ Slow jet

5. Remove the accelerator pump from the No. 2 carburetor by unscrewing the three screws.

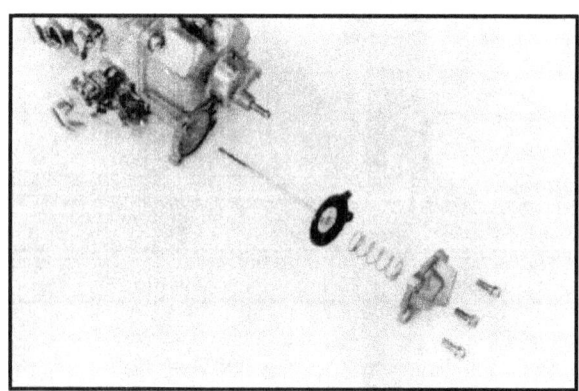

Fig. K7-10 Accelerator pump

24. SUPPLEMENT TO CB750 K7 ('77)

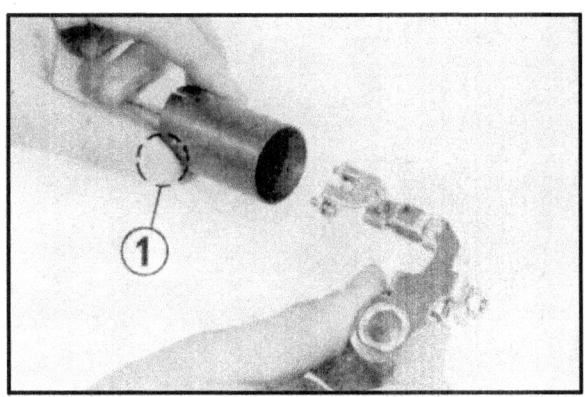

Fig. K7-11 ① Throttle valve cutaway

C. Assembly

To assemble the carburetor, reverse the disassembly procedure. Observe the following notes:

1. Install the throttle valve to the link arm so that the throttle valve cutaway is toward the choke valve when it is installed in the carburetor body.

Fig. K7-12 ① Link arm for No. 2 carburetor
② Link arm for No. 1, 3 and 4 carburetor

2. The link arm which is not equipped with the adjusting screw should be installed in the No. 2 carburetor.

Fig. K7-13

3. Install the choke shaft levers and springs properly as shown in Fig. K7-13.

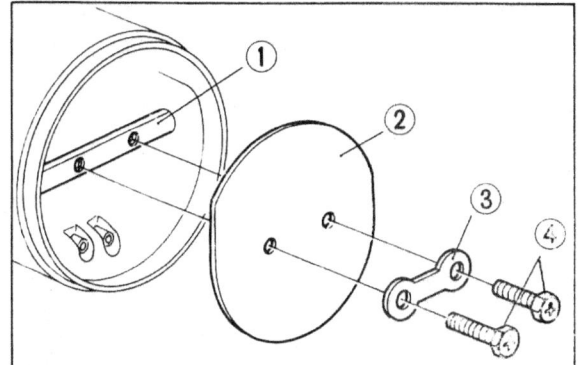

Fig. K7-14 ① Choke shaft
② Choke valve
③ Lock washer
④ Hex. head screw

4. Install the choke valve to the choke shaft by using the lock washer and hex. head screws and bend the lock washer to lock the screws.

   NOTE: The choke valve securing screws are peened when assembling the carburetor at the factory. Discard the used screws.

D. Carburetor setting table

Item	
Main jet No.	#115
Air jet No.	#150
Slow jet No.	#35
Slow air jet No.	#150
Jet needle setting	F2D51E-1
Float height	12.5 mm (0.492 in.)

E. Adjustment

Idle speed:

Make the adjustment after warming up the engine.

1. Adjust the idle stop screw to allow the engine to run at the idle speed of 950 to 1,050 rpm.
2. Turn the pilot screw either in or out to obtain the highest idle speed. Usually the correct setting will be found to be 1 1/2 turns open from a fully closed position.
3. If idle speed changes after adjusting the pilot screw, readjust the idle stop screw.

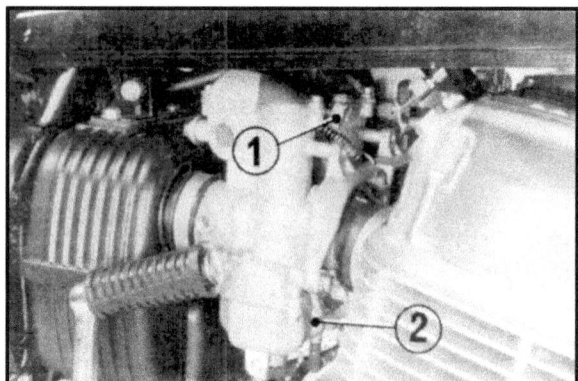

Fig. K7-15 ① Idle stop screw
② Pilot screw

Synchronizing carburetors:

1. Remove the fuel tank. Position the fuel tank higher than the carburetors and reconnect with a longer fuel tube.
2. Connect the vacuum gauge set to the carburetors.
3. Run the engine at the specified idle speed and read the vacuum. The vacuum gauge readings should be the same on all four gauges.
4. To adjust, proceed as follows:
   a. Remove the carburetor tops from the No. 1, 3 and 4 carburetors.
   b. Loosen the lock nut and turn the adjusting screw until the vacuum reading becomes the same as the No. 2 carburetor reading.

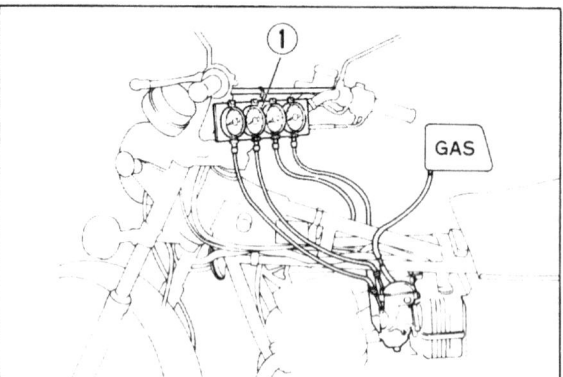

Fig. K7-16 ① Vacuum gauge set

Fig. K7-17 ① Lock nut
② Adjusting screw

24. SUPPLEMENT TO CB750 K7 ('77)

Fig. K7-19 ① Adjusting screw

Fast idle:
1. Remove the fuel tank.
2. Pull the choke knob out fully and turn the adjusting screw until it touches the stopper.
3. Push the choke knob in and turn the adjusting screw in 2·1/2 turns.
Fast idle speed: 3,000~4,000 rpm

Accelerator pump:
1. Remove the carburetor assembly from the engine.
2. Measure the pump rod-to-pump arm clearance with the throttle valve closed. The clearance should be 0 to 0.2 mm (0 to 0.008 in.). To adjust, bend the pump arm tang.
3. Measure the pump arm-to-carburetor stay clearance with the throttle valve closed. The clearance should be 9.5 to 10.5 mm (0.374 to 0.413 in.). To adjust, bend the pump arm.

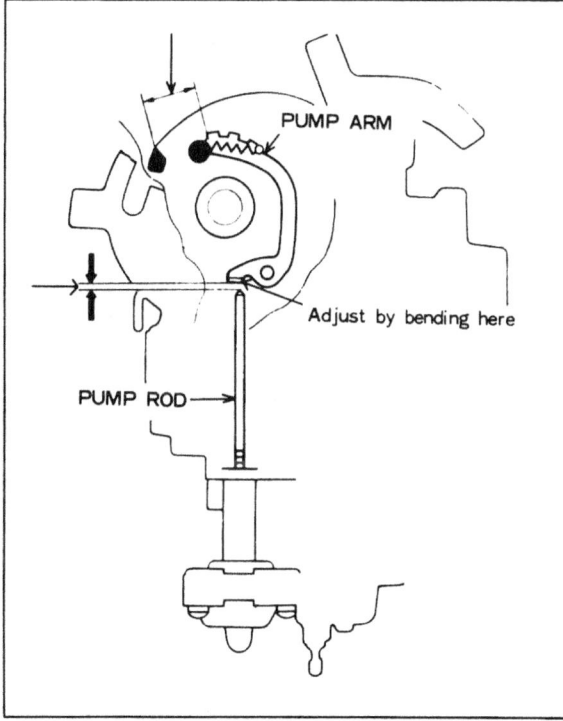

Fig. K7-20

2. DRIVE CHAIN

A. Inspection

1. Check for damaged rollers, loose pins, or missing O-rings. Replace if necessary.
2. Check for kinked, binding, dry, or rusted links. Lubricate only with SAE 80 or 90 gear oil, if necessary.

B. Adjustment

To adjust the drive chain, perform in the same manner described on page 106. Observe the following notes:
1. Drive chain tension: 20 mm (3/4 in.)
2. Check the chain wear label when adjusting the chain. If the red zone on the label aligns with the rear of the swing arm after the chain has been adjusted to 20 mm (3/4 in.) slack, the chain is excessively worn and must be replaced.

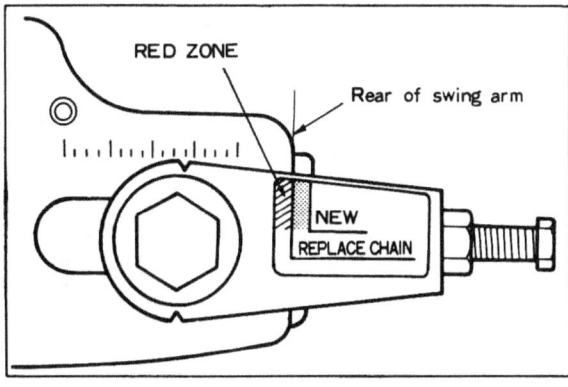

Fig. K7-21

C. Lubricating and cleaning

The drive chain is equipped with O-rings. The O-rings can be damaged by steam cleaning, high pressure washers, and certain solvents. Clean the chain with kerosene. Wipe dry and lubricate only with SAE 80 or 90 gear oil. Commercial chain lubricants may contain solvents which could damage the rubber O-rings.

D. Replacement

The drive chain cannot be replaced by using a drive chain joint tool. Replace using the following procedure.

1. Remove the drive chain case and rear wheel.
2. Loosen the two 10 mm bolts that secure the rear shock absorbers to the rear swing arm.
3. Unscrew the rear fork pivot nut and pull out the rear fork pivot bolt. Remove the rear fork from the frame.
4. Remove the gear change pedal, transmission cover and left crankcase rear cover.
5. Remove the drive sprocket by loosening the 8 mm bolt. Remove the drive chain.
   Replacement chain:
   DID630DL or designation of RK630SD chain.
6. To install the drive chain, reverse the removal procedure described above.

Fig. K7-22 ① 10 mm bolt
② Rear fork pivot nut

Fig. K7-23 ① Rear fork pivot bolt

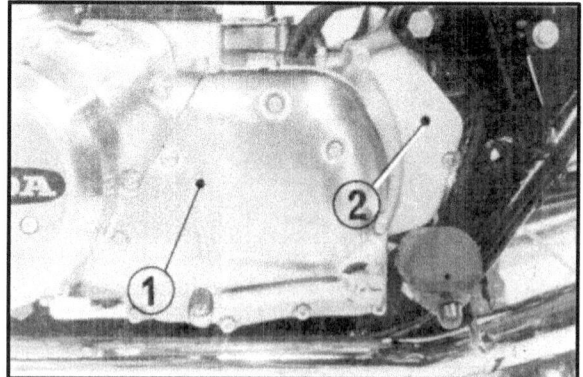

Fig. K7-24 ① Transmission cover
② Left crankcase rear cover

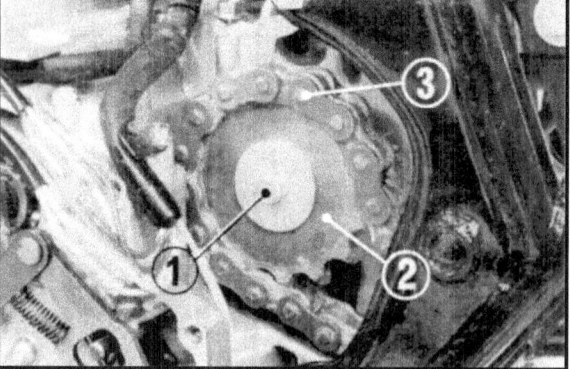

Fig. K7-25 ① 8 mm bolt
② Drive sprocket
③ Drive chain

24. SUPPLEMENT TO CB750 K7 ('77)

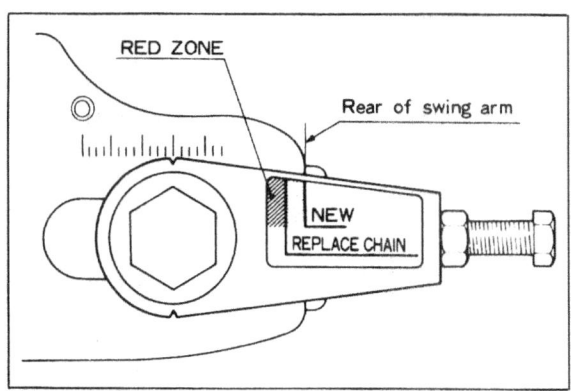

Fig. K7-26

7. Adjust the chain tension properly.
Attach a new label to the left drive chain adjuster so that the right side end of the green zone aligns with the rear of the swing arm as shown in Fig. K7-26.

3. ENGINE OIL TANK

Connect the suction hose to the oil tank as shown in fig. K7-27 to prevent interference between the rear brake middle arm and the suction hose when the brake is applied.

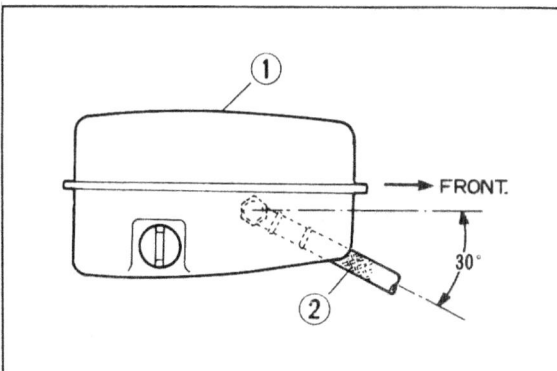

Fig. K7-27 ① Oil tank ② Suction hose

4. REAR BRAKE PEDAL

A. Installation

Install the brake pedal so that the punch mark on the pedal is aligned with the punch mark on the rear brake spindle.

B. Adjustment

1. Adjust the brake pedal height so that the foot peg-to-pedal distance is 10 mm (0.4 in.). To adjust, loosen the lock nut and turn the stopper bolt in or out.
2. Adjust the pedal free play by turning the rear brake adjusting nut.
   Free play: 20–30 mm (0.8–1.2 in.)

Fig. K7-28 ① Punch marks ④ Lock nut
② Foot peg ⑤ Stopper bolt
③ Rear brake pedal

5. SWITCH HOUSING

When installing the right or left switch housing, align the mating edges of the housing with the punch mark on the handlebar and tighten the two screws securely.
The aligning mark on the brake lever bracket holder should be also lined up with the punch mark.

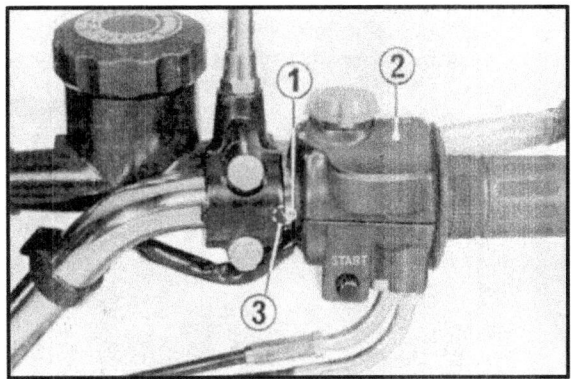

Fig. K7-29 ① Punch mark
② Switch housing
③ Aligning mark on holder

5. SERVICE DATA

A. Service data

	Standard value	Service limit
Front shock absorber spring free length	504.3 mm	480 mm
Rear shock absorber spring free length	232.9 mm	220 mm
Front brake: Caliper cylinder I.D.	42.85–42.90 mm	42.91 mm
Caliper piston O D.	42.82 mm	42.81 mm

B. Torque specifications

Connecting rod cap	7 mm	1.8– 2.2 kg-m	(13.0–15.9 lb-ft)
Cylinder head	8 mm	2.0– 2.5 kg-m	(14.5–18 1 lb-ft)
Flywheel	12 mm	10.0–12.0 kg-m	(72.3–86.7 lb-ft)
Drive sprocket	8 mm	1.8– 2.2 kg-m	(13.0–15.9 lb-ft)
Clutch center	16 mm	4.0– 4.2 kg-m	(28.9–30.4 lb-ft)
Upper crankcase	8 mm	2.0– 2.5 kg-m	(14.5–18.1 lb-ft)
Lower Crankcase	8 mm	2.0– 2.5 kg-m	(14.5–18.1 lb-ft)
Cam sprocket	7 mm	1.8– 2.2 kg-m	(13.0–15.9 lb-ft)

24. SUPPLEMENT TO CB 750 K7 ('77)

6. SPECIFICATION (CB 750 K '77)

Item	
DIMENSION	
Overall Length	2,280 mm (89.8 in.)
Overall Width	880 mm (34.6 in.)
Overall Height	1,185 mm (46.7 in.)
Wheel Base	1,495 mm (58.9 in.)
Seat Height	810 mm (31.9 in.)
Foot Peg Height	330 mm (13.0 in.)
Ground Clearance	150 mm (5.9 in.)
Dry Weight	231 kg (508 lb.)
FRAME	
Type	Double Cradle
F. Suspension, Travel	Telescopic fork, travel 141.5 mm (5.6 in.)
R. Suspension, Travel	Swing arm, travel 101.6 mm (4.0 in.)
F. Tire Size, Type	3.50 H-19-4 PR Rib, tire air pressure 2.0/2.0 kg/cm² (28/28 psi)
R. Tire Size, Type	4.50 H-17A-4 PR Block, tire air pressure 2.25/2.8 kg/cm² (32/40 psi)
F. Brake	Disk Brake
R. Brake	Internal expanding shoe
Fuel Capacity	19 lit. (5.0 U.S. gal. 4.2 Imp. gal.)
Fuel Reserve Capacity	4 lit. (1.1 U.S. gal. 0.9 Imp. gal.)
Caster Angle	62°
Trail Length	115 mm (4.5 in.)
Front Fork Oil Capacity	145~155 cc (5.3~5.4 ozs.)
ENGINE	
Type	Air cooled 4 stroke O.H.C. engine
Cylinder Arrangement	4 cylinder in line
Bore and Stroke	61.0 × 63.0 mm (2.402 × 2.480 in.)
Displacement	736 cc (44.9 cu in.)
Compression Ratio	9.2 : 1
Carburetor, Venturi Dia.	Four piston valve type, venturi dia. 28 mm (1.102 in.)
Valve Train	Chain driven overhead cam shaft
Oil Capacity	3.5 lit. (3.7 U.S. qt 3.1 Imp. qt)
Lubrication System	Forced pressure and dry sump
Fuel Required	Low-lead gasoline with 91 octane number or higher
Air Filtration	Paper filter
Intake Valve: Opens	0° BTDC
Closes	40° ATDC
Exhaust Valve: Opens	40° BBDC
Closes	0° ATDC
Valve Tappet Clearance	IN: 0.05 EX: 0.08 mm (IN: 0.002, EX: 0.003 in.)
Pilot Screw Opening	Fixed by idle limiter (1·1/2 ± 1/2)
Idle Speed	1,000 rpm

Item	
DRIVE TRAIN	
Clutch	Wet multi plate type
Transmission	5-speed constant mesh
Primary Reduction	1.708
Gear Ratio I	2.500
II	1.708
III	1.333
IV	1.133
V	0.969
Final Reduction	2.733, drive sprocket 15 T, driven sprocket 41 T
Gear Shift Pattern	Left foot operated return system
ELECTRICAL	
Ignition	Battery and ignition coil
Ignition Advance:	
"F" mark	10° BTDC
Max. advance	35°
RPM from "F" to max. advance	1,200–2,500 rpm
Dwell Angle	190° ± 5°
Starting System	Starting motor or kick starter
Alternator	Three phase AC Generator 0.21 kW/5,000 rpm
Battery Capacity	12 V–14 AH
Fuse Capacity	Main: 15 amp. Head: 7 A Tail: 5 A
Spark plug	NGK D 8 ES-L ND X 24 ES (U.S.A. model)
	NGK DR 8 ES-L ND X 24 ESR (Canadian model)
Condenser Capacity	0.20–0.24 μF

24. SUPPLEMENT TO CB 750 K7 ('77)

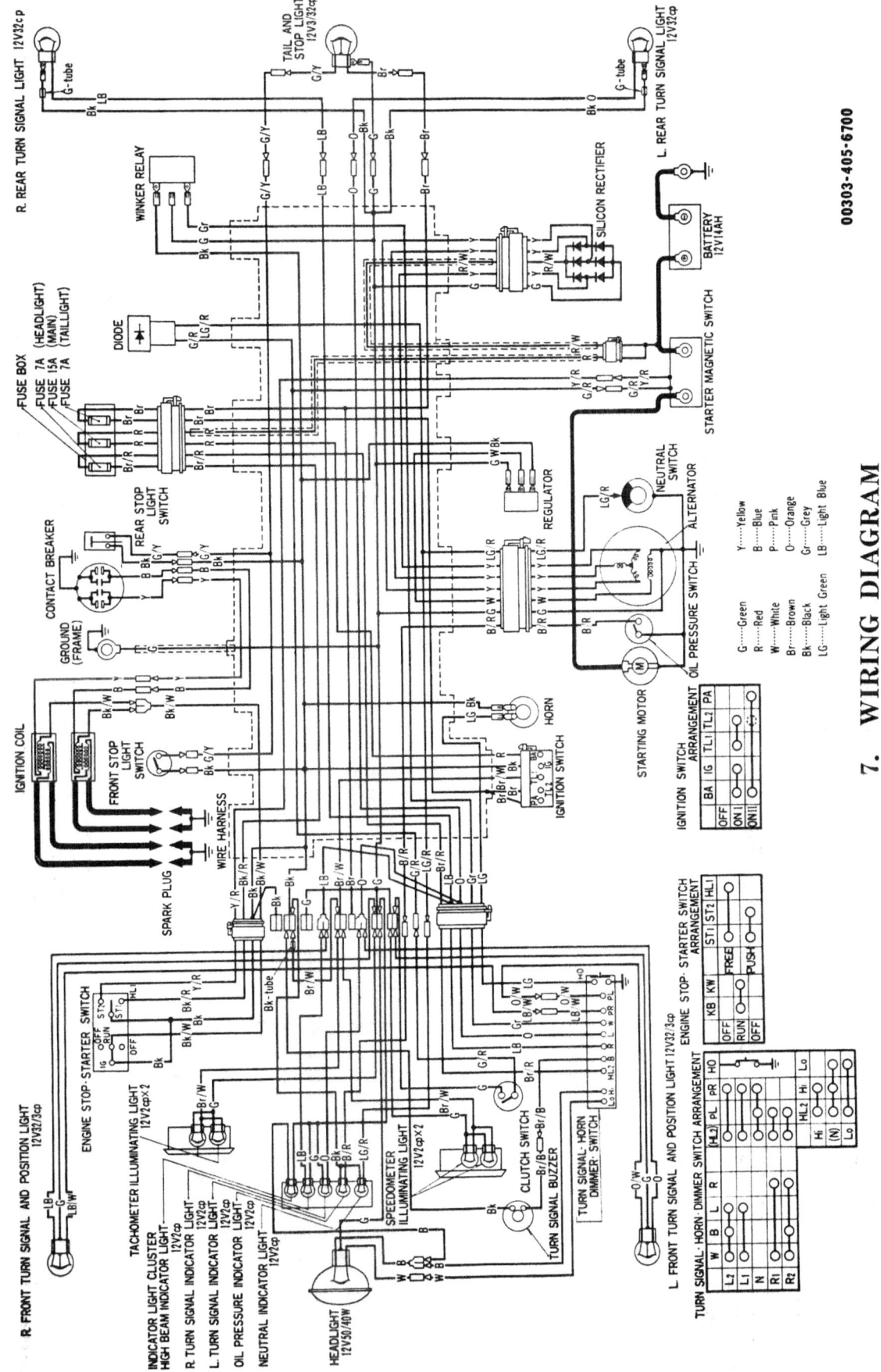

7. WIRING DIAGRAM

SUPPLEMENT TO CB750F2 ('77)

Engine No. CB750E—2600004 and subsequent
Frame No. CB750F—2100001 and subsequent

GROUP 25

1. FRONT BRAKE

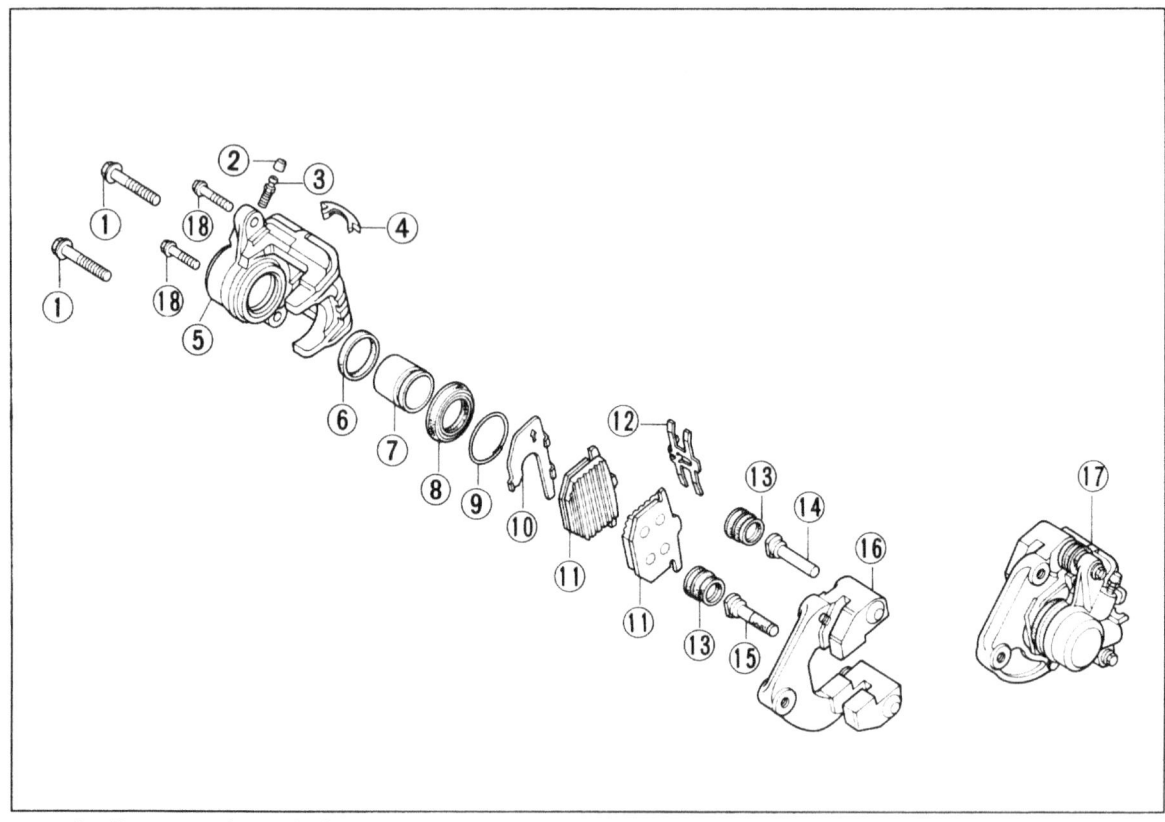

Fig. F2-1
① Flange bolt (10×32)
② Bleed valve cap
③ Bleed valve
④ Indicator cap
⑤ Right caliper
⑥ Piston seal
⑦ Piston
⑧ Piston boot
⑨ Piston boot clip
⑩ Pad shim
⑪ Brake pad
⑫ Pad spring
⑬ Dust cover
⑭ Pin A
⑮ Pin B
⑯ Right bracket
⑰ Left caliper assembly
⑱ 8mm flange bolt

A. Disassembly

1. Remove the oil bolt and disconnect the front brake hose from the caliper.
2. Remove the two 8mm flange bolts and caliper from the bracket.

NOTE: It is not necessary to remove the oil bolt to replace the brake pads.

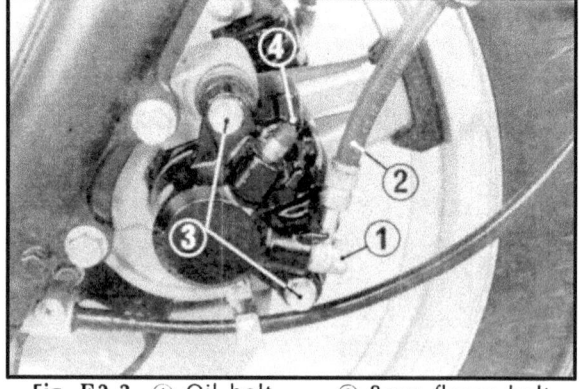

Fig. F2-2
① Oil bolt
② Brake hose
③ 8mm flange bolt
④ Caliper

25. SUPPLEMENT TO CB750F2 ('77)

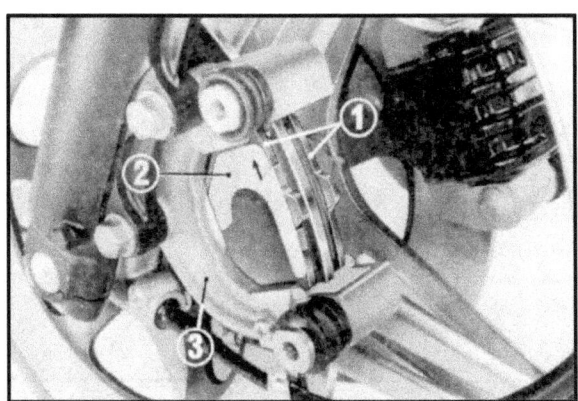

Fig. F2-3　① Brake pad　③ Caliper holder
　　　　　② Shim

3. Remove the brake pads and shim from the caliper holder.
4. Remove the pad spring from the caliper.
5. Remove the boot clip and piston boot. Apply compressed air in the caliper fluid inlet and remove the piston.

Fig. F2-4　① Pad spring　③ Piston boot
　　　　　② Boot clip　　④ Piston

B. Assembly

To assemble, reverse the disassembly procedure. Observe the following notes.

1. Install the shim on the outside pad so that its arrow is in the normal rotating direction.

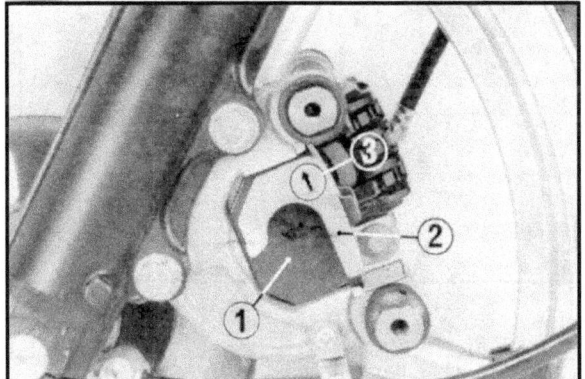

Fig. F2-5　① Brake pad　③ Arrow
　　　　　② Shim

2. Install the brake hose so that the straight side of the hose ends is at the caliper and bent side is at the three way joint as shown in Fig. F2-6.

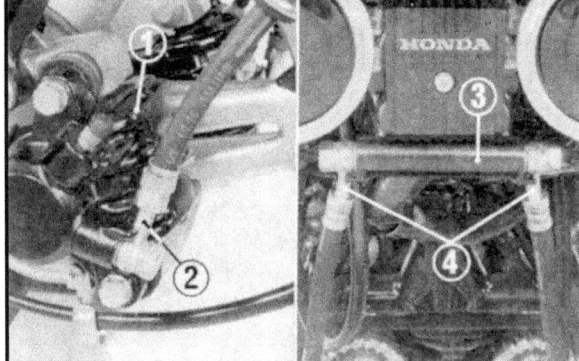

Fig. F2-6　① Caliper　　　③ Three way joint
　　　　　② Straight side　④ Bent side

C. Brake pad inspection

Remove the wear indicator cap and check the brake pads for wear. If the pad is worn to the red line, replace all front pads as a set.

Fig. F2-7 ① Red line   ② Brake disc

2. FRONT BRAKE SWITCH

The front brake switch has been modified from the hydraulic switch to the mechanical switch.

Fig. F2-8 ① Front brake switch

3. REAR BRAKE

A. Pedal free height adjustment

To adjust the brake pedal free height, remove the rubber cap by inserting a screw driver in the groove, loosen the lock nut and turn the adjuster as necessary. Turning the adjuster clockwise will decrease the pedal height, and turning it counterclockwise will result in a increase. After adjustment, tighten the lock nut securely and install the rubber cap.

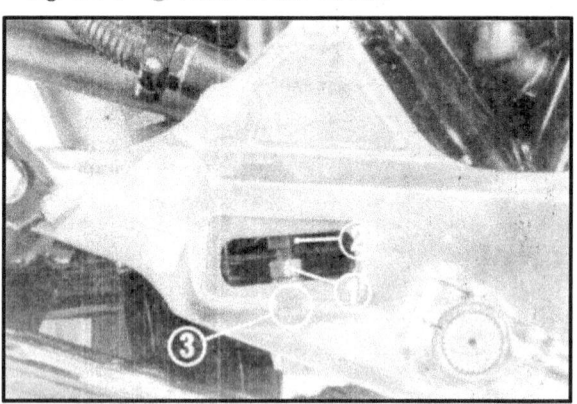

Fig. F2-9 ① Lock nut   ③ Groove
② Adjuster

B. Rear brake hose

The brake hose is installed so that the bent side of the hose ends is at the caliper as shown in Fig. F2-10.

Fig. F2-10 ① Brake hose   ③ Caliper
② Bent side

4. FRONT WHEEL

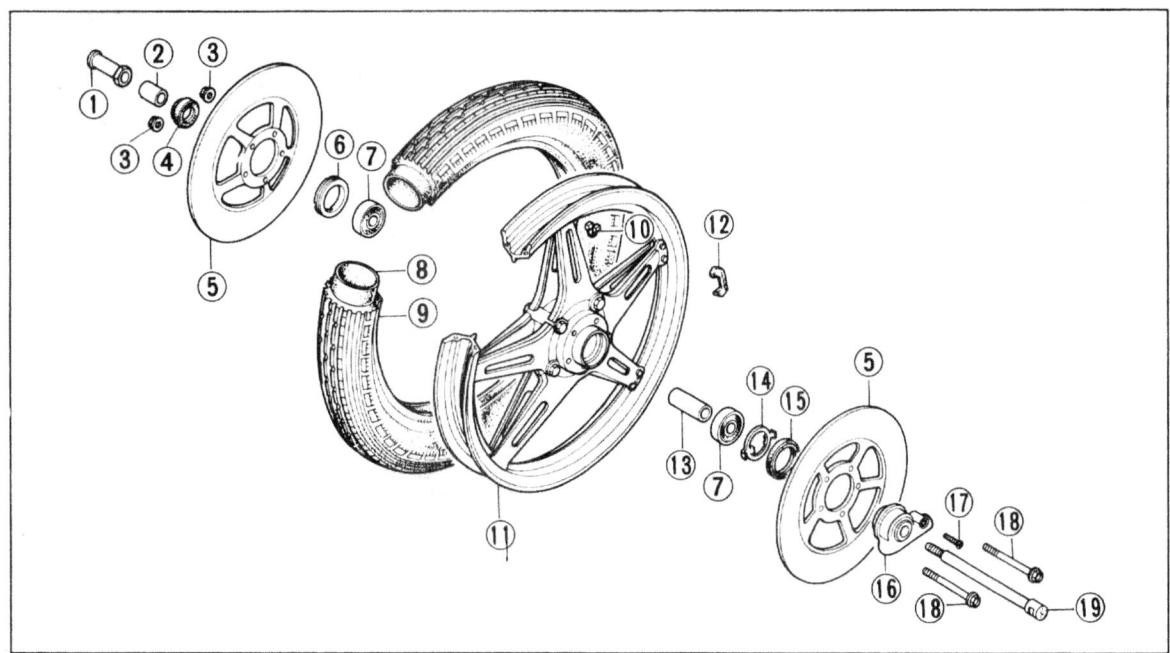

Fig. F2-11
① Axle nut (12 mm)
② Front wheel side collar
③ Hex. nut (8 mm)
④ Dust seal (40×50×5)
⑤ Front brake disc
⑥ Front wheel bearing retainer
⑦ Radial ball bearing (6302U)
⑧ Tire tube
⑨ Front wheel tire
⑩ Wheel balance weight
⑪ Front wheel rim assembly
⑫ Spoke plate mark
⑬ Distance collar
⑭ Gear box retainer
⑮ Dust seal (40×50×5)
⑯ Speedometer gear box
⑰ Screw (5×16)
⑱ Flange bolt (8×100)
⑲ Front wheel axle

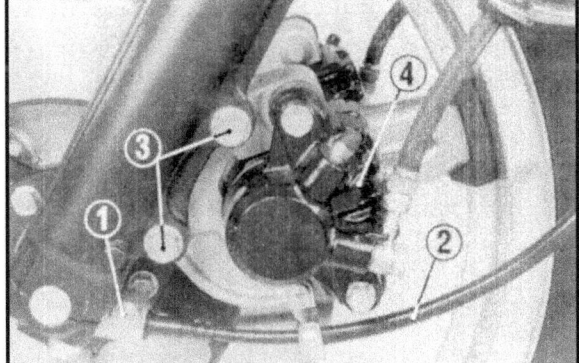

Fig. F2-12
① Screw
② Speedometer cable
③ 10 mm bolt
④ Caliper

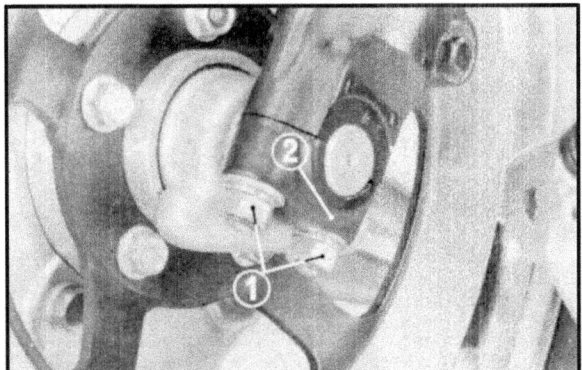

Fig. F2-13 ① Axle holder nut ② Axle holder

A. Disassembly

1. Place a suport block under the engine to raise the front wheel off the ground.
2. Remove the screw and remove the speedometer cable from the gear box.
3. Remove the four 10 mm bolts and caliper assemblies from the front forks.

NOTE: Do not depress the brake lever when the wheel is off the motorcycle.

4. Remove the front axle holder nuts and remove the front axle holders.
5. Remove the front wheel.
6. Remove the front brake discs by loosening the five 8 mm nuts and bolts.
7. Remove the wheel bearing retainer with special tool (Bearing Retainer Wrench; Tool No. HC 37592). Then remove the gear box retainer, bearings and distance collar.
8. Remove the dust seals if replacement is required.

NOTE: Do not disassemble the front wheel rim assembly.

B. Assembly

To assemble, reverse the disassembly procedure. However, install the front wheel assembly as follows.

1. Position the wheel assembly between the fork legs, making sure that the speedometer gear box is properly positioned. Lower the fork lightly so that the hollows in the fork legs rest on top of the axle.
2. Install the axle holders with the "F" mark forward and tighten the forward axle holder nuts lightly.
3. Fit the caliper over the discs taking care not to damage the brake pads. Install the caliper mounting bolts and tighten to the specified torque.
   Specified torque: 3.0–4.0 kg-m (22–29 lbs-ft.)
4. Tighten the nuts on the right axle holder to the specified torque starting with the forward nuts.
   Specified torque: 1.8–2.5 kg-m (13–18 lbs-ft.)

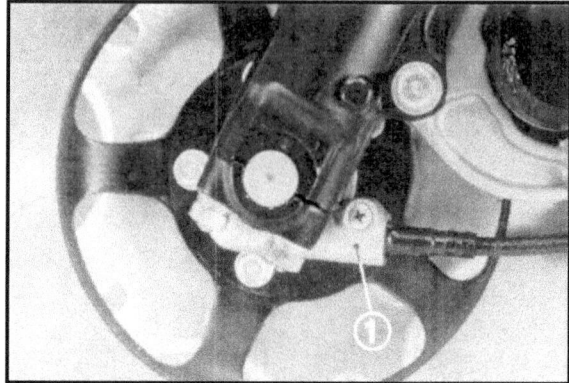

Fig. F2-14 ① Speedometer gear box

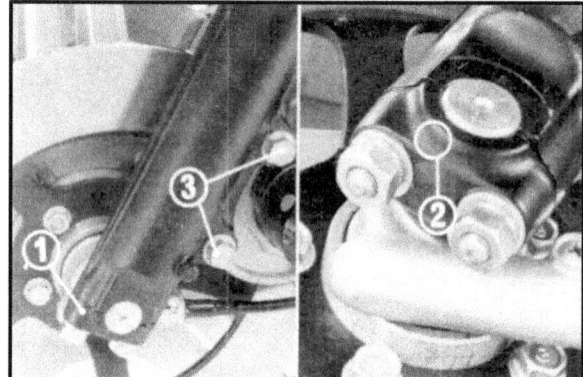

Fig. F2-15 ① Axle holder
② "F" mark
③ Caliper mounting bolt

5. Measure the clearance between the outside surface of the left brake disc and the rear of the left caliper holder with a 0.7 mm (0.028 in.) feeler gauge. If the gauge inserts easily, first tighten the forward axle holder nut to the specified torque, then the rear nut. If the feeler gauge cannot be inserted easily, pull the left fork outward until the gauge can be inserted and tighten the holder nuts with the gauge inserted. After tightening, remove the gauge.
6. Check that the other three corners of the left caliper holder have a clearance of at least 0.7 mm (0.028 in.) between caliper holder and disc.
7. After installing the wheel, apply brakes several times and recheck both discs for caliper holder to disc clearance.

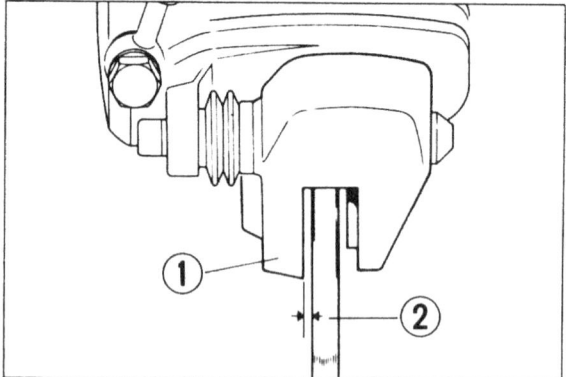

Fig. F2-16 ① Caliper holder ② Disc

Fig. F2-17 ① Feeler gauge

25. SUPPLEMENT TO CB750F2 ('77)

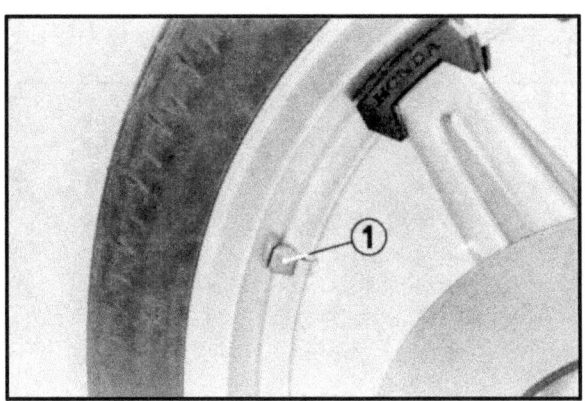

Fig. F2-18 ① Balance weight

C. Wheel balance

(Refer to page 165.)
Install the balance weight on the rim flange as shown in Fig. F2-18.
  Balance weight: 20 g (0.7 oz.)
  30 g (1.0 oz.)

5. CYLINDER

The 12 mm special knock pins and cylinder stud bolt packings have been decreased from eight to four.

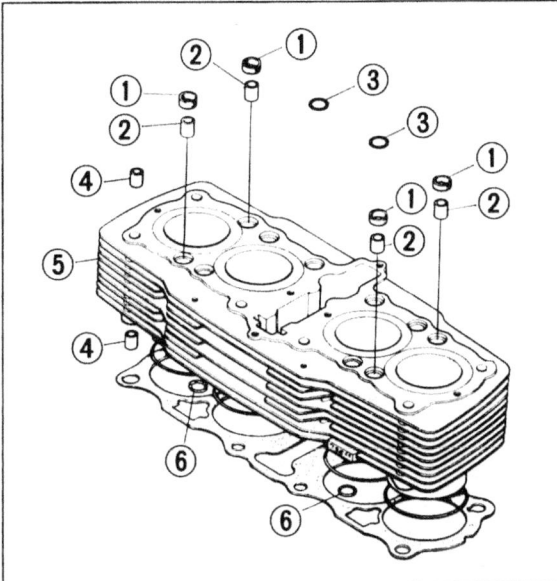

Fig. F2-19 ① Stud bolt packing
  ② Special knock pin (12 mm)
  ③ O-ring (11 × 2.5)
  ④ Dowel pin (12 × 18)
  ⑤ Cylinder
  ⑥ O-ring

6. TRANSMISSION

The countershaft thrust washers have been integrated into the gear bushings.

7. CARBURETOR

Refer to page 190.

Carburetor setting table

Item	
Main jet No.	#105
Air jet No.	#120
Slow jet No.	#35
Slow air jet No.	#150
Jet needle setting	F2051F-2
Float height	14.5 mm (0.571 in.)

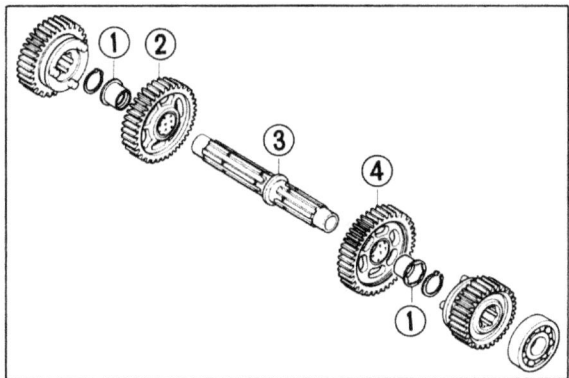

Fig. F2-20 ① 28 mm bushing
  ② Countershaft 3rd gear
  ③ Countershaft
  ④ Countershaft 2nd gear

8. DRIVE CHAIN

Refer to page 195.

9. SWITCH HOUSING

Refer to page 197.

10. SPECIFICATIONS (CB750F2 '77)

Item	
DIMENSION	
Overall length	2,210 mm (87.0 in.)
Overall width	860 mm (33.9 in.)
Overall height	1,185 mm (46.7 in.)
Wheelbase	1,480 mm (58.3 in.)
Seat height	830 mm (32.7 in.)
Foot peg height	325 mm (12.8 in.)
Ground clearance	135 mm (5.3 in.)
Dry weight	232.5 kg (512.6 lb.)
FRAME	
Type	Double cradle
Front suspension, travel	Telescopic fork, travel 141.5 mm (5.6 in.)
Rear suspension, travel	Swing arm, travel 86.3 mm (4.0 in.)
Front tire size, type	3.25H-19-4PR, Rib
air pressure	Up to 90 kg (200 lb) load: 2.0 kg/cm² (28 psi)
	Up to vehicle capacity load: 2.25 kg/cm² (32 psi)
Rear tire size, type	4.00H-18-4PR Block
air pressure	Up to 90 kg (200 lb) load: 2.0 kg/cm² (28 psi)
	Up to vehicle capacity load: 2.8 kg/cm² (40 psi)
Front brake	Disc brake
Rear brake	Disc brake
Fuel capacity	18 lit. (4.8 U.S. gal., 4.0 Imp. gal.)
Fuel reserve capacity	4.5 lit. (1.2 U.S. gal., 1.0 Imp. gal.)
Caster angle	62.5°
Trail length	113.5 mm (4.47 in.)
Front fork oil capacity	145-155 cc (5.3-5.4 ounces.)
ENGINE	
Type	Air cooled 4 stroke O.H.C. engine
Cylinder arrangement	4 cylinder in line
Bore and stroke	61.0 × 63.0 mm (2.402 × 2.480 in.)
Displacement	736 cc (44.9 cu in.)
Compression ratio	9.0 : 1
Carburetor, venturi dia.	Four piston valve type, venturi dia. 28 mm (1.102 in.)
Valve train	Chain driven overhead camshaft
Oil capacity	3.5 lit. (3.7 U.S. qt., 3.1 Imp. qt.)
Lubrication system	Forced pressure and dry sump
Fuel required	Low-lead gasoline with 91 octane rating or higher
Air cleaner	Paper filter
Intake valve: opens	5° BTDC
closes	40° ATDC
Exhaust valve: opens	40° BBDC
closes	5° ATDC
Valve tappet clearance	IN: 0.05 mm (0.002 in.), EX: 0.08 mm (0.003 in.)
Pilot screw opening	Fixed by idle limiter (1.1/2 ± 1/2)
Idle speed	1,000 rpm

25. SUPPLEMENT TO CB750F2 ('77)

Item	
DRIVE TRAIN	
Clutch	Wet multi plate type
Transmission	5-speed constant mesh
Primary reduction	1.708
Gear ratio: 1st	2.500
″ 2nd	1.708
″ 3rd	1.333
″ 4th	1.133
″ 5th	0.969
Final reduction	3.071
Gearshift pattern	Left foot operated return system
ELECTRICAL	
Ignition	Battery and ignition coil
Ignition advance:	
"F" mark	10° BTDC
Max. advance	35°
RPM from "F" to max. advance	1,200–2,500 rpm
Dwell angle	190°±5°
Starting system	Starting motor or kick starter
Alternator	Three phase AC generator 0.21 kw/5,000 rpm
Battery capacity	12 V–14 AH
Fuse capacity	Main: 15 A, Head: 7 A, Tail: 5 A
Spark plug	U.S.A. model: NGK D8ES-L or ND X24ES
	Canadian model: NGK DR8ES-L or ND X24ESR-U
Condenser capacity	0.22–0.26 μF

25. SUPPLEMENT TO CB750F2 ('77)

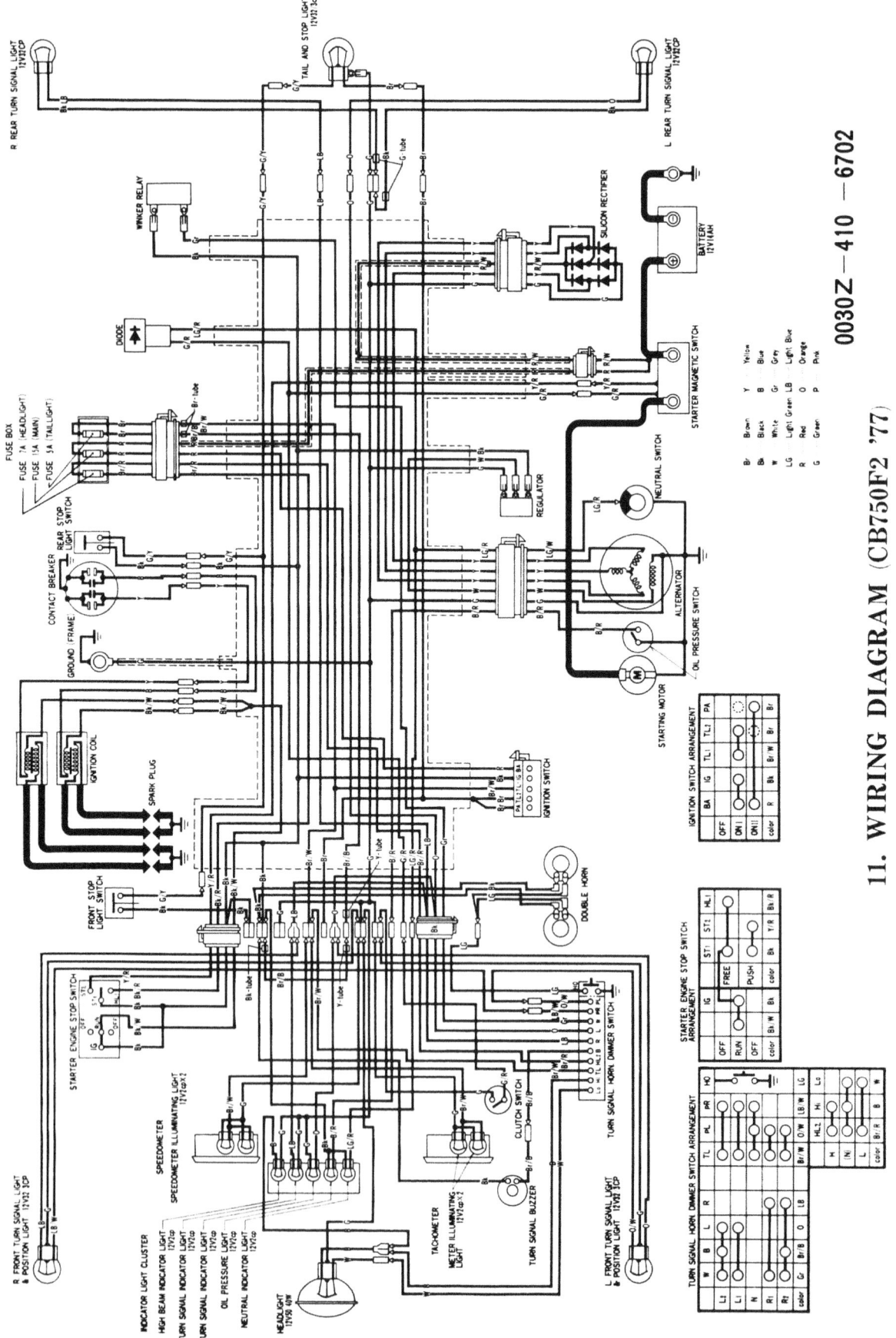

11. WIRING DIAGRAM (CB750F2 '77)

SUPPLEMENT TO CB750K8 ('78)

Engine No. CB750E—3000001 and subsequent
Frame No. CB750K—2800001 and subsequent

GROUP 26

1. AIR CLEANER

Breather Element Cleaning

1. Remove the left side cover, chain protector and diode rectifier. Remove the 6 mm breather element case mounting bolt, disconnect the breather tubes and remove the breather element case.
2. Loosen the four screws and remove the case cover.
3. Remove the retaining plate and breather element from the case.

CAUTION

Be careful not to damage the retaining plate.

4. Wash the breather element in clean solvent and dry the element throughly.

WARNING

Gasoline or low flash point solvents are explosive and highly flammable and must not be used to clean the breather element. Fire or explosion could result.

NOTE: When installing the case cover, position it as shown in Fig. K8-3.

Fig. K8-1   ① Mounting bolt
② Breather element case

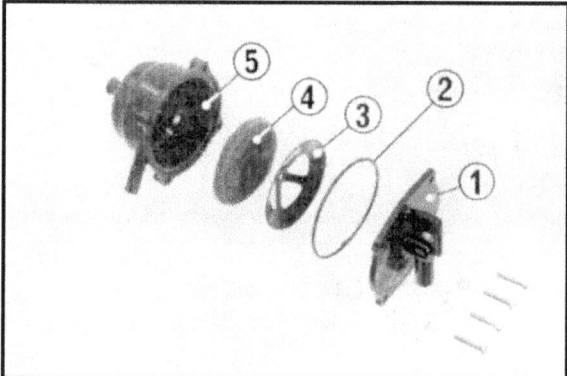

Fig. K8-2   ① Case cover
② O-ring
③ Retaining plate
④ Breather element
⑤ Element case

2. CARBURETOR

Carburetor Setting Table

Setting number	PD 42 B
Main jet	No. 110
Slow jet	No. 35
Pilot screw opening	1-1/2
Float height	14.5 mm (0.571 in.)

Fig. K8-3   ① Case cover
② Element case

3. MAINTENANCE

Perform the Pre-Ride Inspection described in the Owner's Manual at each maintenance period.

I: INSPECT, CLEAN, ADJUST, OR REPLACE IF NECESSARY.
C: CLEAN
R: REPLACE
A: ADJUST

ITEM / FREQUENCY	WHICHEVER COMES FIRST ↓ EVERY	600 mi (1,000 km)	3,600 mi (6,000 km)	7,200 mi (12,000 km)	10,800 mi (18,000 km)	14,400 mi (24,000 km)	18,000 mi (30,000 km)	REFER TO
ENGINE OIL	YEAR	R	\multicolumn{5}{c}{REPLACE EVERY 1,800 mi (3,000 km)}			Page 3
ENGINE OIL FILTER	YEAR	R	R	R	R	R	R	Page 3
* ENGINE OIL SCREEN					C			Page 30
CRANKCASE BREATHER	NOTE (1)		C	C	C	C	C	Page 212
AIR CLEANER	NOTE (2)		C	R	C	R	C	Page 163
* FUEL LINES			I	I	I	I	I	Pages 14, 158
SPARK PLUGS			I	R	I	R	I	Page 5
* VALVE CLEARANCE		I	I	I	I	I	I	Page 10
* CONTACT BREAKER POINTS		I	I	I	I	I	I	Page 6
* IGNITION TIMING		I	I	I	I	I	I	Page 9
* CAMCHAIN TENSION		A	A	A	A	A	A	Page 12
* THROTTLE OPERATION		I	I	I	I	I	I	Page 133
* CARBURETOR IDLE SPEED		I	I	I	I	I	I	Page 194
* CARBURETOR CHOKE/ (FAST IDLE)			I	I	I	I	I	Page 195
* CARBURETOR SYNCHRONIZE		I	I	I	I	I	I	Page 194
DRIVE CHAIN		\multicolumn{6}{c}{INSPECT EVERY 600 mi (1,000 km)}							Page 195
BATTERY ELECTROLYTE	MONTH	I	I	I	I	I	I	Page 84
BRAKE FLUID LEVEL	MONTH	I	I	I	I	I	I	Page 110
* BRAKE FLUID	2 YEARS				R			Page 176
BRAKE SHOE/PAD WEAR			I	I	I	I	I	Pages 154, 204
BRAKE FREE PLAY		I	I	I	I	I	I	Page 113
* BRAKE LIGHT SWITCH		I	I	I	I	I	I	Page 122
* HEADLIGHT		I	I	I	I	I	I	Page 119
CLUTCH FREE PLAY		I	I	I	I	I	I	Page 24
SIDE STAND			I	I	I	I	I	Page 159
* SUSPENSION		I	I	I	I	I	I	Pages 91~99
* NUTS, BOLTS, FASTENERS		I	I	I	I	I		
** WHEELS/SPOKES			I	I	I	I	I	Pages 103~106
** STEERING HEAD BEARING		I		I		I		Page 94

** IN THE INTEREST OF SAFETY, WE RECOMMEND THESE ITEMS BE SERVICED ONLY BY AN AUTHORIZED HONDA DEALER.
 * SHOULD BE SERVICED BY AN AUTHORIZED HONDA DEALER, UNLESS THE OWNER HAS PROPER TOOLS AND SERVICE DATA, AND IS MECHANICALLY QUALIFIED

NOTES: (1) More frequent service may be required when riding in rain, or at full throttle.
(2) More frequent service may be required when riding in dusty areas.
(3) For higher odometer readings, repeat at the frequency interval established here.

4. SPECIFICATIONS

Item	
DIMENSION	
Overall Length	2,280 mm (89.8 in.)
Overall Width	880 mm (34.6 in.)
Overall Height	1,185 mm (46.7 in.)
Wheel Base	1,495 mm (58.9 in.)
Seat Height	810 mm (31.9 in.)
Foot Peg Height	330 mm (13.0 in.)
Ground Clearance	150 mm (5.9 in.)
Dry Weight	231 kg (508 lb.)
FRAME	
Type	Double Cradle
F. Suspension, Travel	Telescopic fork, travel 141.5 mm (5.6 in.)
R. Suspension, Travel	Swing arm, travel 101.6 mm (4.0 in.)
F. Tire Size, Type	3.50 H-19-4PR Rib, tire air pressure 2.0/2.0 kg/cm² (28/28 psi)
R. Tire Size, Type	4.50 H-17A-4PR Block, tire air pressure 2.25/2.8 kg/cm² (32/40 psi)
F. Brake	Disk Brake
R. Brake	Internal expanding shoe
Fuel Capacity	19.5 lit. (5.1 U.S. gal., 4.3 Imp. gal.)
Fuel Reserve Capacity	4.0 lit. (1.1 U.S. gal., 0.9 Imp. gal.)
Caster Angle	62°
Trail Length	115 mm (4.5 in.)
Front Fork Oil Capacity	145~155 cc (5.3~5.4 ozs.)
ENGINE	
Type	Air cooled 4 stroke O.H.C. engine
Cylinder Arrangement	4 cylinder in line
Bore and Stroke	61.0×63.0 mm (2.402×2.480 in.)
Displacement	736 cc (44.9 cu in.)
Compression Ratio	9.2 : 1
Carburetor, Venturi Dia.	Four piston valve type, venturi dia 28 mm (1.102 in.)
Valve Train	Chain driven overhead cam shaft
Oil Capacity	3.5 lit. (3.7 U.S. qt., 3.1 Imp. qt.)
Lubrication System	Forced pressure and dry sump
Fuel Required	Low-lead gasoline with 91 octane number or higher
Air Filtration	Paper filter
Intake Valve: Opens	0° BTDC
Closes	40° ATDC
Exhaust Valve: Opens	40° BBDC
Closes	0° ATDC
Valve Clearance	IN: 0.05 EX: 0.08 mm (IN: 0.002, EX: 0.003 in.)
Pilot Screw Opening	Fixed by idle limiter (1·1/2±1/2)
Idle Speed	1,000 rpm

26. SUPPLEMENT TO CB750K8 ('78)

Item	
DRIVE TRAIN	
Clutch	Wet multi plate type
Transmission	5-speed constant mesh
Primary Reduction	1.986
Gear Ratio I	2.500
II	1.708
III	1.333
IV	1.133
V	0.969
Final Reduction	2.733, drive sprocket 15T, driven sprocket 41T
Gear Shift Pattern	Left foot operated return system
ELECTRICAL	
Ignition	Battery and ignition coil
Ignition Advance:	
"F" mark	10° BTDC
Max. advance	35°
RPM from "F" to max. advance	1,200–2,500 rpm
Dwell Angle	190°±5°
Starting System	Starting motor or kick starter
Alternator	Three phase AC Generator 0.21 kW/5,000 rpm
Battery Capacity	12V–14AH
Fuse Capacity	Main: 15 amp. Head: 7A Tail: 5A
Spark plug	NGK D8EA ND X24ES-U (U.S.A. model)
	NGK DR8ES-L ND X24ESR-U (Canadian model)
Condenser Capacity	0.20–0.24 μF

26. SUPPLEMENT TO CB750K8 ('78)

5. WIRING DIAGRAM

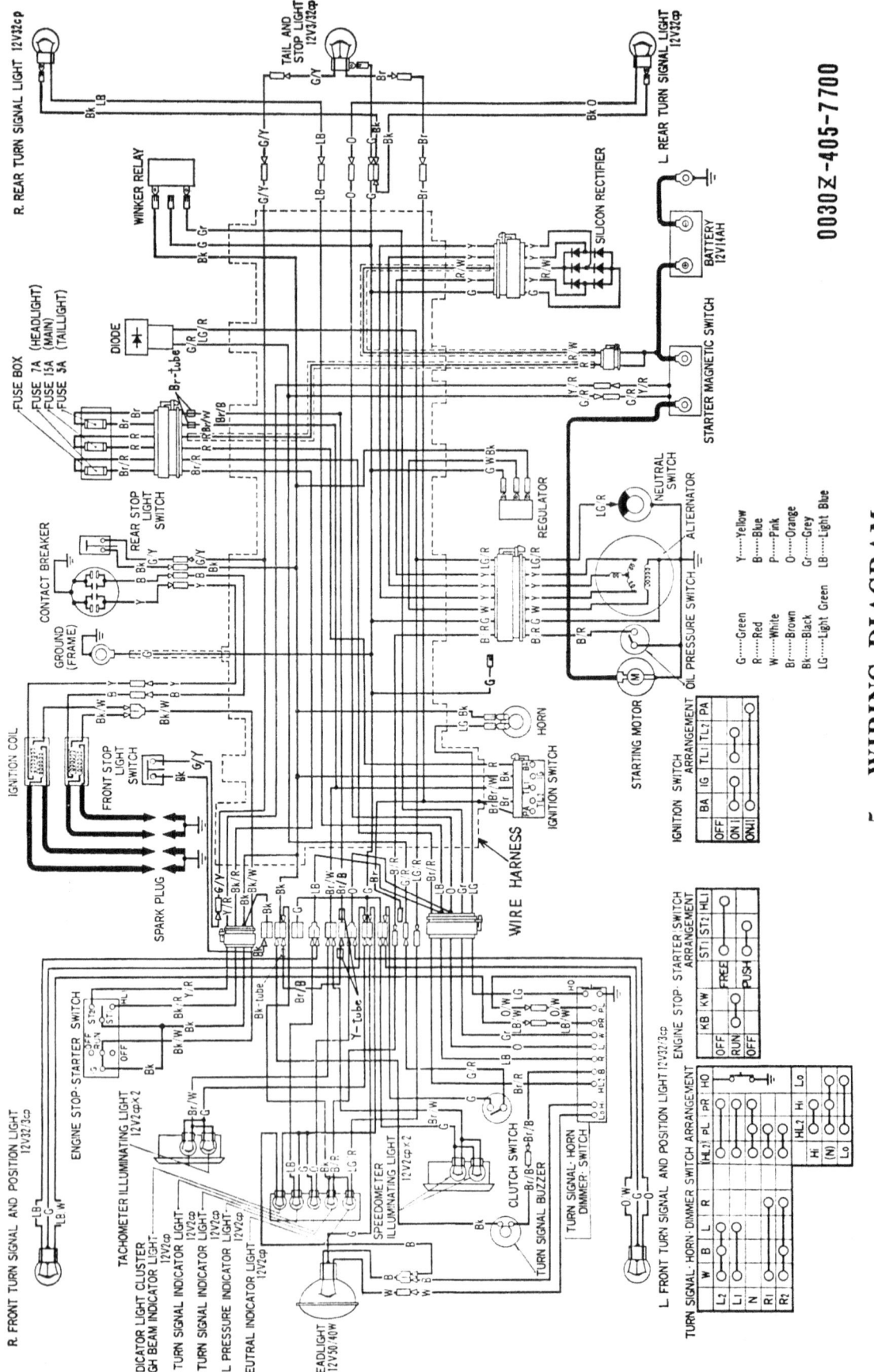

NOTES

SUPPLEMENT TO CB750F3 ('78)

Engine No. CB750E—2200001 and subsequent
Frame No. CB750F—3100002 and subsequent

GROUP 27

1. MAINTENANCE SCHEDULE

Perform the Pre-Ride Inspection described in the Owner's Manual at each maintenance period.

I: INSPECT, CLEAN, ADJUST, OR REPLACE IF NECESSARY.
C: CLEAN   R: REPLACE   A: ADJUST

ITEM	FREQUENCY WHICHEVER COMES FIRST ↓ EVERY	600 mi (1,000 km)	3,600 mi (6,000 km)	7,200 mi (12,000 km)	10,800 mi (18,000 km)	14,400 mi (24,000 km)	18,000 mi (30,000 km)	REFER TO
ENGINE OIL	YEAR	R	\multicolumn{5}{c}{REPLACE EVERY 1,800 mi (3,000 km)}			Page 3
ENGINE OIL FILTER	YEAR	R	R	R	R	R	R	Page 3
* ENGINE OIL SCREEN					C			Page 30
CRANKCASE BREATHER	NOTE (1)		C	C	C	C	C	Page 212
AIR CLEANER	NOTE (2)		C	R	C	R	C	Page 163
* FUEL LINES			I	I	I	I	I	Pages 14, 158
SPARK PLUGS			I	R	I	R	I	Page 5
* VALVE CLEARANCE		I	I	I	I	I	I	Page 10
* CONTACT BREAKER POINTS		I	I	I	I	I	I	Page 6
* IGNITION TIMING		I	I	I	I	I	I	Page 9
* CAMCHAIN TENSION		A	A	A	A	A	A	Page 12
* THROTTLE OPERATION		I	I	I	I	I	I	Page 133
* CARBURETOR IDLE SPEED		I	I	I	I	I	I	Page 194
* CARBURETOR CHOKE/ (FAST IDLE)			I	I	I	I	I	Page 195
* CARBURETOR SYNCHRONIZE		I	I	I	I	I	I	Page 194
DRIVE CHAIN		\multicolumn{6}{c}{INSPECT EVERY 600 mi (1,000 km)}							Page 195
BATTERY ELECTROLYTE	MONTH	I	I	I	I	I	I	Page 84
BRAKE FLUID LEVEL	MONTH	I	I	I	I	I	I	Page 110
* BRAKE FLUID	2 YEARS			R				Page 176
BRAKE PAD WEAR			I	I	I	I	I	Page 204
* BRAKE LIGHT SWITCH			I	I	I	I	I	Page 122
* HEADLIGHT			I	I	I	I	I	Page 119
CLUTCH FREE PLAY			I	I	I	I	I	Page 24
SIDE STAND			I	I	I	I	I	Page 159
* SUSPENSION			I	I	I	I	I	Pages 91~99
* NUTS, BOLTS, FASTENERS			I	I	I	I		
** WHEELS/SPOKES			I	I	I	I	I	Pages 165, 177, 207
** STEERING HEAD BEARING			I		I		I	Page 94

** IN THE INTEREST OF SAFETY, WE RECOMMEND THESE ITEMS BE SERVICED ONLY BY AN AUTHORIZED HONDA DEALER.

* SHOULD BE SERVICED BY AN AUTHORIZED HONDA DEALER, UNLESS THE OWNER HAS PROPER TOOLS AND SERVICE DATA, AND IS MECHANICALLY QUALIFIED.

NOTES: (1) More frequent service may be required when riding in rain, or at full throttle.
(2) More frequent service may be required when riding in dusty areas.
(3) For higher odometer readings, repeat at the frequency interval established here.

2. CARBURETOR

Carburetor Setting Table

Setting number	PD42A
Main jet	No. 105
Slow jet	No. 35
Pilot screw opening	1·3/4
Float height	14.5 mm (0.571 in.)

3. CONNECTING ROD

The connecting rod cap tightening torque is changed from 2.0 kg-m (14.5 lbs-ft) to 2.6 kg-m (18.8 lbs-ft).

4. AIR CLEANER

See page 212.

5. SPECIFICATIONS

Item	
DIMENSION	
Overall length	2,210 mm (87.0 in.)
Overall width	860 mm (33.9 in.)
Overall height	1,185 mm (46.7 in.)
Wheelbase	1,480 mm (58.3 in.)
Seat height	830 mm (32.7 in.)
Foot peg height	325 mm (12.8 in.)
Ground clearance	135 mm (5.3 in.)
Dry weight	232.5 kg (512.6 lb.)
FRAME	
Type	Double cradle
Front suspension, travel	Telescopic fork, travel 141.5 mm (5.6 in.)
Rear suspension, travel	Swing arm, travel 86.3 mm (3.4 in.)
Front tire size, type	3.25H-19-4PR, Rib
air pressure	Up to 90 kg (200 lb.) load: 2.0 kg/cm² (28 psi)
	Up to vehicle capacity load: 2.25 kg/cm² (32 psi)
Rear tire size, type	4.00H-18-4PR Block
air pressure	Up to 90 kg (200 lb.) load: 2.0 kg/cm² (28 psi)
	Up to vehicle capacity load: 2.8 kg/cm² (40 psi)
Front brake	Disc brake
Rear brake	Disc brake
Fuel capacity	18 lit. (4.8 U.S. gal., 4.0 Imp. gal.)
Fuel reserve capacity	4.5 lit. (1.2 U.S. gal., 1.0 Imp. gal.)
Caster angle	62.5°
Trail length	113.5 mm (4.47 in.)
Front fork oil capacity	145–155 cc (5.3–5.4 ounces.)

27. SUPPLEMENT TO CB750F3 ('78)

Item	
ENGINE	
Type	Air cooled 4 stroke O.H.C. engine
Cylinder arrangement	4 cylinder in line
Bore and stroke	61.0 × 63.0 mm (2.402 × 2.480 in.)
Displacement	736 cc (44.9 cu in.)
Compression ratio	9.0 : 1
Carburetor, venturi dia.	Four piston valve type, venturi dia. 28 mm (1.102 in.)
Valve train	Chain driven over head camshaft
Oil capacity	3.5 lit. (3.7 U.S. qt., 3.1 Imp. qt)
Lubrication system	Forced pressure and dry sump
Fuel required	Low-lead gasoline with 91 reserch octane rating or 86 pump octane or higher
Air cleaner	Paper filter
Intake valve: opens	5° BTDC
closes	40° ATDC
Exhaust valve: opens	40° BBDC
closes	5° ATDC
Valve clearance	IN: 0.05 mm (0.002 in., EX: 0.08 mm (0.003 in.)
Pilot screw opening	Fixed by idle limiter (1·3/4)
Idle speed	1,000 rpm
DRIVE TRAIN	
Clutch	Wet multi plate type
Transmission	5-speed constant mesh
Primary reduction	1.986
Gear ratio: 1st	2.500
" 2nd	1.708
" 3rd	1.333
" 4th	1.133
" 5th	0.969
Final reduction	3.071
Gearshift pattern	Left foot operated return system
ELECTRICAL	
Ignition	Battery and ignition coil
Ignition advance:	
"F" mark	10° BTDC
Max. advance	35°
RPM from "F" to max. advance	1,200–2,500 rpm
Dwell angle	190° ± 5°
Starting system	Starting motor or kick starter
Alternator	Three phase AC generator 0.21 kW/5,000 rpm
Battery capacity	12V 14AH
Fuse capacity	Main: 15 A, Head: 7 A, Tail: 5 A
Spark plug	U.S.A. model: NGK D8EA or ND X24ES-U
	Canadian model: NGK DR8ES-L or ND X24ESR-U
Condenser capacity	0.22–0.26 μF

WIRING DIAGRAMS

The Honda CB750 was recognized as the first superbike that was both readily available and reasonably priced to the general public on a worldwide basis. However, no one could have anticipated that it was destined to become a collector's item and, as such, many of them no longer reside in the country where they were originally sold. Unfortunately, as each country had specific 'electrical' requirements, there are also variations in the wiring diagrams within the same models and/or years. Consequently, our goal was to include as many of the different wiring schematics as possible and we urge the reader to determine which one is the most appropriate for their motorcycle. Diagrams included in the supplements are identified (sup).

WIRING DIAGRAM INDEX ~ 750K (1969-1978)

Wiring Diagram for France (1969-70)	Page 222
Wiring Diagram for Germany (1969-70)	Page 223
Wiring Diagram for UK (1969-70)	Page 224
Wiring Diagram for USA (1969-70)	Page 225
Wiring Diagram 750K0 (1969-70)	Page 226
Wiring Diagram 750K1 (1971)	Page 227
Wiring Diagram 750K2 (1972)	Page 228
Wiring Diagram 750K1~K4 (1971-74)	Page 157 (sup)
Wiring Diagram 750K1~K5 (1971-75)	Page 229
Wiring Diagram 750K5 (1975)	Page 161 (sup)
Wiring Diagram 750K6 (1976)	Page 189 (sup)
Wiring Diagram 750K7 (1977)	Page 201 (sup)
Wiring Diagram 750K8 (1978)	Page 216 (sup)

WIRING DIAGRAM INDEX ~ 750F (1975-1978)

Wiring Diagram 750F (1975)	Page 185 (sup)
Wiring Diagram 750F2 (1977)	Page 210 (sup)
Wiring Diagram 750F3 (1978)	Page 230

CB750 (French Type)

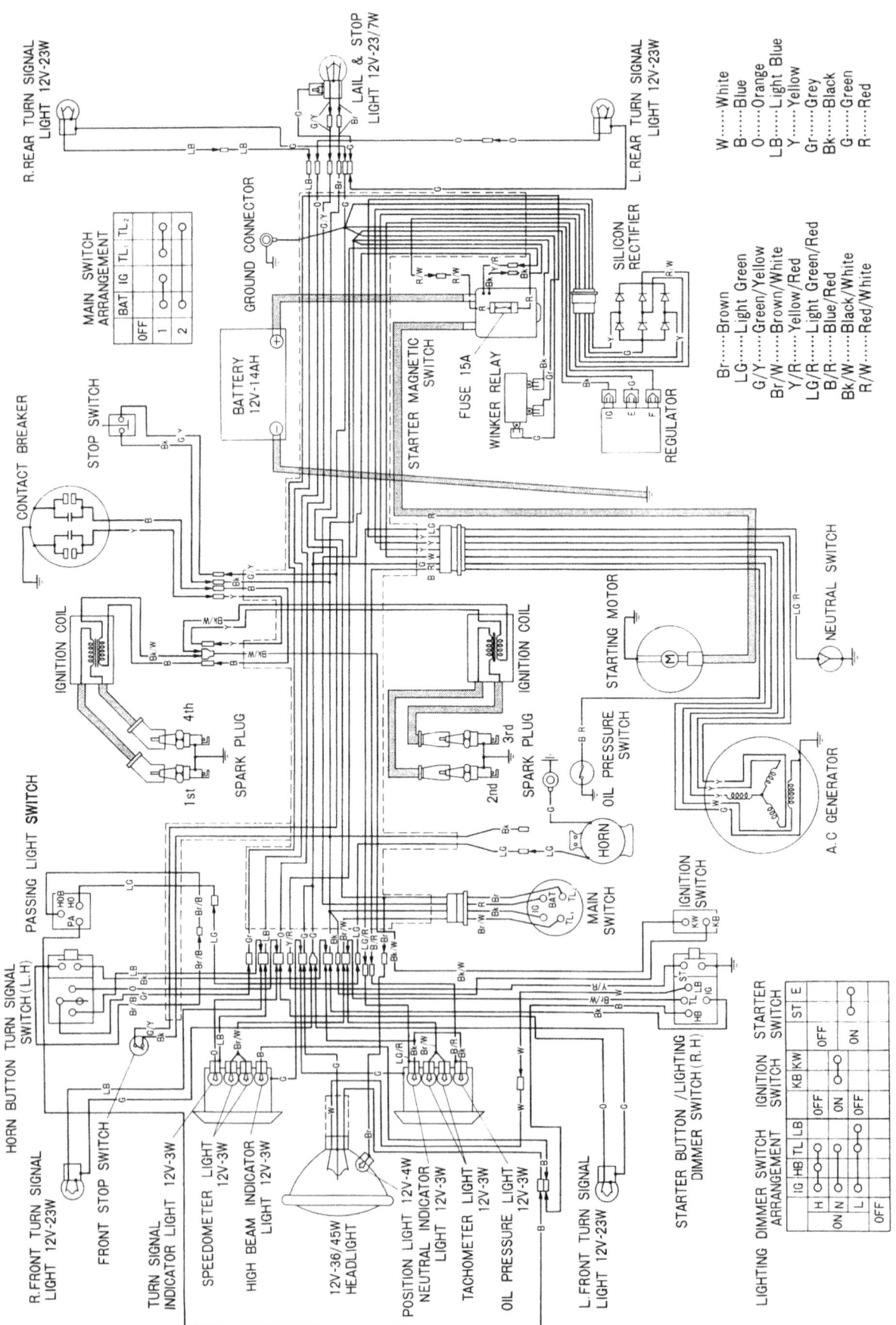

CB 750 (German Type)

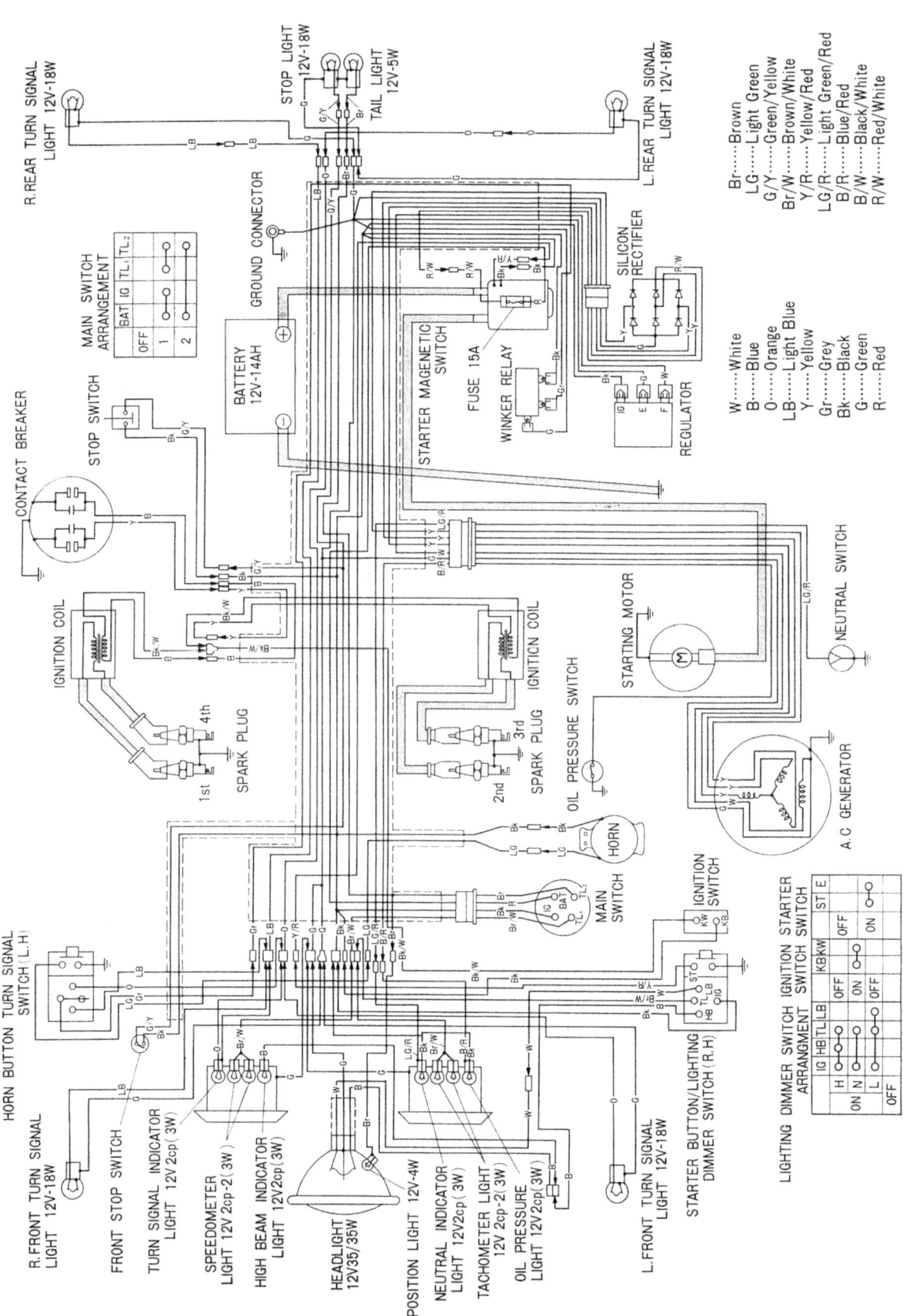

HONDA CB750 — U.K. VERSIONS

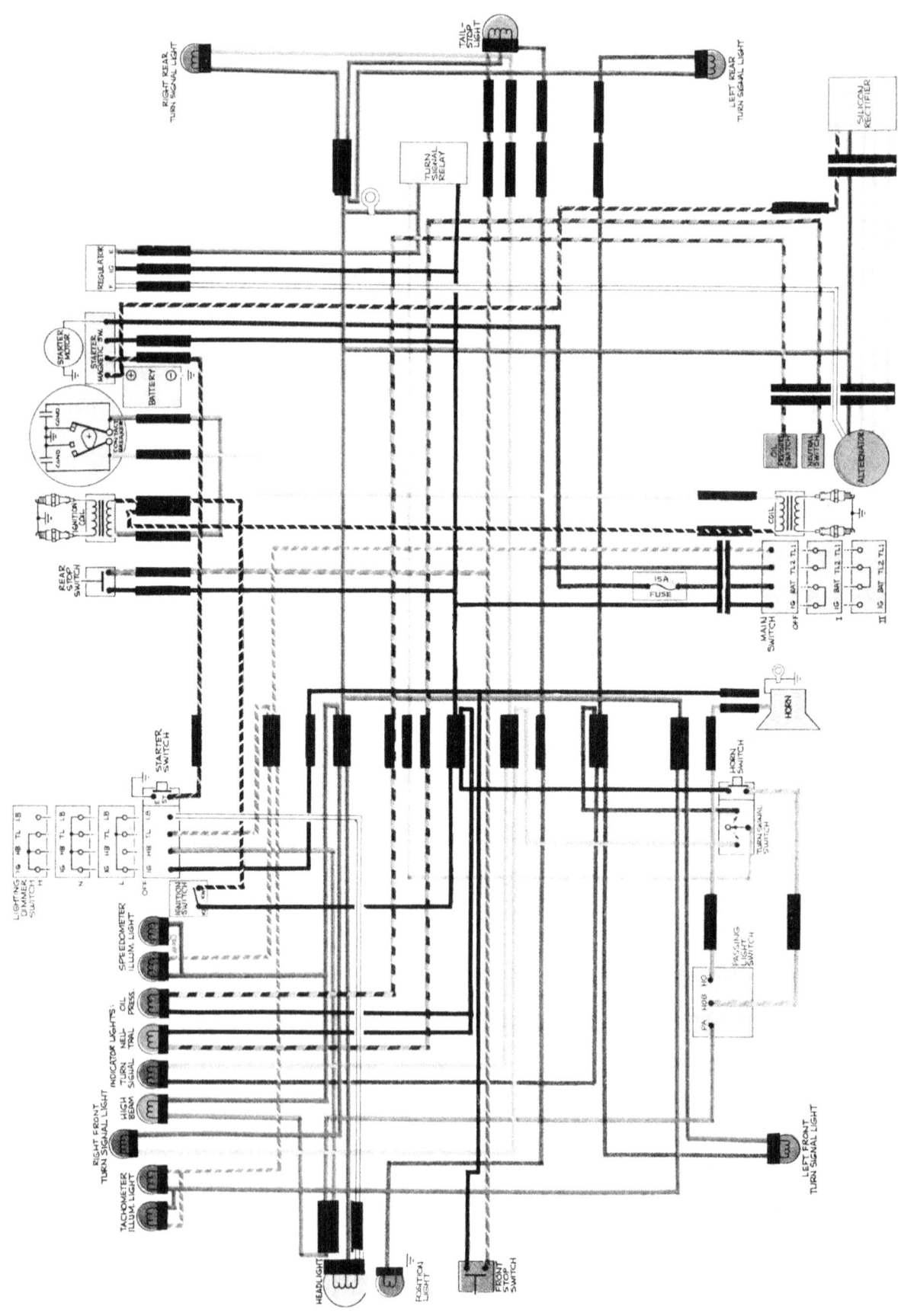

CB750 (U.S.A. Type)

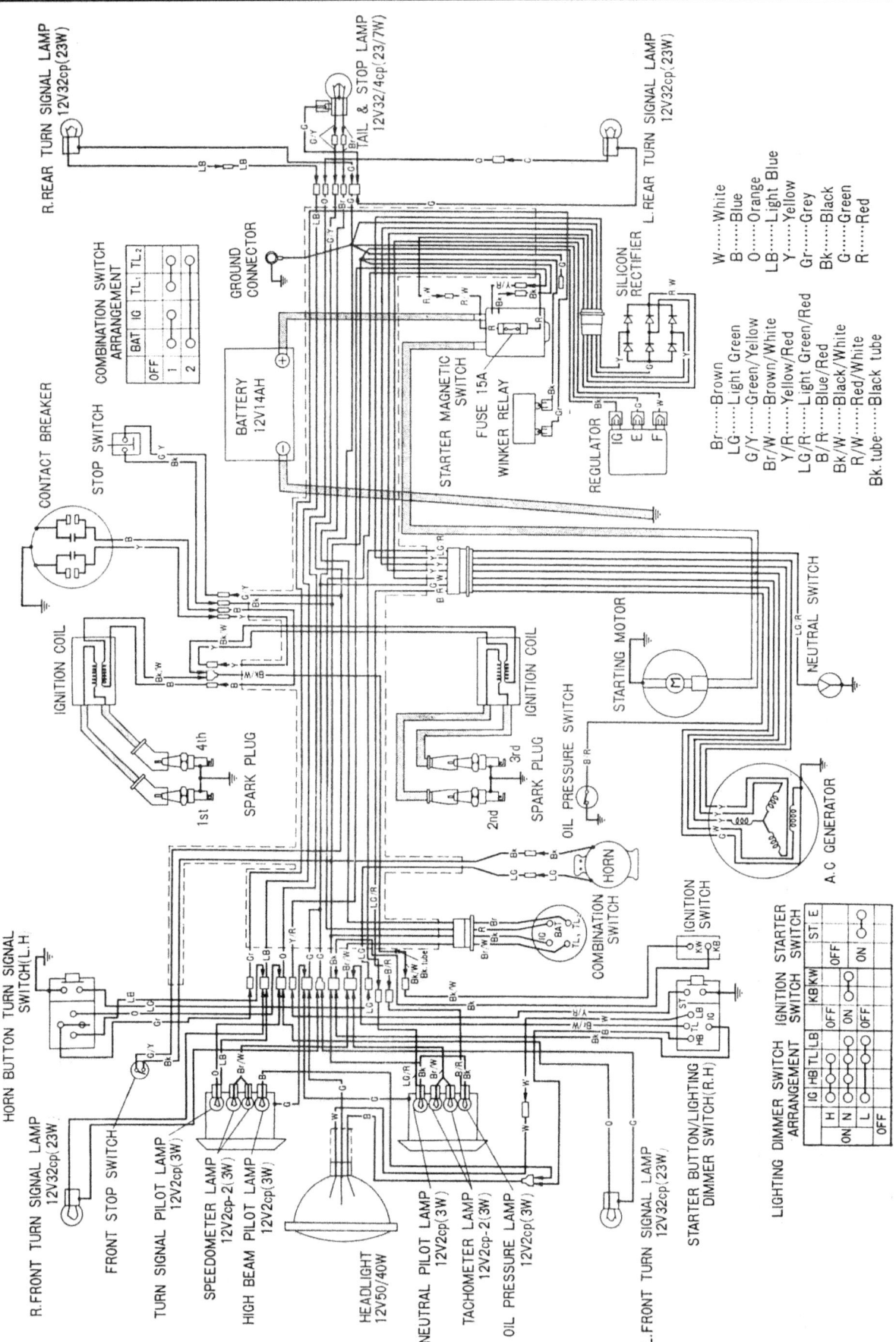

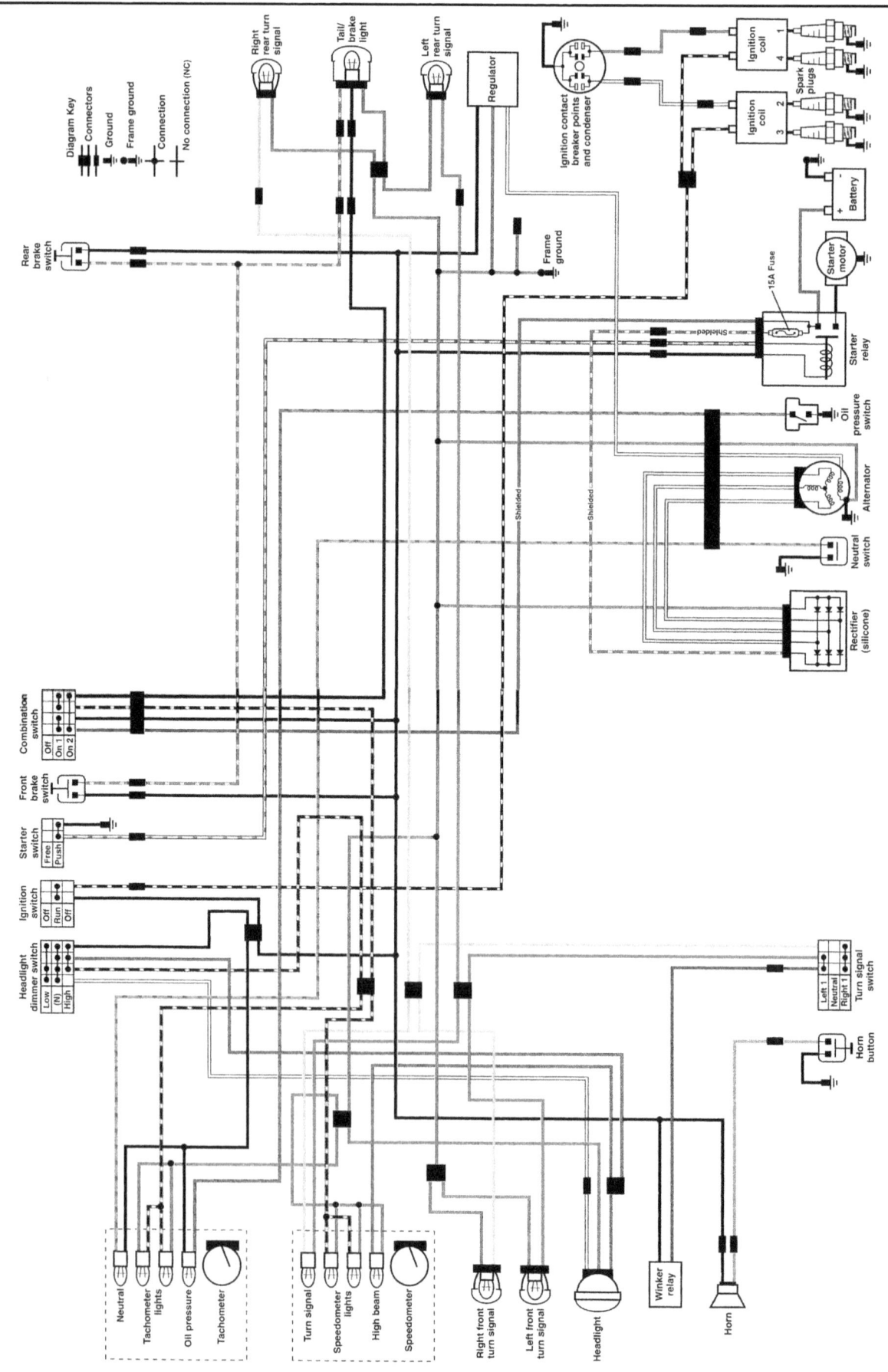

HONDA CB750 K1

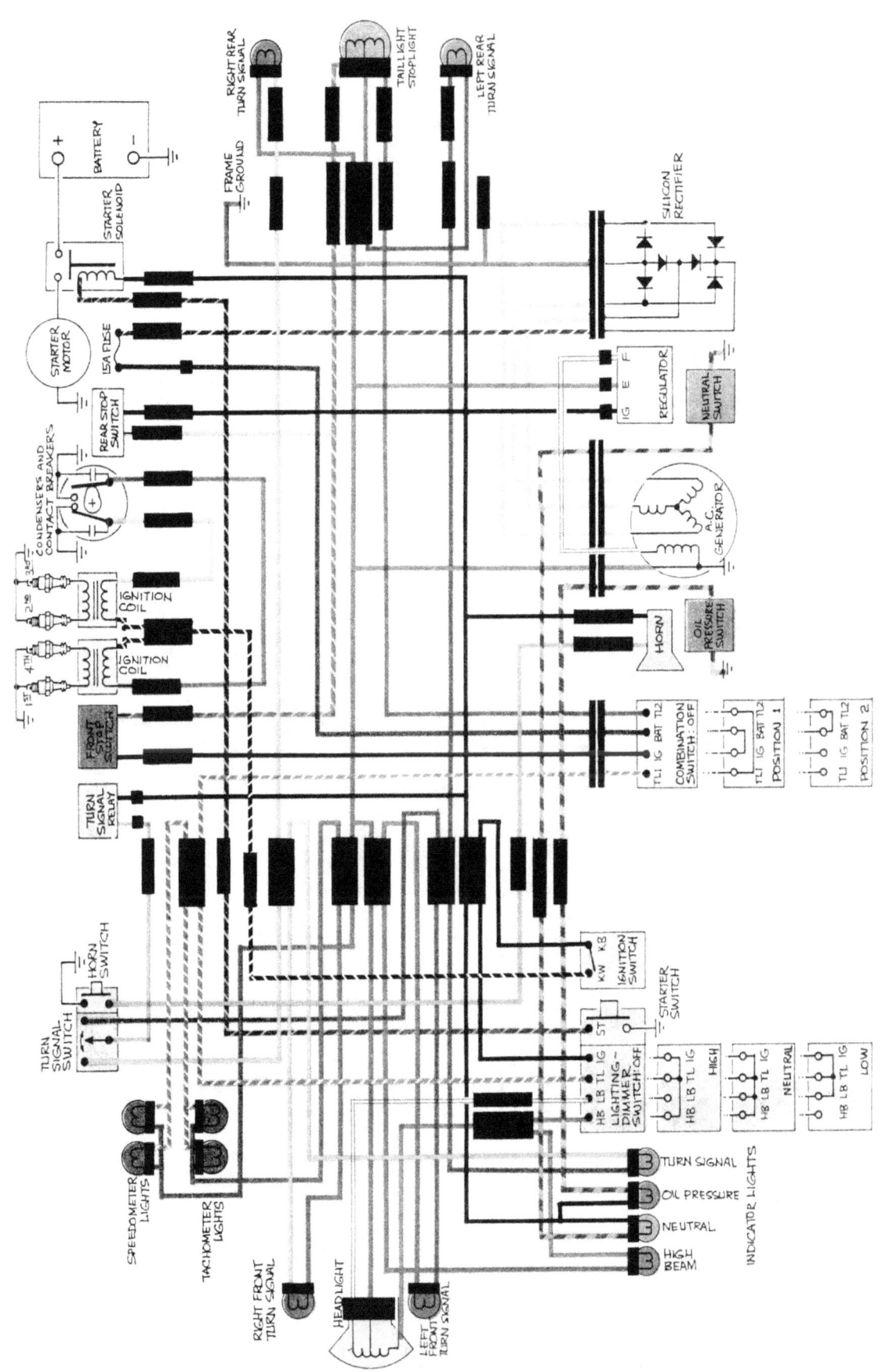

HONDA CB750 K2

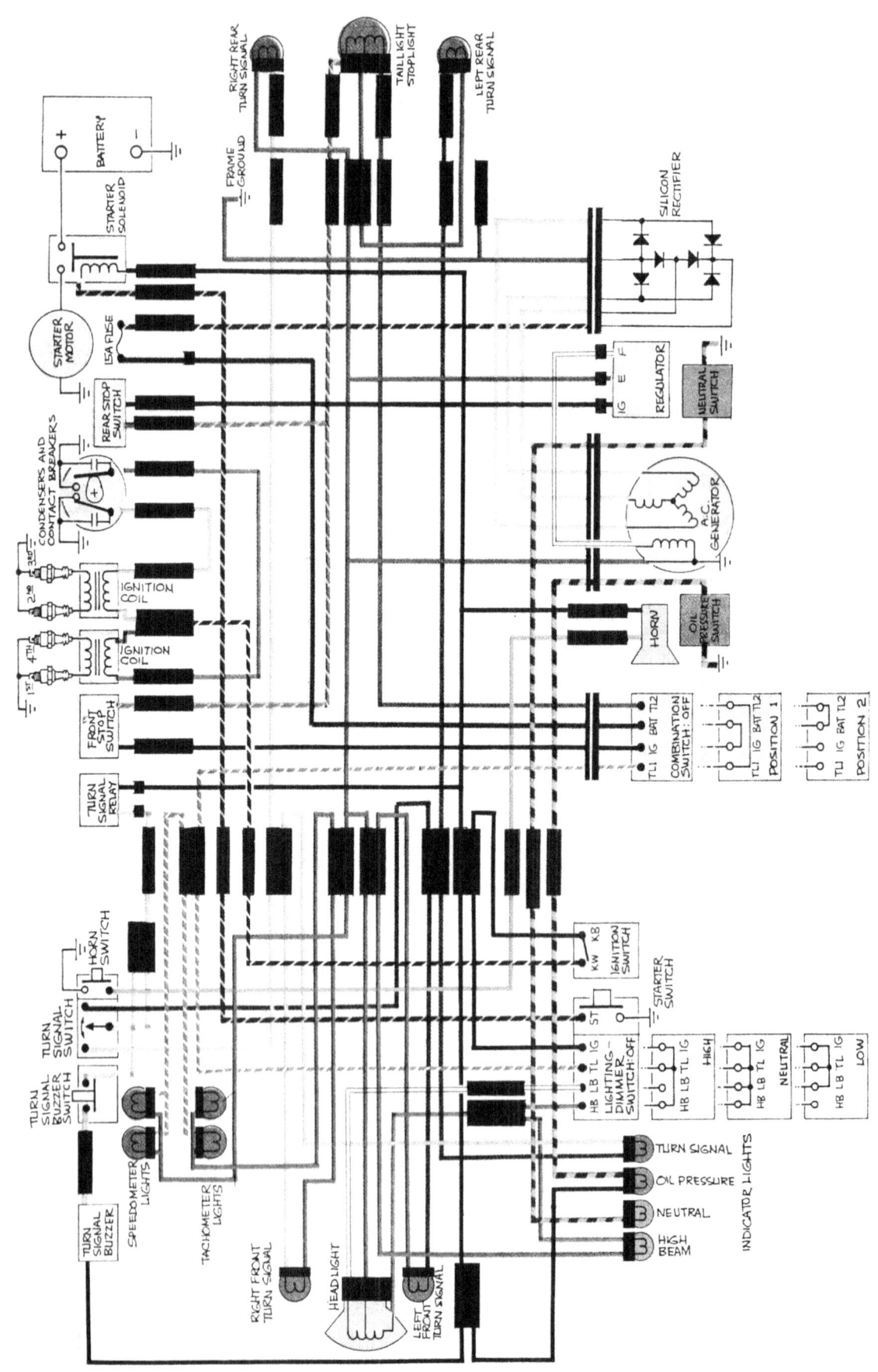

CB750K1-K5 (1971-1975)

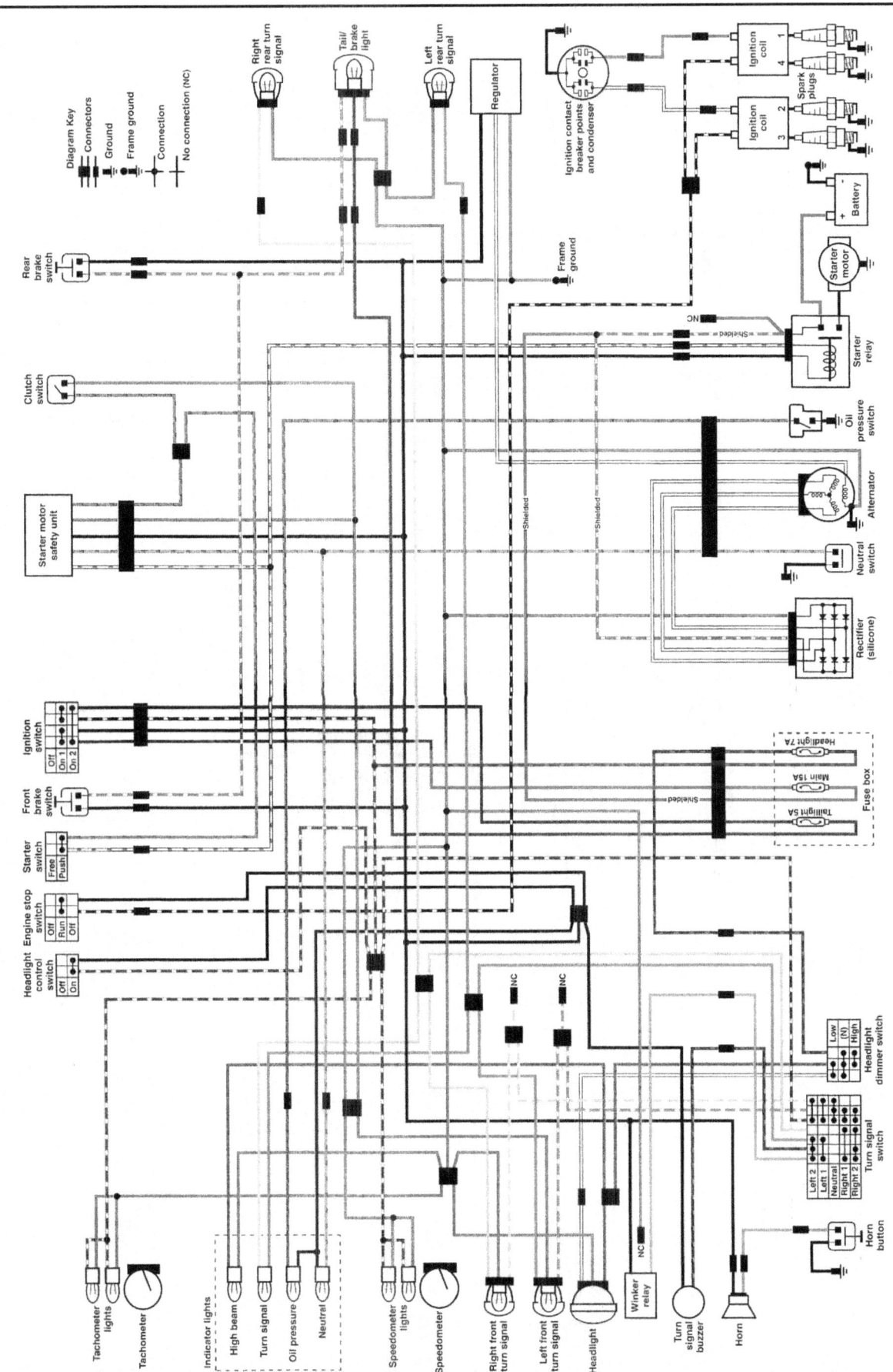

Honda CB750F — 1978

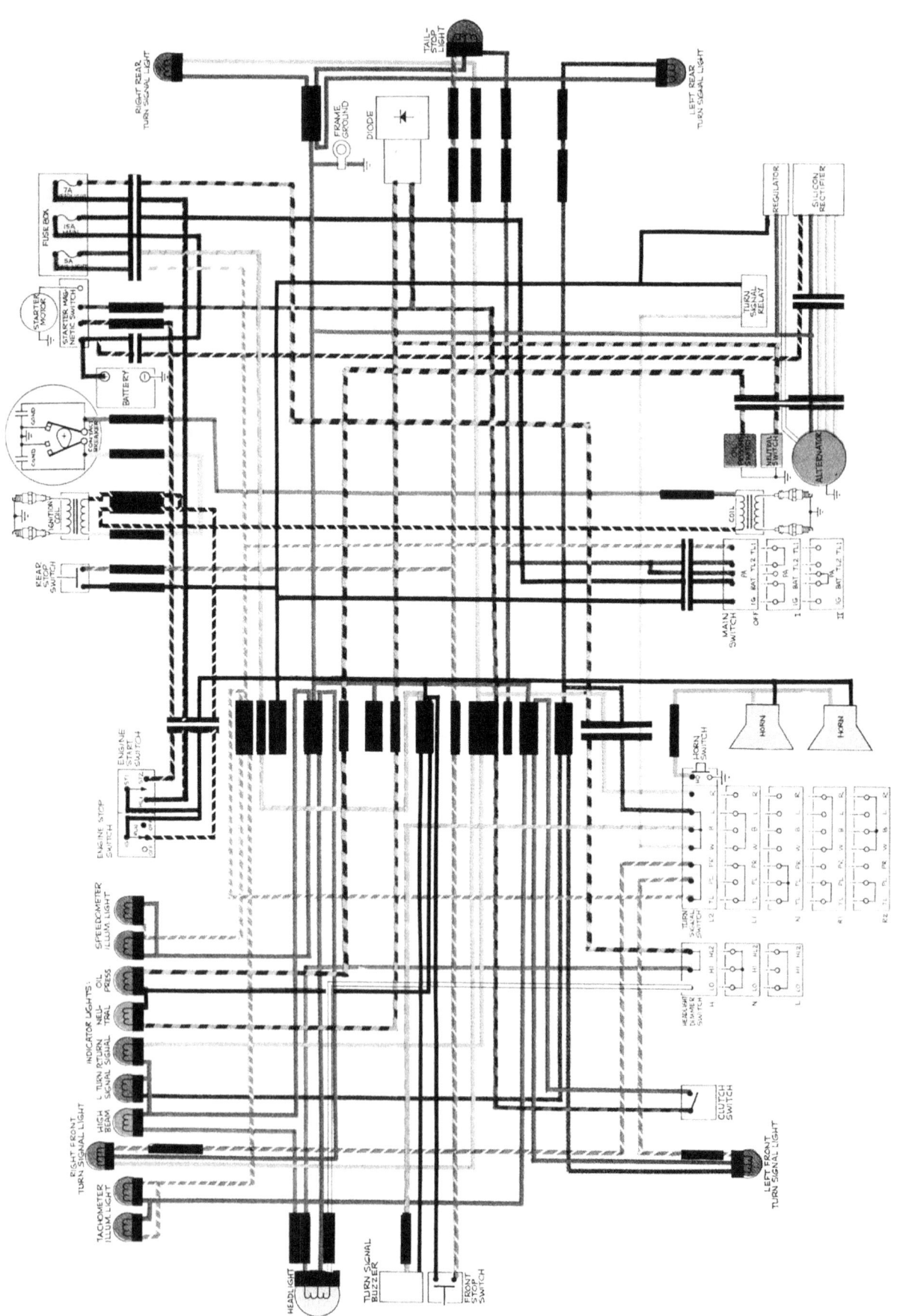

CHAPTER FOURTEEN

TROUBLESHOOTING

Diagnosing motorcycle ills is relatively simple if you use orderly procedures and keep a few basic principles in mind.

Never assume anything. Don't overlook the obvious. If you are riding along and the bike suddenly quits, check the easiest, most accessible problem spots first. Is there gasoline in the tank? Is the gas petcock in the "on" or "reserve" position? Has a spark plug wire fallen off? Check the ignition switch. Sometimes the weight of keys on a key ring may turn the ignition off suddenly.

If nothing obvious turns up in a cursory check, look a little further. Learning to recognize and describe symptoms will make repairs easier for you or a mechanic at the shop. Describe problems accurately and fully. Saying that "it won't run" isn't the same as saying "it quit on the highway at high speed and wouldn't start," or that "it sat in my garage for three months and then wouldn't start."

Gather as many symptoms together as possible to aid in diagnosis. Note whether the engine lost power gradually or all at once, what color smoke (if any) came from the exhausts and so on. Remember that the more complicated a machine is, the easier it is to troubleshoot because symptoms point to specific problems.

You don't need fancy equipment or complicated test gear to determine whether repairs can be attempted at home. A few simple checks could save a large repair bill and time lost while the bike sits in a dealer's service department. On the other hand, be realistic and don't attempt repairs beyond your abilities. Service departments tend to charge heavily for putting together a disassembled engine that may have been abused. Some won't even take on such a job—so use common sense, don't get in over your head.

OPERATING REQUIREMENTS

An engine needs three basics to run properly: correct gas-air mixture, compression, and a spark at the right time. If one or more are missing, the engine won't run. The electrical system is the weakest link of the three. More problems result from electrical breakdowns than from any other source. Keep that in mind before you begin tampering with carburetor adjustments and the like.

If a bike has been sitting for any length of time and refuses to start, check the battery for a charged condition first, and then look to the gasoline delivery system. This includes the tank, fuel petcocks, lines, and the carburetor. Rust may have formed in the tank, obstructing fuel flow. Gasoline deposits may have gummed up carburetor jets and air passages. Gasoline tends to lose its potency after standing for long periods. Condensation may contaminate it with water. Drain old gas and try starting with a fresh tankful.

Compression or the lack of it, usually enters the picture only in the case of older machines. Worn or broken pistons, rings and cylinder bores could prevent starting. Generally a gradual power loss and harder and harder starting will be readily apparent in this case.

STARTING DIFFICULTIES

Check gas flow first. Remove the gas cap and look into the tank. If gas is present, pull off a fuel line at the carburetor and see if gas flows freely. If none comes out, the fuel tap may be shut off, blocked by rust or foreign matter, or the fuel line may be stopped up or kinked. If the carburetor is getting usable fuel, turn to the electrical system next.

Check that the battery is charged by turning on the lights or by beeping the horn. Refer to your owner's manual for starting procedures with a dead battery. Have the battery recharged if necessary.

Pull off a spark plug cap, remove the spark plug, and reconnect the cap. Lay the plug against the cylinder head so its base makes a good connection, and turn the engine over with the kickstarter. A fat, blue spark should jump across the electrodes. If there is no spark, or a weak one, there is electrical system trouble. Check for a defective plug by replacing it with a known good one. Don't assume a plug is good just because it's new.

Once the plug has been cleared of guilt, but there's still no spark, start backtracking through the system. If the contact at the end of the spark plug wire can be exposed, it can be held about ⅛ inch from the head while the engine is turned over to check for a spark. Remember to hold the wire only by its insulation to avoid a nasty shock. If the plug wires are dirty, greasy, or wet, wrap a rag around them so you won't get shocked. If you do feel a shock or see sparks along the wire, clean or replace the wire and/or its connections.

If there's no spark at the plug wire, look for loose connections at the coil and battery. If all seems in order here, check next for oily or dirty contact points. Clean points with electrical contact cleaner, or a strip of paper. With the ignition switch turned on, open and close the points manually with a screwdriver.

No spark at the points with this test indicates a failure in the ignition system. Refer to the Ignition and Charging Systems chapter in this manual for checkout procedures for the entire system and individual components. Refer to the Tune-up chapter for checking and setting ignition timing.

Note that spark plugs of the incorrect heat range (too cold) may cause hard starting. Set gaps to specifications. If you have just ridden through a puddle or washed the bike and it won't start, dry off plugs and plug wires. Water may have entered the carburetor and fouled the fuel under these conditions, but wet plugs and wires are the more likely problem.

If a healthy spark occurs at the right time, and there is adequate gas flow to the carburetor, check the carburetor itself at this time. Make sure all jets and air passages are clean, check float level, and adjust if necessary. Shake the float to check for gasoline inside it, and replace or repair as indicated. Check that the carburetors are mounted snugly, and no air is leaking past the manifolds. Check for a clogged air filter.

Compression may be checked in the field by turning the kickstarter by hand and noting that an adequate resistance is felt, or by removing a spark plug and placing a finger over the plug hole and feeling for pressure.

An accurate compression check gives a good idea of the condition of the basic working parts of the engine—the cylinders, pistons and valves. To perform this test, you need a compression gauge. The motor should be warm.

1. Remove the plug on the cylinder to be tested and clean out any dirt or grease.

2. Insert the tip of the gauge into the hole, making sure it is seated correctly.

3. Open the throttle all the way and make sure the chokes on the carburetors are open.

4. Crank the engine several times and record the highest pressure reading on the gauge. Run the test on each of the cylinders.

5. The normal compression for the Honda 750 is 150 psi to 170 psi. If the readings are significantly lower than 150 psi as a group, or if they vary more than 15 psi between the cylinders, proceed to the next step.

TROUBLESHOOTING

6. Pour a tablespoon of motor oil into the suspect cylinder and record the compression.

If oil raised the compression significantly—10 psi in an old engine—the rings are worn and should be replaced.

If the compression remained the same, the valves are probably leaking and should be reground.

Valve adjustments should be checked next. Sticking, burned, or broken valves may hamper starting. As a last resort, check valve timing as described in the Engine chapter.

POOR IDLING

Poor idling may be caused by incorrect carburetor adjustment, incorrect timing, ignition system defects, an intake manifold leak, or leakage between the carburetors at the balance tube. Check the gas cap vent for an obstruction.

MISFIRING

Misfiring can be caused by a weak spark or dirty plugs. Check for fuel contamination. Run the machine at night or in a darkened garage to check for spark leaks along the plug wires and under the spark plug cap. If misfiring occurs only at certain throttle settings, refer to the carburetor and fuel delivery sections in the Tune-up chapter for the specific carburetor circuits involved. Misfiring under heavy load, as when climbing hills or accelerating, is usually caused by bad spark plugs.

FLAT SPOTS

If the engine seems to die momentarily when the throttle is opened and then recovers, check for a dirty main jet in the carburetor, water in the fuel, or an excessively lean mixture.

POWER LOSS

Poor condition of rings, pistons, or cylinders will cause a lack of power and speed. Check that valves are correctly adjusted. Ignition timing should be checked along with the automatic spark advance.

OVERHEATING

If the engine seems to run too hot all the time, be sure you are not idling it for long periods. Air cooled engines are not designed to operate at a standstill for any length of time. Heavy stop and go traffic is hard on a motorcycle engine. Spark plugs of the wrong heat range can burn pistons. An excessively lean gas mixture may cause overheating. Check ignition timing. Don't ride in too high a gear. Broken or worn rings and valves may permit compression gases to leak past them, heating heads and cylinders excessively. Check oil level and use the proper grade lubricants.

BACKFIRING

Check that the timing is not advanced too far. Check the automatic advance mechanism for broken or sticking parts. Check fuel for contamination.

ENGINE NOISES

Experience is needed to diagnose accurately in this area. Noises are hard to differentiate and harder yet to describe. Deep knocking noises usually mean main bearing failure. A slapping noise generally comes from loose pistons. A light knocking noise during acceleration may be a bad connecting rod bearing. Pinging, which sounds like marbles being shaken in a tin can, is caused by ignition advanced too far or gasoline with too low an octane rating. Pinging should be corrected immediately or damage to pistons will result. Compression leaks at the head-cylinder joint will sound like a rapid on and off squeal.

PISTON SEIZURE

Piston seizure is caused by incorrect piston clearances when fitted, fitting rings with improper end gap, too thin an oil being used, incorrect spark plug heat range, or incorrect ignition timing. Overheating from any cause may result in seizure.

EXCESSIVE VIBRATION

Excessive vibration may be caused by loose motor mounts, worn engine or transmission bearings, loose wheels, worn swinging arm bushings, a generally poor running engine, broken or cracked frame, or one that has been damaged in a collision. See also Poor Handling.

HIGH OIL CONSUMPTION

High oil consumption and loss of compression often go hand in hand. Check condition of rings, pistons, cylinders, and valves. Worn valve stems or valve guides may be at fault. Use the correct grade of oil.

CLUTCH SLIP OR DRAG

Clutch slip may be due to worn plates, improper adjustment, or glazed plates. A dragging clutch could result from damaged or bent plates, improper adjustment, or even clutch spring pressure.

TRANSMISSION PROBLEMS

A grinding when shifting may be a result of worn synchronizers on the transmission gears or a sticking or non-disengaging clutch. Bent or broken teeth may cause hard shifting. A bent shifting rod, mainshaft or layshaft could cause hard shifting. Popping out of gear could be due to worn dogs on the gears or misadjustment in the shifting mechanism.

POOR HANDLING

Poor handling may be caused by improper tire pressures, a damaged frame or swinging arm, worn shocks or front forks, weak fork springs, a bent or broken steering stem, misaligned wheels, loose or missing spokes, worn tires, bent handlebars, worn wheel bearing, or dragging brakes.

BRAKE PROBLEMS

Sticking brakes may be caused by broken or weak return springs, improper cable or rod adjustment, or dry pivot and cam bushings. Grabbing brakes may be caused by greasy linings which must be replaced. Brake grab may also be due to out-of-round drums or linings which have broken loose from the brake shoes. Glazed linings or glazed brake pads will cause loss of stopping power.

LIGHTING PROBLEMS

Bulbs which continuously burn out may be caused by excessive vibration, loose connections that permit sudden current surges, poor battery connections, or installation of the wrong type bulb.

A dead battery or one which discharges quickly may be caused by a faulty generator or rectifier. Check for loose or corroded terminals. Shorted battery cells or broken terminals will keep a battery from charging. Low water level will decrease a battery's capacity. A battery left uncharged after installation will sulphate, rendering it useless.

A majority of light and horn or other electrical accessory problems are caused by loose or corroded ground connections. Check those first, and then substitute known good units for easier troubleshooting.

INDEX

A

Air cleaner
    Replacement 14
Alternator
    Coil testing 82
    Disassembly 82
    Exploded view 81

B

Backfiring 233
Battery
    Charging 85
    Inspection 25, 84
    Installation 85
    Removal 84
Brakes, front
    Adjustment 111
    Bleeding 110
    Description 107
    Disassembly 108
    Inspection and reassembly 109
    Master cylinder, exploded view ... 109
    Pad inspection 108
    Sectional view 107
    Troubleshooting 234
Brakes, rear
    Disassembly 111
    Exploded view 112
    Inspection 111
    Reassembly 113
    Troubleshooting 234
Breaker points
    Cam lubrication 9
    Disassembly 75
    Exploded view 8
    Gap adjustment 7
    Inspection and cleaning 6
    Replacement 6
    Timing adjustment 9

C

Cam chain
    Adjustment 12
    Exploded view 13, 36
Camshaft
    Chain tensioner, exploded view ... 36
    Disassembly 32
    Inspection and measurement 37
    Reassembly 38
    Rocker arm, exploded view 35
    Sectional view 33

Carburetor, CB 750
    Adjustment 17
    Description 17, 64
    Disassembly 64
    Exploded view 66
    Flat spots 233
    Float level adjustment 16
    Idle speed 20
    Inspection and adjustment 67
    Poor idling 233
    Reassembly 69
    Throttle cable 22
Carburetor, CB 750 K1
    Adjustment 20
    Description 17, 64
    Disassembly 65
    Exploded view 68
    Flat spots 233
    Float level adjustment 16
    Idle speed 22
    Inspection and adjustment 67
    Poor idling 233
    Reassembly 69
    Throttle cable 22
Charging system
    Alternator 80
    Battery 84
    Description 76
    Rectifier 83
    Regulator 82
    Testing 80
Clutch
    Adjustment 24
    Cover, exploded view 57
    Description 54
    Disassembly 54
    Exploded view 55
    Inspection and reassembly 56
    Slippage 234
Coil, ignition
    Disassembly 74
    Reassembly 75
    Testing 74
Connecting rods
    Inspection 49
    Removal 47
Contact breaker (see Breaker points)
Crankshaft
    Disassembly 45
    Exploded view 46
    Inspection 48
    Reassembly 49
Cylinder
    Disassembly and inspection 43
    Exploded view 44
    Reassembly 45

Cylinder head
- Disassembly 40
- Exploded view 41
- Inspection 40
- Reassembly 42

D

Drive chain
- Disassembly and inspection 106
- Servicing and adjustment 106

Drive, final
- Disassembly and inspection 106
- Reassembly and adjustment 106

Drive, primary
- Chain tensioner 51
- Disassembly 51
- Inspection 50
- Reassembly 51

E

Engine
- Backfiring 233
- Camshaft 32
- Connecting rods 45
- Crankshaft 45
- Cylinder 43
- Cylinder head 40
- Installation 27
- Kickstarter 52
- Lubrication 28
- Misfiring 233
- Noises 233
- Oil consumption, excessive 233
- Oil filter 28
- Oil pump 30
- Operating requirements 231
- Overheating 233
- Pistons 43
- Power loss 233
- Removal 26
- Sprockets 50
- Starting difficulties 232
- Vibration, excessive 233

Engine lubrication
- Oil filter 28
- System diagram 28

Exhaust pipes and mufflers
- Disassembly and inspection 116
- Exploded view 117
- Reassembly 116

F

Flasher relay 120
Flat spots 233

Fork, front
- Disassembly 91
- Inspection 93
- Oil changing 91
- Reassembly 93
- Sectional view 92

Fork, rear
- Disassembly and inspection 98
- Exploded view 99
- Reassembly 98

Frame
- Component inspection and reassembly 115
- Component removal 114
- Dimensions 115
- Oil tank 115

Fuel system
- Fuel delivery checks 14

Fuel tank
- Disassembly 70
- Exploded view 15, 71
- Inspection 72
- Reassembly 72

H

Headlights
- Disassembly and inspection 119

Horn
- Disassembly and inspection 122

I

Ignition system
- Adjustment 6
- Breaker points 75
- Coil 74
- Description 73
- Spark advance 75

Instruments 118

K

Kickstarter
- Disassembly 52
- Inspection and reassembly 53
- Operation 52

L

Lights
- Headlight 119
- Tail and stop lights 119
- Troubleshooting 234
- Turn signal 120

INDEX

M

Misfiring 233
Mufflers 116

O

Oil changes 2
Oil consumption, excessive 233
Oil filter
    Description 28
    Exploded view 4
    Replacement 3
Oil pump
    Disassembly 30
    Exploded view 30
    Inspection 31
    Reassembly 32
Oil tank
    Description 115
    Disassembly and inspection 116
    Reassembly 116
Overheating 233

P

Piston rings
    Inspection 43
Pistons
    Inspection 43
    Removal 43
    Seizure 233
Poor idling 233
Power loss 233

R

Rectifier
    Disassembly 84
    Testing 84
Rocker arms
    Exploded view 35

S

Shock absorbers, rear
    Disassembly 96
    Exploded view 97
    Inspection 96
    Reassembly 97
Spark advancer
    Disassembly 75
    Inspection and reassembly 76

Spark plugs
    Cleaning and adjustment 6
    Recommended types 5
    Removal and inspection 5
Starter
    Disassembly 86
    Exploded view 88
    Inspection and adjustment 87
    Magnetic switch 89
    Operation 86
    Reassembly 87
    Starting clutch 87
Starting clutch
    Disassembly and inspection 89
    Reassembly 89
    Sectional view 89
Starting difficulties 232
Steering
    Disassembly 94
    Inspection and reassembly 95
Supplements, see 'Contents' at front for page numbers
Suspension, front
    Fork 91
    Steering 94
Suspension, rear
    Fork 98
    Shock absorbers 96
Swing arm
    Disassembly and inspection 98
    Exploded view 99
    Reassembly 98
Switch, magnetic starter
    Disassembly 89
    Inspection and adjustment 90
    Reassembly 90
Switches
    Horn 122
    Ignition 121
    Neutral 123
    Oil pressure 123
    Starter and lighting 121
    Stop, front 122
    Stop, rear 123
    Turn signal 122

T

Taillights 119-120
Turn signal 120
Throttle cable 22
Timing
    Adjustment, static 9
    Adjustment, stroboscopic 9
    Advance mechanism 10

INDEX

Tires
    Removal 101
    Inspection and installation 102
Transmission
    Disassembly 59
    Exploded view 61
    Inspection 60
    Operation 58
    Reassembly 62
    Shift mechanism, sectional view 59
    Troubleshooting 234
Troubleshooting 231-234
Tune-up
    Battery 24
    Breaker points 6
    Cam chain 12
    Carburetor 17
    Clutch 24
    Fuel delivery 14
    Oil changes 2
    Oil filter replacement 3
    Spark plugs 5
    Throttle cable 22
    Timing 9
    Tools required 2
    Valves 10

V

Valves
    Clearances 10
    Exploded view 11
Voltage regulator
    Disassembly 82
    Inspection and adjustment 83

W

Wheel, front
    Balancing 103
    Disassembly 100
    Reassembly 102
    Sectional view 101
Wheel, rear
    Balancing 103
    Disassembly and inspection 104
    Reassembly 104
    Sectional view 105
Wiring diagrams 221
Wiring harness
    Diagram 124
    Disassembly 123
    Inspection and reassembly 125

VELOCEPRESS MANUALS – MOTORCYCLE BY MAKE

AJS 1932-1948 SINGLES & TWINS 250cc THRU 1000cc (BOOK OF)
AJS 1945-1960 SINGLES 350cc & 500cc MODELS 16 & 18 (BOOK OF)
AJS 1955-1965 SINGLES 350cc & 500cc (BOOK OF)
AJS 1957-1966 FACTORY WSM - ALL SINGLES & TWINS
ARIEL UP TO 1932 (BOOK OF)
ARIEL 1932-1939 PREWAR MODELS (BOOK OF)
ARIEL 1933-1951 (WORKSHOP MANUAL)
ARIEL 1939-1960 4 STROKE SINGLES (BOOK OF)
ARIEL 1958-1964 LEADER & ARROW (BOOK OF)
BMW R26 R27 (1956-1967) FACTORY WORKSHOP MANUAL
BMW R50 R50S R60 R69S (1955-1969) FACTORY WORKSHOP MANUAL
BRIDGESTONE 90 SERIES FACTORY WSM & PARTS CATALOGUE
BRIDGESTONE 175 SERIES FACTORY WSM & PARTS CATALOGUE
BRIDGESTONE 350 SERIES FACTORY WSM & PARTS CATALOGUES
BSA SERVICE SHEETS MASTER CATALOGUE ALL MODELS 1945-1967
BSA BANTAM D1 TO D7 1948-1966 FACTORY SERVICE SHEETS MANUAL
BSA BANTAM ALL MODELS FROM 1948 ONWARDS (BOOK OF)
BSA DANDY FACTORY WORKSHOP MANUAL (COMPILATION)
BSA SINGLES & V-TWINS UP TO 1927 (BOOK OF)
BSA SINGLES & V-TWINS UP TO 1930 (BOOK OF)
BSA SINGLES & V-TWINS UP TO 1935 (BOOK OF)
BSA SINGLES & V-TWINS 1936-1939 (BOOK OF)
BSA C10, C11 & C12 1945-1958 FACTORY SERVICE SHEETS MANUAL
BSA OHV & SV SINGLES 250-600cc 1945-1959 (BOOK OF)
BSA C15 & B40 1958-1967 FACTORY SERVICE SHEETS MANUAL
BSA OHV & SV SINGLES 250cc (ONLY) 1954-1970 (BOOK OF)
BSA B31, B32, B33 & B34 1945-60 FACTORY SERVICE SHEETS MANUAL
BSA OHV SINGLES 350 & 500cc 1955-1967 (BOOK OF)
BSA M20, M21 & M33 1945-1963 FACTORY SERVICE SHEETS MANUAL
BSA TWINS A7 & A10 1948-1962 FACTORY SERVICE SHEETS MANUAL
BSA TWINS A7 & A10 1948-1962 (BOOK OF)
BSA TWINS A50 & A65 1962-1965 FACTORY WORKSHOP MANUAL
BSA TWINS A50 & A65 1962-1969 (SECOND BOOK OF)
DOUGLAS 1929-1939 PREWAR ALL MODELS (BOOK OF)
DOUGLAS 1948-1957 POSTWAR ALL MODELS FACTORY SHOP MANUAL
DUCATI 160cc, 250cc & 350cc OHC MODELS FACTORY SHOP MANUAL
HONDA 50cc ALL MODELS UP TO 1970 INC MONKEY & TRAIL (BOOK OF)
HONDA 90cc ALL MODELS UP TO 1966 (BOOK OF)
HONDA 50-65-70-90cc OHC SINGLES 1959-1983 FACTORY WSM
HONDA 125-150cc TWINS C/CS/CB/CA FACTORY WORKSHOP MANUAL
HONDA 125-160-175-200cc TWINS 1964-1980 WORKSHOP MANUAL
HONDA 250-305cc TWINS C/CS/CB 1959-1967 FACTORY WSM
HOHDA 250-350cc TWINS CB/CL/SL 1968-1973 FACTORY WSM
HONDA 450cc CB/CL 1965-1974 K0 TO K7 WORKSHOP MANUAL
HONDA 750cc SOHC K0~K8 4 CYL 1969-1978 WORKSHOP MANUAL
HONDA C100 SUPER CUB FACTORY WORKSHOP MANUAL
HONDA C110 SPORT CUB 1962-1969 FACTORY WORKSHOP MANUAL
HONDA TWINS & SINGLES 50cc THRU 305cc 1960-1966 (BOOK OF)
HONDA TWINS ALL MODELS 125cc THRU 450cc UP TO 1968 (BOOK OF)
INDIAN PONYBIKE, BOY RACER & PAPOOSE ILL PARTS LIST & SALES LIT
J.A.P. ENGINES 1927-1952 & MOTORCYCLES 1934-1952 (BOOK OF)
MATCHLESS 1931-1939 ALL MODELS 250cc THRU 990cc (BOOK OF)
MATCHLESS 1945-1956 350 & 500cc SINGLES (BOOK OF)
MATCHLESS 1955-1966 350 & 500cc SINGLES (BOOK OF)
MATCHLESS 1957-1966 FACTORY WSM - ALL SINGLES & TWINS
NEW IMPERIAL ALL SV & OHV FROM 1935 ONWARDS (BOOK OF)
NORTON 1932-1939 PREWAR MODELS (BOOK OF)
NORTON 1932-1947 (BOOK OF)
NORTON 1938-1956 (BOOK OF)
NORTON 1955-1963 MODELS 19, 50 & ES2 (BOOK OF)
NORTON 1955-1965 DOMINATOR TWINS (BOOK OF)
NORTON 1960-1970 TWIN CYLINDER FACTORY WORKSHOP MANUAL
NORTON 1970-1975 COMMANDO 850 & 750cc FACTORY WSM
NORTON 1975-1978 MK 3 COMMANDO 850 cc FACTORY WSM
PANTHER 1932-1958 LIGHTWEIGHT MODELS 250 & 350cc (BOOK OF)
PANTHER 1938-1966 HEAVYWEIGHT MODELS 600 & 650cc (BOOK OF)
RALEIGH MOTORCYCLES 1919-1933 (BOOK OF)
ROYAL ENFIELD 1934-1946 SINGLES & V TWINS (BOOK OF)
ROYAL ENFIELD 1937-1953 SINGLES & V TWINS (BOOK OF)
ROYAL ENFIELD 1946-1962 SINGLES (BOOK OF)
ROYAL ENFIELD 1958-1966 250cc & 350cc SINGLES (SECOND BOOK OF)
ROYAL ENFIELD 736cc INTERCEPTOR FACTORY WORKSHOP MANUAL
RUDGE 1933-1939 (BOOK OF)
SUNBEAM 1928-1939 (BOOK OF)
SUNBEAM 1946-1957 S7 & S8 (BOOK OF)
SUZUKI 50cc & 80cc UP TO 1966 (BOOK OF)
SUZUKI T10 1963-1967 FACTORY WORKSHOP MANUAL
SUZUKI T20 & T200 1965-1969 FACTORY WORKSHOP MANUAL
SUZUKI TWINS 1962 ONWARDS 125-500cc WORKSHOP MANUAL
TRIUMPH 1935-1949 SINGLES & TWINS (BOOK OF)
TRIUMPH 1937-1951 (WORKSHOP MANUAL)
TRIUMPH 1945-1955 FACTORY WORKSHOP MANUAL
TRIUMPH 1945-1959 TWINS (BOOK OF)
TRIUMPH 1956-1969 TWINS (BOOK OF)
TRIUMPH 1963-1970 UNIT CONSTRUCTION 650cc FACTORY WSM
VELOCETTE 1925-1970 ALL SINGLES & TWINS (BOOK OF)
VILLIERS ENGINE UP TO 1959 INC. 3 WHEELERS (BOOK OF)
VILLIERS ENGINE UP TO 1969 (BOOK OF)
VINCENT 1935-1955 (WORKSHOP MANUAL)
YAMAHA 1961-1967 YA5 & YA6 (WORKSHOP MANUAL & ILL PARTS LIST)
YAMAHA 1971-1972 JT1& JT2 (WORKSHOP MANUAL & ILL PARTS LIST)

VELOCEPRESS TECHNICAL BOOKS – MOTORCYCLE

1930'S BRITISH MOTORCYCLE CARBS & ELEC COMPONENTS (BOOK OF)
1930'S BRITISH MOTORCYCLE ENGINES (OVERHAUL & MAINTENANCE)
1930'S BRITISH MOTORCYCLE GEARBOXES & CLUTCHES (BOOK OF)
CATALOG OF BRITISH MOTORCYCLES (1951 MODELS)
LUCAS ELECTRONICS BRITISH M/CYCLES REPAIR & PARTS (1950-1977)
MOTORCYCLE ENGINEERING (P.E. Irving)
MOTORCYCLE ROAD TESTS 1949-1953 (Motor Cycle Magazine UK)
SPEED AND HOW TO OBTAIN IT (Motor Cycle Magazine UK)
TUNING FOR SPEED (P.E. Irving)
WIPAC (COMBO) MANUAL NUMBER 3 + M/CYCLE & SCOOTER MANUAL

VELOCEPRESS MANUALS – SCOOTERS BY MAKE

BSA SUNBEAM SCOOTER WORKSHOP MANUAL 1959-1965
BSA SUNBEAM SCOOTER 1959-1965 (BOOK OF)
LAMBRETTA 1947-1957 ALL 125 & 150cc MODELS (BOOK OF)
LAMBRETTA 1957-1970 LI & TV MODELS (SECOND BOOK OF)
NSU PRIMA 1956-1964 ALL MODELS (BOOK OF)
TRIUMPH TIGRESS SCOOTER WORKSHOP MANUAL 1959-1965
TRIUMPH TIGRESS SCOOTER (BOOK OF)
VESPA 1951-1961 (BOOK OF)
VESPA 1955-1963 125 & 150cc & GS MODELS (SECOND BOOK OF)
VESPA 1955-1968 GS & SS (BOOK OF)
VESPA 1963-1972 90, 125 & 150cc (THIRD BOOK OF)

VELOCEPRESS MANUALS – MOPEDS & MOTORIZED BICYCLES

CYCLEMOTOR (BOOK OF)
NSU QUICKLY 1953-1963 ALL MODELS (BOOK OF)
PUCH MAXI N & S MAINTENANCE & REPAIR (3 MANUAL COMPILATION)
RALEIGH MOPEDS 1960-1969 (BOOK OF)

VELOCEPRESS MANUALS - THREE WHEELER'S

BOND MINICAR THREE WHEELER 1948-1967 (BOOK OF)
BMW ISETTA FACTORY WORKSHOP MANUAL
BSA THREE WHEELER (BOOK OF)
RELIANT REGAL THREE WHEELER 1952-1973 (BOOK OF)
VINTAGE MORGAN THREE WHEELER (BOOK OF)

VELOCEPRESS MANUALS – AUTOMOBILE BY MAKE

ALFA ROMEO GIULIA WORKSHOP MANUAL 1300 TO 2000cc 1962-1975
ALFA ROMEO GIULIA TECH MANUAL CARBURETED CARS FROM 1962
ALFA ROMEO GIULIA TECH MANUAL FUEL INJECTED CARS FROM 1969
ALFA ROMEO GIULIETTA & GIULIA 750 & 101 SERIES 1955-1965 WSM
AUSTIN-HEALEY SPRITE & MG MIDGET WORKSHOP MANUAL 1958-1971
BMW 600 LIMOUSINE FACTORY WORKSHOP MANUAL
BMW 600 LIMOUSINE OWNERS HAND BOOK & SERVICE MANUAL
BMW 2000 & 2002 1966-1976 WORKSHOP MANUAL
CORVAIR 1960-1969 WORKSHOP MANUAL
CORVETTE V8 1955-1962 WORKSHOP MANUAL
FERRARI 250/GT MAINTENANCE & REPAIR MANUAL
FIAT 500 FACTORY WORKSHOP MANUAL 1957-1973
FIAT 600, 600D & MULTIPLA FACTORY WORKSHOP MANUAL 1955-1969
JAGUAR E-TYPE 3.8 & 4.2 SERIES 1 & 2 WORKSHOP MANUAL
JAGUAR MK 7, 8, 9 & XK120, 140, 150 WORKSHOP MANUAL 1948-1961
METROPOLITAN FACTORY WORKSHOP MANUAL
MGA & MGB OWNERS HANDBOOK & WORKSHOP MANUAL
MG MIDGET TC, TD, TF & TF1500 WORKSHOP MANUAL
PORSCHE 356 1948-1965 WORKSHOP MANUAL
PORSCHE 911 2.0, 2.2, 2.4 LITRE 1964-1973 WORKSHOP MANUAL
PORSCHE 911 2.7, 3.0, 3.2 LITRE 1973-1989 WORKSHOP MANUAL
PORSCHE 912 WORKSHOP MANUAL
TRIUMPH TR2, TR3, TR4 1953-1965 WORKSHOP MANUAL
VOLKSWAGEN TRANSPORTER, TRUCKS & WAGONS 1950-1979 WSM
VOLVO 1944-1968 ALL MODELS WORKSHOP MANUAL

VELOCEPRESS TECHNICAL BOOKS - AUTOMOBILE

FERRARI OWNER'S HANDBOOK
HOW TO BUILD A FIBERGLASS CAR
HOW TO BUILD A RACING CAR
HOW TO RESTORE THE MODEL 'A' FORD
MASERATI OWNER'S HANDBOOK
PERFORMANCE TUNING THE SUNBEAM TIGER
SOUPING THE VOLKSWAGEN
SOLEX CARBURETORS (EMPHASIS ON UK & EU AUTOMOBILES)
SU CARBURETORS (EMPHASIS ON UK AUTOMOBILES)
WEBER CARBURETORS (EMPHASIS ON ALFA & FIAT)

VELOCEPRESS BOOKS & GUIDES - AUTOMOBILE

COMPLETE CATALOG OF JAPANESE MOTOR VEHICLES
FERRARI 308 SERIES BUYER'S AND OWNER'S GUIDE
FERRARI BROCHURES AND SALES LITERATURE 1968-1989
FERRARI SERIAL NUMBERS PART I - ODD NUMBERS TO 21399
FERRARI SERIAL NUMBERS PART II - EVEN NUMBERS TO 1050
HENRY'S FABULOUS MODEL "A" FORD
MASERATI BROCHURES AND SALES LITERATURE

VELOCEPRESS BOOKS – RACING

CARRERA PANAMERICANA - MEXICAN ROAD RACE (BOOK OF)
DIALED IN - THE JAN OPPERMAN STORY
VEDA ORR'S NEW REVISED HOT ROD PICTORIAL

Please check our website:

www.VelocePress.com

for a complete
up-to-date list of
available titles

www.ingramcontent.com/pod-product-compliance
Lightning Source LLC
Chambersburg PA
CBHW060248240426
43673CB00047B/1892